RIDING

with

GEORGE

RIDING
with
GEORGE

 SPORTSMANSHIP & CHIVALRY
IN THE MAKING OF
AMERICA'S FIRST PRESIDENT

PHILIP G. SMUCKER

CHICAGO
REVIEW
PRESS

Published by Chicago Review Press Incorporated
814 North Franklin Street
Chicago, Illinois 60610
ISBN 978-1-61373-605-0

Library of Congress Cataloging-in-Publication Data
Is available from the Library of Congress.

Typesetting: Nord Compo

Printed in the United States of America
5 4 3 2 1

I see our wars will turn unto peaceful comic sport when ladies crave to be encountered with.

—Shakespeare, *King Henry VI*

The King established all his knights . . . gave them lands, and charged them never to do outrageousity nor murder, and always to flee treason; also by no means to be cruel, but to give mercy unto him that asketh mercy . . . and always to do ladies, damsels and gentlewomen succor upon pain of death.

—Thomas Malory, *Le Morte d'Arthur*

Our good people be not disturbed, letted, or discouraged from any lawful recreation, such as dancing, either of men or women, Archery for men, leaping, vaulting, or any such harmlesse Recreation.

—King James, "Book of Sports"

CONTENTS

A NOTE ON SOURCES

IN MY APPENDED ACKNOWLEDGEMENTS, THE reader will get a sense of some of the field research I conducted for this book, which included riding, hiking, and interacting with guides, instructors and historical reenactors. However, my six-year deep dive into George Washington's life as a sportsman and chivalric gentleman also proceeded along traditional academic lines, and so I've created what I hope is a valuable web page for this book: www.ridingwithgeorge.com. The site contains not only links and photos of moments in the journey but also extensive source materials (and end notes) that provided the grist for this story. The reader will also find interviews as well as links to key resources like the Papers of George Washington at the University of Virginia, the Library of Congress, (where my great grandfather, Lawrence Washington, once worked), Mount Vernon's own amazing web pages, exciting links to the Colonial Williamsburg Foundation, and links to a slew of other historical societies and resources, including equestrian and fencing clubs and groups.

In order to explore primary sources, I spent time as a fellow at the newly minted National Library for the Study of George Washington at Mount Vernon but also longer days on the road and in Charlottesville, Virginia, looking into Washington's letters and diaries. Fortunately, when I was away from those locations, the Internet helped transport them into my study, tavern, coffeehouse, or bed and breakfast.

It should be mentioned that it wasn't all straight history that set me hot on the trail of sportsmanship and chivalry. Professor Howard Gardner's theory of multiple intelligences set off sparks in my mind about how young George was more of a kinesthetic (understanding by doing) learner than he was a bookworm, as were most of our other leading Founding Fathers. I pursued Gardner further with his book, *Leading Minds: An Anatomy of Leadership* and found some rather stark parallels between George's early years and the lives of other great leaders. Gardner's theories about how all of us acquire knowledge and wisdom spoke to me about what I had already learned about George Washington, particularly in his own struggles with father figures, mostly British Empire authorities, at a young age. There are so many exciting ways to see history, and the ideas I discovered as a graduate student a few decades earlier from Rhys Isaac's *The Transformation of Virginia* drove me to further explore the context of George's ascent as a man of action, as did Nancy L. Struna's excellent book on the subject of Virginians and the value they placed on prowess.

Much of my research was about teasing out the episodes in George Washington's life that best exhibit his sportsmanship and chivalry, and for this I'm entirely indebted to those who have gone before me. Before Ron Chernow, whose scintillating prose helped many of us better understand Washington in a modern context, two great twentieth-century biographers, Douglas Southall Freeman and James Thomas Flexner, produced lucid, multivolume biographies that delved into the forgotten moments of Washington's life and shined lights on his most gallant and heroic moments. Like almost all modern Washington biographers, I owe an immense of gratitude to both these two men.

Writing this book has been about weaving old (and sometimes frayed) threads into a new carpet. For their labors, I owe a special debt to Thomas Malory, Seneca, and several leading eighteenth-century scribes, including Philip Fithian, Robert Beverley, Andrew Burnaby, John Fontaine, and Hugh Jones. Other more modern authors I'll mention here, and you can find their full works and see how they show up in my book by going to www.ridingwithgeorge.com as often as you like. They are Bruce Chadwick, Fred Anderson, David Clary, Joseph Ellis, John Ferling, David Hackett Fischer, Justin Glenn, Peter Henriques, Edward Lengel, Doug Bradburn, Philip Levy, David McCullough, Mary Thompson, Gordon Wood, Warren Goldstein, Elliott Gorn, T. H. Breen, Stuart Brown, Jane Carson, W. J. Cash, Clifford Dowdey, Alexander Mackay-Smith, Norman Fine, Helen Rountree, Shefali Rajamannar, Kate Van Winkle Keller, Charles Hendrickson, David Zirin, Laura Galke, Richard Gruneau, Shafqat Hussain, Marcel Trudeau, Todd Andrlik, Susan Branson, Cokie

Roberts, Virginia Johnson, Barbara Crookshanks, Laura Auricchio, David Preston, Kenneth Silverman, Dennis Foster, Adrian Covert, Joseph B. Thomas, Don Higginbotham, Gerard Gawalt, Caroline Cox, Tony Horwitz, Paul R. Misencik, Robert Middlekauff, Louis B. Wright, Kathleen M. Brown, Clifford Geertz, and many others.

PREFACE

ON THE PLAIN AT WEST POINT, George Washington sits elegantly on an oversized bronze steed, gesturing gallantly across a long green in the direction of Generals MacArthur and Patton, who are both merely standing in his presence—at the apparent beck and call of the founding father. In this work of art, as in so many others, George is a study of coolness and composure, a man free of fear, entirely at ease atop his noble beast.

Like many Americans, I grew up with this iconic image of George Washington, a chivalric gentleman for the ages. When I acted out, my mother would venture to set me straight, insisting, "Your father and I hope you can start acting a little more like George Washington."

This was disconcerting, to say the least. Even if I did possess a few errant genes of greatness on my mother's side, I thought that was a rather ridiculous standard to hold me to. There were, after all, a lot of indirect relatives of George Washington, our childless founding father, and no one in the extended Washington clan, least of all a black sheep like me, even came close to living up to or, for that matter, even attempting old George's legendary feats. Several of them died trying. One of the general's grandnephews, John Washington Lewis, whom British dragoons had earlier seized to work as a deckhand, sought revenge at the outset of the War of 1812, charging and cursing the invading redcoats on his horse as they attacked the President's House, later named the White House. He fired a few shots in anger, only to fall dead off his horse on Pennsylvania Avenue, just a few miles from my own home, where he was collected the next morning. Gruff old

Gen. George Patton, a first cousin of Washington six times removed, came awfully close to George's heroism on the battlefield and nearly surpassed him as an athlete, finishing fifth in the Olympic pentathlon in 1912 and polishing his fencing skills in France. Unfortunately, his brilliant career was cut short in a car accident.

My great-great-grandfather John Augustine Washington tried, but also stumbled on horseback. The last private owner of the Mount Vernon plantation and no trained soldier himself, Gus, as he was known to his kin, served as an aide-de-camp to Robert E. Lee and was shot dead as he rode past Yankee bushwhackers on only his first reconnaissance mission in the mountains of West Virginia. He was a humble and devout man and, from his embattled and rain-soaked Cheat Mountain redoubt a week earlier, had written forebodingly, "I don't know when I shall leave this region, or indeed whether I ever shall do so, as of course my chances are the same as those of other men, and I know some of us will never get away."

Gus's orphans were raised in Virginia's Piedmont, where my grandmother was born. Of course, horses and sportsmanship still very much mattered in Virginia when I was growing up in the 1970s, at least in a symbolic way. One of my best childhood memories was riding atop a brown-and-white painted pony and looking down on the world, bearing my own coonskin cap. Since becoming a war correspondent in the 1980s, I have ridden, owned, and tumbled off horses of my own in strange places, including in Russia, Egypt, and Afghanistan. I actually only rode horses for pleasure in Afghanistan, making only one brief foray into one of the most violent equestrian sports known to man, *buzkashi*. This is a game brought to Afghanistan by marauding Mongol horsemen over a thousand years ago, a pastime meant to train warriors and their charges for the chaos of battle. I can't recommend the sport even to my fearless foxhunting friends, because this sport for warlords and wild men is just too dangerous. In essence, it involves trying to run with a headless goat carcass, all the while dodging other players, who whip, claw, yank, and try to pummel you with the raised hoofs of their own mounts. When I attempted to take part in a match, I quickly lost my composure. Confronted by a scrum of snorting beasts, I galloped off the playing field as fast as my horse would take me. This game, however, apart from the trepidation it instilled in me, also made me wonder openly about the historical and modern links between sport and war.

Clearly, even with the US military's rare gallops into modern guerrilla war zones, horses and sports once had a closer affiliation with war than they do today. Modern equestrian show jumping is a derivative of foxhunting, which was considered—particularly in the case of George Washington—to be excellent training for war.

Washington's own riding abilities and athletic prowess are legendary. Fellow Virginian Thomas Jefferson insisted that Washington was the "finest equestrian of his day." But Washington, across the arc of his storied career, excelled in almost any and every kind of action he performed, including dancing, throwing, fencing, fishing, and even card playing. With his immense talents in mind—and still hoping to resolve childhood mysteries—I set out to understand how George, not born into one of Virginia's leading gentry families, managed to propel himself through skill and ambition into positions of leadership and eventually become a model of sportsmanship and manners for a new and highly competitive country.

I hope the reader will indulge me as I take some unconventional approaches to unveiling the tale as I chase the gentleman I most often call George—for the sake of convenience and familiarity—along riding trails, on the dance floor, through two wars, as a gentleman farmer, and as president. In order to get closer to my subject, I've tried to use all my reportorial and research skills to the best of my ability. In doing so, I rely on the insights of great scholars, historical impersonators, foxhunters, as well as the dance and fencing instructors I've met along the way. I've also saddled up as often as possible and charged off into Washington's old stomping grounds on the back of a horse. Though I'm only an amateur sportsman, and not an exceptional one at that, seeing what George's woods, byways, and battlefields looked like from atop a saddle—even when time has altered the landscape—has helped me travel back in time to crucial moments in his life. I've not tried to sleep where George Washington slept, so much as ride where he rode, dance where he danced, and walk where he walked, charting out—as it were—where he played and how he fought. On this exciting journey, I've traipsed through the stunning beauty of the Shenandoah Valley and scaled cliffs in the frigid mountains of central Pennsylvania without leaving aside the new urban wastelands that once presented "charming" fields of fire for an ambitious young officer.

*Washington at Verplanck's Point, New York, 1782, Reviewing the
French Troops After the Victory at Yorktown*, Adrian Lamb, after
John Trumbull, 1982. *Courtesy of Mount Vernon Ladies' Association*

George Washington was not born a great actor on the stage of
history. Indeed, he was as flawed and as challenged as any of
his peers, sometimes more so since he did not have their formal
training. Early on, however, he recognized his shortcomings and
began to shape and mold his own image based on the myths and
ideals he had inherited from his forefathers. Only when he had
grasped how his actions were viewed in public did he begin to

successfully shape them to fit the image that remains seared in our minds.

As I delved deeper into the tale, I was struck by Washington's often unheralded skills not only as a sportsman but also in another sense of the same word—as a chivalric gentleman. In a sense, he was an Old World courtier who succeeded beyond all expectations in a New World order. Born in 1732, George Washington possessed a physique and ambitions that were tailor-made for his age—one in which displays of physical prowess were essential to recognition in society. At six feet two inches and with a penchant for rambunctious horse riding, what he lacked in formal schooling, he made up for in physical strength, skill, and ambition.

His tale is, as all historical yarns are, complicated, particularly by mentorships, dodged bullets, and sheer strokes of good luck—all of which also helped him advance and eventually alter the course of history. As I rode with George—in spirit at least—I came to see how he had cultivated and managed his prowess and stamina starting in his teens. There was more, though: invariably, I found that—through the years—not only did he perform at an amazing level in public and on the field, but he also studied his own actions and the public's view of them. If George was a consummate actor, he was also an accomplished director of the man in the mirror. His attention to detail and acquired love of drama in the Augustan Age would eventually make him the preeminent American model of good manners in the public space.

Throughout his life, Washington remained a sportsman. Like his British forefathers and contemporaries, George was also a gambler and a risk taker who relished his chances at a card table, at the races, or on a battlefield. He also loved to canoe, swim his horse across a river, and hunt. Even if today we think of him in superlatives, he was also very much a man of his time, and, though his rise as a young surveyor and then colonial officer still reads like a legend to many of us today, the actual context of his ascent is not exceptional. The British needed young men with George's excellent qualities and skills on their expanding frontier. As one English frontier officer said of a new charge who arrived to help him on the edge of the British India, "I was delighted to get him, for he was a wonderful man on a hillside, a good shot, a hard rider, absolutely fearless, and most cheery." George, even though he had lost his father at the age of eleven, was all of this and a fast learner. With each day in the woods, he became more valuable to the British imperialists who ruled the Old Dominion, including to Lord Thomas Fairfax and the governors of Virginia.

Though he would have little time on his hands to contemplate what his life would mean to the future of America, George eventually helped to define the broader concept of what today we can best call the "American sportsman." If one side of the coin in the age-old controversy concerning the value of sports could be embodied in one person, George came to stand for the virtuous and the well-regulated side of good sportsmanship. Washington's memorable performances on the hunting field and on the battlefield help crystallize his contribution to our modern ideas about athleticism and chivalry—even as they also highlight the intimate ties between sports and war through the ages. Invariably, George's actions, taken individually and seen by others as the core of his being, helped a young nation bridge the old to the new, as well as the aristocrat to the republican.

After my investigations, I truly believe that this story—the biography of a sportsman and gentleman—is essential to deeper understanding of George Washington's ascent and to the legacy he contributed to our national character. That doesn't mean that the subject of this story will cease to be an icon and an enigma, but seeing George primarily through his actions, not his words, I believe, offers a means of deconstructing his life anew and permitting a fresh consideration of a flesh-and-blood American who emerged onto the scene in the middle of the eighteenth century. In the end, I hope my efforts also contribute to our sense of George Washington the founder, who set the bar for our young nation as an advocate of sound competition, honor, fair play, and impeccable manners.

INTRODUCTION

Life, Liberty, and the Pursuit of the Fox

I HAD BEEN WAITING several months to make my first real foray into the strange world of American foxhunting. It still felt awkward. My first real job out of college had been working as an advertising manager for a trade publication, *Fur World*, on New York's Fashion Avenue. I had sold space to Greek and Jewish furriers and offered them photographers and sometimes my own girlfriend to sport their mink, sables, and fox hair coats. I was haunted still whenever I saw a taxidermist's work on display. After New York, live foxes kept showing up in my life at strange moments. On the eighteenth hole in Cairo, I had a friendly encounter with an adolescent fox that ran off with my golf ball, and a lovely red fox occasionally sprinted across my front lawn in Virginia. In Afghanistan, one day my armed guard jumped out of his car with a Kalashnikov and fired repeating rounds up the slope of a mountain at a sleek gray fox. I have to admit that I rooted quietly for the prey to get away. I came to think, rightly or wrongly, of foxes as friendly, even noble creatures.

Then in mid-December word came from the executive director of the Masters of Foxhounds Association of America: "You'll be a guest of Hunt Master Linda Armbrust and you'll be riding Cory," wrote Lt. Col. Dennis Foster, who advised me to report early for duty. I had come to think of Dennis as the 007 of American foxhunting, a gentleman and officer who had worked in espionage for the US army during the Cold War. We had a few war zones in common, and so we became friends. He had ridden camelback in Afghanistan and Iraq and ridden to the hounds on four continents and in eleven countries, chasing stag, wild pigs, and foxes galore. He was also considered an expert in "animal rights tactics"—which is to say he is an advocate for foxhunters. But his job is as an inspector or judge of foxhunts across America with the goal to make sure hunting includes care for the countryside, horses, hounds, and fair sportsmanship in regard to the fox. Some hunt clubs get spooked when he shows up unexpectedly to lay down the law.

Dennis informed me that this would be an official hunt, so I wouldn't be able to get by in blue jeans and a cowboy hat. He had already provided me with a few tips on hunt etiquette, and I was trying hard to digest them. I still hoped that I might be better at foxhunting, George Washington's favorite sport, than I had proven at his other pastimes: ballroom dancing, fencing, and gambling for money. The prestigious Blue Ridge Hunt, with which I would ride, also stressed a few rules to keep in mind. Some sounded logical, like "Never gallop through livestock." Since I don't drive my car through livestock, I thought, surely I would not gallop through a herd of cows.

Other rules were more obscure, and I was sure I would need Dennis's help when push came to shove. For instance, I would not easily "learn the difference between hay fields such as alfalfa and permanent pasture." But it was a special point of protocol that concerned me even more: "When hunting, do not get sloppy with your appearance. Clothes should be neat, your horse well groomed, and your tack clean." I was pretty sure that, with those rules, no cowherds would be allowed to hunt foxes in Virginia. My Afghan buzkashi-playing attire, stashed away in mothballs and consisting of a mangy fur cap and a sheepskin jacket, just wouldn't suffice. These folks wouldn't be barreling into each other, hurling the carcass of a goat. Foxhunting was a royal sport.

For the Blue Ridge Hunt, "in season" you were not to wear "ratcatcher" or any assortment of expensive-looking tweeds. These were acceptable only for informal hunts. Fine, I thought. I was after an authentic look, mostly because I didn't want to draw attention. I also knew I wouldn't be able to just pick up what I needed in an hour at Macy's in the Polo Ralph Lauren department. That was the faux look. No, my hunting attire required a specialty store, and Dennis knew just the place. He sent me to the Middleburg Tack Exchange to get geared up.

I lived out in Middleburg, Virginia, for several months while researching this book, and I already had the impression the whole town

Col. Dennis Foster jumping a stone fence atop his horse, Avalone. *Jim Meads*

was a bit overstocked with wannabe cavaliers and foxhunters afraid of what might be lurking over the next hedgerow. I was a little ashamed that I was about to add my name to the list. The kind of guy walking the streets and hanging out in the historic taverns of Middleburg is usually a bit overly posh, bordering on foppish, and—more often than not—living off a supersized trust fund. There are some other types out there, but they usually fall into the same trap. F. Scott Fitzgerald once landed seven miles farther along Route 50 in Upperville to dry out, and when his editor Max Perkins called from New York, the lady whose old Virginia family was hosting F. Scott in their manor home reassured Perkins that the author had stop drinking whiskey entirely. How was he otherwise, inquired Perkins. "Unfortunately, he is downing a case of beer a day," she said.

Plenty of modern and somewhat hopeless romantics still plied the streets. I recalled one inebriated chap who used to stumble in and out of bars asking ladies if they would like a ride in his horse-drawn carriage, which was waiting outside. Invariably, you could find his downcast coach driver still warming his hands at closing time.

The Tack Exchange was set back snuggly on a side street behind the Fox's Den Tavern. I had arrived for our hunt a day early in order to thumb through the merchandise and maybe get a discount based on my threadbare look. First I needed riding pants.

"What is the difference between the white and the beige?" I inquired.

"The white is for hunt staff," said a tall saleslady who looked like she had just dismounted from a horse.

"Oh."

George Washington's step-grandson wrote that George—in his later years—would ride in a "true sporting costume, of blue coat, scarlet waistcoat, buckskin breeches, top boots, velvet cap, and whip with long thong." Notably, as one of the wealthiest planters in Virginia, he had a purchasing agent in London who did most of his shopping—on very good credit.

I found a pair of riding pants, but in the fitting room I struggled mightily to pull them shut. I finally landed knee-length breeches that had inner-knee protectors and which hugged the rest of me way too tight for comfort. I found deerskin riding gloves and began rummaging through the tall black boots. They were in a musty basement, and they were, I was kindly informed, "experienced." If I had wanted a pair of new ones, it would have run me up to $1,000. For my first real hunt, anyway, I wasn't too proud to go in someone else's boots. I found a pair that fit perfectly.

I was torn over whether or not to buy a new riding crop. Care of a distant relative, I had with me an antique bone handle in the shape of a monkey with a jockey's cap on its head, and so I inquired if I could have someone in the store fit it with a strap of leather so it could serve its original purpose. "Sure, just leave it with us," I was told. The ladies of the Tack Exchange looked pleased when I dropped them a few hundred dollars on mostly used gear. I made a mental note that foxhunting, if you added in the cost of a horse, was probably the most expensive sport on earth, with the possible exception of big game hunting in Africa, which I was averse to for both moral and financial reasons.

Now if only Dennis had a black riding cap, I would be all set with the black cashmere jacket I already owned. After a night prowling George's old haunts in nearby Winchester, I showed up bright and early at Dennis's farmhouse in Millwood for coffee. He greeted me with his ruddy, athletic look and firm handshake, staring me up and down. "Excellent, I won't have to outfit you," he said. "We've got an hour to kill."

"Kill what?" I looked over to his kitchen counter at a well-crafted statue of a modern US Special Forces officer astride a prancing horse, holding not a whip but a machine gun.

I glanced up at the snarling fox heads and felt a tinge of pity thinking I would be going after their kin—hopefully not their cubs—later in the morning. If I kept my mouth shut, I thought, maybe there would be no blooding on my behalf. A blooding sometimes still takes place when a novice hunter witnesses his or her first kill, and the patrons of the hunt smear his or her face with blood. It sounded like a scene out of *Lord of the Flies*, and I was glad to hear from Dennis that it was not much in vogue—at least in the Shenandoah. "We don't recommend it since in today's society, if your nine-year-old daughter shows up for school for show-and-tell with her cheeks blushed with blood, it is hard to explain to anyone who doesn't understand the ritual," said Dennis. "We've had that happen."

Dennis informed me that the day's three masters of the Blue Ridge Hunt were Linda Armbrust (my sponsor), Brian Ferrell, and Anne McIntosh. "Oh, two ladies. That sounds perfect," I remarked. Dennis told me that women were in fact a bit more levelheaded than men in keeping everyone on the scent.

"Women can handle any hunt as well as a man. I thought I knew something about horses until I met my girlfriend, Laura, some years back," Dennis explained, referring to the young lady who would be saddling up our mounts later. "Now, well, I realize I know next to nothing," he deadpanned.

Dennis had picked a near perfect day for our outing. It was brisk and slightly windy, which is good for the hounds searching for a scent. As we bounced over to the neighbors, coffee splattered Dennis's dashboard. Our horses were still en route, but the party was already kicking off. I looked up the hill at a large stone manor with outbuildings and a wooden front portico. Our day's hostess—looking like someone out of a *Town and Country* photo spread—was out on the chilly lawn in a skirt. She offered tiny Smithfield ham sandwiches, hot cider, and a couple of harder options. I noticed earlier that Dennis had packed a flask of Cognac, so I demurred. Foxhunting is one sport, I noted, that permits serious drinking during the actual event. (Teddy Roosevelt's brother and Eleanor Roosevelt's ne'er-do-well father, Elliott, hunted drunk for a good part of his truncated life.)

Despite a hesitant approval earlier from Dennis of my new getup, I noticed that most of the other hunters had a few extra items that I definitely was missing. Like Dennis, they wore spurs and had crops. I asked about the spurs. "They are only necessary if you are in a tight spot or maybe if the horse gets spooked," he told me. No one dared wear a pair of sunglasses, and there were—to my surprise—absolutely no frills worn by the hunters. Flashy jewelry and little dazzles were frowned upon. The main thing was to have "the look," which meant looking pretty much like everyone else. If you wanted to spend lavishly, you could still do that on your horse and saddle. I soon discovered that the saddle I was sitting on was several thousand dollars' worth of English leather. My backside, I knew, would thank Dennis for it.

Laura, as lovely and no-nonsense as I had expected, met us at the bottom of a grassy knoll. She told me that I mustn't take my video camera on the hunt. "You'll need both hands," she said. I nodded and reminded myself that this wasn't a war zone but that it was surely as dangerous if I fell off my mount from a broken stirrup, as I had once done in the sands of Arabia. I was not reassured when Dennis reported to me that he had broken his back and most of his limbs across his career as a foxhunter. He was considered, after all, a master of the masters. "Courage," I said to myself, mounting Corinthian. He was a sleek, coffee-colored horse, groomed and saddled by Julia, a recent graduate of Sweet Briar College, long known as an equestrian stronghold for Virginia's finest.

We set off at a slow pace as the huntsmen, clad in a red coat and wielding a whip, "caste," or ushered, the hounds down into a covert of fallen leaves, ivy, and honeysuckle. The hills, covered in sharp granite outcroppings and light brown grass, ran in quick up-and-down slopes. Looking out across the sunlit winter horizon, I saw endless hills in rapid succession as far as the eye could see, running north along the river and behind me and southwest toward the deeper blues of Massanutten Mountain.

George Washington referred to the Shenandoah as the Garden of America. On his first rides as a surveyor there, he wrote in his diary, "We went through most beautiful garden groves of sugar trees and spent the best part of the day admiring trees and the richness of the land."

Dennis and I were now riding side by side, sandwiched between the ladies in front and behind.

"The region is arguably the best terrain for red foxes in America."

"Why is that?" I wondered aloud.

"Well. It is illegal now, but up until a few decades ago, you had foxhunters constantly importing red foxes from Britain." Still, the red fox did not actually become common in the Shenandoah and its environs until the middle of the nineteenth century. Most American red foxes are, in any case, genetically distinct from their European brethren. A recent study at the University of California suggested that most of the red fox blood in America has been on the continent for at least forty thousand years. Asian and arctic foxes took advantage of the Bering Strait land bridge and populated most of Alaska and Canada early on, migrating in the last several hundred years south and east across the continent. With that in mind, it sounded odd to me that Virginians had sent off to Mother England for fresh foxes. "Wouldn't they eat chickens?"

"That wasn't what they had in mind, Philip," Dennis reassured me. He pointed out that the red fox of any gene is up against stiff competition across the United States in the twenty-first century. Coyotes, often three times the body weight of a fox, are encroaching quickly on their territory.

"If the food chain for the coyote gets scarce, he will attack and kill the red fox, who competes for the same food chain," said Dennis. "Ninety percent of the hunts across the US and Canada now hunt the coyote exclusively, as he is akin to a small wolf, bigger, faster, and tougher than the fox."

We trotted up hills and through narrow ravines. Foxhunters, I soon gathered, aspire to look good only when they set off into the woods. The horses clomped through a stream and splashed everyone. Polished boots lost their sheen, and made-up faces were flecked with mud. Corinthian provided probably the smoothest ride I've ever taken, particularly given the jagged terrain. He fit the description of an excellent hunting horse: he was tireless, had good brakes, was a smooth jumper, and had a demeanor that was entirely calm—almost Zen-like. Unlike some other horses I knew, he clearly enjoyed new riders, and, apart from tripping once and nearly sending me headlong into a field of what looked like alfalfa, he trotted and galloped along with not a flinch or jitter. My Sweet Briar charge reassured me that Corinthian was enjoying the ride as much as I was. I also had good advice from Dennis, who told me to keep the toe of my boot turned out going down hills. It would help with balance. That was easy enough, as I'm naturally bowlegged.

The hounds were down in a hollow nosing about until Julia's horse got spooked and tore off at a gallop. It looked to me for a moment like she was a goner, but she reined him in. Like so many young ladies who love horses, she had extraordinary skills. "Something frightened him," she said of her young mount.

Legend has it that there was not a horse in America back in the colonial era that George Washington couldn't ride, which, as Dennis pointed out to me, is a rather fantastic assertion. He did actually fall off a horse, I recalled, albeit when it had been shot out from under him at Monongahela. Equines are herd animals, and—even when well trained—they are attuned to self-preservation. In other words, they run first and ask questions later, a bit like some of their human cousins. If you are a qualified horse whisperer, which I assuredly was not, none of this bothers you, and the beast usually complies with your wishes.

About an hour into our hunt, the hounds still weren't picking up on a scent. In foxhunting lingo, this is called "drawing a blank." They hadn't stopped trying, though; they nuzzled the earth, their noses sweeping through the leaves, pawing at this and that. It looked as though they were running around helter-skelter, but the huntsmen kept them mostly all on a line. It wasn't always enough, and a couple of the young hounds were lost to the pack sniffing about as the others dashed up a wooded hillside and out of sight.

That is where the "whippers-in" came in. A red-coated equestrian dashed down into the woods to round up the two yelping canines and point them back to their pack. I was starting to get the method to this madness. A huntsman needed his whole pack to properly "draw a line" across the woods. To accomplish this and have all the noses attuned to the prey, you wanted to "give the hounds the wind," making sure that, if there was a draft, which in the Shenandoah there invariably is, they are downwind. A scent will carry well in chilly wind.

Hounds have been bred for centuries to hunt the fox. Mixing it up with other animals is sometimes acceptable, but the best foxhounds want a fox almost exclusively, and, as one accomplished dog breeder suggests, "If you have a hound that likes to hunt whatever comes out of the covert, you may not want to breed that one." Gender isn't an issue, but this is one pastime in which it is acceptable for breeders to remind each other that the strength of their kennel "comes from the bitches."

George Washington paid particular attention to his hounds and became an accomplished breeder. Before the Revolution, he inherited a pack from his good friend and fellow hunter Captain Posey, who appears to have surrendered his hounds out of debts that he owed George.

From his diaries, it is clear that George was on a constant mission to breed a superior hound. On February 18, 1768, he wrote in his diary, "This time a Hound Bitch Mopsey of Mr. R. Alexanders (now with me) was proud, & shut up chiefly with a black dog Taster who lind [fertilized] her several times as did Tipler once, that is known of. The little Bitch Cloe in the House was also proud at the same time—but whether lined or not cannot be known. See how long they go with Pup."

The names for Washington's hounds alone—Sweet Lips, Venus, Drunkard, and Truelove—suggest a special rapport between man and beast, but George was also known to personally attend his pack, particularly when the canines suffered common diseases and infections. He applied medicinal ointments himself.

Several incidents across the course of his life suggest that Washington was an animal lover. One peculiar episode after the Battle of Germantown comes shining through. Whereas many of the legends of Washington's wartime chivalry are hard to nail down, this one isn't: Alexander Hamilton precisely scribbled the events in a note as they unfolded. Among other things, it is also a cautionary reminder to collar your pet.

In the wake of George's defeat at foggy Germantown, a small dog—of an unknown breed—scampered across front lines, lost and unable to find its way home. Soldiers from the Continental Army took it into their custody, considered briefly holding it hostage, but eventually put the fate of the lost dog in the hands of their commander in chief. George quickly consulted with Hamilton and had him write, "General Washington's compliments to General [William] Howe, does himself the pleasure to return him a Dog, which accidentally fell into his hands, and by the inscription on the Collar appears to belong to General Howe."

About ninety minutes into our hunt, the four of us had managed to divide ourselves from the rest of the hunt. We stood slightly bewildered near a fallen log and listened for the cry of the hounds. Nothing. Then came a long, torpid moan, which I thought might be a howl. "That's a cow," laughed Julie. We were lost but having fun.

Dennis to the rescue: he popped out a flask of Cognac and offered me a shot. I figured that with his connections, it was at least a century old, and it certainly tasted that way.

"Is this my cue to start speaking French?" I asked.

We looked behind us and waited. Then we saw a few hounds dash past, and we knew the rest of the gang wasn't long off. There is something majestic about a band of foxhunters, which makes them welcome on almost every farm in the Shenandoah. They came, hoofs pounding, in red coats with whips in the lead and black jackets, all in a grand procession, charging down a hill in our direction. We followed on, lining up to leap a fallen log.

Foxhunting is a British import. English literature is flush with references, so I sidled up to Peter Cook, one of the Blue Ridge Hunt's own imported members, to get an idea of why one Brit called the sport "a hobby which combined the buzz of class A drugs, the adrenaline rush of a Second World War dogfight," involving, among other things, "an incredible leaping beast on the same trip as you, while totally pissed, at the most convivial and glamorous party since the Duchess of Richmond's ball."

"Does it have anything to do with 'mad dogs and Englishmen'?" I asked.

"No, that is another story," he said.

"So what is the obsession?"

"Well, there were a lot of horses where I grew up," Cook told me. "I have a twin brother, and he was good at just about everything, but I took up after my favorite uncle, a foxhunter." Cook rode, while attending the elite boys school Harrow. "There is an old British expression that foxhunting has all the thrills of the battlefield but with only about ten percent of the danger." Indeed, the rigors of foxhunting were once considered ideal as a test of equestrian skills and endurance—an activity that spun off into the sport of steeplechasing. It was easy to see George's own attraction to foxhunting, as well as how the skills he acquired proved of use on a battlefield. Cook informed me that, in his view, American foxhunters are much kinder than British hunters. "From my experience in the US, if someone falls off a horse and is injured here, riders are likely to stop and help," he said. "In the UK, they are more likely to ignore the situation and keep riding."

"That seems a little cruel," I replied.

We stopped again to watch the hounds rooting around in the underbrush. Dennis introduced me to Jeff Lehew, master of the Thornton Hill Fort Valley Hounds, who, when he wasn't foxhunting, could be found floating around in his helicopter. Lehew, a sleek, handsome character, exceptionally attired, was of old French American blood. He informed me that he had only recently commissioned a painting of his ninth great-grandfather meeting up with George Washington on horseback at nearby Front Royal.

"Your people must be very good at both foxhunting and reproducing."

"There is a lot in common," Jeff replied.

Lehew also convinced me that foxhunting was excellent training for making split-second decisions in the high-powered world of big business. "There isn't much time for hesitation when the fox goes one way," he insisted.

After about three hours of trotting around the hills in search of our elusive quarry, the horn sounded. It is a beautiful instrument to listen to. Rounded like a French horn, it takes some talent to play. George's own bugle, along with his silver spurs and other hunting paraphernalia, can be seen on display most weeks at Mount Vernon.

We sallied through an open field, along the fast-moving Shenandoah, and into a small, isolated ravine.

"Tally ho!" Julie shouted, and I cranked my neck to look behind me. Dennis pointed. There on the knoll of a hill, scampering in the opposite direction of the hunt, was a small red fox. Outfoxed, I thought, admitting to myself alone that I was happy to see that fast-moving little creature escaping our hunt party as it crested the sunlit hill and disappeared.

Though I had not suspected it, there was another fox, and the canines were already in full cry. We turned in another direction. Our howling pack had surrounded a fox den or burrow at the base of a large hill.

"Gone to ground," someone shouted.

Dennis asked the hunt master for permission to ride forward and get a better look: Yelps of joy. Earlier I had asked Julia if the huntsman could still save a fox if the dogs were on it. "Well, that is very difficult," she replied. "Usually they take the fox, in any case."

I braced myself. To my surprise, or possibly because American foxhunters aren't really that anxious to see fur flying and blood spilled, the huntsman called off the hounds with his bugle. Mercifully, there would be no blooding—at least on my behalf. I breathed a sigh of relief.

"They'll be rewarded for this," Dennis said. "In America, we never dig a fox out. We don't have many, and we want them to get away so we can chase them another day. The only foxes that are killed are caught above ground before they reach the earth. They are usually sick, lame, or stupid: it is survival of the fittest and helps maintain healthy fox populations."

"I see," I said.

American foxhunting has always been more about the chase than the kill, Dennis reassured me. In his diary, Washington would carefully record the length of a chase, down to the precise minute, but in some cases, having cornered a fox, he also would not bother to kill it, as at the end of a hunting day in December 1785, when he wrote, "We then after allowing the Fox in the hole half an hour put the Dogs upon his trail & in half a Mile he took to another hollow tree and was again put out of it but he did not go 600 yards before he had recourse to the same shift—finding therefore that he was a conquered [the] Fox, we took the Dogs off, and came home to Dinner."

Our own pack obeyed the huntsmen, and we headed back for a late hunt breakfast. I was in some serious pain; we had been chilling our bones and beating up our backsides on our steeds for nearly four hours.

As we galloped the last hundred yards, I commented to Dennis that he would go down in my book as a "very humane hunter."

"We don't usually like to use that word in the context of hunters," he chuckled.

Dennis had himself written about a British hunt he had been on in his capacity as an international hunt master, commenting, "Sometimes the dead body of the fox is thrown to the hounds. This is no different than us carving up a holiday turkey." I had weighed that unusual analogy considerably but decided I preferred the story more about how some foxhunting families had adopted fox cubs and raised them—lo and behold—with their own canines.

During any hunt, the breakfast is the final reward for the hunters. As I looked about the dining room steeped with sterling plates full of pork and beef, dainty rolls, and assorted sweets, I immediately understood

I

Englishman in America

WASHINGTON AND FAIRFAX—FIELD SPORTS

NEW YORK G. P. PUTNAM & CO.

Washington and [George William] Fairfax—Field Sports, engraved by H. B. Halls Sons, after Felix Octavius Carr Darley, nineteenth century. *Courtesy of Mount Vernon Ladies' Association*

why. Riding on an empty stomach with only a shot or two of Cognac is a great way to build up an immense appetite.

Our hostess introduced me to Lucia Herndon, who is the Virginia vice regent for the Mount Vernon Ladies' Association, the group of refined and astute women who bought Mount Vernon from my great-great-grandfather in 1858.

Proprietor of the nearby Chapel Hill farm, Lucia told me that she and her husband raise rare colonial-era cows known as the Randall lineback. Like other members of the Blue Ridge Hunt, Lucia is keen to preserve George Washington's old foxhunting grounds, including the ancient estate of his early mentor, Thomas, Lord Fairfax, Sixth Baron of Cameron, whose five-million-acre Northern Neck Proprietary George helped to survey. "Greenway Court and these hills around us are some of the most important historical landmarks we have in America," Lucia explained.

Lord Fairfax was an unusual character. Curmudgeonly and in love with Virginia, he was also obsessed with fox and stag hunting, so much so that he had his own hounds shipped to America before he met George as a fatherless youth in his teens.

"With neighbors, we raised money to save buildings at Lord Fairfax's Greenway Court, and the Commonwealth of Virginia matched us," Lucia continued. "People sometimes forget that George Washington had his start in life out here in the Shenandoah. He was a brilliant equestrian, and he used all his talents to craft himself into a gentleman and meet some of the most stimulating people in America."

I glanced behind me. Dennis had polished off his Cognac and was ready to feed me to the hounds. I was certainly indebted to him for helping a downtrodden writer to hobnob with the rich and famous in the Shenandoah. I had come away with a few insights. For one, I now knew that foxhunters aren't all rich snobs; the Blue Ridge Hunt had allowed a wretch like me to make a leap—if only for a few precious hours—into their strange world, this "sport of kings."

That was the past, according to my magnanimous host. "Foxhunting is as egalitarian a sport as you can possibly find," he insisted during the ride back to his farm. "In fact, it's not about foxhunting or hunting with the hounds at all; it's all about freedom, liberty, and livelihood."

"Yes," I agreed with a wink. "Life, liberty, and the pursuit of the fox!"

❦ 1 ❧

Passage into the Woods

GEORGE'S FIRST ADVENTURE deep into the Virginia wilderness began amid the now extinct sugar maples and rolling green hills where today's Route 50 sweeps down across the rushing Shenandoah River and over the Blue Ridge and where, on a clear day, even in the twenty-first century, you can see the opaque Alleghenies in the distance. It is here near Ashby's Gap, almost unmarked except for the sign of a modern-day canine kennel, that George, along with George William Fairfax—seven years his elder and the son of Col. William Fairfax—and a motley surveying team, set off to mark the natural landscape and carve out parcels of land on the new American frontier in March 1748. It is also here, a two-day horse ride from Ferry Farm, that I began to carefully retrace the footsteps and hoofprints of young George as he embarked upon his new surveying career and began to record his amusing insights into a new bound diary.

For my own rides through the Shenandoah, I saddled up with, among others, Sam Snapp and her husband, Wayne. The two were old Shenandoah stock, and Wayne still had the 1750 deed provided by Lord Thomas Fairfax, Sixth Baron of Cameron, whose hills and fields these once were. With Sam at my side, I took several rides through this fertile, lush valley, which is in some ways as pristine as it must have been in the eighteenth century. The forest was alive with birds, squirrels, deer, and families of black bear, and its floor was thick with decaying leaves, ferns, and broken branches. These are also the same winding trails that George traipsed, the steep hills and quiet hollows where the war cries of natives and white men on horseback once echoed.

Our rides on Virginia quarter horses began in the crisp air amid poplar clusters and beneath a steep hill marked by jagged limestone outcroppings. Sam, my soft-spoken guide with a broad smile and fancy cowgirl boots, literally grew up on a horse, like so many generations before her. "My brother rode a Thoroughbred, and I can remember racing against him through the woods," Sam told me over a cup of coffee in her barn at her Wagon Wheel Ranch on a windy January day. "My dad wouldn't drive us anywhere, so we had to get there on a horse. If we rode over to a friend's house, we would just put the horses in their barn for the day, or if we went for ice cream at the country store, we would just tie them to a fencepost. Pretty soon I learned to ride competitively. You blink your eyes and a quarter horse is gone. We breed them for hard work and running hard."

Sam was and is a fierce competitor, and when I met her, she had just won the national barrel racing championships held a year earlier in Washington, DC, which test the skill of rider and beast in a series of hairpin turns at short distances. Though I've ridden on three continents, including on the sands of the Sinai and in the Hindu Kush, I felt like a novice riding beside Sam. "When I take someone on a trail ride, I usually go out with a gelding—that's a neutered male—because they have an even keel and don't get overly excited at the sight of a snake or wild animal," she said as we trotted up a barren crest and peered over a caved-in log cabin southwest toward the sprawling Blue Ridge.

George had just turned sixteen years old as he crossed low mountains and the Shenandoah River in the headwaters of the Potomac River. There are no precise pictures of him at this young age, but early descriptions and later depictions show that he had a thick Roman proboscis beneath a wide brow anchored by wide-set, blue-gray eyes. His hair was auburn and tied back behind his muscular neck. George was excessively tall for his time—just a couple of inches taller than his father, Gus, and rather slender at 180 pounds. Yet he had wide hips, powerful legs, and long arms, and he carried himself well—by one subsequent account, as "straight as an Indian." Perched on the back of a horse, George was twice the man and athlete, probably sensing what Winston Churchill would write: that when you are on a horse, "you have the best seat you will ever have" in life.

Yet, apart from the careful sketches of the hills, tree lines, farming plots, and valleys he drew in his early teens, George still lacked the qualifications and formal education to begin work as a surveyor. Most of his survey team's members had field experience, but George was tolerated—likely coddled—because he had been chosen for the apprenticeship by Lord Fairfax and his powerful cousin Col. William Fairfax, whose daughter Anne his older half brother Lawrence had married.

Reading through George's diary entries on this first journey is a little like glancing over the raw script of a slapstick comedy set three centuries ago. His writing, while terse and stilted at times and also peppered with poor grammar, tells us much about his burning curiosity and how he viewed his own emerging role in a world that was entirely new to him. For a sixteen-year-old, he was acutely aware of his natural surroundings, and his early notes are marked by an adolescent exuberance that competes with a classic English deadpan.

On his first trail ride, George rode a saddled and sure-footed horse alongside chief surveyor James Genn, followed by a train of pack mules loaded down with arms, rations, and corn for horses. Four nights in, George wrote, "I not being so good a woodsman as ye rest of my company striped myself very orderly and went into ye Bed as they called it when to my surprise I found it to be nothing but a little straw-matted together without sheets or anything else but only one thread bare blanket with double its weight in vermin." On a subsequent night, his bed under the stars "catch'd a fire," and a snoozing George was rescued when another in the surveying party woke up and extinguished the blaze. The incidents expose Washington's inexperience and surprise over the rough conditions, surely harsher than what he had faced as a child back at Ferry Farm.

George was not out of his own element for long, and after several days of camping in the open air, he landed in "a good feather bed with clean sheets." That night the survey party had what the equestrian wrote of as a "very agreeable regale," which included a "good dinner prepar'd for us Wine & Rum Punch in Plenty." The surveyors carried ample supplies of alcohol on their journey, and George was already enjoying social drink, which he would imbibe, distill, and serve his friends—within limits—all of his life, including as a soldier and commander. Though New England Puritans often considered this a vice, an occasional "agreeable regale" with plentiful supplies of alcohol was a ritual Virginia gentry enjoyed shamelessly on the frontier and in the manor house.

As days of steady rain overtook George's small caravan, the rising waters of the Potomac delayed the surveyors, and so they made a short detour to the "Fam'd Warm Springs," at present-day Berkeley Springs. The small West Virginia town had earlier been known as

Bath, after the lively English town described comically centuries earlier by the poet Geoffrey Chaucer. I spent several days here on my own, riding around in the forest where George had surveyed plots. From the valleys, one looked up at steep cliffs above the warm springs. It was easy to imagine George young and lost in thoughts of his ensuing adventures as he waited for the high waters of the upper Potomac to recede. This lush valley at the foot of a small mountain had a reputation with white settlers and Native American Algonquin tribes for curing numerous ailments. I climbed the wooden stairs to the town's museum and discovered a recently removed road sign indicating that the springs could indeed cure everything from "infantile paralysis to rheumatism and diabetes." Judging from the run-down spa rooms, which looked oddly like stalls for hosing down livestock, and a minor trickle of tourists from Philadelphia and Washington, the magical powers of the waters were finally receding into the past.

As the rains subsided for George, the survey team proceeded over steep, small mountains to a point not far from present-day Paw Paw, West Virginia, where they crossed the Potomac in wooden canoes and, as George described it, "swam our horses over." Washington and the survey party made their way up the opposite side of the river to present-day Oldtown, Maryland, where they stayed for several nights in the well-fortified cabin of Thomas Cresap, a land agent for Maryland's Lord Baltimore. He'd been arrested in Pennsylvania a decade earlier on the charge of murder. As I glanced at the foundations of Cresap's home, overgrown with vines now, I wondered what relish George would have found in the stories of Cresap's fights with the law.

The survey party stopped nearby, meeting up with Native Americans, whose returning warriors clutched a prize. Excited and amused, Washington wrote what some historians have called one of the better accounts from this era of an Indian dance: "We were agreeably surpris'd at the sight of thirty odd Indians coming from war with only one scalp. We had some Liquor with us of which we gave them part—it elevating their spirits put them in the humour of daucing of whom we had a war daunce. Their manner of Daucing is as follows Viz. They clear a circle & make a great fire in the middle then seats themselves around it, the speaker makes a grand speech telling them in what manner they are to Daunce after he has finish'd the best dauncer jumps up as one awaked out of a sleep & runs & jumps about the ring in a most comical manner he is follow'd by the rest."

George's account of the performance, which runs on to include their music making, is laced with grammatical errors. George and young Fairfax gawked and laughed, but what they witnessed was a dance custom that often followed the conquest of a foe—in this case at least one. For me, it brought to mind the arrowheads and ancient stone hatchet heads that I unearthed as a youngster on a mound on the lawn of my own Virginia home. It also recalled the mock warfare rituals I'd seen enacted in the highlands of Asia.

George's youthful air of superiority did not stop him from getting to know the Virginia woodland natives. He was entertained in their company even as uncertainties lingered ahead. Back on the trail, he wrote, "with Indians all day," suggesting a complex, close relationship between the survey party and the tribesmen.

Though Englishmen in North America, including George, looked down their noses at these so-called savages, they shared a fair bit in common, whether they wanted to acknowledge it or not. For their part, the natives hunted for a living, waged incessant war, and tried to rise within their own ranks based on their prowess as warriors and hunters. Their customs included bloody rites of passage and were influenced by sacred beliefs that gave meaning to the trees, streams, and animals. They were required to prove themselves as competitors, and to do so, they wrestled, fought, and danced—ritual activities laced with deeper meaning.

These moments with the woodland Indians were new for George but not for earlier explorers. Englishmen and Spaniards elsewhere in the New World had already witnessed Native Americans painting their bodies and decorating their playing sticks before lacrosse games, an indigenous American sport. In 1763 one tribe in upper Michigan invited British soldiers to play a lacrosse match with them in a ruse that worked as well as a Trojan horse. The natives joyfully played the match, edging closer to the gates of Fort Mackinac, only to enter and commence a bloody battle that would end in a massacre of their foe.

Virginia's woodland native people already had their own sporting history with whites. Three decades before George launched his survey-ing career, Virginia governor Alexander Spotswood, whose business interests were responsible for helping to settle Fredericksburg, took several forays across present-day Virginia and into the Shenandoah. In a humorous gesture to the past, Spotswood founded the Knights of the Golden Horseshoe, which, in the name of expanding the Virginia frontier, amounted to something more akin to a drinking party of gentlemen and their porters gallivanting around the woods and pretending to be the knights of Sir Lancelot—or an eighteenth-century Monty Python version thereof. John Fontaine, the French Huguenot assigned to chronicle the journey, described one drinking regale as follows: "We drank [to] the King's health in champagne, the Princess' health in brandy, and the rest of the Royal family in claret." This constant toasting took place at each campsite along the route.

Fontaine's lucid account reads even today like a fraternal band of brothers run amok on the frontier. Spotswood, a descendant of King Robert II of Scotland, was born in British-run Tangier, Morocco, in 1676, and he had won plaudits in Williamsburg before his journey into the woods. He had dispatched a ship, the *Ranger*, to hunt down the infamous pirate Blackbeard, whose throat was cut and whose severed head was hung on the ship's bow. Spotswood had an adventurous and eccentric flair: on one of his early expeditions, he sponsored a sporting event for young Indian warriors, outside the gates of one his own wilderness forts. As Fontaine recounted, "The governor sent for all the young boys, and they brought with them their bows, and he got an axe which he stuck up and made them all shoot by turns at the eye of the axe, which was about 20 yards distance. The governor had looking glasses and knives, which were the prizes." He added, "They were very dexterous at this exercise and very often shot through the eye of the axe." Following this display of prowess, the natives then "danced all around endeavoring who could outdo the one the other in antic motions, and hideous cries."

Spotswood and his party likely did not understand—as sixteen-year-old George did not either—the significance of what they were observing, but they certainly were familiar with the sport of archery and knew that it had amused Englishmen for centuries. Even King Henry VIII had designated his own club of Round Table archers, named in honor of King Arthur. Accuracy with the bow was more than a mere *sport* for these young woodland warriors, however: in many cases it meant the difference between an honorable livelihood and poverty or brutal death. As an expert in the native Powhatan Indians of Virginia wrote, "The consequences of failure as a warrior were ignominy at best and horrible death at worst."

While I was on horseback with Sam in the woods, on several occasions we sprinted playfully toward herds of bounding whitetail deer, and I was reminded, as Spotswood's scribe had chronicled, that natives who stalked deer with their bows in the Shenandoah often did so by pretending to be deer themselves, disguised in "two deer skins sewed together" and mock antlers. Their bodies greased with bear oil, bows in hand, they crouched on all fours behind trees and rocks, licking themselves like deer in pretense if one glanced over. Spotswood would have been wise to keep a few of the native warriors at his side as he continued on into the Shenandoah. A few weeks later, when his gallants were attacked by several bears at the Mason Camp, named for his fellow traveler George Mason, the father of the author of the Virginia Declaration of Rights, they fought the animals off, but Fontaine wrote that some of "the dogs suffered in the engagement."

On a subsequent trip into the Shenandoah, young George openly praised the natives for their skills. But this time, he observed them as they stalked, and when possible, he also tested his own improving hunting abilities. Keeping exact score one day on his journey, George wrote that he shot at wild turkeys and "missed twice," adding the next day that he "killed two" wild turkeys. Each man in the Fairfax survey party cooked his take on spits, eating from wood chips for plates. Though the surveyors had packhorses with provisions, the team lived off the meat they hunted in the wild.

Washington was born at the right moment, both for his own sake and the sake of an unborn nation. He took his first breath in Virginia, whose residents aspired to mimic the pastimes of Great Britain. As a subject of the Crown living on the edge of a rapidly expanding empire, he began to engage in English games and pastimes, or their colonial equivalents, and like the native games he now witnessed in the Shenandoah, his own sports and games held real and symbolic meaning.

For centuries, sports and pastimes had helped to define British culture. In the sixteenth century, a century before any Washington arrived on the shores of Virginia, King Henry VIII's royal hunts through the English hills displayed a relevant microcosm of society, with kings, princes, and even princesses taking charge of steeds, riding across their own surveyed dominions while servants toiled in the stables and commoners looked on in awe or envy. Sports, believed to improve strength and character, also came with their own rules, defined and enforced by the upper classes to bolster their authority. The same Tudor dynasty also encouraged varied blood sports, including jousting and fencing, sponsored by the monarchs to stress their authority but also, and as crucially, the courage and martial skills of participants. In Britain, and across much of Europe, equestrian instruction was essential to the career of a young nobleman. Riding a horse well went hand in hand with fencing, dancing, and other displays of skill.

Yet, in the century before Washington's own birth, English sporting traditions were riven by turmoil. An ongoing struggle pitted Royalists and their Cavalier supporters against Puritans and their own backers, unfolding with nasty insults on both sides. The Crown weighed in as the ultimate authority. Specifically, King James wrote a kind of defense of sports and good fun in 1618. His decree, which would come to be known as his "Book of Sports," insisted that "our good people be not disturbed, letted, or discouraged from any lawful recreation, such as dancing, either of men or women, Archery for men, leaping, vaulting, or any such harmlesse Recreation." These words, suggested for Sunday enjoyments, would hardly appear, on the surface, to be controversial. The sponsorship of sports was, King James knew, sound politics and good training for war.

But ideologues of the Reformation had other ideas. King James's decree came as England's Puritans were rounding on their opponents, accusing them of "revels, with dancing, drinking, whoring, potting, piping," and debauched "gaming" of all sorts. The rising tide against having too much fun—which usually meant having a few too many drinks as well—forced Archbishop William Laud of the Church of England to reissue James's decree nearly two decades later in 1633 in a move meant to back contestants and their admiring public. In a tit for tat, with the rise of the Puritans, Parliament issued an order in 1643 to have the "Book of Sports" publicly burned in a symbolic denunciation of sports and the allegedly bad behavior that came with them.

Oliver Cromwell's Roundheads—who derived their name from the short, cropped hair of the Puritans—succeeded in establishing the Commonwealth and cracking down on gaming and otherwise lascivious living in 1649. The fun was put on hold, but only temporarily. It was not long before Great Britain recovered its gusto and continued with the sporting traditions that had characterized the

Middle Ages, particularly at the tournaments that featured equestrian sport, archery, and versions of rugby—or what would evolve into our violent modern-day American football—played with a pig's bladder. Even the church jumped back into the fray, again sponsoring pagan-like Maypole events around the time of Easter, which featured games of running, jumping, throwing, and wrestling.

Since Americans are indebted to the British for many of our strange sporting traditions, it may come as no surprise that our nation also inherited the English dissonance over the value of sports. Indeed, some believed the first surviving European colony in the New World, Jamestown, was almost destroyed by overindulgence in play. In 1611 newly arriving governor Sir Thomas Dale arrived in Jamestown to find residents engaged in "their daily and usual works, bowling in the streets." Far from praising them for their sporting values, Sir Thomas was appalled and disappointed by what he saw as the dissipation of his embattled lot, even as the colony was then teetering on the edge of starvation and extinction. An immediate crackdown on bowling and gaming ensued, but the New World's love of sports wasn't going to be banished by an ill-tempered governor.

Early on, Virginia's Anglican stock adhered closely to long-standing English sporting traditions. One of the *Oxford English Dictionary*'s past definitions of the word *sport* also curiously included the idea of "amorous dalliance," a reference to the romantic aspects of chivalry. In William Shakespeare's plays, for example, further connotations of the word embrace pastimes, pleasures, outdoor sports, games of hazard, jest, even mockery, and, as importantly, the theatrical play. A refined sportsman was a man who excelled at these games and understood the delicate art of chivalry, a word that derives from the idea of a gentleman on a horse. Accordingly, Virginians, who saw themselves as Englishmen living abroad, liked to refer to themselves as Cavaliers in the Old Dominion.

Everything from horse racing, the "sport of kings," to knocking an opponent over the head with a stick or cudgeling soon arrived on American shores. In Virginia, frivolous card games and British sports meant to defend a man's honor and train for war were present from the start, even if the daily grind prevented a boom until the middle of the eighteenth century. New World sports also evolved along new and different lines. Sports and games became signs of freedom and gentility, as opposed to actual labor, which colonists associated with suffering, even servitude.

As George Washington emerged onto the scene, riding horses and dancing at balls became the quintessential expressions of the contentious nature of colonial Virginia in the eighteenth century. His was a world where prowess was of immense consequence. Virginians of all ages brought their competitive spirits to the ballroom, and in scenes that would have amused the modern creators of *Dancing with the Stars*, attendees and participants delighted themselves with the fine dancing as much as with watching others slip up or otherwise entirely embarrass themselves on the floor. In the same vein, an exciting horse race in eighteenth-century Virginia was a special form of nonverbal communication, with riders testing their speed and often elbowing one another to oust an opposing jockey from his saddle.

In 1732, the year of George's birth, the Reverend Doctor James Blair was officiating horse races at the College of William and Mary and settling racing disputes whenever riders were accused of unsportsmanlike conduct. This included mean-spirited elbowing, but also even betting on fixed horse races. The Scottish Blair, who was president of the college, came to be known by some as the school's "sporting parson," but his successor as president weighed in with a stern antiracing resolution, threatening students with the "pain of punishment" for "race horses, kept in ye neighborhood of ye College, and belonging to any of ye scholars." This latest American flirtation with Puritanism didn't last long though, and a path to equestrian glory was soon again cleared for young scholars. In many ways, all of colonial America was a defiant free-for-all whose regulation would define the power of some and pose challenges to the pursuit of happiness for many.

Though Washington's rise as a young surveyor and then colonial officer is the stuff of legend, the actual context of his ascent is not exceptional. The young Virginian was a talented woodsman and a fast learner. He marked the mountain passes and noted the water sources, even surveying the views of the Indians and white settlers in his midst. With each day in the forests and fields, he became more valuable to the British imperialists who ruled the Old Dominion.

On his first treks into the Shenandoah, Washington learned from experienced men the essence of carefully walking a tract of land. He determined its boundary lines by reading the bearings on a circumferentor, a magnetic compass mounted on a tripod. When he went off on his own to survey, George almost always had the help of two chainmen who ran lines as he recorded the gradations and variations of the terrain, including the ridges, streams, and clusters of foliage.

There was probably no other occupation in the 1740s that could have made a man a better master of his world. Washington's surveying gave him a strong idea of the land and its every fixture: the hills, the valleys, the names of all species—what you can cultivate and even what you can hunt. It guaranteed that he would become an outdoorsman and a lover of nature. The life of a surveyor also allowed George to catch the first glimpse of his surprising future, but before we beat down that path, we must slip back in time to Virginia's low country to understand George's unique family roots and understand the first outlines of his character.

2

Born on an Empire's Edge

ON THE FARM WHERE WASHINGTON forged his character as a young man, the arc of early colonial history is still palpable 270 years on. The tidal waters of the Rappahannock whisper by, and if you listen attentively, you can almost hear the clanking wagons being loaded with pig iron set to be shipped back to Mother England. Imagine a little more, and you can hear the echoes of merchant ships unloading rum and sugar, the squeaking wheels of a wagon, and the ribald talk of seamen across the waters that guided ships up from the Chesapeake Bay. Glancing westward back up the river toward the rapids, young George surely would have wondered—between shooting at imaginary foes and hiding behind trees with his three younger brothers—what lay deeper still in Virginia's dense pine, maple, birch, and oak forests inhabited by strange native peoples and settlers.

When I walked down to the river, I passed the foundations of the smokehouse where the Washington family slaughtered and cured their hogs and then passed the plantation outbuildings where some twenty slaves lived side by side with George's relatively small family, which also included his full siblings John, Charles, Samuel, and Betty. As I continued, several groundhogs waddled into the woods and down to the river's edge. Upon reaching the shore, I thought to look for a stone large enough to toss across the river and match the legend of George's great arm, but I decided not to make an utter fool of myself. It was only one of so many legends about George's athletic abilities, a tale told by a distant Washington cousin, Lewis Willis. He had claimed to one writer that George could toss a stone across the river at the ferry landing, a reasonable distance but not an impossible feat for a strong young man. He was proud of his throwing arm, and claimed to his biographer later in life that he never in his life met a man "who could throw a stone so great a distance as himself," citing a high natural arch in the Shenandoah, which stood at a height of some 215 feet, that he had cleared one day.

From the age of six, George Washington grew up on a small plantation now called Ferry Farm. Until George turned eleven, his father, Augustine "Gus" Washington, was present and working to expand horizons for his children from two marriages. He was earning a good living on the backs of black slaves, which made him similar in some ways to other ambitious members of Virginia's middle and upper gentry in the eighteenth century.

But that's not how life started for the Washingtons in the New World.

The emigration of the first Washington, John—a full three generations before the birth of the first president—to Westmoreland County, Virginia, is a story worth retracing, as it informs George's early standing among his fellow Virginians. It also speaks to the acquisitive ways of his forefathers in a milieu of frontier savvy, competitiveness, and disease. For this venture back in time, just an hour down the road from Fredericksburg, I left a message on the phone of Westmoreland's leading genealogist, Dalton "Dal" W. Mallory.

He called me back the next day and in a lovely southern twang began an impromptu explanation of my own genealogy. He pointed out to me that I was related to several local characters I hadn't known about, said they were "good folks all around," and promised to meet me in town for a drive down the peninsula.

Blessed like many of his fellow southerners with loquacity and charm, Dal had recently written a dense history of the county's numerous cemeteries. He had had his work cut out for him centuries back: Westmoreland produced our first and fifth presidents, the Lees of Stratford Hall, and the Carters of Nomini Hall. "As a child, a distant cousin of yours would take me around the Washington family graveyards, point to a grave, and ask me if I knew who this one or that one was," he chuckled when I met him. "She was about four feet tall and couldn't see over the steering wheel, but she knew her Washington family tree!" Dal caught on and discovered that the county's dead white men were at least as interesting as any of its living ones. When he got a bit older, Dal, who wears his long hair tied back, became a historical impersonator. He referred to it as "first-person living history" and noted that he had once "ridden with the hounds," playing the person of Lord Thomas Fairfax, one of George's first benefactors and mentors. As we stopped before our tour of the region to collect his mail, I noted that Dal's actual mailing address was "Washington's Birthplace, Virginia."

Westmoreland County is today popular with not only colonial and Civil War history buffs but also an unusual modern crowd that moves with ease between interests in drag racing at the local car track and in drag queen shows on the beach. A few miles from Washington's birthplace, the gargantuan off-track-betting hall, Riverboat on the Potomac, advertised FEMALE IMPERSONATORS AS SEEN ON *AMERICA'S GOT TALENT*.

Washington's birthplace, though well marked, is not as well known to Virginia's tourists, most of whom come to Westmoreland County for—apart from the aforementioned activities—boating, wine tasting, or pilgrimages to Stratford Hall, the birthplace of another famous Southern son, Robert E. Lee. I had already taken a tour of the mansion on my own and was impressed with the long flowing locks in the portraits of progenitors and stories of the Lee family's soirees held on the rooftop of the grand house. Back down on the water, I discovered that Westmoreland is one of Virginia's nicest counties, thick with history and thin with people. Steeped in tradition and southern hospitality, you can still drive for miles without seeing another human. As we drove toward an ancient church steeple, a mature bald eagle broke through the branches, a white tail fluttering beneath a snowy gray sky narrowed on either side of the road by immense pines and overhanging oaks.

Westmoreland County is a part of Virginia's Tidewater region, which gave rise to Jamestown in 1607. A year later, John Smith explored the shores near several of the Washington family's future homes, continuing in a boat up the Potomac near present-day Washington, DC. A few short decades after that, back in England, Rev. Lawrence Washington, the father of the first Washington, ran into trouble with a band of feisty zealots. An Oxford-educated master of divinity, a former college fellow, and an avowed Royalist, Reverend Washington, born in 1602 at the stately Washington family manor at Sulgrave, had been assigned to a parish in Purleigh, England, due east of London. Puritans weren't impressed with his reverence, though, and charged him with being a "common frequenter of Ale-houses." Worse, they said he was "oft drunk" while performing the Lord's work. Despite protestation of the charges from a supportive congregation at his All Saint's Parish, Lawrence was forced out as rector. The church reassigned him to a distant and smaller parish, where he died with little to his name in the early 1650s.

With Roundheads seizing power in 1649 and initiating an interregnum that would last over a decade, Lawrence's son John would seek a livelihood as a seaman on the *Sea Horse of London*, captained by John Prescott. The trading ship set sail from Danzig, Poland, and navigated through the Baltic Sea, eventually meeting John Washington in Elsinore, Denmark—a town earlier made famous in Shakespeare's *Hamlet*—after he had traveled there to secure trading deals. In the late winter of 1656 the *Sea Horse* embarked for Virginia to fill fresh tobacco orders. In one of those serendipitous moments in American history, court records show that "ye Vessell was cast away" on a sandbank in the shallows of the Potomac River along the shores of Westmoreland County. The ship lost its returning cargo and suffered extensive damage. The crew escaped and began a lengthy process of repairs.

We walked down to the shore and looked at the calm ripples across the Potomac. There wasn't a ship in sight, and the muddy waters spread out as far as the eye could see. It would be hard to run anything aground here, except at night. George's great-grandfather apparently liked what he saw, though, as he struck up conversations with local plantation owners who had begun to settle the new county. John Washington soon befriended an established colonial, Nathaniel Pope, who owned tracts of land in the area and had an alluring daughter, Anne. Pope understood John's budding wish to remain in Virginia, and he invited both Captain Prescott and Washington over to his home to talk about their impending separation. Attempting to resolve a roiling dispute between the two men, Westmoreland County records show that he stepped in to help his future son-in-law. The documents read, "If ye said Washington did owe ye said Prescott anything he ye said Mr. Pope would give ye said Prescott ready paymt in Beaver at eight shillings per pound." Although, in what wreaked of revenge, Washington would later accuse Prescott of wrongfully murdering an accused "witch" aboard one of his ships, he jumped on the deal in beaver skins that day and shortly thereafter asked for Mr. Pope's daughter's hand in marriage. Some eighteen months after his ordeal with Captain Prescott, John was married in 1659. The newlyweds had seven hundred acres of their own near Pope's Creek, Virginia, and a solid loan of eighty pounds sterling to start their new life.

Like his great-grandson George would do one day, John Washington moved rapidly up the social ladder, obtaining the post of justice of the peace in 1662, gaining jurisdiction over financial affairs, land disputes, and some—but not all—legal affairs. Elected to the Virginia House of Burgesses in 1666, John also attained the rank of colonel in the local militia and in 1674 purchased much of the land, a former Native American hunting ground, which one day would become George Washington's Mount Vernon estate. Only a year later, in 1675, John was asked to lead a force to investigate recent raids of Iroquois Indians from across the Potomac in Maryland.

When he arrived in Maryland, at least five natives being held by the Maryland militia were killed in captivity. Though John was cleared in Westmoreland County of any wrongdoing, Virginia's governor, William Berkeley, reprimanded him for what Berkeley deemed to be overly aggressive tactics. In the process, the tribe's members gave America's first Washington a dubious moniker that translated roughly as Destroyer of Villages, a nickname that the woodland natives of Virginia and into the Ohio Valley would remember for generations.

John Washington died in 1677 at the age of forty-six, with some 8,500 acres to his name and enough of a nest egg to guarantee his short-lived son, Lawrence, a good start. Though George's grandfather, Lawrence, died at age thirty-eight, Dal reminded me that Lawrence married well, to one Mildred Warner, whose family traces its roots directly back to the fourteenth-century British king Edward III (the son of Queen Isabella of France), whose reign transformed the Kingdom of England into one of the most formidable military powers in Europe. George's own twenty-fourth great-grandmother was a notable equestrian and rebel, as I discovered while examining his British genealogical records with Dal. This was none other than Lady Godiva, who—as legend has it—rode naked through the streets of Coventry, England, in support of the tenants who were protesting the overtaxation imposed by her own husband. "George had a lot of interesting and royal bloodlines, but he either did not know it, or he simply paid almost no attention to it in his lifetime," Dal told me. In his later years, George did begin to mark many of his possessions, including his coach and silver plate, with his Washington family coat of arms.

Dal walked me down to the Washington gravesite. Behind us was a functioning National Parks Service colonial-era plantation, flush with oxen, plows, and, well, slave laborers. It was a blustery day, and the cold winds made an extended vigil unlikely. John and Lawrence were buried together in a family crypt a few hundred meters from George's birthplace. The crypt also contains the bones of George's father, Gus. I stood for a moment in a flurry of melting snow, thinking not only of the challenges for the Washingtons in the seventeenth century but also of the history of Virginia, a state that produced eight—or seven, depending on your analysis—US presidents, not to mention a fair share of writing that set America on its current course. As Dal and I turned and walked against the wind and snow, a father and son arrived to pay their respects, the only other visitors in sight.

Next we were off to see where George was born. "We don't know nearly as much as we would like to about George's father, Gus, but we know he inherited the ambition and drive of his grandfather, John," Dal told me. Blond-haired and six feet tall, Gus was, according to acquaintances, "mild, courteous, and gentle." Though he likely suffered from debilitating gout in his later years, he was known to have "raised and placed in a wagon a mass of iron that two normal men could barely raise from the ground." The story does not sound like a stretch given that Gus recorded sending regular twenty-ton shipments of pig iron from a furnace he operated. He took pride in never having used his immense strength to fight in anger with another man over any petty dispute. Gus, who was only four years old when his own father died, was educated at the Appleby School in Derbyshire, England, before returning to Virginia to live with Westmoreland relatives and help settle his father's estate.

Augustine Washington became justice of the peace in 1716, speculating on land in Westmoreland County, the third member of the Washington family to hold such a position. Though he had a successful career and a family in his wife and two sons, Lawrence and Augustine "Austin" Jr., his fortunes eventually turned in 1730: upon his return from a trip to enroll his sons at his old Appleby School, he found that his wife, Jane, had died unexpectedly in his absence. The men in George's family, particularly the heads of households, usually did not live to an old age, but they were often widowed. A year after the death of his first wife, Gus wed twenty-three-year-old Mary Ball, the daughter of Col. Joseph Ball, who hailed from a family of well-educated Englishmen and planters on a farm on the Corotoman

River in nearby Lancaster County, Virginia. Mary's dowry, which included two plots of land near Gus's iron mining venture, and her equestrian skills, no-nonsense view of life, and devout nature made her an appealing choice for Gus.

Dal and I paid a visit to Yeocomico Church, where Gus and Mary are believed to have married. Some of the bricks dated to 1706, and I was reminded as I gazed through the chapel window that the early Puritans, who had harassed Gus's great-grandfather, Rev. Lawrence Washington, were nowhere to be found in this grave-yard. Oddly enough, it held the remains of American novelist and Hemingway contemporary John Dos Passos alongside those of several famous Virginians.

With his new wife, Gus decided to further expand his family, and on a frigid day in February 1732, six years prior to the family's arrival at Ferry Farm, Mary gave birth to George Washington in a small wood-frame home in Pope's Creek, Virginia, some thirty-eight miles east of modern-day Fredericksburg and quite near the home of the first Washington settler, John Washington. Midmorning on that winter day, relatives dropped by—as tradition had it—to raise a hot toddy to the newborn's health. Months later at the break of spring, George's name would be inscribed into the family Bible with details of the time and place of his birth. "George was not born into wealth, but he was born surrounded by the wealthiest families in Virginia," Dal reminded me.

George had been born in an auspicious year both for Virginia and for his own prospects. A few months after George's birth, Virginia's wealthiest landowner, Robert "King" Carter, died possessed of £10,000, 300,000 acres of land, and some 1,000 slaves. Carter, and his father before him, had accumulated much of the massive fortune, as Thomas Lee of Stratford Hall had done, by overseeing the lands of the Culpepper family, which, by marriage, became the lands of Lord Thomas Fairfax. Fairfax's five-million-plus-acre royal land grant was known as the Northern Neck Proprietary. Still in England and alarmed that the Carters had obtained such wealth dealing on his own lands, Fairfax moved his cousin Col. William Fairfax, a former tax collector in Barbados, down from Boston to manage his precious Virginia accounts. The powerful Fairfax and his extended clan would take up residence beside another Washington home at Little Hunting Creek, the future Mount Vernon. In time, George's half brother Lawrence would marry a Fairfax, knitting the yarn of wealth and connections tighter for an aspiring young boy in Fredericksburg.

Anxious to exploit his own growing investments, Gus had moved the family twice after George's birth—the first time to Little Hunting Creek and the second time to Fredericksburg when George was just six years old. When the Washingtons arrived there, the port town was already a growing hub of English-inspired civilization on a sparsely inhabited frontier.

3

Mother, Manners, and Cockfights

GEORGE WASHINGTON'S BOYHOOD HOME, SOON to be rebuilt in its original form, sits across an interstate highway from a bustling McDonald's. When Walmart sought to build a massive outlet on the doorstep of the home, the Daughters of the American Revolution fortunately rose to the occasion, buoyed by local small business owners to put a screeching halt to that idea. Today the site remains poorly marked, and I had to swerve quickly off the highway through an open gate and in past a split-rail fence before I realized where I had landed. What unfolded before my eyes in a series of subsequent meetings was a tableau of clues to a childhood that remains arguably more mythologized than that of any other American.

With the help of David Muraca and Laura Galke, archaeologists who live in nearby Fredericksburg, I was able to examine and sometimes handle Ferry Farm's delicate artifacts, many of which suggest that Washington's life as a young sportsman was well under way by the time his father died in 1743—the year he turned eleven.

David and Laura started work in 2001 after years of trying to pinpoint the precise location of the Washington home. After several failed attempts, David, who is the site's director of archaeology, and historian Philip Levy announced to the world that they had discovered the farmhouse in 2008. Set well above the Rappahannock, the house had a view of the bustling city across the river.

When he moved his clan to Fredericksburg, George's father, Gus, had settled on the previously owned farmhouse, later renamed Ferry Farm. The crowded house was not large—about fifty-four by twenty-eight feet, with two floors and only a few rooms. It had a hall and parlor as well as an excellent view of the Rappahannock, which snaked across the Northern Neck of Virginia to the Blue Ridge.

Discovering the foundations of the old home was only the start. The earth there holds hundreds of years of mixed artifacts. As they unearthed the foundations of the Washington home, archaeologists discovered a Civil War–era military trench cutting through the foundations. Nearby outbuildings, including a kitchen, a smokehouse, a dairy, and slave quarters are still being sifted.

David's and Laura's work shows that George, taught by his father and likely also his older stepbrothers to ride, found encouragement in his love of horses from his mother, Mary. Inside the dusty artifacts laboratory at Ferry Farm, Laura handed me a plastic bag containing a rusted swivel stirrup, the kind often used on a lady's sidesaddle. Though leading historians have made only vague references to Mary's fine equestrian skills—pointing out that she rode her own horse to market—we do know for certain that her own mother, Mary Walker, showed an interest in her riding. Walker, who made out well in two marriages to established gentlemen, stated in her last will and testament that she was giving her daughter "a young mare . . . which I formerly gave her by word of mouth." She also instructed the executors of her will to buy her daughter "a good young pace horse together with a good silk plush sidesaddle." Her father also left his daughter a "young dapple gray riding horse," giving her a total of three riding horses at a young age. This suggests that her relatives were well aware of her love of horses and riding.

Though an acquaintance described Mary Ball Washington as "majestic and venerable," she was probably not so unlike other sturdy colonial Virginia mothers who lived on farms and managed, when necessary, from the saddle. One Col. Philip Ludwell, auditor of royal revenues, described another Virginia matriarch of the same era (1710) as one who "shews nothing of ruggedness, or immodesty in her carriage . . . yet she will carry a gun in the woods and kill deer, turkeys . . . and perform the most manful exercises." Mother Mary may not have been quite the roughrider, but she knew her way around the stables, particularly when eleven-year-old George was the oldest relative around after her husband's sudden death.

One thing we may never discover is why George Washington never talked about his own upbringing in any detail. Was there something in his childhood that prevented him from wanting to discuss it much?

His silence, in any case, has helped contribute to the myths that grew up around his childhood.

I did not ask Laura or David for special access to their work, but both were happy to provide it, inviting me into their offices and workspace to look at what they found and discuss what it meant. Laura, in particular, told me she wanted to clarify what some of the recent finds tell us about Mary Ball Washington's interest in making her modest home a shining example of good manners and decorum.

Along with balancing the books, Mary also made sure that brass buckles adorned shoes, and carefully mended what had been damaged, including a broken punch bowl adorned with cherries, a possible intimation of the distorted origins of the cherry tree legend. Five years into George's stay at Ferry Farm, his father died unexpectedly. Mary proceeded to do what she could to care for five small children and keep up appearances in a home that was quite modest compared to the great manors of Westmoreland County or the stately plantation homes in the lowlands along the James River. Mary's aspirations of genteel living held out "the hope of elevation from ordinary existence into an exalted society of superior beings." This was a way of living a better life on an equal footing with wealthy merchants and aristocrats, even if only by mimicking their ways.

The way the Washingtons tried to live in the wake of Gus's death was rooted in an ancestral and far-flung world of courtiers and knights—a world George embraced at a young age. Mary asked that George pay attention to protocol even when luxuries were hard to come by. In a tiny room lined with shelves and rusty, fragile artifacts, I asked Laura about ways in which George's mother would have influenced his upbringing. "She was concerned the children be present and be presentable in public," she said, unveiling a special tea set, parts of fans, numerous wig curlers, and ornamental ceramic figurines. Much of what has been discovered suggests a woman's delicate touch, one that conveyed a message. "The artifacts show the Washingtons' desire to remain sophisticated and communicate their membership in the gentry class despite the stress from her husband Augustine's death," she added.

Laura and David also found remnants of an eighteenth-century sword, musket balls, parts of an old gun, dozens of horseshoes, and a lone spur, quite possibly used for riding by George or one of the other Washington boys.

"We can say from the evidence that George was constantly working to better himself while he lived here," said David, a disheveled and self-deprecating scholar who knows as much as anyone about George's early days. Sports, particularly riding horses and wielding a sword, he said, were expected, "something you needed to know as a gentleman."

George and his brothers were fast at play in their early years and into their teens. With playmates and brothers—and probably a few children of slaves—George swam, fished, tossed balls and metal bars, and hunted turkey and deer in the woods. Recently, Laura and David unearthed a set of old stone and clay marbles in the Washington house's cellar, the sight of which made me chuckle, remembering the sandbox where I grew up playing the same game.

Fredericksburg is today a modern town that cherishes its present along with its past. Modern gun shops and antique shops line the city's old Caroline Street. In one shop, I found an owner who had an eighteenth-century ironworks document signed by George's father. Though Fredericksburg is better known as a Civil War battlefield than it is as a former playground for young George, there are several colonial museum gems, including an apothecary store once owned by George's good friend Dr. Hugh Mercer, with, no kidding, live Swedish leeches.

"I had one leech who lived to the age of seven," chimed the lovely lady in a bonnet and long dress.

"Right," I interjected. "Was it living off human blood, or . . . ?"

She insisted on opening a glass jar with a perforated lid, pulling one out, and showing it to me. I backed away. Leeches were bad enough, but long-living European leeches? That was something to avoid.

By comparison to what it was in the eighteenth century, Fredericksburg today actually feels a bit sleepy. It is too far from Washington, DC, to buzz with tax dollars or raucous oyster bars. Not so in the mid-eighteenth century, when several dozen ships from Europe arrived in port every week, unleashing scores of rowdy sailors to drink and play.

Fredericksburg was a bustling enclave on the edge of a growing British Empire, which in the 1740s already extended up and down the American colonies' east coast. The lively colonial hub offered coffeehouses, drinking holes, shopping, and some of the liveliest sporting events in Virginia.

From the windows of his home, George could see and hear the bustle in the distance. As a teen, he could step onto the ferry below him for the five-minute ride into town. The Washingtons weren't strangers to the townspeople and were in fact close to one of the city's most prominent families, the Lewises. George's great-aunt and godmother, Mildred Washington, was married to Col. Henry Lewis. And George's sister, Betty, would eventually marry her own second cousin, Colonel Lewis's well-to-do son Fielding. Having arrived in town in 1734, the Lewis family ran a fleet of seaworthy ships and for a time operated a popular "ordinary," or tavern.

Josephine "Jo" Atkins stood in the doorway of the Rising Sun Tavern dressed in a lace bonnet, a blue chemise, and a long white apron. An unassuming grandmother, amateur historian, and former schoolteacher, Jo jumped from the eighteenth century right into my story. She listed several reasons for me to first accept and then ultimately reject the contention by Puritans that Virginia taverns were "dens of iniquity." Fredericksburg's tavern owners, I soon learned, not only tolerated gambling and gaming but also found it in their financial interest to promote everything from horse racing to bowling to cockfighting. The tavern now functions as a museum.

"Business was business—this wasn't Philadelphia or some other city run by Quakers or Presbyterians," said Jo. "The doors of any tavern in Fredericksburg would have been open to everyone, but mostly men of some means and standing, including George Washington in his late teens," she said. "He would have been part of the bustle." She curtsied and ushered me into the main dining room, where a mock meal was being served and where menfolk would have sat around talking politics, travel, religion, and sports.

It was fancier than I had expected—more like a home. It had place settings and proper seating around a wood table. The scene was indicative of southern gentility in the eighteenth century, a place where the ordinary became the extraordinary in an attempt to mimic life back in London. The embellished environment helped to change ordinary forms of vulgar entertainment into cultivated expressions of enlightenment and civilization. As one expert in American gentility noted, "Cards played on a mahogany table by the light of candles in silver holders, the genteel must have believed, was different from cards in the greasy hands of a day laborer in a dark tavern with a mug of beer at his elbow. The beautiful objects, along with the clothes and manners, transformed card playing, as they did eating, drinking, and dancing, into an activity performed with the 'utmost decency and decorum.'"

The Rising Sun Tavern was only a replica, but Jo assured me its proprietors had tried to re-create the world George would have known on his trips into town. Despite its prim interior, it still preserved some of the rough-and-tumble air popular with colonial sailors and frontiersmen. In fact, it had actually been a home to George's brother Charles in the 1760s before becoming an actual tavern.

Out back, in the cobblestone streets named after English kings, queens, and princesses, George acquired a taste for one very special blood sport: cockfighting, a pastime he would continue to enjoy for years to come. As Jo explained the nuances of cockfighting to me, she smiled a toothy grin and chuckled from behind her wire-rimmed spectacles. "Why just yesterday I made a cock-a-leekie soup," she said. This favorite colonial dish was made with leeks, carrots, barley, and, she added, "the losing cock, of course."

For further insight into this aspect of tavern life, I culled the city archives and history books, since cockfighting is (fortunately) now illegal in most states, including Virginia. In most fights, cocks, armed with razors attached to their feet, invariably maim or kill one another. Depicted in the unearthed mosaics of Pompeii, cockfighting is a sport with a long global history, and anthropologists have spent many hours and chapters analyzing the significance of the sport, including as it relates to male virility. A simple description of an eighteenth-century fight makes clear the wild popularity in George's day. A traveler to a nearby Virginia town described a "cockpit; surrounded by many genteel people; promiscuously mingled with the vulgar and the debased. Exceedingly beautiful cocks were produced, armed with long, sharp, steel-pointed gaffs, which were firmly attached to their natural spurs. The moment the birds were dropped, bets ran high. The little heroes appeared trained to the business, and not the least bit disconcerted by the crowd or shouting. They stepped about with great pride and dignity; advancing

Card table at the Rising Sun Tavern. *Phil Smucker*

nearer and nearer." Such mixing of the classes in colonial America was common. George was genteel—or his mother hoped he would be one day—but he also relished excitement and public theater. Personally, I'm not much for modern blood sports, even boxing, but I can still imagine that, in the light blue eyes of young George, it was a thrill that he couldn't pass up. The imported English sport was popular in Williamsburg as well, and the president of the College of William and Mary would eventually ban students from taking part in cockfights in 1752, when George was twenty.

George also became a small-time gambler at a young age. In 1748, for instance, at sixteen, he noted in his own rough accounts that he won two shillings and three pence from his sister-in-law at whist and five shillings at loo from his brother. Jo walked me out of the dining room over to the Rising Sun's gaming room, where a game of loo, an early forerunner of American poker, was already set up. In her hand she held out the tiny, delicate, fish-shaped mother-of-pearl chips used to keep score. The game is believed to have arrived in England about 1660, when the Roundheads ceded power back to the Crown. Loo was a contentious card game, humorously described by Alexander Pope in his mock epic "The Rape of the Lock": "Even mighty Pam, that Kings and Queens o'erthrew, And mow'd down armies in the fight of Lu." It wasn't the first or last time in history that someone imagined a game of cards to be a bit warlike.

Life in Fredericksburg was London Town in miniature. That great city's well-appointed betting parlors were in full swing during George's youth. Fredericksburg's little tavern games must have paled by comparison, but Virginians tried hard to have as much fun as their English cousins. They bet on everything from jumping frogs to dogs and, yes, rat fights—even betting on the precise day and hour of an expected child's birth. Gambling was not only fashionable but also allowed as "a framework for skilled decision-making in an uncertain life that was itself a gamble." In other words, gambling often imitated real life, and for George, gambling in measured and large doses would remain an influential aspect of his own life.

The residents of Fredericksburg copied the traditions of their English cousins, and in both the spring and summer in the 1740s—when George was between the ages of eight and eighteen—Fredericksburg was a venue for entertainments of all kinds. Included in local festivities were horse races, dances, cockfights, sack races, and even greased-pig chasing. These events were the equivalent of similar, if often more elaborate, fairs and festivals popular in Britain and across Europe. In the Middle Ages, feudal lords and kings paid lavish sums to impress subjects with their interest in pleasure and the public good. The fes- tivals were the community's means of discovering and promoting the best performers, male and female. Moreover, competitive displays, some of them bloody, were a way for men to highlight their power and skill—and also prepare for war.

Games and sports in early Virginia spoke to deeper communal bonds. They embodied everything from "honor, chivalry, paternal obligations, [and] noblesse oblige" to "ancestral pride." Like Jamestown's famous bowling league before them, Virginia's eighteenth-century denizens, by engaging in fun leisure activities, were thumbing their noses at the Puritan work ethic; they simply did not let work rule their moral universe.

Strains of classical music and violins had filled Fredericksburg and its environs with an upbeat air of amiability. Spontaneous dancing could erupt at any time. Virginia's wealthiest plantation owners had their own small events. For instance, in George's home county of Westmoreland, only half a day's horseback ride from Fredericksburg, Stratford Hall's Philip Ludwell Lee put together his own band made up of slaves and indentured servants, who would often perform inside and outside, according to my guide to the Lees' mansion. Dancers at the lavish estate spun and shuffled the night away in the manor's immense ballroom well into the morning hours.

Musical performers and dance instructors of this era were itinerant, traveling from town to town and tavern to tavern. Instructors were easy enough to find in almost any large town in Virginia, particularly in the capital, Williamsburg, where Mary and Charles Stagg started both a dance school and a public theater in 1716. Yet there is curiously no record that George was "ever in the hands of an instructor of dance," according to colonial dance expert Kate Van Winkle Keller, who thinks George studied in his teens at his half brother Lawrence's Mount Vernon estate as well as with the Fairfax family. (By age nineteen, George was dancing regularly, notably on a trip to Barbados with Lawrence.)

Festival days, which originally coincided with court days, were also a time for presentation of horses and riders. Like dances, horse-riding events and races were a means for the gentry to exert their social status while entertaining others. Horse ownership in George's youth was, and sometimes still is today for Virginians, a matter of personal pride. As one visitor in that era noted, a man sometimes spent hours in the paddock chasing down his horse just to ride it two miles to church on Sunday.

George's teen years preceded the golden age of Virginia horse racing, when equestrian sports grew to dominate the sporting scene well into the nineteenth century. Along with nearby Williamsburg, Fredericksburg was one of the most established racing towns in Virginia in the eighteenth century. Races were "combat by proxy," a test of "not only the speed of the horses but the daring and combative skills of the riders." Only established gentlemen were allowed to enter a horse in a race. Any violation of this rule could lead to imprisonment, public flogging, or humiliation in the stockade. In these disputes, judges— sometimes including the powerful bishop of Virginia and Rev. James Blair of William and Mary—wielded authority, which made clear to everyone the dominance of the upper classes.

It was against this backdrop that George Washington became determined to become a polished equestrian, and he would eventually become secretary of the Fredericksburg Jockey Club. Because he spoke so little about the details of his youth when he became famous, we remain in the dark about his equestrian training, when, for instance, he broke in his first horse, a skill he would carry into his old age.

The three eldest sons of Augustine "Gus" Washington all inherited viable estates upon his death, and for George, at just eleven, that meant the advantage of servants and horses. This didn't mean he was rich or well provided for, though. By his midteens he already had a horse but did not always have food for the animal. He wrote his wealthy half brother Lawrence that he could not join him in Williamsburg as planned, possibly with a mind to dance and socialize, saying, "My horse is in very poor order to undertake such a journey, and is in no likelihood of mending for want of corn sufficient to support him."

George Washington may have been traumatized by the death of his father, but there is little evidence to suggest this. It is hard to make the case that his father was his mentor. He gave scant mention of Gus is either because he had little time to get to know him or because—far less likely—he did not admire his father. Even up to his death, Gus traveled often, including abroad, and was burdened with constant bookkeeping and business affairs.

The same cannot be said of George's close, sometimes tempestuous relationship with his mother. Mary Ball Washington was at George's side through the first half of his teens and later on his trips home. Leading Washington biographers have sometimes written her off as overbearing and undereducated, but I didn't hear that line at Ferry Farm. On the contrary, Laura was beating the drum for the historically maligned Mary, insisting that mostly old (and dead) male historians misunderstood her.

There is strong evidence that George's mother mentored him in many ways, including spiritually. In her book *In the Hands of a Good Providence*, Mount Vernon's leading research historian, Mary Thompson, has carefully examined texts that belonged to Mary. This includes religious texts, such as *The Christian Life* by John Scott, which Mary signed in 1728, and two titles that George signed. Thompson asserts that Mary almost certainly instructed her son directly on the books' contents. As a young surveyor, George likely continued his spiritual studies on his own, once noting in the margins of his diary, "If you can't find it in the Book of Ezekiel, look for it in Israel."

Mary's Christian beliefs were in keeping with an Anglican tradition in the colonies that accepted life's trials with stoicism and discouraged the overt expression of grief and zeal. With numerous and sudden deaths in her family, she had learned to disguise her own fragility and cultivate a stern presence in front of her children and servants. George listened to his mother, and her presence in his life, which lasted well into his twenties, appears to have been crucial to the development of his stoic, British-inspired demeanor. He was, after all, still facing a frontier rife with brutality and disease—a life that would require immense fortitude. Her influence extended to all aspects of behavior as well, with George learning to master his gangly arms and legs, to bow down to persons of rank, and to not pick his nose in public.

As I strolled around Ferry Farm, I imagined a young George copping the occasional glance into the Washington family's pricey wall mirror that hung in the dining room. George might have adjusted his collar or tied back his red hair in a knot, knowing he was in training for the life ahead. It was a future that would require modesty and the skills to negotiate his way and remain competitive in a new culture. Maybe he even recognized early on when he gazed into the wall mirror that he was putting on a public face for which his mother's stoic resolve served as a model. Maintaining a seriousness and an air of devotion provided a veil for George to disguise his own limits, including his nascent understanding of social graces. That same face bought him time in public while he endeavored to improve himself in private.

After the sudden death of her husband, Mary did not have the funds to send George abroad for a formal English education.

Unexpectedly, he would have to seek on his own the "panache and finishing" that would "serve as a sort of entry into a club—the fellowship of genteel Britons." George worked to both improve his manners and to pick up skills that he would need as a surveyor, a job he apparently was already considering in his early teens.

"You see this in practice even in George's survey of his brother's garden at Mount Vernon," David Muraca explained, directing me to one of George's first attempts to sketch a plot of land, dated February 27, 1748. I noticed that George's handwriting was impeccably neat. He titled the survey quaintly "A Plan for Major Lawrence Washington's Turnip Field as surveyed by me, George Washington."

A profession and a trade, one his father had dabbled in, surveying offered itself as a possibility. But there were no assurances. In 1746 Washington was confronted with another opportunity that nearly squelched his chances in the Virginia wilderness. Already a tall, strapping child, he was given a chance to board a British Royal Navy ship docked off the sandy banks of the Potomac near the future town of Alexandria (Belle Haven), Virginia. His older half brother, Lawrence, now married into the wealthy Fairfax family, agreed with Col. William Fairfax that George would make an excellent naval officer. Lawrence had served in a Virginia foot regiment aboard a British flagship at the Battle of Cartagena and later in Guantánamo Bay, Cuba. Though Lawrence had written home to his parents and siblings with a touch of bravado about becoming acclimated to the roar of canons, the mission left over three-quarters of the Virginians dead, mostly from disease. He was lucky to have survived. Glory was clearly held in higher regard than was death in the Washington family, and fourteen-year-old George needed to earn a living.

To further that end, Colonel Fairfax made a business trip to Fredericksburg, met with George, and wrote Lawrence an upbeat letter about George's budding interest in the proposition. "George has been with us," Fairfax reported to his son-in-law, "and says he will be steady and thankfully follow your advice as his best friend."

In a fortuitous turn, Mary hastily asked for the advice of her cousin Joseph Ball. Somewhat belatedly, he would warn her that George would begin his service as a "common sailor before the mast," subject to the whims of captains and first mates who, he claimed, might "cut and slash him and use him like a negro, or rather a dog." It was true, of course, and Joseph and Mary both understood that the prospects in the middle of the eighteenth century for a Virginian with budding talents were at least as good at home as they were facing the vagaries of empire building. Thanks to his protective mother, George never stepped foot on the docked British naval vessel. His great-grandfather John may have crossed the Atlantic to land on the banks of the Potomac, but this Washington—for what it was worth to the future of the New World—wasn't taking the family name back to sea. In a manner of speaking, George had made a great escape, and just in time to further his own career. This was only the first of a rapid succession of events in George's life, however, in which the Fairfax family took interest in him.

George was now free to enter into a vocation that would require the brawn of an equestrian and the brains of a good accountant. Surveyor was the ideal profession for him, a test of the rugged sporting skills he was fast acquiring in and around Fredericksburg and on visits to his two half brothers' homes at Pope's Creek and Mount Vernon. As he embarked for the frontier, he was about to gain entry into a gentleman's club that controlled an elaborate game of colonial Monopoly. He would ride out with friends and associates of an aristocratic circle of Virginians, who maintained top-down control of a vast real estate business—everything from surveying to the final bill of sale and quitrents on new properties.

After his initial foray into the wilderness with George William Fairfax, Lord Fairfax helped approve George at the mere age of seventeen to be the official surveyor for Culpeper County and parts beyond, including the Shenandoah. After that successful foray, the Fairfax family helped him become an official Crown surveyor. George's superiors would quickly recognize that his newfound familiarity with hard living and precise observations were just what were needed to further their own property interests.

4

Blood Sports in the Shenandoah

IN THE SPRINGTIME, with snow still melting in the shadows, I rode again through the Shenandoah Valley with my newfound foxhunting friend Lt. Col. Dennis Foster. This time, though, we weren't on the trail of the fox. Having boned up on accounts of Native Americans and the region's first settlers, I wanted to get a better idea of what George had faced on his surveying adventures.

My right leg had stiffened severely on me two nights earlier, and Dennis was kind enough to offer a bolster to help me slide onto the back of an obedient brown-and-white gelding. The Shenandoah wasn't the Wild West, but it had been once, my friend assured me. With Dennis in his leather chaps in the lead, we set out along cracked gray stone walls that zigzagged up and down the valley, opening into vistas of blue-shaded hills sprinkled with purple and yellow wildflowers.

On his first treks into the Shenandoah, Washington learned from experienced men the essence of carefully walking a tract of land. He determined its boundary lines by reading the bearings on a circumferentor, which sits today in the museum at Mount Vernon. George almost always had the help of two chainmen, who ran lines as he recorded the gradations and variations of the terrain, including the ridges, streams, and clusters of foliage.

There was probably no other occupation in the 1740s that could have made a man a better master of his environment, which then remained a densely foliaged rural scape. "Washington's surveying gave him a strong idea of the land, its every fixture—the hills, the valleys, the names of all species—where you could go and where you

49

couldn't go, what you can cultivate, and even what you can hunt," said Dennis. "You get attuned after a while and start to think just like a hound," he chuckled.

"Ha-ha."

I wasn't convinced that we mere humans had the olfactory instincts of a hound, but the crackle of the leaves, the scent of pine, and the crisp air helped the metaphor ring true.

It would take time for George to meld his studied parlor manners to the rough ways of the wilderness. "He could ride a horse well, which would have helped him immensely to win favor with German and English settlers," said Dennis. "In the woods, a man is no better than the horse he rides in on."

The sporting life in the Blue Ridge was as rich and amusing for its more plain-spun settlers as it was for the gentry back in the Tidewater regions of Virginia. Just as George's friends had fun racing in sequestered grasslands, the Scotch-Irish and Germans of the frontier sprinted on horseback along narrower paths hacked out of the wilds of Appalachia: one man against the next, and the winner would be rewarded with a bottle of liquor, which he would pass around for good cheer.

Americans, despite what one hears from whiskey-doused punters at the Kentucky Derby, didn't invent horse racing, but in the 1740s European settlers, including horse-crazed Virginians, were already giving their sport its own uniquely American flavor. The Virginia quarter horse, bred to work and run hard, had been named for the usual length of a race in the forest. Virginian masters bred these horses for their speed and power from English imports and native horses of Spanish origin, some of which had arrived with conquistadors or swum to shore from sinking galleons.

Sam Snapp, who had quarter horses, had earlier recounted for me her own participation in reenactments of seventeenth- and eighteenth-century Virginia quarter horse races—straight sprints to the finish. "I've been slapped across the face with a whip," she explained. "That is the nature of these races, every man—or in my case, every woman—for himself!" An observer of an eighteenth-century race noted that "jockeying for advantage" was one of the great entertainments of the sport, with two horses often "closely locked, jostling and fowling." A mean rider was far more likely to finish in first place than one of today's smooth derby riders.

George encountered frontiersmen who fought for a leg up and the upper hand; they were defining their own statuses and identities in the same way he hoped to. These unscheduled meetings with rough-hewn European settlers would prove, in the long run, to be as invaluable as his observations of Native Americans. After all, these were the same farmers and frontiersmen who, like the natives, would fight alongside him in battle.

But although the teenaged George's superior height, strength, energy, and coordination aided him in this strange new world of men wielding muzzle-loaders and bows, he was not a classical frontiersman by any measure. When he first set off, his outlook was that of a fourth-generation son of a settled and established family.

Due in part to his own preferences for genteel manners and the help he had from his mother, Mary, George started his adventures as a rather recognizable snob. As one expert in eighteenth-century manners put it: Washington assumed his "superiority based not on his riches but on his refinement. Genteel dress, furnishings, manners, and speech implicitly passed judgment on the world and always in the gentry's favor."

While George's language regarding Native Americans and some black people is condescending, his attitude toward some of the white settlers he met was at least as patronizing. Indeed, in 1749 in a letter to a friend, George complained that he had been forced into the uncomfortable company of "Barbarians and an uncouth set of People."

When his surveying party came across a group of non-English-speaking "Dutch"—likely German—settlers, Washington writes that they "went shewing their antick tricks" and continues, "I really think they seem to be as Ignorant a Set of People as the Indians." This is a revealing first glance at George in the company of the whites who made up a struggling but powerful lower class on the frontier. These men were not the white indentured servants he had crossed paths with in Fredericksburg, nor were they related to European gentry. They were fiercely independent men living off the land and hoping to make ends meet. Few, if any, of them held the ties George now did, necessary to help them secure a powerful colonial post.

George may well have caught wind of the antics of these European settlers from the travelers' tales he had heard down at the ferry crossing where he grew up. Back home he had listened to exciting stories of sports like boxing and cudgeling, which also took place on the edge of town. In the Shenandoah, the scent of wood smoke and sweat would have mingled in the air as men tossed or pummeled one another in the pine needles in bloody games that made George uncomfortable.

Though he loved gazing down on a good cockfight, fistfights and other "outlandish" behavior were not acceptable for George. For most of his adult life, Washington avoided direct and violent fighting off the battlefield, even making an effort to break up fistfights. According to Ed Lengel, a renowned Washington scholar in Charlottesville, "On one occasion in December of 1755, Washington declined to strike back when a much smaller man knocked him down with a stick during an argument. Instead he left the room, pondered his conduct, and later apologized for his words." On first thought, it is striking that George would have backed down, but then when you consider that manners and honor meant more to him than winning a personal dispute, his actions make more sense.

Fights—even those begun in fun—could lead to a quick death. One of Washington's contemporaries said that participants in boxing matches he witnessed "conduct themselves with the barbarity worthy of their savage [Native American] neighbors." Such behavior was ingrained in the struggles of early American life, at least in the hinterlands. George's own games would draw the line at outright brutality toward other humans, at least until he entered official military service.

George was born into an era in which the trusted gentry, including his own relatives, wrote the actual rules for rough blood sports. Sports and games were inextricably tied to power and to politics. His father, grandfather, and great-grandfather had all served as justice of the peace in Westmoreland at one time or another, putting them in a position to regulate other men's actions, including their gaming activities. Country justices, judges, and even Anglican clergymen had a mandate to provide order and encourage so-called fair play—just as George would attempt to do as he grew older. In making these rules, the gentry asserted control over other men who sought fortune, fame, or a chance to display their courage. Yet, as the Rev. James Blair in Williamsburg had relished a chance to officiate at horse races and insert himself into disputes, most of the laws regarding proper human behavior and even hand-to-hand combat were being written by men who had an interest in keeping the middling and lower classes from engaging in too much rowdiness on any given occasion. In the shadow of the Puritan reproaches of too much fun and games, which often targeted sports and dance for encouraging debauchery, Virginia's authoritarian and controlling gentry had an interest in, on the one hand, permitting pastimes authorized in King James's "Book of Sports" but also, on the other hand, moderating behavior so contests and contestants did not get wild and unruly. Exerting control was paramount. Contestants and spectators were encouraged to enjoy their sports and games but also to not shed too much blood in the process.

But in the Shenandoah, such reasoning did not always prevail. Whereas the gentry fenced with polished swords, these frontiersmen relished the cruder sport of cudgeling, performed with stout wooden sticks and patterned after the traditional sport in England. "The players are called 'old gamesters,' why, I can't tell you," wrote one flabbergasted observer of the brutal sport, adding, "and their object is simply to break one another's heads: for, the moment that blood runs an inch anywhere above the eyebrow, the old gamester to whom it belongs is beaten and has to stop." The objective was pretty simple: to brain an opponent. Fortunately, as I had observed, the reenactors of cudgeling in Colonial Williamsburg didn't go so far as to brain one another.

More violent still, eye gouging was openly allowed in some approved sporting matches, but in 1748, at the precise time of George's first wilderness trip, the Virginia legislature saw fit to pass statutes against "malicious maiming and wounding." In a sign that not much has changed, when I was riding through the Shenandoah with Dennis and Sam, officials in the county where I was at the time decided to outlaw cage fighting—a popular professional pay-per-view sport whose amateur members fight around the country still. I was reminded as I tracked in the hoofprints of young George that popular American sports are still a societal mirror held up before a cruel and sometimes pitiless world. Why, I asked myself, do some fathers allow their sons to play American football, a sport that is documented to cause severe brain injury, when other—often wealthier—families send their kids to play slightly less violent sports, such as lacrosse or polo? Had today's limits on brutality improved much over those of other eras? I wondered about arguments on both sides of the debate, then and now, as well as the immense financial interests involved.

In George's day, a new Virginia law also made it a felony to "cut out a tongue, put out an eye, slit or bite a nose or lip, or cut off or disable a limb," and a special amendment added to the list wounding by "gouging, plucking or putting out an eye." Even in our modern era of televised blood sports like full-body boxing and cage fighting, it is sometimes hard to imagine that such laws are really necessary.

Even if George preferred the moderation and so-called gentlemanly behavior his mother had encouraged him to embrace, his competitive spirit had much in common with that of the "uncouth" woodsmen he mingled with. Their competitive spirits were as strong as those of any man he met within the taverns of Fredericksburg. Though their own sports were arguably wilder than those he played (and was playing) as a teen, they were also a means of negotiating rights, privileges, and status. For settlers, the forest was their proving ground, and the sports they valued—hunting, riding, cudgeling, and wrestling—were as utilitarian as they were symbolic. Not unlike the occasional Virginian plantation owner who had his honor impugned and challenged a neighbor to an outright sword or pistol duel to the death, these settlers were also satisfied that a man's physical agility could and would prevail as the best form of judgment, often as the ultimate verdict in a verbal dispute. Like formal and informal dance, these wilderness games in the Shenandoah were also a means of making an assertion in public—albeit sometimes with a gory exclamation point.

In 1747, by George Washington's midteens and just before his first wilderness foray, Lord Thomas Fairfax, an enthusiastic English sportsman, unloaded his foxhounds on Virginia soil. Though Fairfax was not the first to hunt foxes in Virginia, he took special care of his English foxhounds. He sent, via one Captain Cooling of the ship *Elizabeth*, "two dogs and a bitch" in advance of his own arrival on this occasion, his second visit to the colonies. Another British visitor to Virginia, Andrew Burnaby, was impressed with Fairfax's demeanor. He observed that Lord Fairfax was a polite man of "modest and unaffected" manners, whose "chief, if not sole amusement was hunting," and that he also "carried his hounds to distant parts" of Virginia. Despite Burnaby's sense that Fairfax was mainly in Virginia to chase wild animals, the Sixth Baron of Cameron also had pressing and massive financial interests and was keen to pursue them, whether on horseback, in a simple chariot, or in a fancy coach.

The sprightly, at times cranky, aristocrat did not have to try hard to impress colonists. He was an accepted paragon of authority in

Virginia by virtue of his control of the Northern Neck Proprietary, a Crown land grant bestowed on his mother's relatives and inherited by him in 1719. Still, if you looked at his portly and truncated stature, or his gawking brown eyes and long nose set above a double chin, it would have been hard to tell that Lord Fairfax was an accomplished horseman. (Fortunately, foxhunting is a bit like golf in that, although special skills are required, it is not prohibitive to have a strange physique.)

The portly British peer also was heir to the medieval-era Leeds Castle in Kent, England, set in the middle of the River Len not far from London and still a stunning structure today. Its walls whisper stories of brave knights and fair damsels in distress. Born into nobility and the life of a courtier, Fairfax apparently avoided large social gatherings growing up, and, by some accounts, did not have much luck with women. He may even have been jilted on at least one occasion, but that story is of nebulous origin. Nevertheless, when he took up full-time residence at his cousin's newly built Belvoir Manor in Virginia, he left behind five decades in England, including early years that epitomized the life of a young British sportsman and landed aristocrat.

Lord Fairfax was an aristocrat to the bone. He received an education at Oriel College, Oxford, where he studied a broad range of English and classical literature. In Oxford and London, he hung out with witty, poetry-loving sons of blue bloods in coffeehouses and befriended the playwright and editor of the often satirical *Spectator* magazine, Joseph Addison. Though he was not a writer himself, Fairfax's associations with people like Addison gave him a literary outlook on life, which likely encouraged George's curiosity about arts, drama, and books. Possibly by no coincidence, Addison's best-known play, *Cato*, would become one of George's favorite productions.

With no children of his own, the fifty-four-year-old baron—who was the only British peer residing in America at this time—had already taken an interest in the upbringing of his own extended Virginia clan. While visiting his lands in 1735, he helped ship his cousin's eldest son, George William, off to England, with instructions that he be taken in by "the Cornet of Leeds Castle, there to be disposed of as thought proper," for a decent education. In this formal and deliberate way, Fairfax gave George's future friend and surveying partner an introduction to a courtier's life, with all the manners, mindfulness, and movements that implied.

In 1747, while at Belvoir with his cousin Colonel Fairfax, Lord Fairfax took a direct liking to the fatherless adolescent George, a frequent visitor who was also—from the collective viewpoint of the Fairfax family—in need of serious edification. He apparently saw in George the making of a young gentleman, and he weighed in with his support almost immediately. This included the idea of providing the young Virginian with pastimes that would assist in his growth as a suitable Englishman. In this way, George also became an obvious choice as a sporting companion. For a man who had misspent much of his youth hunting stag and drinking port at cricket matches, George presented a charming New World project.

Foxhunting is not a sport for the faint of heart, nor has it historically been for commoners, myself included. I had taken it up to satisfy my curiosity about George's own love of the sport, but what I discovered in the process was that foxhunting is an acquired taste. My friend Dennis had several good stories about how he got hooked.

"I learned to ride when I was about ten, jumping on mares bareback and holding on to their manes for dear life," he told me. "My father was a roofer, and so I was a poor kid in a neighborhood with a lot of Ivy League sportsmen. I fell off a lot of those mares because I didn't have a saddle. A few years later, when I saw the local foxhunt pass, I followed along on a horse to have a look but was shooed away." That did it for Dennis; he wouldn't be looked down on by a bunch of lousy Ivy Leaguers. I imagined that foxhunting was like that for George, too, in some respects, given that it was a leisurely pastime more likely to be indulged in by Cambridge and Oxford types than, say, colonial farm boys.

After he joined the US Army, Dennis ended up in intelligence, working as a special agent in the company of British allies, one of whom was an important cavalry officer. It was not until he needed to gain insight into a special weapons system that the army became interest in his foxhunts. There was some weird correlation, I suppose, in the parallel notion that a modern army officer had become a foxhunter to better fight the Cold War when, in another age, George Washington had used foxhunting to become one of the nation's greatest field commanders.

George had recorded the number of turkeys he killed in the forest with Native Americans, so it didn't surprise me that in his diary

entries he also carefully marked down the exact times that a fox was taken, dead or alive, as well as his outright anger at not catching one. "More than anything, Washington was a hunter," said Dennis, twisting back in his saddle and ducking under a tree branch. "That is what he loved. Sometimes that can get lost in the formalities and social events surrounding a hunt, but that is what he always really cared about."

Foxhunting has a long and storied tradition in European and British lore. English poet Geoffrey Chaucer makes a fourteenth-century reference to an entire village shouting "Ho! Ho! The fox!" before chasing it with the next best thing to hounds—cudgels. The sport has had strong advocates in the upper classes of the British Isles (as well as in France) for centuries. In the eighteenth century, the sport became all the rage with "young men of fashion, who took great pleasure in jumping their horses."

Baron Robert Baden-Powell, otherwise known as the founder of the modern Boy Scouts movement, believed that foxhunting was some of the best training a young man could have for war. "The nation really owes much to foxhunting [for] what it has done to help our cavalry to compensate for its small quantity by its excellence in quality, and this without any extra call upon the taxpayer," he wrote.

Another of Baden-Powell's favorite martial sports, I noted while combing his extensive writings, was "pig-sticking," or wild boar spearing on the frontiers of the British Raj. In 1992 I had managed to accompany a group of vodka-swilling Russian hunters in the city of Moshaisk, some seventy miles outside of Moscow, for a story I was writing at the time on poaching, so I was already somewhat familiar, if in a different age and form, with the dangers and alleged attractions of pig hunting. What Baden-Powell advocated was a more extreme, arguably primitive, variety. He asserted that the sport helped to bond Indian aristocrats with their British Empire contemporaries. Killing wild boar, I noted, was also a sport King Henry VIII took pleasure in during the Tudor Era. (Indeed, the first recorded incident of hunting on horseback goes back much further, to at least 1300 BC.) Along with foxhunting, Baden-Powell, a general in the British Army, advocated mounted pig-sticking as "par excellence a soldier's sport" because it "tests, develops, and sustains his best service qualities, and stands without rival [in the British colonies] as a training school for officers." His descriptions of the sport made the founder of the Boy Scouts sound a bit too overjoyed, I thought, as he advocated the thrill of the kill when, "spear in hand, you rush for blood with all the ecstasy

of a fight to the death." At least he didn't beat around the bush, I guess, and pretend this wasn't a sport that lusted after blood. Notably, pig-sticking provides its participants some nourishment, but the same can't be said for foxhunting, as the carcass is usually discarded or just fed to the dogs.

If you consider that many, if not most, of the battles fought in eighteenth-century warfare made use of cavalry, it is easier to understand why some Brits saw foxhunting as quite useful in a martial context. Participants must stay on a horse, leap over unknown obstacles, and do all this across challenging terrain and in all variety of weather conditions. "What better way to learn to ride?" Dennis remarked. "There are obstacles you would never see, including stone walls, creeks, and hills. It requires you to be courageous. Some of the best foxhunters I know have incredible charisma."

I agreed, but I wasn't looking for any stone walls to leap over.

Foxhunting was thought to impart essential qualities of leadership and courage, but it also spawned elitism. Participants lived in a storied world above the concerns of the middling classes. Paintings and sketches of eighteenth-century hunts provide insight into the sport, which over two centuries later still takes place with only slight variations in the foggy moors of Scotland, the rocky hills of Kent, the Loire Valley, and into the rolling hills of the Blue Ridge. As I studied depictions of English and American foxhunts in Dennis's house or on the walls of the National Sporting Library in nearby Middleburg, Virginia, I noticed the outlines of an exclusive society. In some pictures, country squires stood casually discussing the hunt in the company of their pedigreed horses and well-bred hounds. The paintings presented a microcosm of a gentleman's life—a veritable theater of upper-class pleasures. Where were the pigs, chickens, and common laborers in these pictures? There were few hints of the toil—often by slaves—that went into planting and harvesting, nor of the squalor of everyday life for the masses. These were ignored, or at best overlooked, by haughty eyes.

Naturally, depictions of foxhunting have always been wildly popular with those who love the sport. The scenes of foxhunters in tricornered hats leaning against their steeds as hounds lap water present an idealized view of English and Virginia country life, the very style of life that well-to-do folks—even in modern Virginia—aspire to. The more I contemplated these scenes of racing horses and salivating dogs, the more I came to see this as a surreal world, or, as one British art

historian put it, "an almost magical world with its own inherent logic." And I could see in these portraits how foxhunting became the iconic genteel sport of royalty.

But there was a lot more going on during a Blue Ridge hunt and its associated social encounters in the eighteenth century. There was also a logic that defined authority. This appealed directly to George's ambition and his acquired love of order. "Foxhunting is a gentleman's sport, and you are required to abide by rules and ethics," said Dennis. "The first time I hunted I asked if I would have to wear those silly white riding pants, but now I understand why. A hunt is always well organized, and you have what amounts to a field commander, the master of the hounds. When you ride, you also learn how to trust a horse—and to understand the limits of animals and humans."

Foxhunting also provides a broader collegial atmosphere and, if you don't mind hunting furry creatures, a sense of shared mission.

As I rode with Dennis through America's most cherished foxhunting territory, I tried to imagine, with the help of several accounts of hunts from the same era, just what the scene would have looked like over 265 years ago. We stopped for breakfast on a hillside, and Dennis introduced me to a huntsman in a tight red jacket perched on an Arabian horse. Whip in hand, he rounded up his yelping hounds in a cornfield and prepared to start out into the wintry air. Someone offered port wine, which I thought an odd elixir for nine in the morning.

The first hunts that George participated in took place in and around the Fairfax home at Belvoir Manor and his brother Lawrence's home at Mount Vernon. The foxhunting season—as it does even today—began in the autumn, a half dozen English foxhounds sniffing the fresh air, licking their snouts, and jumping up and down, excited for the thrill of a morning run through the fields and woods that stretched across hills and down through the small streams that run into the Potomac River.

Lord Fairfax, or Colonel Fairfax if he was present, led the hunt. Typical hunting gear in this day included a knee-length coat, often black or blue with embroidered cuffs, a vest inside, lengthy kid gloves, a tricornered hat, leather riding boots, and a requisite whip for some or a stag-horn riding crop for others. Lord Fairfax, who would have performed as master of the hunt, was known to shun overly formal dress.

"He would have shouted, 'Hounds, please!' as the huntsman, the keeper of the hounds, unleashed the dogs," Dennis explained. In an instant, the horses would have plunged ahead, hooves thumping the earth as birds scattered in the skies above. When the lead hounds, running along, muzzles to dirt, caught a solid whiff of the fox, the master lifted an arm and shouted out the order "Hold hard!" as his hounds huffed in anticipation of closing in on the fox.

Dennis explained to me that a foxhunt, taken as a whole, is a kind of opera. For the gentry, the howls of their beloved dogs were music to the ear. In Shakespeare's *A Midsummer Night's Dream*, Theseus, Duke of Athens, boasts about "the music of my hounds," saying his dogs were, "matched in mouth like bells, / Each under each. / A cry more tunable / Was never holloed to, nor cheered with horn." I think I got the idea of the "music" of a nice dog, and I've had a few of my own who made sweet sounds. At the same time, the howling of the hounds is likely a hauntingly similar cacophony to what most runaway slaves heard just before surrendering to their masters and to the inevitability of dozens of lashes.

In a typical eighteenth-century hunt, hounds dashed onward, tumbling over rotten logs and clamoring one over the other to get closer to the prey. Up another hill and down through the sparse brush of a hollow beneath oak and chestnut trees, the hunting party would trot along behind the drooling hounds. The end game of most hunts, of course, was ugly, often bloody, a day's denouement aptly described by Richard Beverley, a Virginia planter and historian from near Fredericksburg: "And then they detach a nimble Fellow . . . after it, who must have a scuffle with the Beast, before they can throw it down to the Dogs; and then the Sport increases to see the Vermine encounter those little Curs [hounds]."

In such a scenario, the "nimble Fellow" could well have been George. Foxhunting also could be a perilous sport, according to Dr. William Beebe, who resided in nearby Maryland, noting:

> Frequent instances have occurred, where in leaping
> the fence, or passing over gullies, or in the woods,
> the rider has been thrown from his horse, and his
> brains dashed out, or otherwise killed suddenly. This,
> however, never stops the chase—one or two are left
> to take care of the dead body, and the others pursue.

Writing well before the aging Lord Fairfax's first hunts in Virginia, Beebe added presciently, "I have seen old men, whose heads were white with age, as eager in the chase as a boy of 16." It was at

They were as much tests of manhood as those parallel rites honored by native woodland tribes and rough-hewn frontier settlers. His advantage, however, was that he was forging a distinct character. He was becoming a sportsman with his own unique prowess, melding the precision of a surveyor with the backwoods know-how of a Daniel Boone and Native American warrior while at the same time garnering the studied equestrian skills of an English foxhunter. In everything he did, George Washington strove for proper manners and bold actions. As a fourth-generation Virginian, he was well on his way to becoming a first-class Englishman in America.

5

A Gentleman's Code

I KNEW THAT IN ORDER to penetrate the world of eighteenth-century dance, I would need a proper tutor. In my hometown of Alexandria, Virginia, which Washington's half brother Lawrence founded and seventeen-year-old George sketched a neat grid for, there is but one admired master of colonial dance, Corky Palmer. He instructs classes of loving couples and historical reenactors at Gadsby's Tavern, where the entire staff lives and breathes the eighteenth century.

Corky wears his long hair in a ponytail, and he knows how to raise a "Huzzah" toast in a crowd. Though he walks with a noticeable limp, he has twinkling eyes and can dance an impeccable French minuet. As an instructor, Corky is patient and forgiving, and as a historian who understands the attraction of a pastime considered essential for young colonials, he has no peer in Virginia.

"George Washington would have had most of his experience, early on, dancing at plantation homes," Corky explained to me over coffee. "He was doing all in his power to become a gentleman. Proper dance steps were a chance for him to show off some education, even if it hadn't been a formal one."

"It is funny," I said. "I think I had more of a formal education than him, but no one bothered to teach me to dance."

"Well, if you couldn't dance, you didn't have an education."

"Oh?"

"But dance is something you can learn," Corky reassured me. "Just as today when you see someone dancing and a man who really knows how to lead a lady, you can't help but be impressed and know that he has learned that somewhere. In Virginia, dance, unlike in puritanical New England, was both accepted and encouraged. Young people in New England, for their part, did sometimes dance, but usually only, as a rule, with the partner that brought them."

"That doesn't sound nearly as fun as mixing it up," I commented.

"In Virginia the rule was, you danced the first dance with your partner and returned to the 'one who brung you' for the last dance," he explained.

By the middle of the eighteenth century, dancing had become, for Virginians including George, a passion that was one of the most acceptable forms of social interaction. Anyone who danced poorly, like me, would have been a virtual social outcast. Like their English cousins, Virginians preferred the playful steps of a French minuet set to Handel over, say, a battle in the woods. Many would have chuckled knowingly at Shakespeare's lines in *King Henry VI* when Burgundy says, "I see our wars / Will turn unto peaceful comic sport / When ladies crave to be encountered with." This is, by the way, an excellent use of the age-old British idea of sport—and one that George would have understood innately—as it incorporates both theatrical and romantic notions of the word. It wasn't, to my mind, such an arcane idea after all when you considered that any chivalric gentleman of this era would really rather make love than war—or at least dance with a lovely lady if he could not do the former.

Over several weeks of troubled learning, Corky helped me try my own feet out on the dance floor, crossing me over to the correct partner and trying, with little success, to get me to "listen to the rhythm of the music."

Colonial-era dance requires dexterity and an ear for music, which is something my own mother always reminded me that I had simply not inherited. My problem with the harpsichord and violin, I explained to Corky by way of excusing myself, was that I could not detect a rhythm in either instrument. All I heard was strings. I'm sure now in retrospect that I was also rather intimidated.

Fortunately, Corky yelled at me only once, when instructing me not to trip over my shoelaces.

"How did you get started?" I asked.

"I think military personnel recognize this form of dance because it is about keeping in step," he said. "The first time I heard colonial-era music, I kind of just envisioned the whole scene: the participants and what the composer wanted when he wrote the tune."

"I can see that now," I said.

I had never considered that the orchestration of a dance could appeal to military officers in any special way, but his points made sense, particularly as I thought of all the marine balls I had attended as an overseas reporter. However, though they had required some waltzing, they hadn't required minuets or reels.

Virginians found excuses to dance whenever and wherever possible. Andrew Burnaby, a British visitor, described Virginians of this era as "immoderately fond of dancing," saying, "towards the close of an evening, when the company are pretty well tired with country dances, it is usual to dance jigs; a practice borrowed, I am informed, from the Negroes. These dances are without any method or regularity." Americans' lasting affection for formal dance today, especially competitive ballroom performances, first emerged in the New World, particularly Virginia, as early as the late 1600s. Dance melded the New World's contrasting and diverse genres of music, and for Virginians was understood to be as or more expressive than mere words. In the town of Fredericksburg and at surrounding plantations, residents danced in classic European styles and also invented new and lively dances of their own. There were formal dances, like the minuet; country dances, which exchanged partners; and wilder, heel-tossing numbers.

Dexterity on the dance floor maintained social status, and also allowed for proper courtship. Dance represented an elaborate world of nonverbal signs, a system of gestures, starting with curtsy and bow, which derived from an ancient, sometimes forgotten European court life.

A test of my own acquired and very unnatural acumen presented itself on February 14, at Gadsby's Tavern's Birthright Ball. I arrived with my tall and exquisite date, Barbara, who was clad in a long yellow gown. Somehow my own eighteenth-century getup didn't match and made me look more like an eighteenth-century John Travolta in *Saturday Night Fever*. I doffed my hat and met Corky for a glass of wine. I managed to keep up with a few of the reels, feeling like I was in the middle of a Jane Austen novel, but tripped up on a partner switch and ended up mortified and paralyzed at the thought of the whole room laughing at me. I had to concede that it just wasn't in my DNA. Meanwhile, I kept thinking of what Jo, my guide to tavern life in Fredericksburg, had said: that if she could have one wish before she died, it would be for a chance to dance with George Washington. "I think he would have put any of those competitors on *Dancing with the Stars* to shame," she had remarked during our tavern tour.

For George and his contemporaries, dance was refined flirtation and a means for Virginia's men to express their adoration of and interest in ornately attired women, the loveliest of southern belles. Learning the art of proper comportment—"complaisance," as it derived from the French equivalent—was as much about Darwinian mate selection as it was about being seen as well mannered and presentable in society. Courtly dancing, popular with royalty in Europe and Britain, had begun as a pastime for wealthy men and women who had long hours of leisure on their hands. By the eighteenth century, versions of this same court dancing had grown popular in most towns and spread across the Atlantic.

Through dance, second and third sons, like George, gained the chance to find proper mates and move up in a world that was less and less about primogeniture—the tradition of the first son inheriting almost everything. George, while he inherited land and slaves, was not born a Lee, a Mason, or a Fitzhugh. His physical prowess, be it on a horse or on a dance floor, was something that made men of wealth—who might one day help him—raise their eyebrows and take notice of him.

After a few drinks at the Birthright Ball and a few minutes to recover from my humiliation on the dance floor, it was all starting to make sense. I was beginning to understand how dance offered a chance for upward mobility through mixing and matching. Yet that was still a poor explanation of how dancing caught fire in Virginia just in time for George to display his talents to the world. I thought there might be something more, and Corky confirmed my suspicions: "In the same way it is today, if there is a fiddler in the room, people just wanted to move to the music."

"Oh. I think I get it now," I said.

By his midteens, George was taller than the varied members of the Fairfax clan. Thanks to the detailed order he wrote to a London tailor, we have a reasonable idea of how he might dress on formal occasions. His hands would have swung beneath the cuffs of his frock coat, marked by five-inch lapels and six buttons on either side, dropping just to the crease of his large knees. He no doubt cut a sharp figure in riding boots and hat. Such meticulous attention to male clothing was encouraged among Virginia's gentry, and both his outfit and his brother's ornate military uniform were "smart and fashionable, sometimes almost theatrical" in design. Appearances mattered for George because he hoped, one day, to fully enter into the idealized world of the gentry around him.

At Ferry Farm and visiting his cousins in Westmoreland County, George had already begun to cobble together his own code of behavior, a special set of rules to live by. This personal protocol, which would guide George in the homes of Virginia's elite, as a sportsman in the field, and as a soldier on the front lines, fleshed out his first ideas of gallant behavior.

George Washington knew he wanted to be perceived as a chivalric gentleman in the Old World sense of the idea; he just needed a means to get there. Anglo-Saxons in America, despite the rugged nuances of their existence, still grew up dreaming about the heroics of their forefathers, and, indeed, the Lees of Stratford Hall and the Carters of Nomini, who had long pedigrees and wealth beyond that of the Washingtons, encouraged the mimicking of British custom. Middle-ranking gentry, which included George in the years before he made his mark as a surveyor, wanted to be seen playing the same sports and parlor games as more landed aristocrats. And they knew they also needed to behave in such a manner as to be looked upon not as social climbers but as well-behaved men.

Anglo-Virginians, more than any other group in colonial America, seized on the long-standing myths of the medieval knight, or chevalier, and in some cases they promoted their own heroes to fit the feudal mold. These myths also offered a commonly accepted social outlook. For George's generation, the time-honored values of honor, valor, and geniality played a key role in societal acceptance and in a young person's standing among his peers. This cult of courtesy, a product of English and French ideals of accepted behavior at the royal court, esteemed, among other attributes, good deeds, competition, physical skills, and service to a higher cause. These ideals have weathered the centuries fairly well, I noted. Even if they are Americanized and watered down in our modern era, we still recognize them as traits of good character and leadership today.

In George's world the concepts of a proper gentleman and noble warrior were inseparable. And they started with good manners and a bit of humility, two things that Mary Ball Washington appears to have been keen on helping her children acquire. Fortunately, she had help.

When I had checked into a bed-and-breakfast near George's birthplace in Westmoreland County, I was a bit surprised to find a copy of George's *Rules of Civility and Decent Behavior* in my desk drawer, a local substitute for a Gideon Bible. It made sense. Over the course of his life, George appears to have contemplated proper and decent public behavior in much greater depth than he did chapters of the Bible. As a mere child about the age of twelve, George copied the rules from an English translation of those composed in a slightly different version by French Jesuits in 1595. These rules were then as much for French and Italian courtiers as they were for British aristocrats, and in copying them, George was regurgitating a shared French and British heritage that had already found a way into popular culture in colonial America. And George's attraction to these manners and rules made even more sense when one considers that it was the Norman invasion and French court that influenced the development of the British monarchy.

For his part, George tried hard to memorize these guidelines: a set of deferential manners that he could put to practical use in his daily life. A few of these instructions, in particular, stand out as governing the behavior of young Washington for years to come. Among these are instructions to look serious, behave with deference and modesty, be thankful of admonitions, and not to engage in unseemly pastimes. He paid careful attention to these rules, even when he did not live up to them, and his own development—well into his old age—reflects their pithy prescriptions. My favorite six rules are worth considering across the course of Washington's entire life:

Rule 19: "Let your Countenance be pleasant but in Serious Matters Somewhat grave." After he lost his teeth—maybe because of it—George looked grave most of the time. His serious demeanor would serve him well later in life, as well as early on.

Rule 20: "The Gestures of the Body must be Suited to the discourse you are upon." George became a master of the right moves, not only on the dance floor, but also as a politician.

Rule 24: "Do not laugh too loud or too much at any Public Spectacle." George laughed rarely, but when he did it was in the company but not at the expense of others.

Rule 42: "Let thy ceremonies in Courtesy be proper to the Dignity of his place with whom thou converses for it is absurd to act the same with a Clown and a Prince." George did not suffer fools well; he found them insufferable, but he still tolerated them.

Rule 63: "A Man ought not to value himself of his Achievements, or rare Qualities of wit; much less of his riches Virtue or Kindred." While he did take some pride in his achievements, George did not care to discuss his family lineage nor his net wealth.

Rule 109: "Let your recreations be manful not sinful." George was never caught out committing an egregious sin.

The 110 rules of civility—none of which George thought up on his own—were penned neatly, as an elder might well have asked him to do. They were a means of expressing selflessness, charm, and even compassion, albeit with reserve and limited emotion. These guidelines, as they did for many of his young colleagues in Virginia, assisted George in gaining acceptance, and they also helped him to reflect on what he valued in his own behavior from a very young age.

The rules and George's interpretations of them were crucial to his rise, but they were probably not as significant as the older male models in his life. His father, Gus, was dead by the time he scribbled down his rules, so it was other individuals who provided admonitions, set examples, and gradually began to help mold George's actions. Within his own family, he came to idolize the military exploits of the round-shouldered, cleft-chin older half brother Lawrence, who became a key exemplar of old-school English chivalry. Lawrence, fourteen years older than George, was an accomplished storyteller and had a decidedly romantic view of war. In a letter home from South America, he recounted for the entire Washington family his "disregard" for "the noise, or shot of cannon" fire at a famous naval battle near Cartagena in 1742. Lawrence named his inherited Washington family estate, Mount Vernon, after naval commander Admiral Vernon, who led him and his fellow Virginians into a losing battle. Lawrence was not only a leader of men but also, by several accounts, widely admired for his steady demeanor in public and well liked in Virginia society.

With his newfound profession in hand, George had begun to expand his ideals through reading books, something the Fairfaxes encouraged. For instance, he combed through the biography of Frederick the Great and read his own copy of the works of Seneca, the Roman Stoic. There is also another book—more of a pamphlet—that he purchased apparently from a cousin when he was just fifteen and that appears to have impacted his early vision of decent behavior and ideals of a military officer's duty. H. de Luzancy's *A Panegyrick to the Memory of His Grace Frederick, Late Duke of Schonberg* is a eulogy about the life of French Huguenot Friedrich Herman, who followed his own rules of civility probably similar to those that George became familiar with. Several of the passages in the pamphlet, which is written in direct and simple prose, speak presciently to events in Washington's life over the next several decades. The author, a priest who followed the duke's military exploits, recounts that the duke, "sate an horse the best of any man; he loved constantly to be neat in his clothes, and in his conversation he was always pleasant." The duke is said to have had a "robust and strong body," and to have had a "great love of exercise." In keeping with what was expected of an officer fighting for the British Crown, in the duke's case King William III, Schonberg exhibited no fear in the face of danger and fought through to victory against the odds. He was also just an all-around magnanimous *nice guy* who found it hard to be cruel to anyone. As the author states, he was "affable, candid, and [of an] Obliging Nature. It is harder for him to deny a Favour, than to another be deny'd," adding that when he could not deliver, they "refus'd with extreme Civility, what he could not grant." Furthermore, Schonberg was "free from the duplicity and emptiness," as well as the "affectation of Mode and Gallantry," which Luzancy believes characterized modern gentlemen in the seventeenth century. In other words, the duke was no fop; he was a man's man, which is precisely how he won love and respect over a long and successful life. It is not hard to imagine George, nestled behind a tree, book in hand, trying to envision his own future along the lines of the Duke of Schonberg's.

When he would eventually set out into the forests along the Blue Ridge on his first military mission, George already would have decent manners, but he was still no exemplar of greatness; he would often forget his own code of civility when speaking or writing directly to his superiors. As a young man and soon-to-be officer, what he arguably valued more than any of his rules of civility were the most crucial aspects of a soldier's code: courage, perseverance, and martial exploits. In his Pulitzer-winning *Washington's Crossing*, historian David Hackett

Fischer expands further on what he calls George Washington's "code of honor" as one that "assumed that a gentleman would act with physical courage and in the face of danger, pain, suffering, and death." The code, based on creeds of ancient and Stoic warriors, developed over time into a broad philosophy for a life that would guide and challenge him to test his acquired physical skills against the fates. This early worldview—spoken, unspoken, mimicked, and acquired by rote—would help harness his fierce passions, but not necessarily his untamed eye for the opposite sex.

6

The Sorrows of
Young George

GETTING PAST THE GUARDS at the high-security gates of Fort Belvoir,
the modern military facility where the foundations of Belvoir stood,
wasn't going to be easy. I phoned my friend Col. Paul Ung, who had
once spent two months eating coconuts as a castaway on a remote
island in his quest to get to America. I knew he had a special knack
for getting into difficult places, so I asked him to swing by and pick
me up.

At the fort, Paul flashed his credentials, and we were onto the
macadam maze of an immense US military base, a self-contained
minimetropolis with shopping, swimming, tennis, dining, bike trails,
and its own hospital. After locating the posh officer's club and finding
the bar closed, we drove farther down the road toward the remains
of the manor, asking a young officer working on his lawn for advice.
"Just down there!" he offered, waving us through with his rake.

The fog was just rising off the water beyond the brick foundations
of the old Fairfax home, built in 1741, when George was only nine.
I reached down and ran my palm over the crumbled brick as Paul
stood attentively by wondering what all my excitement was about.

Sketches and descriptions show that the Fairfax family's Belvoir
Manor, a symmetrical Georgian mansion, was set amid manicured
boxwood gardens complete with stables, walkways, and a shaded sitting area. In its prime, the estate teemed with servants, including
footmen, parlor maids, and cooks. In the full basement there was a
servant's hall and cellars. The home had, by visitors' accounts, uphol-
stered chairs, immense sideboards, inlaid mother-of-pearl tea tables,

and imported mahogany. Off the long hallway, which ran the width of the home, there were four high-ceilinged rooms, two parlors, and a well-appointed dining room. At the entrance, a curved staircase ran to the second floor of bedrooms with windows that opened onto the river. It impressed just about everyone—except some of its own wealthy residents. Colonel Fairfax's own son George William Fairfax, who had grown fond of his former aristocratic life at Leeds Castle, joked about Belvoir Manor in classic English dry humor, calling it on one occasion a merely "tolerable cottage" in a "wooded world." Now it was a shadow outline of red bricks inside an immense, high-security US Army installation.

As a teenager George often rode his horse here from Ferry Farm or after spending the night with Lawrence at Mount Vernon. It was a quick, slightly meandering jaunt south along the Potomac, but it was also accessible from Lawrence's home in a small boat, which was a more direct trip. I conjured the two tall, neatly attired Washingtons stepping out of a rowboat or handing their steeds to the stable boys and mounting the manor's brick stairs. Lawrence, the debonair veteran of the War of Jenkins' Ear with Spain, had returned to Virginia in 1741 and been quickly appointed adjutant of all Virginia armed forces.

Lawrence's comforting presence at Belvoir reminded George of his own still-middling place in the pecking order of the gentry, but it also offered George entry into the cultivated and rarified world that his mother had only hinted at with her neat table settings, wall mirrors, and English tea ceremonies.

Belvoir Manor, for a teenage George, turned out to be much more than another stopover. Time spent with the Fairfax clan also offered a foray into a garden of exclusive delights, and, as Mount Vernon's Mary Thompson explained to me, it contained within its walls "the outlines of a good Jane Austen novel set on the banks of the Potomac."

George always prepared meticulously for his visits to Belvoir, packing everything he would need and practicing to be a gentleman in advance. Here at Belvoir, he was immersed in constant social interaction, including riding, dancing, and card games with light betting. There were also light theatrical performances, or selected play readings, at the manor, during which the sexes mingled openly. Crucially, at Belvoir, young George had a chance to put his acquired understanding of good behavior into practice. Taking careful mental notes of affectations and courtly gesture, he began to imitate others and fit in alongside a set of resplendent and sometimes older friends and acquaintances at Belvoir.

In the two main parlors of the manor, dances would have unfolded on long winter nights with a small ensemble, sometimes consisting of two violins, a French horn, or possibly a harp. As the musicians struck up a chord, couples on the dance floor would stand smiling and facing one another in anticipation of the next dance, often a Scottish reel, an up-tempo number.

Up until his death in July 1752, Lawrence assumed his place facing his partner and wife, Anne Fairfax Washington. Beside Lawrence, George William Fairfax—betrothed after his first surveying forays with George Washington—would have stood poised opposite his new wife, Sally. In existing portraits, George William Fairfax has a rather timid appearance, flush with a sad and drooping mouth and his forefather's hooked nose, which, in my view, made him look a tad haughty. An honored member of the Virginia House of Burgesses in this same era, he had a special burden to bear from the British Empire's legacy of racism, which looked down on persons of "mixed parentage."

Belvoir Manor, along with its young married couples, also came with its own "grizzled master" in the form of Col. William Fairfax. The colonel would become a close mentor to George even in advance of Lord Fairfax's permanent arrival in Virginia in 1747. He was a worldly and jovial man who served as a royal customs collector in Barbados and Boston. He and his wife, Sarah, had three children.

Though the Fairfax family was the wealthiest and arguably most aristocratic clan to be found in Virginia's Northern Neck, they had a clear affection for the less well-off Washington family. Colonel Fairfax regularly referred to himself in his correspondence with George as "your assured and loving friend." Fairfax shared his copies of Julius Caesar's military writings and a copy of *The Life of Alexander the Great*, offering George an introduction to a world of noble deeds and encouragement for his own future martial exploits. In sharing his library with George, as Lord Fairfax would also do, Colonel Fairfax turned his own home into a much-needed schoolroom for his new friend. In their affections and concerns, both Fairfax men, as well as Lawrence, acted as surrogates for the father that George had lost at a young age.

Not born into a manor home, George still needed to negotiate his way into the upper ranks of the powerful Virginia elite. A few years later, he would write to his younger brother John, whom he called Jack, "I shou'd be glad to hear you live in Harmony and good fellowship with the [Fairfax] family at Belvoir, as it is their power to be serviceable upon many occasions to us, as young beginners." He clearly saw the Fairfax family as a springboard for his and Jack's futures.

At Belvoir, Colonel Fairfax and George William Fairfax watched over George's development. On the surveying trail after he turned seventeen, Washington was more likely to run into or ride with Lord Fairfax, whose sporting character left an indelible impression on him. As one of Fairfax's senior surveyors, an unofficial representative of the Crown on a vast frontier, George was free to let his spirit roam.

Lord Fairfax ran his affairs out of Greenway Court, down the road from Winchester, Virginia, and along what is now called Lord Fairfax Highway. Legend has it that George planted the original surveying post to mark Fairfax's estate, providing the town's current name, White Post. Beyond the white post, which is certainly not the original, I came upon an ancient oak tree near a classic automobile shop, where I stopped to ask a mechanic for further directions to Lord Fairfax's estate. I took a sharp right at a gigantic boulder and drove cautiously back past a sign reading BEWARE OF DOG. Set back in the woods on a dirt track, a limestone commercial office glinted at me in the noonday sun. Farther back was a carriage house, built with stones from the original home, which Fairfax began in 1749 just as George was setting out as a surveyor. I was a little surprised the site wasn't better marked for curious visitors like me. Maral Kalbian informed me that the estate remained closed to the public.

George sometimes worked out of Greenway Court for days on end when Lord Fairfax was present, and he may have written several letters and diary entries as his guest. Here in the woods, George learned all he needed about an eccentric model of British aristocracy with a man who spent his mornings in the field hunting and his evenings pipe smoking and toasting the Crown with posh travelers and local ruffians. The aging sportsman's choice of lifestyle in the American wilderness was extremely rustic considering his patrician origins; his early life in England epitomized almost everything a spoiled aristocrat could have hoped for. "However, there were lots and lots of slaves," said Kalbian, whose own research and study suggests that the estate changed considerably in the 1750s and 1760s.

Despite some climactic similarities with Mother England, life in the Virginia backwoods bore only a vague resemblance to the traditional sportsman's life Lord Fairfax had known there. It was far more isolated. He settled first into his small twelve-by-twelve cabin, whose logs were "hewn square and fitted closely upon each other," forming the body of a home with a stone chimney. In the next few years, drawing on the skilled labor in the region, he assembled a staff, which included relatives, and had a hundred-foot-long manor built with two chimneys, two belfries, and a "heavy beatling porch" out front. The sprawling estate did not make up a manor house in any real sense of the word, though. It was far more of a gigantic hunting lodge with numerous beds for land speculators, surveyors, huntsmen, and for Lord Fairfax's own extended family.

Lord Fairfax was in all apparent respects a feudal landowner, and he lived well off the rents that his tenants paid him. In a sign of his devotion to his new authority, Lord Fairfax, Washington would write on one occasion in 1749, "My Lord . . . I shall wait on your Lordship at Frederick Court in November to obey your further Pleasure and am my Lord & c." It sounded to my ear to be right out of a scene from the court of Elizabeth I, but it would have been the only real way for George to address the great man. Such Old World mannerisms still regulated human relations in pre-Revolutionary America. Colonel Fairfax was his friend, and Lord Fairfax was more his master. The Old Dominion was still a genuine patriarchy, and the biggest patron was the old sportsman himself.

Lord Fairfax entertained and staged hunting forays in the nearby woods. If he wasn't pleased with what he caught, he could put his hounds in a carriage or run them down the road for fresher ground. He was not in danger of running out of real estate; his royal land grant was "roughly the size of Massachusetts, and it included all of the land between the Potomac and the Rappahannock rivers from the Chesapeake Bay to the crest of the Appalachians."

Lord Fairfax, forever the prankster and jovial sort, offered one settler free rent if he would deliver him "one large, fat turkey ready for roasting" every year on December 25. On another occasion, the English peer shot and stuffed a great horned owl from the valley and sent it off to the Earl of Burlington, who shared an interest with him in natural history. None of the hunting of wild fowl or game was new for Fairfax, who had grown up chasing fox and stag on the grounds of Leeds Castle and continued hunting even as a student at Oxford.

Fairfax made sure his Virginia residence had the necessary imports to make his colonial hunting utopia replete. His stables included kennels for his imported English hounds, a powder magazine, a carriage house for his horse-drawn chair and his coach, and a library, which his own estate records indicate carried classics and the racy modern tomes of eighteenth-century English literature, including the lusty 1749 novel *The History of Tom Jones, a Foundling.*

The mystery that had surrounded Lord Fairfax's own romantic interests persisted in the wilds of the Shenandoah, and George's own early love interests are only slightly better documented, if even less understood. A frequent guest of Lord Fairfax's immaculate man cave, he began to entertain some of his first romantic dreams in the company of the Fairfax family. These come to us in a series of melodramatic letters, the kind that blustering teenage boys have been writing about unrequited love for centuries. The letters cast a light on George's quieter personal longings and, in doing so, provide a prism through which to see his struggle to control his bubbling passions. Likewise, these awkward days and tender nights before George obtained any fame also contribute, in a small way, to a better understanding of a complex character.

George's emergent code of honor implied decency, but only rudimentary, still unformed notions of how to interface with young women. Even the sight of a lovely lady could launch George into a state of agitated alarm. In 1749 or 1750 (the letter is not dated), after he was well into his surveying career and had taken up one of several residences with Fairfax, he wrote the following to a former playmate, Robin:

> My place of residence is at present His Lordships where I might was my heart disengag'd pass my time very pleasantly as There's a very agreeable Young Lady Lives in the same House but that's only adding Fuel to the fire it makes me the more uneasy for by often and unavoidably being in Company with her revives my former Passion for your Low Land Beauty whereas was I to live more retired from Young Women I might in some measure eliviate my sorrows

by burying that Chaste and troublesome Passion in
the grave of oblivion or eternall forgetfulness.

As do his copied and sappy lines of bumbling poetry from the
same era, the note puts on display George's angst-ridden passions.
In this telling note, he is trying hard to dampen his attraction. He
refers to his own passion as "troublesome," a signal that he is still
not at ease around women. His other romantic writings are rife with
a sense of anguish and self-pity over being denied love. For instance,
in a poem discovered stashed away with his earliest diary entries, and
never delivered to the lady of his affection, one Frances Alexander,
George wrote, "Ah! Woe's me, that I should Love and conceal /
Long have I wished, but never dare reveal," and further "That in an
enraptured Dream I may / In a soft lulling sleep and gentle repose /
Possess those joys denied by Day."

As it turns out, and in striking contrast to the future admiration
he would gain from the opposite sex, the ladies of Virginia were
showing little interest in the young chivalric George, who was still not
anyone's hero. He may have gleaned early on that he needed more
in his personal arsenal to succeed with the fairer sex.

In September 1751, at the height of surveying season, a dying Lawrence Washington called on George to travel with him by ship to the
distant colony of Barbados, as an antidote for his worsening cough.
It would be the only trip abroad that George would ever make, and
it is one that helped further refine his own ideas about how gentlemen behave.

Lawrence remained the adjutant of Virginia forces as the two half
brothers embarked by ship at the height of hurricane season. George's
tattered diary of the trip speaks of severe weather, fishing from the
deck, and dolphins circling playfully below. It was exciting to finally
be at sea with his brother but bittersweet to be on a mission to save
Lawrence's life. Upon arrival in the British port of Bridgetown—far
and away the largest city George had ever seen—the two checked
in with Col. William Fairfax's brother-in-law. Describing an initial
ride into the cane fields with Lawrence, George wrote, "In the cool
of the evening we rode in the country and were perfectly enraptured
with the beautiful scenery." Lawrence and George were welcomed
into a neighborhood supper society known jovially as the Beef Steak

and Tripe Club. Immersed in the hospitality of the island's wealthy planters and public servants, George praised the Barbadians' "genteel behavior," which was "shown to every gentleman stranger." The breezes and warm air would provide a sprinkling of hope for Lawrence's recovery, as an examining doctor would announce that, given proper care, Lawrence might well survive the cough that was slowly destroying his lungs.

First settled by the British in 1627, Barbados was a wealthy example of British imperial rule. It had a chummy and clubby air at the top, but it was a strict hierarchy, and slave owners often took advantage of their holdings in exceptionally cruel ways; in his diary, George notes his dismay at the lack of a guilty verdict in the rape trial of one wealthy slave owner.

With Lawrence at his side, George, nineteen, set out upon their arrival to explore the island. By his and Lawrence's account of the journey, he danced at social gatherings, took in the sights and sounds, and fell in love with exotic food, including the mysterious avocado. His brother's letters home illustrate that the Washington brothers exhausted themselves while enjoying the attention of local admirers, including the island's leading ladies. George commented, "The Ladys Generally are very agreeable," noting, though, that they "affect the Negro style." This latter observation probably reflects the fact that many residents in this old Caribbean colony were multiracial, and despite the harsh rule of the cane plantations, blacks and whites mixed more socially in Barbados than they did in Virginia, particularly through a close melding of African and European music and dance.

Hit with a severe case of smallpox soon after his arrival, George was confined to a bed. Continuing his diary, he penned a telling 750-word essay to sum up some of his key observations about Barbados and in doing so paid particular attention to the British governor's ruling style, noting, in an unusually lucid passage, that "it is said" that the governor lives "at little expense," and "it is said he is a gentleman of good sense as he avoids the errors of his predecessors he gives no handle for complaint but at the same time by declining much familiarity is not over zealously loved." The reflection speaks to George's nascent political interests and suggests, given his close attention to the character of the ruler, that the governor is a model of stoic resolve, aloofness, and verbal restraint. His lesson was that absolute power—above the fray and even unfettered by criticism—may be less admired but also can be sensible and effective.

While making such observations about authority, George also took time to explore the island's military forts and plunged into a lifelong fascination with dramatic performances, attending his first full theater performance, *The London Merchant, or the History of George Barnwell*, in Bridgetown. The play is about a decent man drawn into the snare of a harlot—not an uncommon theme for that day and age. British authorities and elders approved of the seedy subject matter since it served as a cautionary tale for aspiring young men. English colonies, unless they were excessively influenced by Puritanism, like some of the northern American colonies, accepted the benefits of drama and encouraged it as entertainment and instruction. Such a melded view of both the amusement and beneficial value of the theater would stick with George across the course of his life, particularly during and after the Revolution, when events allowed him to become a staunch patron of the arts.

Unfortunately, Lawrence's consumptive cough showed no signs of improving. Depressed and tired from the socializing, Lawrence made a decision to send George home and depart, on his own, for Bermuda. Within months, he would be forced home to Virginia to serve out what he described in a letter home as an impending death sentence.

On his own, and likely disturbed by what he had seen of Lawrence's failing health, George sailed for Virginia on December 21, 1751, managing to have his berth robbed before landing in Yorktown on January 28. He bore Lawrence's ill tidings back to his family and peers, hired a horse, and rode to Williamsburg to the Virginia Governor's Mansion. As he walked through the garden and imposing gates of the Robert Carter House to see Lieutenant Governor Robert Dinwiddie—the acting governor—he knew his lot in life was already in transition. (The governor and George would, in fact, dine at the Robert Carter House on this particular occasion since the Governor's Mansion was under renovation in January 1752.)

Williamsburg was Bridgetown in miniature: a vibrant, bustling colonial capital with all the outcroppings of royal authority. The Virginia Governor's Mansion was—though it was being spruced up when George would first visit—far more imposing than Belvoir Manor in its prime.

It consisted of ten acres of manicured gardens, three brick stories, twenty-four rooms, and eleven thousand square feet of wood-paneled splendor. In the entrance hall stood the symbols of power that would have confronted George as servants ushered him in. This includes a door crest with dozens of crossed swords and pistols surrounding the king's coat of arms and the French inscription DIEU ET MON DROIT, a reminder of the Battle of Hastings that signifies the divine right of the British monarch. The architecture and artifacts together conveyed social and political values, including "a strong sense of gradations of dominance and submission." When his mansion was in full use, the governor entertained his guests in the ballroom and nearby room where there was an assortment of musical instruments, including pianos and harps. In the main dining hall he treated visitors to the best sterling silver and imported libations available in England.

Off visiting his estate at Green Spring six miles from his mansion when George showed up on his doorstep, Dinwiddie apparently had not been expecting him, and George had to wait several hours. Upon his return, Dinwiddie welcomed Washington, and during the first solemn dinner between the two—of which nothing formal is recorded—George likely did little but behave with deferential modesty. Already trained and coached by mother and mentors, he likely put his best table manners on display as he explained his brother's dire state. Naturally, Lawrence's health was of interest to Dinwiddie, a wigged, dapper, and cherubic Scotsman of nearly sixty years, who along with Lawrence—and George Mason and the entire Fairfax family—happened to be a prime investor in the real estate venture known as the Ohio Company. The consortium of Virginia gentlemen was determined to exploit land opportunities across the Appalachian Mountains within Virginia's fast-expanding borders.

This dinner with George, and further recommendations from Lawrence's associates, undoubtedly helped plant the seed in Dinwiddie's mind to find a use for the young Virginia surveyor in the Ohio Company's investment schemes in the year ahead. Even if Washington remained soft-spoken at the dinner, he had arrived at the governor's table with strong recommendations, a healthy physique, and knowledge of the frontier. Just by showing up, he made a strong impression.

When George left Williamsburg the day after dining with the governor, he returned by horse to Yorktown and with a friend attended a rowdy cockfight, probably betting something along the lines of a typical five pistols per bout on the best-looking hen, which would have attempted to cut its opponent to death with its attached razors. A Virginia cockfight was, of course, yet another expression of dominance and submission—the thrills of winning and the agony of defeat in colonial society.

George now openly wanted to become a hero in the service of the Crown. There is little written evidence of this early on, yet his anxious acceptance of the ensuing assignments Dinwiddie gave him make it clear that he valued distinction at least as much as he did the small fortune he had already made as a surveyor. A yearning for fame through service to the British Empire was nothing to be ashamed of, particularly by a young man steeped in European traditions. If anything, George was encouraged in this goal; leading social and political minds in this era, including that of Francis Bacon, believed that "aspirations of glory" were a solid raison d'être for any young man. Tied to glory, but not necessarily riches, ambition became a useful character trait within the empire's own broader aspirations of control and conquest. Military service to a higher cause went hand in hand with a British ideal of honor, but it also had much deeper roots in Greco-Roman culture. The classics George was reading about Alexander the Great and Caesar's campaigns had more than enough vainglory in them to inspire any young colonialist with a bent to arms. George knew innately through the lessons he had picked up since his father's death that to become a leader of men he needed to garner both awe and love through actions, not words or money.

Though he still did not yet have the debonair and disciplined air of command that he would carry into the Revolutionary War, George had the raw talents required for good soldiering. No doubt, along with his sterling recommendations, George impressed the plump, aging Dinwiddie as a physical specimen. He already could ride, hunt, and parley with natives in the woods. His rough-hewn body and powerful limbs spoke, in their unique way, to the endless possibilities of an expanding western frontier. He had narrow shoulders and a modest chest, accompanied by massive thighs that put him in firm control of a horse and gave him a noble appearance in the saddle. Though he may well have looked clumsy at times in his size-thirteen boots, George was no slouch. He had lived efficiently in the wilds of the

Shenandoah Valley and performed backbreaking work for weeks at a time.

A year later, after Lieutenant Governor Dinwiddie had selected George for a special Crown mission into the wilderness to ask the French to abandon the Ohio Valley, London's *Gentleman's Magazine* attributed this to George's being "used to the woods" and also being known as "a youth of great sobriety, diligence, and fidelity." George later claimed that he could not believe that anyone would think him capable of the mission at hand. Indeed, he would write—with a hint of feigned humbleness—that his selection to lead the mission to warn the French off their own expansionist intentions came about "by some extraordinary circumstance," adding that it was astounding "that so young and inexperienced a person [as him] should have been employed on a negotiation with which subjects of the greatest importance were involved."

In February 1753, Dinwiddie appointed George as a major in the Virginia militia for the southern district, his first formal military post and one that brought into play contradictions, some of which would be considered "conflicts of interest" in our own day. Even as a newly honored Major Washington was displaying fresh instincts, he was now a paid soldier charged to serve greedy Crown policies that demanded western expansion in America, ran roughshod over Native American interests, and would spark bloodshed across Europe. Washington heroism was about to be built on the back of British imperialism. His admiration for everything that the empire stood for, however, embodied in his rock-solid friendship with the loyal-to-the-Crown Fairfax clan, prevented George, for now, from suffering any dissonance or moral crises. He knew the new boss, so to speak, because it was the same as his old boss.

II

War Games and Folly

Washington the Soldier—Battle of the Monongahela [July 9, 1755], engraved by Claude Regnier, after Junius Brutus Stearns, 1854. *Courtesy of Mount Vernon Ladies' Association*

7

Mission for a
Flawed Hero

A FEW HUNDRED FEET FROM ME, a young lady in a light blue dress, red apron, and bonnet squatted in the tall grass, taking aim. She pulled the trigger, and the flint hit the lock. The kick from the gun's butt sent the muzzle in the air and her apron flying high, but she quickly recovered her composure and reloaded her musket as her terrified-looking colleagues ducked incoming fire. The settlers were shooting at Native Americans, which included one Mike Shafer, whose grandfather had been a full-blooded Wyandot tribesman. Mike looked the part with a feather through his nose, a blackened jaw, assorted silver earrings, a bludgeon in one hand—which functioned, he said, "to brain" his opponents—and a musket in the other. Mike the Wyandot and his fellow tribesmen, including his son-in-law, were slipping behind trees and firing back, moving closer in an attempt to seize hostages. After shooting several males through and through, the natives grabbed white wives and daughters by the hair and began yanking them into the woods. The ladies howled in piercing wails as their foes dragged them up a hill in the direction of a lean-to strung with coyote skins. I was not surprised to hear the word "Savage!" cried at a very high pitch.

The twenty-first century American passions for reenacting the French and Indian War—the conflict for which George Washington achieved his first international notoriety—were higher than I had imagined. A day earlier, I had driven four hours north from Washington, DC, into the woods of western Pennsylvania to retrace his steps. The participants I met over the next several days were dead serious about re-creating the realities of what for most Americans remains a

A soldier takes fire at the enemy during a French and Indian War reenactment.
Phil Smucker

long-forgotten conflict. Through their attention to detail and the complex personas they attached to frontiersmen, British officers, Indians,
and Frenchmen, the reenactors were keen to get the story right. In
case I had missed anything as a war correspondent in the Balkans
and the Mideast, they also were determined to make me understand
that wars in the eighteenth century were just as hellish as those in
the twentieth and twenty-first centuries.

My own role in their conflict was suspect, at least at the start. I
tried to pass myself off as an eighteenth-century battle scribe, but my
uniform, I quickly learned from unsolicited style tips, wasn't nearly
dirty enough, and my cowhide boots needed more scuff marks before
they would be acceptable to the Virginia militia leader. I had to concede early on that I was far more adept at the eighteenth-century
technique of turning up a clay jug of Caribbean rum than I was at
shooting a musket at a fleeing foe.

Nearly everyone I met had a view on George Washington's role
in the war. Of George's early penchant for dashing through incoming fire on horseback, Tom Hinkelman, a hulking Native American

reenactor, said, "I think it was just shit luck. Washington had that special gift, and he was just destined for greatness." Shaded in black and maroon war paint, Hinkelman, an "Injun," as the white settlers called him, leaned on a post hung with skulls and animal skins. As he spoke, he passed me a cast-iron mug of rum spiced with cinnamon, inviting me to toast a fellow reenactor who had died not of war wounds but of old age.

Some were less impressed and referred only to George Washington's "alleged heroics." A tall, hollow-cheeked chap dressed in a Scottish kilt, upon hearing that I was writing a book about Washington, ripped off an extended invective directed at George. It was one that I imagined the young Virginian might have heard himself, after some of his early battlefield blunders: "Washington was a self-promoting, rich, spoiled brat! People don't realize what kind of family he was from. As a surveyor and officer he was out for one thing—himself."

He was armed with a musket, so I held my tongue.

I weighed these views, as both a mirror of what we have become as a nation and as insight into the misconceptions that still surround the ascent of George Washington. I knew, without a doubt, that George would not have kidded himself that he was anything like the average soldier or settler. Certainly, however, when he first stepped into the fray, he was sympathetic toward the frontiersmen of the Shenandoah and Ohio Valleys. Many of their families were under attack as he embarked on his first mission, but the simple truth was that he could not empathize with them, because he was not—nor had he ever been—one of them. He was, I had to admit from my own research into his teen years and close ties to the Fairfax clan, emerging onto the world stage as a slightly condescending son of good fortune.

For their part, the Ohio Valley's first settlers, many of them having fled into exile after royal and religious persecution in Europe, were helping to open the frontier to others through their homesteading, parleys, and conflicts with natives. Their new trading posts and open houses of worship created a unique fellowship on the frontier that had little to do with George's own first surveys of royal land grants. Their lot included British, Scotch-Irish, German, Swiss, and liberated indentured servants from other parts of Europe. Theirs was a world apart from the coddled life of wealthy plantations lining the Potomac and James Rivers. In 1744 John Hampton and his two sons reported living the greater part of one winter in the wilds of Virginia in the "hollow of a sycamore tree." Other settlers, required to pay annual quitrents to wealthy landowners like Lord Fairfax, resided in log cabins with floors made of "split puncheons a little smoothed with a broad-axe." They slept on mattresses stuffed with straw, and after a long winter their windowless homes, by some accounts, "smelled like goat pens."

Across the Shenandoah and into the Ohio Valley, British and German traders were facing new attacks from an aggressive French and Indian alliance. These skirmishes included kidnappings in which colonists had been paraded through Indian towns and French forts on their way to jail in Montreal. Diseases that had their origins in Europe had already ravaged native communities. Their white foes did not think of these darker-skinned people as "noble savages," and, for that matter, Mike the Wyandot wasn't hearing anything of the "politically correct Native American" label either: "*American* isn't what I like to call myself! Americans took everything we had or wanted to have," he insisted. "Yes, there were atrocities on both sides, but in the end we were squeezed out."

George embarked on his first official government mission in the woods to do the bidding of another class of colonists and British aristocrats. Since his first dinner with Lieutenant Governor Dinwiddie, he had become an insider in the power politics of the day, and now—less than a year on—a scheming Dinwiddie asked him to deliver what amounted to an ultimatum to the French and also to try his hand at espionage by assessing alliances with Native Americans and measuring the size of the French garrisons in the Ohio Valley. The governor's urgency in delivering his message to the French was underwritten by his own personal financial interests in the Ohio Valley in the form of lining his own pockets through the Ohio Company.

Although the mission was self-serving for Dinwiddie, he did value the young major's life, and in a prescient warning that took into account the distrust between Virginians and Native Americans, he carefully instructed George to ask the French, after telling them to back off their own claims on the Ohio Valley, for a "proper guard" to guarantee George's safe return to Virginia. This was to ward off, he said, "as you may judge for your safety, against any straggling Indians, or hunters, that may be ignorant of your character and molest you."

The cherubic Scotsman also instructed Washington to enlist the services of Christopher Gist, a former neighbor of Daniel Boone in the Carolinas and a principal real estate agent for the Ohio Company. A year earlier, while exploring the Ohio Valley for the Ohio Company, the forty-six-year-old Gist had cemented alliances with local tribes. He had already monitored the duplicity of frontier players, and in his absence from the Carolinas his own family had come under attack from angry tribesmen. He was a backwoodsman and diplomat with a serious edge.

Along with three dedicated servitors, a language interpreter, and a fur trader, Gist and Washington, a mere twenty-one years old, set off on their mission with pack mules and horses on November 15, 1753. Late in the year, when most frontiersmen had already begun to hunker down for winter, it was an odd time to take to the woods. As he made his way toward the Shenandoah, George found himself riding along the familiar banks of the Potomac, through the river port of Alexandria, and then onward to Winchester, Virginia, not far from Lord Fairfax's expanding country estate at Greenway Court. Here he helped procure a tent, weapons, ammunition, gifts for the native tribesmen, and deerskin leggings and shirts that mimicked the attire of the fur traders and natives he would interact with on the journey.

At the French and Indian War reenactments in western Pennsylvania, I ran into Dr. Carl Robertson, a local historian who often "interprets" the role of Christopher Gist by dressing as he would and playing his character in reenactments of Washington's first mission into the wilderness. A rustic eccentric who lives in a replica plantation house in the area of George's early exploits, Robertson dresses in colonial frontier garb: a broad-rimmed hat, a blue vest, and pants tucked into tall work boots. At his home, he often throws parties during which Indian and white settler reenactors interact cordially and enjoy an authentic frontier meal washed down with home brew. Carl kindly agreed to travel with me to retrace portions of the route that Washington and Gist traversed. "Washington's goal was to make this trip in as short a time as possible," he explained while sipping coffee at a wooden table in his eighteenth-century farmhouse before our departure. "When you read George's journal, you can almost see him straining at the bridle, even when the weather is being uncooperative. He never stops long anywhere, and at every step of the journey, we see him taking steps that strike notes of efficiency." But Carl, who has studied Gist's life and account of the journey inside and out, likes to keep George and anyone else—including local Pennsylvanians trying to exploit George's footprints and hoof tracks for tourist dollars—honest about what really happened along the trail on the wilderness trek.

In what he described in his journal as "excessive rains and a vast quantity of snow," George and a party of six left Winchester, Virginia, riding single file over ridges and down through wet gorges. The party trudged along slick, icy trails for a week to cover the first seventy-five miles as the crow flies. George began to show impatience with the harsh conditions, and when he found the Monongahela River flooded, he parted with the pack animals and took a canoe with the currents to the forks of the Ohio River. When the horses and pack animals caught up, he jumped on his steed and urged it on across the Allegheny River, cajoling the animal into the icy waters as he straddled it, swimming the beast across to the opposite shore.

The party moved onto to Logstown, where the French had established a trading post in 1747, building sturdy log cabins to attract Delaware, Iroquois, Shawnee, and Ottawa families with an eye to expand their trade. This trading post was now the domain of Chief Tanacharison, a Catawba Indian who claimed to have been adopted by the Seneca tribe as a child. A year earlier, the native leader had gone out on a limb opposing the French encroachment into the Ohio Valley, holding his finger up to the face of Philippe-Thomas Chabert de Joncaire and warning him to leave Logstown during a summit of several tribes. Known to the British as Half King, in recognition of his tribal authority, he served one of the representatives of the British-allied Six Nations in the Allegheny Valley. Just over fifty years old, he had sworn his loyalty to the Crown in Gist's presence a year earlier, and he now stood as the most influential Native American ally that Washington would work with through thick and thin for the next two years. The two men would develop an unusual symbiotic friendship that would come to bedevil George in the weeks and months to come.

Though more open-minded than some of his wealthy British mentors, George carried a standard European bias against natives. Like his colleague Gist, he had already established a working relationship with natives prior to his first formal meetings as an envoy. He admired them for their fighting and hunting skills, but there was a legacy he could not change or outlive: his family already had four generations of interactions with the eastern tribes, experiences that posited more prejudice than insight in his mind.

Despite a reputation as harsh fighters, Ohio Valley natives were cautious and rarely faced off directly with a more powerful foe. When dealing with the white man, they engaged in careful negotiations and ceremonial gift giving. Frequent meetings with both French and British leaders and varied promises suggested they had learned to play both sides of a conflict in order to try—in vain as it turned out—to preserve their long-term interests. To this end, the Delaware and Shawnee tribes in the Ohio Valley were already flying both British and French flags over their towns in recognition of the fact that so-called friendships and alliances were fleeting at best. Due to past betrayals, they had little reason to trust either side, especially a young upstart major who now pleaded with them for their loyalties.

Wearing a turban, deerskin leggings, moccasins, and furs, Washington's soon-to-be ally in arms, Half King, arrived to meet George in Logstown. Upon the major's urgings to speak out, the chief launched into a revealing account of his last meeting with the French. He recounted how during the past September he had been to Presque Isle, a fertile peninsula that shoots up from present-day Ohio into Lake Erie, to talk to the French commander Sieur de Marin, presenting him with a wampum peace belt of beads and polished shells woven into patterns representing goodwill and commitment. He claimed he had told the French, "Now Fathers, it is you that is the disturber in this land by coming and building your towns," adding that, "both you and the English are white. We live in *a country between*, therefore the land does not belong to either one or the other; but the great being above allowed it to be a place of residence for us." Half King made a point of reminding Washington that he also told the French, "We have told our brothers the English to withdraw," adding, "They have done so," a less-than-subtle hint of what embattled Native Americans wanted from both the French and the English.

To Half King's protests, Marin reacted swiftly and, according to the chief, referred to the Indians as mere "flies and mosquitoes" before he allegedly tossed the wampum belt back at its maker. This had been an unforgivable affront to Half King's pride.

Washington understood that the natives were out to protect their interests, but as the drums of the approaching French and Indian War beat louder, he accepted their vows of allegiance despite his distrust of them. He recounted later, asserting broadly, "The Indians are mercenary—every service of theirs must be purchased and they are easily offended." Yet the young major admitted in his subsequent account of the expedition that he had concealed the true intent of his mission to the French from Half King, who agreed, in any case, to work as his guide.

Accompanied by Half King and two other senior warriors, Jeska-kake and White Thunder, Major Washington again set off on horse-back with Gist to deliver his terse message to the French command. His first obstacle came on December 4 at Venango, a small French for-tification at the confluence of the Allegheny River and French Creek. Here George met the French captain de Joncaire, the offspring of a Seneca squaw and a French military officer. Captain de Joncaire was, of course, the same French leader whom Half King had insulted with a finger in the face at an earlier summit in Logstown. Invited to dine in style with the French, Washington refrained from heavy drink, remarking, "They dosed themselves pretty plentifully with it," adding with a flourish that "it gave license to their [French] tongues to reveal their sentiments more freely." Washington wasn't a teetotaler, but he was well aware that alcohol could conquer one's mental and physical discipline. For some men it served as a truth serum.

At the dinner, the French spat on British intentions and vowed to hold their ground. Seeking to control the players as much as pos-sible at this stage of the mission, George purposefully kept his Indian friends at bay in the woods. This did not succeed for long, and when Joncaire discovered his half cousins hidden away, he invited them in for a round of drinks. According to George, Half King and the natives, despite their disdain for the French, imbibed "liquors so fast, that they were soon rendered incapable of the business they came about."

George gathered his trekking party together and made a bee-line through the snows for his destination, finally arriving at Fort Le Boeuf. With his usual good manners and bright cheer, the Virginia major called on the silver-haired, one-eyed French commander Jacques Legardeur de Saint-Pierre, whom he compliments in his journal as possessing "the air of a soldier." The Frenchman reciprocated with equal praise, later asserting that Washington had comported himself with "quality and great merit." Left alone for more than a day while the French digested Dinwiddie's statement, George, taking care-ful notes, assessed the French fortifications and counted birch-bark canoes.

Saint-Pierre came back to him with an answer, dismissing Din-widdie's letter and its assertions that the French had encroached on the Crown's property and should leave without hesitation. The

Frenchman then suggested that his lieutenants lure Half King and his warrior friends into yet another round of drinking. Though Half King had sworn to Washington earlier that he intended merely to return a peace wampum he no longer respected, he contended the morning after his drinking spree that Saint-Pierre "evaded taking it, and made many fair promises of love and friendship."

It was the first clear indication that Half King was playing both sides, or at least wavering. At the same time, George fell into a restless funk over the French efforts to win over his newfound Native American friends with guns, powder, and liquor, writing, "I can't say that ever in my life I've suffered so much anxiety as I did in this affair." George, obsessed with remaining in control, was angry that his own efforts to persuade the natives to leave were failing. He and Gist thoroughly scolded Half King and accused him of betrayal before finally convincing him to depart in their company as a guide, as agreed.

But George had only the loosest grip on Half King and his whimsical ways. In his haste to bid farewell to the French, Washington, throwing caution to the wind, did not follow Dinwiddie's specific advice to petition the French for a guard to accompany him on his return journey, which would soon take him into uncharted territory. As the canoes departed over icy shoals, Washington wrote that his canoe was "staved against the rocks," forcing his party to wade in the shallows of the icy waters. The travelers spent a night trying to hack through thick ice.

Worried that his message for Dinwiddie might get lost in the snow and ice, George again expressed dismay as Half King and his fellow warriors sat down casually—and somewhat comically—to consume a bear at their first resting spot. Frustrated by this behavior, Washington and Gist continued on their way, with the natives still gnawing gleefully on bear bones, happy to have a hearty meal as the befuddled major focused on his taxing return to Williamsburg. Half King and company soon rejoined, along with four canoes full of Frenchmen tipping over in the current and setting brandy and wine bottles floating past the Virginians, who snickered and left them to fend for themselves.

Dr. Carl Robertson pointed out to me that Major Washington's party had also, to this point, been having some fun. "The fact that they found it so amusing the French had tipped their canoes tells you that they weren't deadly serious—that they weren't sourpusses," he said. "They could see humor in the bottles and the French bobbing up and down in the river."

"It wasn't slapstick comedy, but it was fairly amusing, I suspect." I nodded.

Arriving back at Venango, Washington's horses, which had trod along beside the canoes, were now collapsing and unable to continue without rest. "Later, we do find out that the horses all died, which probably devastated George, considering his love for animals," said Carl. Half King, who was enjoying himself far more than George, argued to remain in the company of Joncaire, who had been so generous with his liquor earlier in the journey. The chief now bid George adieu and abandoned his commitment to accompany the young major, with the excuse that a sickly elder in his party could not move on.

Gist and George left their horses with colleagues and pressed on. Concerned about worsening weather, the Virginia major also left behind his heaviest bags and stepped into the previously purchased "Indian walking dress" of deerskin leggings and a knee-length fur coat belted around his waist. Gist then remarked—prematurely as it turns out—that the major "showed signs of wearing out," adding, "I was unwilling he should undertake such a travel." After another day and night in which Washington appeared again to Gist as "much fatigued," the two pushed on through Murdering Town, a desolate outpost named for past and forgotten deeds.

Carl and I arrived in Murdering Town—which he explained was the white settlers' name for a native town—in the late afternoon about the time that Gist and Washington arrived on their own journey. Above us, on the crest of a nearby hill, were the wagon wheel ruts of the old Venango trail, sunken two and three feet deep in the ground. "See how deep this is," said Carl, measuring it by hand and pointing to the sides of the old road at the top of a hill. "From up here, you can see clear across to Murdering Town. Beyond that, you can make out the horseshoe bend in the creek—it is about two miles across, and the Venango road went right through it."

Carl and I descended a hill and crossed a bridge over Beaver Creek, where we then stood at the foot of the old town itself. "If you were to dig up there about six inches down, you would turn up a lot of interesting native artifacts," Carl said.

"So these were permanent native settlements?" I asked.

"Yes. The homes would likely have been huts, not teepees, including possibly a longhouse for meetings. Along the water here would have been vegetable and corn gardens."

George and his savvy guide had been hiking all day when they arrived and, according to Gist's journal, met with an Indian whom he recognized as having seen earlier at Joncaire's Venango post. "We asked the Indian if he could go with us, and show us the nearest way," he wrote. The native, possibly a wandering Wyandot and not from Murdering Town, was "happy" to guide the two men, Gist wrote. The three men marched toward the forks of the Allegheny, but Gist also remarked in his journal that he distrusted the Indian. Major Washington "soon mistrusted him as much as I," he added.

Both men followed as they left Murdering Town, with Gist noting, "The Major's feet grew sore, and he very weary, and the Indian steered too much Northeasterly." When Washington refused to give their guide his gun to carry, the native man grew "churlish," Gist wrote. The men had at least one compass and knew they were off the trail they had taken on the way to Venango much earlier. As the three reached a clearing, their guide broke forward, spun around, and assumed a shooting position with his rifle. At fifteen paces, about forty to fifty feet, he turned and fired in the direction of his two charges. George hadn't been daydreaming, though, and had seen the guide turn in his tracks. "The Major saw him point his gun towards us and fire," wrote Gist.

It was to be the first of many bullets fired in anger at George Washington, and this one could well have killed him, but like dozens more flying lead shots, the slug missed the mark. "Are you shot?" cried Washington in the direction of his companion. Within an instant, Gist, Washington, or both—it is not clear from the two journal accounts—pounced on the Native American as he rushed to reload his single-shot. Gist remarked, "I would have killed him but the major would not suffer me to," suggesting that Washington did not want to take a prisoner's life at close quarters, despite the circumstances. It is worth considering that Major Washington had still to engage in his first battle, and, as such, was a raw novice but managed to dissuade Gist from killing the man. Though there were no other adversaries lurking near them, a move to kill the guide could have meant retribution either on settlers, or themselves.

Carl took me down to an unmarked meadow, the alleged "scene of the attempted murder." A grove of oak trees can still be seen several hundred paces before a small stream where, traveling by foot and with their guide now in their captivity, Washington and Gist stopped briefly to rest after their traumatic moment. The small meadow, which slopes down toward a stream called Breakneck Creek, is well off the Venango trail, and it is clear that from a map of the earlier route that George's guide tried to trick and misdirect the two of them. Carl and I worked our way down to a bend in the stream. "I think Washington was giving the impression that he was a naive white man, but he had already begun to appreciate the theater and theatrics, and my own impression is that his whole routine on the hike was designed to allow the Indian to think just that," said Carl. "You'll note that it was George, not Gist, as Gist wrote in his account, who spotted the Indian as he wheeled around to shoot."

Gist tried to calm the situation. He told the captive, "I suppose you were lost, and fired your gun," while offering him some food to eat. It was a strange face for the seasoned woodsman to put on the event, but it worked. At dusk, the two released the native, but not before heaving his gun into the underbrush, and they set off themselves at a brisk clip to complete their journey. The two hikers had reason to suspect they were about to be ambushed; upon finding fresh moccasin tracks and fearing the worst, they separated and trudged forward through the snow on different paths toward the same fork of the Allegheny, finally reuniting and camping for a few short hours.

The next day, December 29, 1753, having trekked most of the night, the two sped up through the snow only to find that the Allegheny River was flowing with broken sheets of thick ice atop it. The only means of crossing would be on a raft, which Washington and Gist began to build with "one poor hatchet." As the sun set, the travelers took a calculated risk, holding two long poles for propulsion in their hands and launching their rickety mass of loosely bound logs into the river. Neither Gist nor George had slept for over thirty-six hours, but the threat of an attack inspired them to work as fast as possible.

George's narration of what happened next rings with intense detail: "Before we were halfway over, we were jammed in the ice, in such a manner that we expected every moment our raft to sink and ourselves to perish. I put out my setting pole to try to stop the raft that the ice might pass by, when the rapidity of the stream threw it [the raft] with such violence against the pole that it jerked me out into ten feet [of] water, but fortunately saved myself by catching hold of one of the raft logs." He added, "We were obliged, as we were near an island, to quit our raft and make [swim] to it."

The crossing point taken by Gist and Washington is visible from the Fortieth Street Bridge, also known as Washington Crossing Bridge, just outside Pittsburgh. The Allegheny is wide but shallow at this point, dredged significantly in the nineteenth and twentieth centuries, so even the "island" has now merged with the older embankment. This makes it difficult to gauge the strength at which the water would have flowed, in Carl's view. In any case, hypothermia would have killed both men within minutes had they failed to make dry ground. Washington was a swimmer from his days growing up on the Rappahannock, and with his previous struggles through the snow, he must have been incredibly depleted. Despite falling in up to his neck, he still fought his way ashore.

Though some elements of the mission to Fort Le Boeuf are still lost in the fog of differing accounts, little is left to the imagination in George's journal as he crosses the Allegheny. The athleticism Washington displayed at the time of the Allegheny River crossing was nothing short of amazing. In recounting the story, Washington does not tout his own physical prowess, but from his account of the icy plunge and his survival of a night on an island, a solid picture of an indomitable young man in a harsh wilderness emerges. Though it is easy to question some of George's naive personal choices at moments in the journey, which Gist's own careful account of the trip also renders suspect, almost everyone, including Washington's fellow colonists who learned of the hardships of the return from Fort Le Boeuf, marveled over the daring Dinwiddie's envoy displayed.

Carl pointed out to me one more astonishing thing as he bid me adieu to finish a book he was writing. "The letter that Washington was carrying has not been smudged," he said. Sure enough, back in Richmond, Virginia, I discovered that the French commander's rejection of Dinwiddie's demands was intact and legible, with no water stains. In retrospect, the sum of the feats was greater than each small accomplishment along the way. Washington had commandeered his horse across icy waters, canoed down rushing rivers, swum to safety amid ice jams, and literally dodged a bullet. He had performed all this while scribbling in his journal, dealing with Half King's quizzical and often booze-inspired antics, and engaging with two alien cultures. In a final and published report, Washington comes across as undaunted, obsessed with the completion of his mission, and, in my view, even slightly humble in his telling of his own two near-death experiences, however intent he was on including them in the final report. His stamina and courage, given the parallel account written by Gist, which confirms most of the key facts, are obvious.

Over the course of the mission, Washington emerged as the undisputed master of his environment and acted without getting swept away by diversions. One has a persistent sense that George understood that this first mission was going to define him in some way, which it absolutely did. He was particularly disciplined in his dealings with the Native Americans, and he displayed an unusual sense of protocol for a twenty-year-old, paying close attention to his own words and to native customs, even when his "allies" were being less than direct. In completing his mission in the wilderness through physical duress, he was living out his own code of conduct and sportsmanship.

To be clear, none of his accomplishments were wildly out of character for a Virginia lad who wanted to be seen as a hearty English gentleman with great fortitude under extremes. Such toughness was very much encouraged in this mid-eighteenth-century colonial culture, but George was a particularly polished exemplar of physical virtues, and he excelled where others might have failed—even when Christopher Gist believed he was in a state of utter exhaustion.

As he did later during the actual combat of the French and Indian War, George actually relished the challenges thrown at him. His attitude was in keeping with the Roman Stoic Seneca's guidance on the importance of stamina and determination. In his writings, which Washington admired and acquired, Seneca advises that "the bodies of sailors are hardened by enduring the sea; the hands of farmers are hardened by work; the arms of soldiers are strengthened to hurl darts, the legs of racers are kept agile" when exercised. Accepting a challenge—a symbolic gauntlet thrown down at one's feet—and overcoming it was as important in the New World as it had been in the Greco-Roman or Judeo-Christian cultures of the Old World. Seneca also wrote in one of George's favorite texts that "strength weakens without adversity." This was an age-old idea that men build character by struggling and overcoming a challenge, a concept that George embraced with gusto. Epictetus, a similar-minded Greek sage and Stoic philosopher who had been born a slave, also employed language about sportsmanship, advising that "when some difficulty befalls you, remember that god, like a wrestling-master, has matched you with a rough young man. To what end? That you may become an Olympic victor, and that cannot be done without sweat." Against great odds on the frontier, George was proving his intelligence as much by his action and endurance as by his words, which were often still bumbling by comparison.

Back in the bustling streets of Williamsburg, the towering Virginian had his first fleeting taste of celebrity. He had succeeded in asserting King George's claim to the western frontier and thrown down a proverbial gauntlet at the feet of the French. There was no parade or official award presentation, but the capital was abuzz with the news of his mission, its political implications, and the suggestion that he had accomplished the goals of the king with flying colors. He had shed no blood and sidestepped only one bullet, but he still had much to boast about. His account, written on deadline and imperfect in many ways but published in a pamphlet immediately made available in the streets of Williamsburg, described well the challenges he had faced and overcome, and did not leave out the moments when the mission might have failed. In a sense, the major's official journal was a unique adventure tale told by a determined young man coming of age in an extreme, harsh environment. The story sold, and the praise that followed gave George a big, dangerous-for-his-own-good ego boost.

Nevertheless, the account and his letters to friends also expose a startling paradox. The writings explain the thoughts of a young man still not quite comfortable with the service he had signed up for nor with the code of honor he has devised for himself. In some of his words, we see George's selfish ambitions still struggling to reconcile his sense of service to a higher cause. His journal exposes solipsistic ramblings that come across almost as whining but that Dinwiddie and others likely ignored as small parts of the more important and successful story. Early on, George writes, "Throughout the whole journey we met with nothing but one continued series of cold wet Weather, which occasioned very uncomfortable lodgings; especially after we had left our tent." Such comments appear aimed at gaining sympathy from his superiors and peers. In my view, glancing over the complete evidence, it looks as though George protests a little too much about both the harsh conditions and, to friends in private, about his own eventual pay. In other words, he knew what he had signed up for.

Buried behind these minor complaints is the slightly spoiled ego of Dinwiddie's new golden boy. George's letters to his family display the emergence of another private persona, a man who craved still more praise and reward than his political masters and mentors had offered to him. (Arguably this is a sign of a healthy ambition and can be seen as a decent trait as well.) When Williamsburg's Virginia Assembly voted to give Washington a fifty-pound-sterling reward for the successful completion of his mission—no small sum in this era—he grumbled in a letter to his sixteen-year-old brother, Jack, "I was employed to go on a journey in the winter (when I believe few or none would have undertaken it), and what did I get by it? My expenses borne." In my view, the dismay is strikingly reminiscent of a young Winston Churchill complaining vehemently to his American mother of the poor paychecks he was receiving from the *Telegraph* newspaper in London while reporting on the British Empire's perilous skirmishes on the Pakistan-Afghan borderlands at the turn of the nineteenth century.

George's confidential note to Jack, which fortunately was preserved for posterity, makes clear that he is learning to behave one way in public but vent his private concerns through other channels, a pattern that will recur and evolve through the years. In a sense, the public persona and private views are to be expected, but to understand how Washington came to view his own public performance on the stage of history, these private thoughts are crucial. Though George had accepted a mission and sought to perform beyond expectations, his attitude toward authority—as expressed to Jack—already suggests that the glory of the British Crown would not be enough to sustain his immense ambitions.

8

Charms of War

VERY FEW OF THE FORMER BATTLEFIELDS on which George Washington fought are so well preserved as is the densely wooded site several miles northwest of Washington's camp at Fort Necessity, where he fought his first encounter. The glen, which Half King's allies had referred to as a "gloomy hollow," presents a natural cathedral: an enclave marked by a long ravine running down the side of a small mountain and lined with sharp granite cliffs atop giant boulders. The ground is flush with ferns and fallen logs covered in dewy moss. When I visited, small birds were flitting about beneath a thick forest canopy, and a brown-and-white-striped chipmunk was foraging in the escarpments. As I walked across the humid grounds, I was struck by how this same prehistoric forest must have remained virtually silent as George's force crept up on the French military party on the morning of May 28, 1754.

I carefully descended from the granite cliffs and stood for a time in the heart of the ravine, where most of the killing took place. The ground was cold and damp, as it had been on that day over 260 years earlier. Outgunned and surrounded on ground lower than their attackers, the French had attempted to surrender, they insisted, but the Virginians and Indians had closed on them for what quickly became a hand-to-hand slaughter.

According to one of George's senior lieutenants, the French troops had been lazily preparing for their day, rolling out from under lean-tos made of bark and brush. Oddly, they had posted no sentinels. Before any shots were fired, Washington sent two columns along different routes. Fighters for his close friend, Maj. Adam Stephen, took the cliffs above and opposite him while Half King's ten men quietly slipped down around both sides to the base of the ravine to complete an encirclement.

George crept from behind trees to get a better look at the French camp. Within range and with a full view, which slanted down the mountain, he looked over a contingent of soldiers occupying a small space no larger than a modern football field in width or length. He would claim he watched the French scramble to grab their guns. Washington wrote to Lieutenant Governor Dinwiddie, "I was the first man that approached them, and the first whom they saw, and immediately upon it they ran to their arms, and fired briskly." As fire broke out on both sides, the natives, led by his ally Half King, closed off any hope French forces had to exit at the bottom of the glen. Indians present at the slaughter say they quickly killed eight Frenchmen attempting to run down and out of the ravine. At least one claimed that Lieutenant Colonel Washington had fired the first shot, a fact he may have chosen to conceal from Dinwiddie but that, oddly, he probably would have mentioned in a subsequent and private letter to his own brother if he knew it to be true.

Due to the fog of war—and a dearth of reliable accounts—the remainder of the battle is confusing at best. Though Washington states that the shooting engulfed the ravine and that his men easily defeated the French from their higher ground, the sole French soldier who slipped past the Native Americans told another story entirely. He said he saw Joseph Coulon de Villers, Sieur de Jumonville ask one of his soldiers to read an official diplomatic summons that charged the British with, among other things, "coming armed with overt force." Washington denied this, but it is quite possible that, amid the mayhem, a French diplomatic overture was made, particularly with hand-to-hand killing taking place at the bottom of the ravine. Jumonville's superiors had instructed him to deliver a message.

As soon as the shooting erupted, however, Washington had the battle he had longed for, writing exuberantly in the aftermath to his brother Jack, "I heard the bullets whistle, and, believe me, there was something charming in the sound."

The folly of war was not yet apparent to Washington, and what happened after the first fusillades in his initial battle is a subject that is heatedly debated by American, British, French, Native American, and Canadian historians even today. It still—in any version of the events—reflects poorly on Washington's storied self-discipline and, in other respects, on his evolving personal code of honor.

George Washington had been attracted to war for years in advance of his first skirmish, and when he finally came upon the chance, he plunged somewhat recklessly into a storied world where prowess and skill soon become inseparable from barbarity and blood lust.

The relationship between sports and war started, of course, in the Stone Age. The ties are apparent in ancient artistic depictions wherein the slaying of a wild animal is often interchangeable with the slaying of a menacing human foe. The hunt, at the start, was very much about sustenance. In the ancient art found in Chauvet Cave in France and the Cave of Altimra in Spain, for instance, we see wild animals painted dark red with arrows sticking out helter-skelter from their bodies. (These paintings have been carbon-dated to about thirty thousand years ago.) Hunting was usually for food, but conflict could also involve the harvesting of meat for ritual purposes, including cannibalism. There are strong and irrefutable scientific hints that these passions evolved over time. If you subscribe to the theory of evolution, which I tend to, it is worth noting that modern chimpanzees hunt down, murder, and sometimes, albeit rarely, eat one another to protect their own valuable hunting grounds. Tribes I've visited with in New Guinea had similar, but highly ritualized, tactics. Nevertheless, modern men sometimes trick themselves into believing through the promotion of "rules" of war that all the visceral and violent impulses of warfare can be contained within a rational prism. Of course, history—ancient and medieval—tells another, far more barbaric tale.

Hunting heroes and military leaders are interchangeable on Grecian urns and Roman vases. Egyptians trained wild cats to hunt and kill for them, and some cultures domesticated and trained animals to go to war. The Romans combined the two and created a spectator sport for humans to watch lions shred and eat the corpses of men thrown into their den. This appealed to base impulses and became a wildly popular blood sport.

Battles were not "sport," at least not as we use the word today, nor was war in the eighteenth century—or even today—endowed with an adequate set of rules defining fair play. But Roman and Greek soldiers, leaders included, were duty-bound to perform well at war and in times of peace, and they were trained in sports that provided sets of overlapping physical feats, including riding, fencing, and thrusting or shooting, skills required to do well at war and play. Like many ancients, the Greek writer Xenophon considered sport to be an excellent school for war, and he actively promoted sports and fitness to this end, making him a modern thinker in his day. Over two thousand years ago it was a given that excelling at sports and physical feats, in and of themselves, gave men confidence to achieve greatness. As an epitaph on his tomb, the warmongering Persian emperor Darius I, born 550 BC, had someone write, "I loved my friends; I was an excellent horseman, and an excellent hunter; nothing to me was impossible."

History's varied notions of skill and daring form the backstory for George Washington's rise as a gentleman warrior in the New World. In the wilderness, he had already tested and improved skills that would serve him well in battle. Even when he was back home at Mount Vernon or Ferry Farm, he was often in the field, riding rough as a foxhunter, leaping over unexpected obstacles, and chasing down a quarry.

But there was one mental leap that George had yet to accomplish: he did not understand the art of war or the strategic thinking required to win on the battlefield in the same way he might have known how to win in a foxhunt or a game of cards. So, as he headed off to fight, he faced a new quarry but also new and daunting quandaries.

With his journey to Fort Le Boeuf, George had launched his personal odyssey and escaped the perils of Scylla and Charybdis. His return had opened doors. Lieutenant Governor Dinwiddie, who had gambled on Major Washington during the journey, was pleased with what he had seen of the young man's documented escapes and sheer determination.

Meanwhile, French intentions to try to hold the Ohio Valley had become clear. The same fleet of canoes that George had counted in number on his mission to inform the French command had been readied for an invasion of the Ohio Valley. Dinwiddie again called George into his quarters, this time to accept a mission with far more pugilistic ends. Subsequently, as George rallied a ragtag force of heavy drinkers, few could have predicted the approaching storm or the words of British pundit Sir Horace Walpole, who would write, "The volley fired by a young Virginian in the backwoods of America set the world on fire."

George had no idea that he was about to strike the flint that would ignite a tinderbox. He was under vague and slightly contradictory orders not to initiate hostilities, but at the same time Dinwiddie also wanted him to build defenses and "in case of resistance to make prisoners of [his foe] or kill and destroy them." For a young man itching to prove himself in battle, the orders were as close to a license to kill as any young officer could ask for.

George was just twenty-one years old when he prepared for his first war, and this was to be his first real command. He had already been welcomed into an elite group of powerful patriarchal players in Virginia society, gentleman landowners who were asked to raise arms and mobilize the broader masses. Yet he soon discovered that his potential new recruits were, in his words, "loose, Idle Persons, that are quite destitute of House, and Home. . . . Many of them without Shoes, other's want Stockings, some without Shirts." Offered fighting men from the local Alexandria jail, George wrote to his brother Jack, comparing it to a futile "attempt to raize the Dead to Life again, as the force of this Country." War was not a popular imperative, particularly in areas already made safe from raids through the expulsion of Native Americans. Local farmers did not line up to go to war, and they did what they could to hide their horses and carts from George's prying eyes. Incentives were required, and so George's superiors had agreed to hogsheads of rum and the lure of near-constant libations to sustain these "idle persons" in the thick of battle. Not surprisingly, this often proved to be a recipe for less discipline, not more.

Lieutenant Colonel Washington rode out of my hometown, Alexandria, Virginia, on April 2, 1754, at the age of twenty-two in a "red coat with lace cuffs and black boots," on a tall horse, and commanding a sloppy force of 159 men wearing moccasins and homespun linen. This first fledgling corps of fighters boasted in their arsenal hunting rifles and a few small-caliber swivel guns. Within hours, the force began to carve out a route to the front, George's men beating back the underbrush with axes and machetes.

George hadn't seen his closest Indian confidant, Half King, since he left him drinking merrily from Joncaire's ample supplies of rum along the shoals of an icy river a year earlier. Since then, his old colleague had invited both the Virginians and Pennsylvanians to build forts in Iroquois country, promising food and warriors (whom he claimed to control) in return. But now, Half King sent two young warriors to confront Washington with a fresh wampum belt and an urgent message: "If you do not come to our assistance now, we are entirely undone, and I think we shall never meet again." It sounded oddly like a swoon from a lonely lover, but the message veiled Half King's calculations. He saw an opening for his own sagging authority, and he no doubt believed that he could strengthen his power base by spurring on the young Virginian to engage his French foe.

As George approached the valley of the Ohio River region, he assembled his forces at Wills Creek, well south of present-day Pittsburgh. At the same time, some one thousand French troops were pushing south on foot and in canoes with loads of ammunition and artillery, setting the stage for a showdown. The young Virginian's replies to Half King's pleadings had a quizzical air to them. He wrote that since "our hearts burn with love and affection" for Virginia's Native American allies, he would dispatch "a great number of warriors" with "our great guns . . . to assist you, whose interest is as dear to us as our lives." This was the language of phony affections, a standard and almost always highly condescending approach representatives of the British Empire used in the seventeenth and eighteenth centuries. By no coincidence, perhaps, a cocky George signed his correspondence to Half King with the nickname "Destroyer of Villages," a moniker the Seneca had given to his great-grandfather John. George even sent what he called "bunches of wampum, to assure you of the sincerity of my speech, and that you may remember how much I am your Friend and Brother."

Despite his words, Washington's Crown mission had little to do with Native American interests, and, as other letters indicate, he distrusted the tribesmen at least as much as they doubted him. The pretense of great friendship continued anyway. Half King's next communication amounted to a poorly written, somewhat quaint, but predictably dire warning to his friend "Mister Georg[e] Washington," advising him to "beawar of them [the French] for deisin'd to strik ye forist English they see ten deays since they marchd," and adding that he was ready to immediately meet with the Virginia forces to guide them forward.

Back at a new base camp, George's Virginia forces began to dig trenches that would eventually become the foundation of a small fortress at Great Meadows, some forty-five miles south of the current city of Pittsburgh. He wrote in giddy terms to Dinwiddie about his intended actions, explaining, "We have with nature's assistance made a good entrenchment and by clearing the bushes out of these meadows prepared a *charming* field for an encounter."

Washington was probing for a clash, and his suspicions were further stoked when his former guide to Fort Le Boeuf, Christopher Gist, arrived to tell him that he had spotted fifty Frenchmen on the prowl near his own home. Leaping to a convenient conclusion, Washington reported to Half King's roving messengers that the French were lurking nearby with the clear intention to "kill the Half King." The enemy of his French enemy had been warned.

As a young commander enamored of his own half brother's war stories, George now actively sought out his foe. His eagerness was to be expected. It was in keeping with the needs of young British and Virginian officers who desired to prove themselves in the field and, thereby, impress their political and military masters. George, in essence, was about to risk his neck for the lieutenant governor and his aristocratic good friends, all of whom sought a greater dominion for themselves and the Crown. These mentors and bosses were practiced at disguising their personal interests beneath a call for "victory, honor, and glory" in the name of the empire.

Keen to know more about the available attack routes, in case he would need them, Washington broke off with a small party to explore and test the navigation possibilities on the Youghiogheny River. On May 20 he paddled a canoe down a set of rapids but was warned off his adventure by a local fur trader at the Ohiopyle Falls in the heart of present-day Ohiopyle State Park. Washington returned on foot, concerned that his party might drown while facing off against a drop of forty-six feet in the rapids.

Reciprocating with intelligence of his own, Half King's messenger, Silver Heels, informed the Virginians that French forces had encamped in a rocky ravine six miles as the crow flies away from Great Meadows. Though British and North Carolina reinforcements were still on the way, George gathered forty of his best fighters and crept toward a rendezvous with Half King. His description of the march conveys unusual detail. It states that his forces moved forward "in a heavy rain and in a night as dark as pitch, along a path scarce broad enough for one man. We were sometimes fifteen or twenty minutes out of the path before we could come to it again, and we would often strike against each other in the darkness. All night long we continued our route, and the 28th, about sunrise, we arrived at the Indian camp."

He also remarked that after he met Half King and exchanged intelligence, "we concluded to attack them together." So he admitted he was on the offensive, but he also made it clear he thought that the French forces he was about to confront were out to strike his own forces and that he was only intercepting them in advance in a kind of preemptive strike against an assumed aggressor. Standing against

this contention, however, are the original orders for the French contingent led by the young officer Joseph Coulon de Villers, Sieur de
Jumonville. Though these orders threaten the eventual use of arms,
they also provide a written summons for Jumonville to deliver to the
ears or eyes of the commanders of the British King's forces to evacuate
the area first. Claude-Pierre Pécaudy de Contrecoeur, the senior commander who wrote the orders, ended them in no uncertain language
for the opposing officers he would meet, addressing them directly: "I
am convinced you will show M. Dejumonville all the consideration
that he deserves and send him back at once to inform me of your
intentions."

When the fighting commenced, the fusillades from Washington's
side intensified as Native American fighters moved forward. What
precisely happened amounts to a still-to-be-solved historical whodunit.

French accounts state that Half King, who spoke broken French,
approached Jumonville from behind, shouting, "Tu n'es pas encore
mort, mon père!" (You are not yet dead, my father!) Half King "swung
his tomahawk and split Jumonville's skull, which killed him instantly.
Then, as the horrified Virginians and their French prisoners watched,
[Half King] scooped out a handful of Jumonville's brains and washed
his hands with them." Such ritualistic killing was not frowned upon
in native circles, but Washington and his men do not corroborate
the account. One possibility is that Jumonville was brained as he fled
down the hill in an effort to escape.

Washington's initial account suggests that the French leader was
more likely killed in gunfire, since he says Half King's men "scalped
the dead." He wrote, "We killed Mr. de Jumonville, the Commander
of the party, also nine others, we wounded one and made twenty-
one prisoners." Then he states, "The Indians scalped the dead and
took away the greater part of their arms." But in another Washington
account of the same moment, George leaves no doubt that the natives
slaughtered some of the Frenchmen after they had been wounded,
stating that Half King's men proceeded "to knock the poor, unhappy
wounded on the head and bereave them of their scalps." This is
arguably, on the one hand, an unusual way to describe such a horrific event, particularly in light of George's letter to Jack describing
the actual shooting as "charming." Certainly, the wounded French
soldiers would have felt more than "unhappy" as they were being
slaughtered. On the other hand, that George even uses the phrase

"poor, unhappy wounded" suggests he feels for his foe and knows precisely what he is witnessing.

Accounts of who killed Jumonville differ, but it is clear that he died either at the hands of Half King and his men, who gouged out his brains, or he was shot by a Virginian or Native American. It is, of course, possible that he was first shot and that is why Half King shouted that he was "not yet dead," and then simply brained him. Regardless, Washington soon would stand accused of assassinating a high French military envoy in direct violation of eighteenth-century martial law.

In letters back to Williamsburg, Washington effusively denied the notion that he oversaw the assassination of the French officer. His strident explanations, which highlighted his notions that the French were bald-faced liars, did not fall on deaf ears. Dinwiddie's final account to King George's court insists that Washington's men were under the control of the native warriors, which would not have been in keeping with normal protocol. In a dubious attempt to defend his own appointed field commander, Dinwiddie wrote, "This little skirmish was by the Half King and their Indians. We were as auxiliaries to them, as my orders to the Commander of our Forces (were) to be on the defensive." These words, particularly the use of the phrase "little skirmish," so far removed from the actual event, strike me as a lame attempt to cover up an attack gone awry, and which had clearly not—especially by George's own account—been defensive in nature. On the other hand, Dinwiddie's defense of his protégé suggests he was not unhappy that a war that embodied his own imperial interests had now begun. He actually also wrote to George congratulating him for the "very agreeable Acct of Yr killing."

Though a handful of French historians have insisted Washington was responsible for what we would term in our day a war crime, the known facts from this eighteenth-century battle simply do not prove this. And at least one leading Canadian professor of history familiar with all the French versions of the battle, Dr. Marcel Trudel, has supported much of Washington's argument, insisting that George "had every reason to be suspicious" given his own near-death experiences in meetings with the French and Indians five months earlier. In truth, Jumonville was operating well south of the French-designated "lands of the King" and could have used a Native American runner to convey his message or announce his presence if he had wanted to do this.

Dinwiddie accepted Washington's account of the battle in an apparent case of believing what he wanted to hear, and went so far as to describe Washington as "prudent," which was a clear stretch of the truth by any measure. Though their manipulations of Half King are obvious, there may be substance to Dinwiddie's contention that the older native warrior led George into the slaughter. Half King actively deceived Washington, which raises questions about his professed loyalty to the man he called "Mister George." George's competency, in light of war crimes that were committed, cast a cloud over his own code of honor during the Jumonville Glen attack. When and if he harbored major doubts about what to do, he ignored or successfully hid them. As he allegedly enjoyed the whizzing of bullets, he would soon be the butt of jokes in England for playing the part of a foolhardy young officer. Upon hearing of Washington's "charming boast," Britain's own King George purportedly sneered that the young Virginian would "not say so if he had been used to hearing many [bullets]."

Even if we did not have George's heady assertion in writing, it is fair to ask what precisely might have been going on in his mind as those first bullets whistled past his ear. The shots, which likely sparked a dollop of apprehension, marked a young officer's baptism by fire into a profession that embodied the dominance of empires, the promise of conquest and riches, but also unpredictable punishments for bad decisions and vainglory.

George now had a taste of the glory of war he had longed for as a teen. It became, in essence, his rite of passage into manhood. While at Ferry Farm, despite his mother's reluctance to unleash him, he had relished the chance to fight, and as his life as a Crown warrior finally got under way, he had no reason to believe that a fight for British dominance in the Ohio Valley held hidden drawbacks for him. He did not have time for idle speculation. The prize of military service was too great in and of itself. Besides, he must have thought the prospect of fighting an armed foe a hundred yards in the distance was far more exciting than standing in a grove of trees and inspecting a survey line with an assistant.

Even if he was still unsure of what his future held, not much had changed since Alexander the Great conquered Asia, Caesar's campaigns faced down the Gauls, or Henry V beat the French at

Agincourt. For young men not born into ruling clans but hoping to make their name or prove the nobility of their character and exhibit the courage of their forefathers, warfare offered a path to magnificence. A life of arms offered membership in a new family of men, a set of thinkers who agreed on principles and codes of honor. These men adhered to the idea that the force of arms, with God's blessing, would win the day and, even if they fell in battle, bring *glory* to its participants. The Church of England, the imperial state's religious arm, provided hymns enough to affirm these communal notions.

As much as a Native American teen sought to prove his manhood by hacking off the scalp of a foe and raising it to the heavens, George knew that in war he would have a chance to prove and define his manhood to others. His rides through the forest on foxhunts, bayonet drills in the heat of the summer sun, pleas with Dinwiddie for better pay and a higher rank, and rounding up of drinkers and ruffians to join him all led straight to what he really wanted in life: a war he could call his own.

As any soldier is aware, military life is steeped in boredom and routine until those moments that test one's mettle. The British officer corps' standards to which George aspired—but which he would never quite attain in the eyes of his royal masters, who would refuse him an official commission—were geared toward instilling discipline and rewarding those moments when a young officer was asked to stand tall and face the bullets of a foe. For these chaotic and uncertain moments, the empire trained its soldiers to take "pleasure" in war, not unlike a young man's training as a hunter asked him to steady himself in the saddle and relish the moment of the kill. Naturally, as with the imperial penchant for pig-sticking, there was a visceral, almost barbaric emotion bound up in these split seconds. So the British Empire, as much as the US Marine Corps today or any other unit in need of hardened killers, encouraged the emotional high of that moment. In social circles, it was repeated that war presented a fine, maybe the finest, path to glory for young men.

It wasn't such a hard sell after all. If today we recognize that war is promoted by savvy propagandists and can be extolled by a nationalistic media, there were as many or more proponents (proportionally speaking) of war in George's era as there are today. The powers-that-be encouraged participants at every turn through rewards, as well as through indoctrination, including the idea that only cowards turn and run. These incentives and disincentives were a part of the cultural fabric into which George had been born in 1732. From cradle to grave, men living under the British Empire were asked to be brave and to face death as a means to an end: *glory*. To aspire to glory, in and of itself, did not imply vanity. Yet, as in any era, some young men followed such encouragements more seriously and fearlessly than others did.

George had a special interest in arms and war, admitting he had a "bent to arms." Early on, he looked on war in an extraordinarily positive light—maybe because no one had bothered to explain all the pitfalls and drawbacks. When he wrote to his younger brother Jack, he had used the word "charming" as in the definition of the French word *charmant*, meaning alluring or sexy in the modern sense. But the word's roots are also grounded in a medieval era of knights and fair damsels. The idea that war might be exhilarating is not so counterintuitive to those—myself included—who have experienced the thrill of live fire and the adrenaline rush of a close call.

For others, a call and a race to arms masked and still mask a deeper, more sinister human urge. A colleague of mine from the Balkan Wars of the 1990s, Chris Hedges, once wrote, "War is an elixir. It gives us resolve, a cause. . . . It is peddled by mythmakers—historians, war correspondents, filmmakers, novelists, and the state—all of whom endow it with qualities it often does not possess: excitement, exoticism, power, chances to rise above our small stations in life, a bizarre and fantastic universe that has a grotesque and dark beauty." George's attraction to battle, while likely stronger than that of many of the officers he rode alongside, is also in keeping with greater universal patterns of men at war. In line with this theme, the most thrilling moments I can remember have come to me while working as a war correspondent obsessed with getting closer to the action. This came in the line of my assigned duty, as well, so it came with an imprimatur of what was expected of me as a professional war reporter. As other correspondents and soldiers at war, I've done my share of mindless things to gain proximity to the action. In one case, in Kosovo I drove purposefully through incoming fire to a besieged police station to report from inside the station on what it was like for those getting shot at from all sides. At the gates of the station, we skidded to a halt, and a seventeen-year-old ran out and stuck a machine gun to my head, his finger shaking on the trigger as he screamed at us wildly. Moments later, he led us inside, and we came away with an amazing glimpse into the fear and anger exhibited by men about to die. In another case, I defied a gang of paramilitary thugs to cover a funeral, only to have someone stand at point-blank range and try to put a bullet through my head, barely missing and skipping the bullet off the roof of my car, two inches above my scalp. I'm almost ashamed to admit it, but war does offer all of us a kind of perverse excitement, and, yes, even *charm*.

None of my attraction was unique or new to persons taking an interest in war. For example, French prime minister George Clemenceau, "who having barely escaped" enemy fire in World War I, told Winston Churchill, "It is my great pleasure." People who abhor war or have never experienced it can't easily understand this attraction. War isn't a game of Russian roulette, after all, despite what some winners and survivors might insist.

Some who leave for war want glory and thrills, others just a closer look at what it means to be human. Winston Churchill noted that an observer of battles has a unique window into the human spirit. It is hard to disagree with such assertions. He wrote that his first war provided him with a chance to "remark occasions of devotion and self-sacrifice, a cool cynicism and stern resolve," adding that an or observer "may participate in moments of wild enthusiasm, or of savage anger and dismay—the skill of the general, the quality of the troops, the eternal principles of the art of war," adding that "to others—spectators, perhaps—[war offered] the pleasure of the play, the knowledge of men and things." In short, there is an education of sorts to be had at war. George Washington's own front-row seat early on to human savagery would serve him well several decades later as a leader of men seeking peace and prosperity and even steering his nation away from war.

It is hard for me to believe that George Washington, whom the American people know more as a Founding Father than as a young officer, sought war merely for the thrills it provided. Though some men do, other societal forces were at work inexorably pushing George toward his first engagement. I think that he also felt a need to prove himself, to actively display his personal code of honor. And if, like Churchill, he merely sought excitement and glory at first, there are signs later in his life that war schooled him and offered him an inordinate amount of wisdom that would be useful to him as a general and president. For that, we should be glad he saw battle at a young age. Yet in 1754, as is the case today, the character of a gentleman was not made merely from physical strength and prowess; while brave in battle, George still had much to learn about self-discipline, field tactics, and the duplicity of both his enemies and his would-be allies.

9

Brave to a Fault

DRIVE INTO BRADDOCK, PENNSYLVANIA, on the banks of the Mononga-hela, and you may well be overwhelmed by the desolation and the lack of greenery. The scene of Gen. Edward Braddock's mortal wounding and bitter defeat, once a wooded hillside along the southern bank of the river, is now a decadent landscape of rancid streets, falling doors, and shattered windows, a memorial to the demise of America's steel industry. The city is abandoned and shuttered except for some three thousand residents who live mostly hand to mouth or needle to arm in two-story dilapidated townhomes. I saw immediately why it had been chosen as a backdrop for a post-Armageddon Hollywood thriller about man's barbaric nature. One local writer had called the town, appropriately, "the nightmare at the end of the American Dream." In the nineteenth century, Andrew Carnegie sent an armed contingent across the river to put down a steel workers' strike but afterward built a lovely Victorian brick public library, easily the most beautiful building in town. In the city's archives, I began to dig further into George's exploits at the Battle of the Monongahela during the French and Indian War.

It was, appropriately maybe, also an ancient hunting ground. The slope that shoots up from Carnegie Free Library, rising to some three hundred feet on red brick streets in the distance, served Native Ameri-can hunters as a gathering point as they whooped and chased deer and bear down the hill to the river, flushing the animals down to a natural killing field. In 1755 the hillside served French and Indian forces for the killing of King George's loyalists, an encounter that ended in one of the worst single-day defeats for the British Empire in the eighteenth and nineteenth centuries. In hunts and battles with animals and humans, the tribesmen picked off their quarry with equal ease.

At the Battle of Monongahela reenactment, General Braddock's forces, surrounded by Native Americans, fire back in desperation. *Phil Smucker*

On March 26, 1755, huge British transport ships landed at the base of Oronoco Street in Alexandria, Virginia, not far from where George had assembled his first small army of ruffian rum drinkers. Some sixteen hundred British soldiers and sailors disembarked along with heavy artillery. Many of them set up camp nearby while officers, including General Braddock, commandeered taverns and private homes. Prominent Alexandrian John Carlyle later provided a scathing review of the general's comportment, writing that he had taken "everything he wanted abused my house, furniture, & made me no satisfaction [payment]." Commenting on the character of the old warrior, Carlyle added that he was an "indolent" man, who was "Slave to his Passions, Women & Wine." (Braddock had stayed in his home, so Carlyle's complaints, though mostly unsubstantiated, represent a credible critique.) General Braddock—who would march forth out of Alexandria in the company of his brightly clad aide-de-camp, George Washington, in the spring of the same year—also had harsh words for his hosts, referring to them as the "Spawn of Convicts."

From the outset, Braddock hadn't intended to get embroiled in a guerrilla war, nor serve as a living example of imperial folly, but that is just what he was poised to do, particularly in the eyes of colonists. His first mistake was to underestimate the harsh terrain. Benjamin Franklin, who would help Braddock gain the transport he needed, gave him fair warning, recalling that he told Braddock about "Ambuscades of Indians, who by constant Practice are dexterous in laying and executing them." Taking axes to the forest, the general's army engineers and scores of common laborers, including a twenty-one-year-old Daniel Boone, helped clear a path toward French fortifications. Its outlines still visible today, Braddock's rough road into Ohio country shot west from Alexandria, crossing the Shenandoah and passing through Lord Fairfax's holdings, now Winchester, Virginia. Deeper still into the dense forests, it split a line through "Injun Country," where English, Scotch-Irish, and German fur traders were already offering goods at better prices than their French competitors, whose bases were farther north in present-day Michigan and Canada.

I left steamy Alexandria and arrived just north of Pittsburgh for a reenactment of the Battle of the Monongahela, a battle after which twenty-three-year-old George's legend grew to a level that would propel him one day into leadership of the American Revolution. The French and Indian War junkies I would hang out with had chosen a wooded hillside several miles from the original scene of the battle—an area that better resembled the terrain of the 1755 clash than did the decomposing steel city of Braddock.

The reenactment encampment was rough, dirty, and well supplied with rum. Fresh legs of venison turned on iron spits above open fires. The fighters themselves—divided into Frenchmen, Indians, British, and Virginians—dressed in scruffy, soiled linens. Bleary-eyed and sweaty, but still smiling, many of them looked as though they had made the march on foot from Virginia to Pennsylvania. I knew it was going to be an entertaining week when a French officer, dressed neatly in silk and a tricornered hat, raced down a hill on his horse at a canter, slipped, and plunged into a mud puddle. I approached him to check on his health, but he ignored me out of embarrassment, looking mortified at his muddied outfit.

Apart from a flintlock that misfired, requiring a modern ambulance to extract its victim, the reenactors did manage to get most of the details right. As their only designated scribe, I noted that each member of Pennsylvania's Washington County Militia, led by commander Bob Tohey, had to not only play a role but also memorize a unique imagined family history. For instance, you might be a lumberjack or an ironsmith, as some of the soldiers who fought with Braddock and Washington were, or even a sailor from the Atlantic coast, and you had to know your part perfectly and dress, for example, in a hunting shirt and deerskin leggings with your tobacco pouch and medicine bag swung around your neck. And if you were playing a prim British officer, you did not mix well with this local riffraff. For their own role-playing, Native Americans painted their faces with natural dyes and tried with little avail to hide beer bellies drooping over belts above leather loincloths.

"We require a lot of training and initiation by fire," Commander Tohey told me.

"Yes, there is some drinking," said an associate, almost apologetically. "But there is also the torture part—which can get pretty real too!"

I knew that as an unarmed male, I would be a loner and a virtual outcast in this group, so I resigned myself to the curious stares at my freshly washed Virginia militia outfit and too clean tricornered black hat. I had initially assessed this mixed and raucous crowd to be closed shop, but I turned out to be mistaken. After some bargaining and tale swapping from varied war zones, the Washington County gang allowed me to carry on in the woods with them, steal an occasional sip out of their rum flasks, and pretend, as best I could, that I was some kind of eighteenth-century war reporter bent on covering a British military debacle. The reenactors were all really Americans, I noted, and they had a natural aversion to British snobbery—so at least we had that much in common.

After an initial victory at Jumonville Glen that gained him high praise from his mentors, George's soldiering career took a turn for the worse. As he scribbled off letters about the thrill of war, he put his men to work completing a rudimentary defense, appropriately named Fort Necessity, at Great Meadows. It was Washington's first fort and had a paltry, horrendous design that left its defenders open and exposed to the enemy. Today, with the help of the National Park Service, an accurate replica stands at the same location. The fort's split wooden tree trunks look from a distance like a half circle of halved clothespins. To complete their defenses, Washington's men covered the interior, some two hundred feet in circumference, with tree bark and animal skins. Several small cannons on swivels pointed off into the dense surrounding forest.

Though reinforcements were on the way, Washington already knew his foe had some one thousand soldiers and scores of Shawnee, Delaware, and Mingo massing against him. If he had been older, wiser, and more experienced, and if this had been the Revolutionary War, he likely would have chosen a strategic retreat moving back south to Wills Creek, drawing the French into a more difficult expedition.

On Saturday, June 1, 1754, Half King arrived with Queen Aliquippa, an aging native matriarch to whom George politely had given a bottle of rum on his earlier return from Fort Le Boeuf. A forlorn-looking group of only eighty-five men, women, and children accompanied her; clearly George had sadly underestimated the Native American support he had garnered in recent months. In a last-ditch attempt to meld colonial and Native American cultures to strengthen ties, he decided to reward Half King, the queen, and the queen's son Chanachquasy with new British-sounding names. In a formal ceremony, he distributed medals and wampum, giving Half King the ceremonial name of Dinwiddie, which he said meant "the Head of All." On the queen's son, he bestowed the name Colonel Fairfax. This, Washington made clear, translated into "The First in Council," which sounded equally powerful to Half King and, by accounts, "greatly irked" him. George then invited his old ally to meet with his namesake, Dinwiddie, in Winchester, but the chief balked, insisting he preferred to attend to the security needs of his tribe.

George's gestures of solidarity had fallen short of the mark, and his good intentions hurried along the inevitable. Half King, the queen, and her son soon packed up their meager belongings and fled the scene. Before his own untimely death from pneumonia, exacerbated by alcoholism, in October of the same year, Half King would denounce George's fort as "that little thing upon the meadow" and accuse him of treating Native Americans like slaves. Clearly there had earlier been unexpressed tensions between the two. The chief originally had allied himself with the British, hoping to both enhance his authority and oust the French, but Washington's strength, common sense, and strategic thinking proved even worse than his erstwhile ally had imagined. Though British regulars eventually arrived, nearly doubling his overall troop strength at Fort Necessity, George remained the de facto commander of all forces. And his decision to fight in a clearing surrounded by trees would prove both foolish and deadly.

On the morning of July 3, 1754, George's scouts reported that French forces were on the verge of attacking. They soon appeared from behind trees with their native allies as shots rang out at 7 AM. The foe remained in the shadows of the forest, denying Washington's hope that they would emerge onto the meadow and attack his riflemen and fort. As the fighting wore on, the circle began to close, and intense rains set in, turning the inside of George's rickety stockade into a sea of mud, blood, and maimed bodies.

If the events at Jumonville Glen hadn't shocked George into a recognition of war's horrors, what he witnessed at Fort Necessity surely must have. Major Stephen, a fellow Virginian who fought at Jumonville Glen and would fight at George's side again in the Revolution, described the end game: "Rains and Water in the Trenches, the most of our Arms were out of Order, and we had only a Couple of Screws in the whole Regiment to clean them. But what was still worse, it was no sooner dark, that one-half our Men got drunk."

It was a worst-case scenario. Nearly a third of George's forces would be killed or injured, and a good portion of the rest of the men, soldiers in the fort charged to shoot at moving targets hiding behind trees, had broken open rum supplies to numb the pain of impending defeat. Their desperate antics inside the small fort in the presence of a commander speak to the issue of sound leadership and suggest that George, despite his brave face, had lost control not of the natives this time but of his own men.

The French, led by Jumonville's vengeful half brother, may have perceived that they were up against an inexperienced foe in Washington and they could have intensified the slaughter. Instead, possibly because there was still no formal declaration of war between France and Great Britain, the French sought to force a rapid surrender. Washington, working with fencing instructor Jacob Van Braam, examined the terms of capitulation, which included a direct reference to the death of Jumonville. A rudimentary knowledge of French was not enough, since the French verb for "to kill" can be confusing. Van Braam interpreted *l'assassinat* not as the "assassination of" but as "the killing of," giving rise to one of history's most famous lost-in-translation moments on a rain- and blood-soaked woods. By signing the terms of surrender, Washington provided a propaganda coup for the French. He was openly admitting that he had committed a heinous crime of war at his first encounter. As George prepared his retreat, French officers turned their own native allies loose to pillage his supplies and harass his limping and dying forces as they moved off toward Wills Creek.

Fort Necessity would be George Washington's only military surrender, which says something about what he learned from it. And the irony of how this blundering defeat was perceived at the time says as much about George's failure to live up to his own ideals as it does about the British Empire's hubris and dogged belief in its own superiority. In his own defense, George would make the undocumented and false claim that his French foe had lost three hundred killed in action. (It was probably under a dozen.) Strangely—but maybe not surprisingly given Dinwiddie's intentions—he also managed to avoid a public scolding for some very dubious decision making.

There may have been justice in George's narrow escape of a public rebuke. It had been Dinwiddie, after all, who had sent a young officer champing at the bit into the fray with an inadequate and ill-supplied force. Washington's forces may well have suffered defeat at Necessity even with a more experienced commander at the helm. The goading on of the Virginia lieutenant colonel was an act of bad leadership from on high, but as I found as a war correspondent, young American officers are quite often honored with awards even when their superiors have made fatal strategic decisions. Perhaps in keeping with the notion that authority figures more often than not dodge responsibility for sending ill-prepared young men to war, Williamsburg's House of Burgesses paid tribute to George and his fellow officers for their "late, gallant, and brave behavior in the defence of the country."

So even an outright defeat had turned in George's favor. If Dinwiddie wanted a war, and it is clear he did, he now had Washington to thank. The young lieutenant colonel's role in many ways had been to supply a steadfast example of courage and resolve. This he had accomplished in spades. His narrow escape was viewed a bit counterintuitively back in Williamsburg as the success of an underdog. Almost despite his rashness and bravado, Washington's conduct in the field—even to a fault—had served him well in his career. He had been otherwise humiliated in defeat, even tricked into admitting in writing to Jumonville's assassination, but he still managed to increase his personal renown.

As he relished a moment of fame in Williamsburg and with his family and friends at Belvoir and Mount Vernon, George had taken the opportunity to temporarily resign from the military and bolster his wardrobe with "six yards of gold regimental" cloth and "a hat adorned with gold lace." The list of acquisitions ran on at length. If George hadn't yet achieved everything he wanted at war, he was certainly still determined to look the part of a soldier.

Even as he took a breather and visited with the Fairfax family, Washington kept an eagle's eye out for his next opportunity. In 1755 he had written Gen. Edward Braddock in an excessively humble tone. He implicitly acknowledged his own lack of experience while not mentioning his defeats, stating, "I wish earnestly to attain knowledge of the military profession." Soon after, he agreed to serve as an unpaid aide-de-camp for the British general. Elated, he wrote to his mother, "I am very happy in the general's family, being treated with a complaisant freedom which is quite agreeable to me, and have no reason to doubt the satisfaction I hoped for in making the campaign." In light of the close calls her son had in his two years of service, which he had proudly acknowledged to her in writing, Mary complained that George should remain close to home and take care of his kin. I'm not sure how some leading, notably male, biographers interpret that to mean she was standing in the way of her son's ambitions, but this is still a widely held view of Mary's attempts to persuade him not to go back to the front. The accusation seems unfair to me. If a bullet didn't kill you, deadly diseases were rampant during the French and Indian War, and any mother protective of a son knew this.

George's new relationship with General Braddock developed along cordial but curious lines. Knowing that his words would be kept in confidence, he wrote to Colonel Fairfax at Belvoir, stating that his boss was a stubborn man and that "we have frequent disputes on this head, which are maintained by warmth on both sides, especially on his who is incapable of arguing him out, or of giving up any point he asserts, let it be ever so incompatible with reason." It is not too much to imagine George, an unpaid aide-de-camp, riding alongside the general and hanging on his every word but also adding his own opinions when at all possible. It was this kind of back-and-forth and active learning that George needed at this stage in his life. Braddock apparently knew when to commend and when to shut down the loquacious young Virginian, but like Lord Fairfax before him, the general enjoyed George's company.

Braddock's goal was ambitious: to destroy French positions in and around present-day Pittsburgh, specifically at Fort Duquesne. Yet from the start, it didn't look good for the British and colonials who had hacked their way over the Blue Ridge on a rough unpaved road in ninety-degree summer heat. An adolescent fife-and-drum squad played a lively number alongside a jolly and stout General Braddock, who was determined, come hell or high water, to face off against an amorphous French and native foe. He and his fellow officers were decked out in brilliant red-and-white uniforms that glistened in the sunlight—a kind of "shoot me now" invitation to the French and their painted friends camouflaged in the leaves a few miles to their front.

For some before-battle insight into George's next flirtation with disaster, I sought out Jeffrey Graham, a Pennsylvania military historian, a short teddy bear of a man who was playing the role of General Braddock. I also knew from the historical evidence that in the subsequent reenactment I would witness, Graham would be falling off his horse, shot in his back. He was playing the same British character, I noted, who had distinguished himself for his rakish and boorish behavior both in my hometown and earlier in London by challenging a fellow officer to a duel in Hyde Park.

When I walked up for an interview, Jeffrey, who managed the historical archives at nearby Fort Ligonier in western Pennsylvania for several decades, was sitting beneath a canvas awning and beside a table stocked with fruit and cheese. The layout was meant to mimic an elite British officer's battlefield repast. On my arrival in my usual guise of a scribe, Jeffrey called out to a nice and rather well-rounded young lady, referring to her as a "kind wench" and asking her to search for something "back in the tent." Graham, who used eighteenth-century military language, gave off the air of a polite, erudite, and misogynistic British general. I judged him to be an excellent—albeit undersized—match for the real Braddock. After what Alexandrian John Carlyle had said about Braddock's lusty ways, I wasn't so shocked.

With little prompting, Jeffrey, or rather the general, launched into a scholarly take on why an inordinate number of women had been taken prisoner during the Battle of the Monongahela. "Why, they are not just in our company to wash our shirts," he told me without cracking a grin.

During the French and Indian War there had been a series of letters between British officers discussing the relative attributes of the female camp followers, who had been nicknamed the Dulcineas in accord with Cervantes's humorous novel *Don Quixote*, a text George would eventually own two copies of. In that novel, Don Quixote states that Dulcinea is his muse, saying, "Her rank must be at least that of a princess, since she is my queen and lady, and her beauty superhuman." The don's sidekick, Sancho Panza, knew the ways of knights and had other views. He describes Quixote's Dulcinea somewhat more mundanely as "a brawny girl" who likes to mock the soldiers, adding, "She will know how to keep her chin out of the mud with any knight errant who ever has her for his mistress."

Jeffrey offered me a small glass of rum, which he said was meant "to honor the fallen beauties." I pressed him on what would have possessed Braddock to march his troops into a wooded ravine thick with "Injuns" and why so many of the British regulars had "panicked and run." His retort, not surprisingly, was to defend his men.

"Yes. Well, I wouldn't exactly call their behavior 'cowardly'—cowards don't take eight hundred casualties. Yes, it was a disorganized rout, but few of the soldiers cut and run until almost all of the officers had been shot. Then, of course, it became a rout, before George Washington led them back across the river to safety. You can't blame them, after fighting for three hours in the stinking heat, for thinking at some point that this is a losing zero-sum game. I think they just said that if we don't leave now, we are going to die," he insisted, refreshing my cup.

"Men were dropping like flies, and it didn't help that the Indians were wailing these blood-curdling screams," he continued. "Some of the Virginians are used to it, but it filled the regulars with the fear of God. For many of them, fresh off the boat, it was their first taste of combat. No one had seen this kind of wilderness warfare before."

"True, but some of them still wilted like wildflowers," I interjected.

With that, Jeffrey, disturbed by my suggestion, stood up abruptly to take his place at the head of the army. He called out to his "wench" to bring him his sword. He stepped up on the stirrups and onto a stallion, and, with the fife-and-drum corps twittering and beating away, he rode off to a predictable and humiliating demise.

The real Battle of the Monongahela began just as abruptly. The French commander, who would die in the fight, brought his men out of Fort Duquesne directly, but his real strength was the command he orchestrated over several hundred Native Americans. Pushing through the oaks and maples, a British provincial officer commented on the gusto of the British forces he had seen cross the river in all their glory. Across the river, he also noted the steady and upbeat thump of the drums until a guide "in front of me above ten yards spyed the Indiens lay'd down before us. He immediately discharged his piece, turned his horse (and) cried, the Indiens was upon us."

As initial shots rang out from behind trees, the French forces, who initially assumed a blocking position at the top of a hill, were astounded to meet their foe so early and in such sturdy form. Several of them turned to run as British forces shouted, "Long live the king!" British troops were only part of the way up the massive hillside, which proved a dreaded impediment. Within minutes, Native American fighters crept down through the forest from two directions, positioning themselves in gullies and behind trees, firing against their entrapped and panicked foe, whose colors were far easier to distinguish than the brown and black hues of their usual quarry. As they bunched in circles to avoid shooting one another, the Brits and Virginians became even better targets for Native American snipers, who unleashed a flurry of musket balls.

A French officer described the ensuing slaughter: "The enemy was attacked on all sides, but fought with unyielding stubbornness. Entire ranks fell; all the officers perished." Indeed some fifteen of eighteen British officers soon were killed as their panicked fighters shot wildly at shadows or at nothing at all. As musket fire intensified and two of Braddock's close aides, Orme and Morris, fell, the general moved into the heart of the mayhem. The French and natives fired relentlessly, and an even more panicked British retreat ensued.

George would later describe a bold effort by a portion of the colonialist fighters "in the early part of the Action," to advance "to the right, in loose order, to attack; but this, unhappily from the unusual appearance of the movement being mistaken [by British officers] for cowardice and running away was discountenanced, [or ended]." He also insisted that the cowardly behavior of the British regulars had "exposed all others . . . to almost certain death."

Indians slipped around both sides of the British column from behind trees to seize the fleeing and wounded, with one witness, hiding in a hollow tree, recounting that "yelping and screaming," the Indians "began immediately to scalp the dead and wounded."

Again George was face-to-face with an outright slaughter. His first crucial set of orders during the surprise attack at the Battle of the Monongahela had been to rally the troops and keep the forces of two regiments from firing on each other. He and a handful of remaining officers found this order nearly impossible given the configuration of their men in a column and the advantages held by a foe perched on hillsides and hidden in dense foliage.

After a first, second, and then third and fourth musket ball ripped through his uniform, George fought back just to keep his wits about him. Despite his being one of the largest and most obvious targets during the battle, none of the riflemen shooting from gullies or from behind trees managed to hit his torso or even scrape his leg. He just kept riding, turning, twisting, and dashing in and out of fire. In nearly three hours of fighting, Washington lost two horses. Still, he carried out every order that Braddock gave him—which included calling Virginians, who had taken to the trees, to reemerge into the open, only to suffer more carnage.

As Native Americans crushed the skulls of fallen British soldiers with their tomahawks, Braddock lost at least three horses of his own before he finally tumbled and fell. He was reportedly in the process of mounting a fourth horse as a musket ball hit him in the back. George looked over to see Braddock knocked off his horse and sprawled out, bleeding from his side. After dismounting, he leaned over the general to help. With colleagues, Washington placed Braddock in a wagon and wheeled him away from the ongoing massacre. He then remounted his horse and momentarily attempted to stop the panicked flight of British regulars. Plucking an appropriate analogy from the slaughter at the hands of the Native Americans on their own killing grounds, he wrote to his brother Jack that his efforts to stop the exodus met "with as much success as if we had attempted to have stopped wild bears."

When he finally crossed the river himself, George discovered that his now injured fellow officer and future Revolutionary War rival Lt. Col. Thomas Gage was already across. Relying further on his Virginia aide, a feeble Braddock ordered Washington to ride forty miles the same evening back along British lines to Col. Thomas Dunbar's rear base camp to send up food, rum, and hospital supplies for the dead and dying. For this last task, George had to rely on an infusion of adrenaline and his best equestrian skills, for he accomplished it while suffering from an abysmal bout of dysentery, which had forced him to ride into—but not out of—battle with pillows on his saddle.

Again it was more than luck, though there had been much of that, that helped George Washington at the Battle of the Monongahela. The precise details of every turn, halt, and gallop George made on his horse that day are not documented, but numerous sources indicate that he did extraordinary things, almost all of them on horseback. Unfortunately, Washington was too busy corresponding over human affairs to ever document or explain to anyone the tricks of his equine successes. As a bullfighter does not describe his profession, George left his equestrian exploits for historians to muse over at length. For him, it had come naturally, a skill that had become second nature and instinctual for a young man who already had spent much of his working life on a horse.

A master of his beasts, George was also affectionate toward them and knew how to start, halt, and run with them without leaning too much on the reins or stirrups. This is not to suggest that George Washington was an eighteenth-century horse whisperer, but, as any skilled equestrian knows, controlling a horse is more a matter of understanding its temperament and fears than of using force or strength to command it. George is said to have loved all his warhorses, keeping them on the plantation for years after his great battles. Indeed, some observers paid special attention to how Washington's horses ran to him in glee whenever he appeared.

Col. Bob Ferrer, a longtime equestrian and foxhunter from Orange County, Virginia, explained the challenges of riding a horse in battle when I first met with him on his farm near Ladysmith. "Going into battle on a horse is considerably different than going into battle on foot, because you are having to make sure that your horse can stand when fired at," he explained. "Smoke and noise will frighten a horse.

They are herd animals, and they have to be brave enough not to turn and run when another—say a horse ridden by your foe—gets scared and dashes off in one direction." Ferrer's father rode in the now defunct US Cavalry and also trained warhorses for the US military. "The way you train a horse is to help it stand against its fear—that's how the cavalry has always trained them, with actual live fire. They would put powder in the cannon, make it *boom*, and let the horse stand and make sure it was OK with that. My father went through this using both rifle and pistol fire. In one exercise, he even had horses lie down in a prone position so he could fire over them."

Controlling a horse under fire is the essence of equestrian warfare, and throughout history there are other examples of warhorses being trained and acclimated for such encounters. Especially calm horses were bred for war, but good training was considered the only antidote to panic. The first actual manual for training horses for chariot fire, written by a Hittite equestrian named Kikkuli, appeared in 1350 BC. In 360 BC a Greek cavalry officer wrote another guide for training a riding horse for war. Riding skills were further refined in French and Spanish equestrian schools to emphasize the rider's mastery of a horse but also to display the horse and rider at "their harmonious best." In a classic "levade," which Washington performed in battle on several noted occasions, the rider draws the horse's head and forelegs into the air—something twentieth-century television viewers recall the Lone Ranger also being adept at.

There are good reasons the modern Olympic equestrian sports were both created for and dominated by military officers. Controlling a warhorse is a matter of life and death, and so the training is intense. Just as I had seen horses in Afghanistan rage through the scrum of a wild and violent buzkashi match, horses can, with practice, become incredible performers amid chaos and outright combat. For instance, the two horses that I owned in Afghanistan had both been trained—well before I bought them—to stop in an instant and also to rise up on their hindquarters in a levade to intimidate an opposing player as necessary. In this way, a horse is an extension of a warrior.

Certainly, George had an amazing gift for riding and training. Decades after the French and Indian War, the Marquis de Chastellux described in detail Washington's horses and his excellent control of them. One morning after breakfast, General Washington offered the marquis his best warhorse, which by then was retired. Chastellux stated, "I found him as good as he is handsome but above all, perfectly well broke and well-trained having a good mouth, easy in the hand, and stopping short in a gallop without bearing the bit." The marquis's letter continued his account in a careful examination of Washington's equestrian skills: "I mention these minute particulars because it is the General himself who breaks all his own horses, and is a very excellent and bold horseman, leaping the high fences, and going extremely quick, without standing upon his stirrups, bearing on the bridle, or letting his horse run wild."

"Warhorses are trained to perform to easy and light commands, and to be less responsive to the reins than to the legs and the hips of a rider, who often had to otherwise have his hands available to engage his arms with a sword or a gun," explained Ferrer.

In the heat of the battle, George's wide hips and long legs would have aided him as he galloped or leapt over obstacles. But with two horses shot out from under him at the Battle of the Monongahela, Washington most likely ended his battle on an unfamiliar horse, almost surely a greater challenge to control than one of his own favorite steeds. Riding a horse well was one thing, but ducking bullets was equally a matter of good luck.

George's performance alongside General Braddock was also a defining moment in his development and understanding of his own role in history. In his letters to family members, he explained in some detail how the Virginia forces fighting alongside him behaved with courage in the face of heavy fire. To his mother, he wrote that the Virginians "behave'd gallantly in order to encourage their men, for which they suffered greatly, sixty of them going down." The behavior of the colonials stood in stark contrast to the fleeing Irishmen he had failed to stop on their panicked retreat. The letter to his mother served as a first draft for a subsequent account to the Virginia House of Burgesses and to the governor, and it is yet another indication that, even after he moved out of her house, Mary Washington remained close in her son's thoughts. In contrast to the British regulars, who panicked and ran, as documented by their own scribes, Virginia troops "shew'd a good deal of bravery, and were near all kill'd," George wrote. He also noted that Virginians lived up to his own ideal of courage, as they "behaved like men and died like soldiers."

His own survival and the daring of his colleagues confirmed for him that bravery was at the very core of what he admired the most in any man. Courage in war mattered, at least for a young Washington, even more than tactics. Indeed, this became his greatest takeaway amid the pandemonium. After he buried his commanding general secretly on the road his men had taken to Monongahela and disguised the grave from marauding Indians by crossing it with wagon tracks, Washington held onto Braddock's bloodied battle sash as a memento. Echoing a common theme from his own early days at war, he would write that the old general was, in contrast to many of his own men, "brave even to a fault." Others could say what they wanted about his overall performance—and the criticism could be scathing—but what made the young Virginian feel invincible was this idea of unwavering bravery, gleaned from his upbringing and from classic tales of soldiery.

Writing again to Jack, he made light of his survival, joking that his younger brother should disregard "circumstantial accounts of my death" and adding, "I take the early opportunity of contradicting [the accounts], and assuring you that I now exist and appear in the land of the living by the miraculous care of Providence." This jesting missive came on top of the earlier boast that at Jumonville Glen he had "escaped without a wound, though the right wing where I stood was exposed."

Youth, of course, is always a good excuse for feeling immortal. Decades later, when Washington revisited the region, a Native American warrior is said to have approached him in awe, pointing out that to have survived the Battle of the Monongahela, he must have been protected by the "Great Spirit" in the sky. George's own reference to the will of Providence would echo across his long and storied military career and come to define his broader spiritual viewpoint, some of which was probably acquired at a young age from family members, including his own mother. This spiritualism was grounded in ancient Roman and Greek views, which advise a calm, courageous, and dispassionate demeanor in the face of death and tragedy. Yet after Jumonville Glen, he had dared even to boast of his strength in the face of adversity, telling Lieutenant Governor Dinwiddie that he had a "constitution hardy enough to encounter and undergo the most severe trials."

One of his first biographers and a close friend of the Washington family, Chief Justice John Marshall, writing at the turn of the century, stated that in the French and Indian War George had "manifested that coolness, that self-possession, that fearlessness of danger which ever distinguished him, and which are so necessary to the character of a consummate soldier." It was how he imagined he should live, and it was what George had long cultivated in his own character. Though an animated debate still rages as to how devoted George was in his later years to the Christian faith, he clearly felt in the wake of the Battle of the Monongahela that God, or Providence, which he viewed as a force for good, had rewarded his courage, and preserved him to live and fight another day. Before the start of the Revolution, boosting his chances to take complete command, several poets would agree with this notion in flowery language of their own.

In *Seneca's Morals*, on George's reading list from his late teens, the Roman sage advised scholars, "I have armed your minds against all things. Bear them bravely: This is the way in which you can surpass God: He is beyond suffering, you are above it." Though the statement, taken too literally, could lead to an Icarian fall from grace, it is hard to imagine that young Washington was not inspired by the Stoics as he galloped back down Braddock's road unscathed to Dunbar's base camp and heard "the dying, the groans, the lamentations, and crys along the Road of the wounded for help." Otherwise the toll had been devastating and hard to fathom: Native Americans and French forces had slaughtered over 500 British, and another 520 or so were wounded and maimed. As he would do later in life, George remained mentally, if not physically, above the fray, exhibiting no signs of trauma from the horrors he witnessed.

George's foxhunts with Lord Fairfax had only been a warm-up for what he experienced firsthand in the French and Indian War. In the human hunt at Monongahela, he had ridden astride the Crown's own commander, who did not survive the battle. Even at this early stage in his career as a gentleman-warrior, Washington had seen great men wield power, and he had found much to admire in even their stubbornness. He had further remarked on Braddock's qualities as a leader that "his attachments were warm—his enmities were strong—and having no disguise about him, both appeared in full force. He was generous and disinterested—but plain and blunt in his manner even to rudeness." These were excessively kind words from a colonial, especially when compared to John Carlyle's earlier assessment of Braddock in

Alexandria. Like he did of the governor of Barbados, George was developing his own critique of authority figures and of how an efficient leader could wield power even while appearing disinterested. To be a nice guy wasn't always essential, he learned. More crucially, George had begun to grasp the complexity of human character, the multi-layered aspects of any man's personality. It follows that anyone who can understand the intricacies and contradictions of others is better equipped to understand his own virtues and foibles. In short, George was becoming a far better judge of character through experience.

Still in his midtwenties, Washington had begun to see himself as the peer of any British soldier or commander. Some Brits had looked down their noses at the young man whom they saw as a Virginia upstart, but it was becoming clear that George was not in awe of them and that his ego was big and bold enough to match wits with them. Having watched the Battle of the Monongahela unfold, he could say that he now knew at least as much as the dead general about how to fight a war in the woods. Now a friend and associate of several leading players in Virginia commerce and politics, he began to increasingly challenge and even dispute the acting governor of Virginia, Robert Dinwiddie. While he directly emulated and lauded the irascible behavior of the fallen Gen. Edward Braddock, he did not hesitate to complain, lambast, and criticize the views and orders of Dinwiddie. That these men were both British and that he was a fourth-generation colonist would be a key equation in George's evolution. He might have had a chip on his shoulder, but it was a chip that provoked bold views and brazen acts.

George clearly liked the reflection of his fame he saw in the mirrors lining the corridors of power in Williamsburg. That his name was on the tongues in the courts of Europe also gave him an increased self-awareness and brought his self-image into focus. There is also evidence that George, in the wake of Monongahela, had begun to think not just about his courage and honor but also about specific character traits and how he wanted to be thought of by those around him. In his letters to detractors and mentors, George struggled to correct his critics and combat their stories with his own version of events. After the battles of Jumonville Glen and Fort Necessity, he had been accused of overseeing the assassination of a French envoy, but he wrote at length to try to amend that perception. He did not settle for mere words, though, and had volunteered to fight as an unpaid aide for Braddock. Through deeds, not words, he believed he could and would refute his detractors.

The rewards for his bravery came swiftly. Since George had been, in a sense, the last young officer—albeit still not commissioned as he was—left riding at Monongahela, important players, including those in the Fairfax family, petitioned for the young lieutenant colonel to remain at the forefront of the struggle against the French. To this end, Dinwiddie asked him to usher the First Virginia Regiment into being. For this charge, George returned to his former stomping grounds in Winchester, Virginia, just down the road from his old sporting mentor, Lord Thomas Fairfax, Baron of Cameron. Though his command would not begin well, it could not have been a better fit: few young officers were as familiar as George with the lay of the land and the ways and eccentricities of the local residents.

10

Cavalier in Love and War

WITHIN DAYS OF BRADDOCK'S CRUSHING DEFEAT and George's heroics on horseback, word trickled back to the north of Virginia, including to his close friends at Belvoir Manor. On July 26, 1755, George William Fairfax wrote from Belvoir to his good friend George, who had just arrived back at Mount Vernon. While George William had been enjoying a rather serene domestic life, his old surveying buddy, George Washington, had become the talk of all Virginia. He was anxious to see his old friend, writing that the ladies were frantically searching for horses to hook up the chariot because they wanted to see him, and joking that all his female admirers wanted "to have an ocular Demonstration of your being the same Identical Gentn that lately departed to defend his Country's Cause." In the same letter, his wife, Sally Fairfax, added a lighthearted note of her own: "After thanking Heaven for your safe return I must accuse you of great unkindness in refusing us the pleasure of seeing you this night." Speaking for a group of female admirers, she added, "If you will not come to us tomorrow Morning very early, we shall be at Mount Vernon."

George was still recovering from his ride and serious digestive issues. He would see the Fairfax couple in short order, in any case. He was, after all, still single, and there was no better time to start casting about for a wife in a more serious way, but first he had to overcome his long-standing teenage infatuation with none other than Sally Fairfax.

The best remaining image of Sally is rudimentary but revealing. It is a painting of an elegant, fair-skinned, and slender young lady in a low-cut dress, her hand daintily clasping a rose. My own eyes were drawn to the fine lines in her soft face, her narrow lips, and her smart gaze above willowy shoulders framed in white lace. Her face exudes charm and outright intelligence, which she had acquired at an early age as a member of one of Virginia's prominent families on the James River—not far from the original settlement at Jamestown.

As an eldest daughter with beauty and wit, Sally had been wooed by dozens of young men before finally settling on a Fairfax. Her grandfather Col. Miles Cary was an influential burgess and one of the original trustees, named in the royal charter, at the College of William and Mary in Williamsburg. Her father, Col. Wilson Cary, studied there as a young man but finished at Trinity College, Cambridge, later taking an interest in science, including meteorology, a subject that he wrote about at length.

Sally Cary's own education left her fluent in written and spoken French, and included regular access to her father's extensive library, which included many of the English literary recommendations from leading London magazines. If she was a flirt, as some historians contend, she was certainly a refined and well-educated one.

It is hard to know the precise moment that George was smitten by Sally's charm, but the two would have been present together on numerous occasions, particularly as George's ties through Lawrence with the Fairfax clan deepened. He was by no means her social peer when he first met her. Their origins had been far too different. Whereas George studied the rules of proper comportment within the confines of his rather austere farmhouse, Sally had the best etiquette tutors in Virginia to help her along from an early age in the halls of a luxurious plantation house. Fortunately for George, the great social equalizer among the Virginia gentry was not so much education as action in the form of equestrian skill, dance, and, of course, courage in the field.

"There is no doubt that George fell in love with Sally early on," Professor Peter Henriques, George Mason University's preeminent Washington scholar, told me. "But George also knew that this attraction could be as lethal as a bullet through his heart." As Professor Henriques explained the romance to me in his plush sitting room with a pleasant view of an attractive seventh hole on the edge of the Shenandoah, my first thought was, Then why would he even try? The alleged love between Sally and George had always been, and will probably forever be, at least for me, one of American history's most inexplicable romances. But since my book was in part about chivalry, I anxiously set out to better understand George's special attraction to Sally.

From the start, there had been much more at play than mere hormones. With time on her hands and a nod from her own husband to her new friendship, Sally set out to help instruct a teenage George in the art of gracious behavior. Fortuitously, she had arrived at Belvoir at almost the same time George was launching his surveying career. That she wanted to help George is not surprising given that other members of the Fairfax family were making a point of doing the same. But whether the friendship should be characterized as mostly platonic in nature or as one fraught with secret desire—an interpretation that dovetails well with some of Washington's own sometimes cryptic writings—it is indisputable that George was mesmerized by Sally's charms.

Still, an immense obstacle loomed: Sally Fairfax, as the wife of another man and a member of George's own mentor's household, epitomized what was out of his reach. This may explain the lack of directness in some of George's letters and other writings, but it did not keep him from making his interests known to her.

Sally, though she jested and likely also dallied with George in public, did not always return his letters. At one stage she even directed him, as might any married lady, to send his cheeky notes through a friend in hopes that he would ease up on his all-too-obvious desire for her. In keeping with what would be a careful editing of his own legacy, Washington destroyed most of the letters he received from Sally and did not copy most of his outgoing correspondence to her, so we can't be sure of all—or possibly most—that he had to say in this relationship. After Sally wrote that he should send his correspondence through the third party, George replied, on the way to Braddock's Defeat, that he knew well in regard to his letters to her that she "desired it might be communicated in a letter to somebody of [her] acquaintance," adding with clear disappointment to Sally, "This I took as a Gentle rebuke and polite manner of forbidding my corresponding with you." George sensed that Sally had denied him, a recurring theme in his earlier romantic writings. He struggled with the letter, rewriting it considerably, offering his regards for Sally's friends but notably not her husband on this occasion.

In his known correspondence with her, George tried but failed to mask his bubbling passions. Sally and George both knew that even a whiff of an affair would have ruined his friendship with George William Fairfax and destroyed his relations with both Lord Fairfax and Colonel Fairfax. It's important to remember that in this era, it was not only a sin to covet another man's wife but also simply bad manners. George was a young man who prided himself on being an exemplar of socially acceptable behavior in public. It wasn't that men didn't have affairs; it was just that these liaisons usually involved more convenient and arguably safer partners, such as servants, slaves, and ladies of the night.

There is no evidence that George Washington ever loosened his morals enough to sleep with a slave or even a servant. And if there was any hint of escapism in George's pent-up attractions to the opposite sex, it may well have been expressed in his special affections—as far as history tells us—for cultivated and high-brow women. Until his marriage, none of these relationships ended well for him.

Curiously, the romantic aims George documented in letters stand in contrast to the upbringing he had known as his mother's first child. As a hardworking and single mother, she must have stood out to George as a no-nonsense matron amid the fragile, often exquisite damsels who paraded their good looks before him at Belvoir Manor, Greenway Court, and in the Governor's Mansion.

Clear evidence suggests, however, that George was not above groveling at the feet of beautiful women and their guardians. In a letter penned to Esquire Fauntleroy, a wealthy planter who lived near Richmond on the Rappahannock, nineteen-year-old George stated that he hoped Fauntleroy's daughter Elizabeth would reconsider her recent jilting of him. She never did. In a tizzy over his rejection, and still hoping to win a lover's reprieve, George wrote, "Sir: . . . I was taken with a violent pleurice which has reduced me very loe; but purpose, as soon as I recover my strength, to wait on Miss Betsy in hopes of revocation of the former cruel sentence, and see if I can meet with any alteration in my favor. I have enclosed a letter to her, which should be much obliged to you for the delivery of it. I have nothing to add by my best respects to your good lady and family." George, already in the process of building an admirable fortune as a surveyor for Lord Fairfax, at this moment was not too proud to beg. His comic politesse veils a burning intent to obtain a well-bred beauty of his choice. On this occasion, he failed.

The loves of George, though so little is understood concretely about them, should instruct all of us. In my view, his romantic aims bear a heartfelt pleasantness that derives from another age. Despite often being rejected early in his romantic life, George appears to have maintained good manners toward the opposite sex on almost all occasions, across his entire life, and well into his old age. From an early age he wanted to be polite and to treat others with respect, particularly women. Almost certainly because they were first penned by a group of French monks, George's cherished *Rules of Civility* make no mention of a man's obligations of courtesy toward the opposite sex. But this courtesy is very much in keeping with English cultural traditions. In this regard, George was a product of an Old World and Western outlook that, while patriarchal, put women on a pedestal as persons—and in some cases as objects of intense desire—to be fought for and cherished.

To understand George's old-school devotions to women, it is useful to dig back briefly into the repository of legends and myths that influenced a young Virginian's view of women in the eighteenth century. Parallels can be found in allegorical English tales that remained fashionable in the New World then and now. Full disclosure: as a former English major, I stand guilty of a personal affection for ancient tales of chivalry, which, in any case, educated Virginians in the eighteenth century were familiar with and often quoted at length.

In 1590 Edmund Spenser published the epic poem "The Faerie Queene," which he informed his readers aimed "to fashion a gentleman or noble person in virtuous and gentle discipline." The poem was very much in the tradition of English literature from Chaucer to Shakespeare, favoring moral edification through words. In "The Faerie Queene," Spenser describes the actions of a knight who exemplifies such virtues as temperance, chastity, friendship, courtesy, justice, and magnificence—Elizabethan virtues that were held in high esteem across the whole of the Tudor dynasty. Spenser's other characters alternately embody these virtues or suffer falls from grace and face consequences.

English royals, though their personal lives were often disasters, sought to uphold values of decency and chivalry as a means to project authority and also as a way to highlight their own glory. In keeping with this tradition, it would be hard to underestimate the influence of another text, which Spenser modeled some of his own writing on: *Le Morte d'Arthur*. This lively compendium of English legends penned by Sir Thomas Malory in the 1450s, mostly in a jail cell, set forth the ideas of chivalry better than any text before it. It would influence men and their romantic aspirations for centuries to come. American author John Steinbeck once stated, "I think my sense of right and wrong, my feelings of noblesse oblige, and any thought I may have against the oppressor comes from *Le Morte d'Arthur*." Steinbeck's comment is a sure exaggeration even in relation to his own values, but the traditions and outlook found in Malory's book had an immense impact—albeit one that is sometimes overlooked—on the views of literate Virginians, particularly in the founding generations.

Le Morte d'Arthur relates tales about King Arthur's knights, often focused on the character of Sir Lancelot du Lac. These knights are obsessed with servitude and women, or in Lancelot's case, one particular woman. In carrying out their loyal duties, King Arthur's knights slay lowly characters, tricksters who attempt to steal the virtue of "damosels," and at the same time they give mercy, when it is deemed viable or begged for, to their defeated battle foes. In short, they are the very definition of chivalric gentlemen as defined by deed—ideals widely understood and admired in colonial Virginia.

Malory's writings provide what is probably one of the earliest and most nuanced depictions of what would later evolve into our own American concept of good sportsmanship. Depictions can also be found in the first book George ever bought, a eulogy of a loyal knight, the Duke of Schonberg. A knight's prowess is crucial to all of these legends, and *Le Morte d'Arthur* goes on at length with descriptions of jousting, the ancient equestrian sport that pitted two knights in front of a public, usually including female spectators. It was a direct showdown that required participants on horseback to charge one another and stab at each other with their giant lances. Jousting was, of course, a spinoff of war, a spectator's blood sport that allowed for a "mediated and virtuous" form of human violence on a carefully designed field. In the same way that hunting in the forest bore direct resemblances to warfare, jousting pitted gallant men against one another in a kind of duel that would, according to fate, provide victory for the best man. There was, of course, a payoff in popular appeal as well: winners, not losers, were rewarded with the affections of lovely ladies. (Yet even losers, if they obeyed rules, could die honorably or live to joust another day.)

The sport embraced elements of courtly love as well. Notably, in a jousting competition, men were allowed to express adoration for ladies they could not necessarily obtain as their own. Knights could beg favors—in the form of a ribbon tied to their lances or arms—from the objects of their devotion. A victorious jouster would then do honor to a lady by winning a match. In this way, honor and a man's attraction to lovely women were intricately woven into the ceremonial tapestry of good sportsmanship.

Not surprisingly, jousting remained immensely popular in courtly circles, including during the sixteenth-century reign of King Henry VIII, who suffered a severe leg injury during one match. By no mistake, Henry's father had named his firstborn Arthur, but the boy died before inheriting the throne. Henry's desire to link himself to King Arthur compelled him to have a court artist paint a picture of Arthur on his own court's "Round Table," bearing vainly his very own face. Henry had an archers' club named after the Knights of the Round Table, and his daughter, Queen Elizabeth, held an Arthurian costume party to further promote the same traditions—also proving that historical reenactment has a long and important tradition in Mother England as well as in her former colonies.

Carefully reading over key scenes in *Le Morte d'Arthur*, I came across some striking similarities to moments that spoke of George's own code of conduct and to his unusual relationship with, among others, Sally Fairfax. They help, I believe, to make George's own old-school values and sometimes awkward Virginia courtships resound with an ancient romantic note.

In Malory's version of Camelot, King Arthur gives his Knights of the Round Table a specific code of decent conduct. Malory writes that "the King established all his knights, and gave them that were of the lands not rich, he gave them lands, and charged them never to do outrageousity nor murder, and always to flee treason; also by no means to be cruel, but to give mercy unto him that asketh mercy . . . and always to do ladies, damsels and gentlewomen succor upon pain of death." Clearly, being loyal, kind to others, and sympathetic to ladies are high virtues in this imagined world.

In "Book VI," the author says of Lancelot that it is "certain he loved the queen again above all other ladies and damosels of his life, and for her he did many deeds of arms, and saved her from the fire through his noble chivalry." Lancelot boasts, himself, of the virtues of the queen, asserting that she is "the truest lady under her lord living." Also known as Sir Galahad, Lancelot informs a group of ladies, after boldly preserving their honor, that he isn't one to settle down into a domestic life, claiming that "to be a wedded man, I think it not; for then I must couch with her, and leave arms and tournaments, battles, and adventures; and as for to take my pleasaunce [pleasure] with paramours, that will I refuse in principal for dread of God; for knights that be adventurous or lecherous shall not be happy nor fortunate unto the wars." Lancelot wasn't the first knight in history, of course, whose fall from grace was tied to an overly enthusiastic pursuit of fair damsels; Malory was merely adding to older legends of men and their tumbles from grace.

But what would a splendid myth be without an illicit affair to make it a cautionary tale for a man who lusts after another man's wife? Despite Lancelot's claims of virtue, he finally ditches his abstinence and "went to bedde with the Queen and toke no force of his hurte honed, but toke his plesaunce." In other words, he didn't rape the queen, who admired him so much, but "took his pleasure" with her. It is still a miserable deed done to another man's wife, and, notably, it ends in a disaster for the entire kingdom. King Arthur orders Queen Guinevere burned at the stake for her adultery, and Lancelot is compelled to try to rescue her. After this, their affair flounders, spelling an end to the era of the Round Table.

The parallels between English mythology and George's own behavior toward Sally Fairfax are far too obvious to miss here, in my view. Though it's not known if their relationship came to kisses or more, some evidence suggests Sally stopped George in his tracks if he did try to consummate his love. In the few letters that have been preserved, Sally manages to entertain George's deep and steady devotions and keep him on the hook while not giving in entirely to his desire to flirt by mail or to engage in a more disastrous forbidden love affair. As their friendship deepened, Sally became more and more impressed with George's exploits as a courageous royal knight in the woods. "She is—eventually—also very attracted to him," Professor Henriques insisted to me in our discussion.

"Well, she seems to have moved to the very edge of the abyss," I agreed.

Sally's language in her letters is playful, flirtatious, and carries hints that George is her own knight in shining armor. But the special moments George would come to cherish for the remainder of his life, and which took place at Belvoir Manor, remain elusive. He regularly saw Sally at Belvoir, and he dropped in to visit on key occasions, including for a day upon his return from delivering Dinwiddie's message to the French command asking that they remove their forces from the Ohio Valley. Belvoir was an easy ride down a dirt road from Mount Vernon, and he also paid the Fairfax family the occasional tea-drinking visits on his jaunts back and forth to Williamsburg. His letters show that George sometimes pined for Sally while on the front.

Sally was an ideal partner and a very unobtainable one, a notion that would have fueled the flames of his desire even more. Again, the historical parallels are useful: just as Helen of Troy, who was married to King Menelaus, represented the aspirations of the Trojan and Spartan warriors, and just as Arthur's leading knight held Queen Guinevere on a pedestal, George had what can be viewed as an epic love for a beautiful, virtuous, and as it turns out very intelligent and forbidden queen. Sally may have been a southern belle and the wife of his friend, but this did not prevent George from casting her in a mythical light in his imagination.

At the same time, before and during the war, Sally was evolving into the refined first lady of Belvoir, responsible for much of the entertainment in the manor house as well as for the guest list. A typical social engagement at Belvoir would have been enlivened by a small musical ensemble, often consisting of violins, a French horn, and possibly a harp. As the musicians struck up a chord, couples on the dance floor would stand smiling and facing one another in anticipation of the next dance, often a Scottish reel. George William Fairfax would have been poised on some nights opposite Sally. Early on, George Washington would have appeared as a fifth wheel, but that would change substantially over time.

Yet, if George's interest was growing every time he saw Sally, he also checked his passion for her in public. Maybe because he knew his love for Sally would be unrequited, he never swore off the company of other women. (He was no Sir Lancelot in this respect.) From his early copied-down love poems, it's clear that George harbored an immense interest in women, and he may well have slept with one or two before he finally married Martha Custis at the age of twenty-seven. "You can be pretty sure that he wasn't a virgin when he married," Professor Henriques told me. (Personally, I don't think there exists enough evidence one way or another.)

Starting with the mystery of his love interests at Greenway Court, there are some clues that Washington had other opportunities to amuse himself with the opposite sex even as he was leading troops. This could well have come in the early years of the French and Indian War, where there were documented camp women who trailed military campaigns to earn money sometimes approved of by the governor's budget. Senior officers also enjoyed the company of these women trailing. Along with calming soldiers' nerves by whispering sweet nothings or doing more, these ladies also washed clothes and provided medical assistance.

Colonial Virginians embraced devotion and strong morals, but they weren't saints, and philandering behind closed doors was not uncommon in the eighteenth century. Men also objectified women in private male-only settings and in public. As a French officer wrote shamelessly to George during the French and Indian War, "I imagine you By this time, plung'd in the midst of delight heaven can afford and enchanted by Charms even stranger than to the Ciprian Dame." As a postscript, the same officer, hinting at a liaison he imagined Washington already had going, dared name a would-be Washington paramour as "Nell," yet another lady linked to George but lost now to history. A Cyprian dame was no ordinary lady; she was usually a lusty woman, often a prostitute, Professor Henriques explained to me. This was a sin in the eyes of some but not a breaking of the Ten Commandments, so to speak. Virginia, despite producing some of the best minds of the Revolution, did not moralize about prostitution in the same way as did many of the northern colonies. As with Thomas Jefferson's famous love affair with Sally Hemings, what went on in the back rooms often stayed in the back rooms, at least until modern DNA technology became available.

But George's love for Sally Fairfax was on an entirely different plane from any camp mischief. George, as I discovered in his subsequent letter writing, continued to maintain a special fondness for smart and elegant female socialites across the course of his life. Though he may have stumbled in the presence of beauty as a youth, as he acquired greater social skills, he came to cherish the company of smart women.

In return for George's adoration, Sally paid him special attention for several years, and at crucial stages in his early military career. Near to the end of 1757 and with Washington on leave from the army and deathly ill at his inherited Mount Vernon estate, Sally is believed to have visited him, in response to one of his letters, to prepare "jellies," soft foods prescribed by a doctor in Alexandria to nurse him back to health. A less-than-subtle plea dated November 15, 1757, from a bedridden George asks for Sally's help with hints that only she can assist him. George bemoans, "My sister is from home and I have no person that has been used to making these kind of things and no directions." Sally must have mused heartily at the prospect of a military hero bereft of decent instructions for jelly making. Her husband happened to be away in England at the time. In a private moment, the two could well have stolen secret embraces—or more—behind closed doors as George recovered his strength from a harsh stomach ailment. We'll simply never know. Coincidentally or not, a heartfelt confession was about to appear several months after the jellies letter. It contained a shocking confession on the eve of his marriage to Martha Dandridge Custis.

"Tis true, I profess myself a votary of love, I acknowledge that a lady is in the case, and further confess that this lady is known to you. Yes, Madame, as well as she is to one who is too sensible of her charms to deny the Power whose influence he feels and must ever submit to." Though it sounds like George—ordinarily far more direct in his language—is beating around the bush, his next line makes matters clear when he adds, "I feel the force of her amiable beauties in the recollection of a thousand tender passages that I could wish to obliterate, till I am bid to revive them," further interjecting that, "the world has no business to know the object of my Love, declared in this manner to you, when I want to conceal it." The language, while still cryptic and archaic in tone even for the eighteenth century, is difficult to mistake for anything but love for a woman, in this case Sally. It is an affection that George still felt obligated to disguise, if no longer to repress. What he meant by the term "a thousand tender passages" is not clear, but the hyperventilating language is far more typical of George's earlier infatuations than anything found in his often excessively dry diary entries. I think it is safe to say his heart was aflutter.

But why would George fire off such a love letter just as he was about to marry another woman? This was not the first time in history that a man about to be married went to his first love and queried her in desperation, hoping either to fulfill a subconscious yearning or at least to learn some intimate truth. As one of Washington's leading biographers, Douglas Southall Freeman, cogently stated in respect to this same letter, George "was hopelessly in love with Sally and wished above everything else to know whether she loved him." That sounds like a logical explanation to me. Who of us hasn't behaved, at least once, in a similarly foolish manner? If he had lived in our era, George might have merely replied to a public inquisition with a stern "It's complicated" or, if pressed, referred reporters to his personal press secretary.

With this authenticated love letter from George to Sally now secure in the archives of Harvard University's Houghton Library, George's often disguised affections for Sally are on full display. Sally's specific reply to the 1758 letter is lost, but Washington's next return letter suggests that she pretended in her response to not understand his sentiments, as he wrote to her tellingly, "Dear Madam: Do we still misunderstand the true meaning of each other's letters?" As any man who has been in an unrequited relationship can help testify, it is at these precise moments that women invariably confess ignorance or dismiss a man's affections. Sally, married to another man, had only one choice in this instance: leave George hanging in advance of his own announced wedding to another woman. Anything other than feigned ignorance could have altered the course of Washington's rise to fame and brought disgrace to the entire Fairfax clan.

In hindsight, Sally's well-professed confusion looks commendable, another sign of her solid character. Though she disposed of almost all her correspondence with Washington, she curiously chose to keep the now famous "tender passages" letter until she died at eighty-one years of age in England. Politely and in good confidence, she apparently also never revealed its contents. Only a dropped hint in another letter from Sally to a friend suggests regret over the course of her early romantic life. "I know now that the worthy man is to be preferred to the high-born," she wrote. George William Fairfax, though the son of a Caribbean mother of mixed blood, was nevertheless "high-born." Tragically, George William—likely due to his mixed-race appearance—did not inherit the family estate, and when he died at the age of fifty-eight, a childless Sally had to resign herself to spend her final years as a widow in Bath, England. The image of her as a Miss Havisham in Chaucer's favorite town is, unfortunately, hard to put aside.

Some would characterize—wrongly, I believe—Washington's relationship with Sally as merely a light romantic interlude. To me, there is more intriguing substance to what they shared, suggesting something more profound but still in keeping with accepted chivalric behavior of the day.

As George launched his military career, he was enjoying a modish life in Williamsburg and in the parlors of elegant plantation homes along the Potomac and James Rivers. By the 1750s, nearby Williamsburg was fully immersed in the Augustan Age of literature, which witnessed an explosion of satire, fiction, and both high- and lowbrow drama marked by scathing satires, often with ironic twists aimed at highlighting or pillorying societal norms. George's personal development ran parallel to this vibrant age of wit and wisdom. Notably, the students of the College of William and Mary, which dominated the center of Williamsburg, were on the cutting edge of this dramatic era. The *Virginia Gazette* noted on September 10, 1736, that "the young gentlemen of the College . . . will perform . . . the Tragedy of Cato," a play written by a friend and former colleague of Lord Thomas Fairfax.

Through light theatricals or readings at Belvoir or Mount Vernon, both George and Sally became familiar with the play *Cato*, written by Joseph Addison, the cofounder of the still-thriving British journal the *Spectator*. Penned in the early eighteenth century, *Cato* was a vessel tailor-made for young Virginians to express their sentiments behind a veil of Roman antiquity and high ideals. Amanda Carson, an expert in Virginian pastimes in this era, points out that "the elevating effects of the play [*Cato*] made it especially suitable for young people." The play's main protagonist, the rebellious Cato, would serve as an icon for Washington for decades. In the performance, Cato's character embodies the ideals of Stoicism, aspirations for liberty, and republican virtue set against the imposing tyranny of Julius Caesar.

George's love of the ideas contained within this script of *Cato* evolved over the years as he would later revisit the play in some of his darkest hours. Cato, in similarity to George's own future revolutionary character, is a devout Stoic whose deeds display an unflinching resistance to Caesar's authoritarianism. Yet the scenes that pricked his imagination and George's playful use of the name Marcia to describe Sally evolve from the subplot of forbidden love between Cato's daughter, Marcia, and the Numidian (African) prince, Juba. These scenes also oddly mirror and echo George's problematic relationship with Sally. As they are written for the enjoyment of English audiences, many of the lines contain a style of flirtatiousness and double meaning that was widely popular in the Elizabethan and Stuart eras of English courtship and extended well into eighteenth-century Augustan literary circles.

Within weeks of his stunning confession that he was a "votary of love," George referred to the Addison play in yet another letter. If they had ever actually performed this well-known theatrical at Belvoir—as is believed by several leading Washington experts, including those at Mount Vernon—George would have no doubt played Juba, and Sally would have played Marcia, whom the playwright describes as consisting of "inward beauty, unaffected wisdom and sanctity of manners." In his jesting aside about the play they both knew so well, Washington teased Sally in September 1758 with the line "I should think our time more agreeably spent, believe me, in playing a part in Cato with the Company you mention, and myself doubly happy in being the Juba to such a Marcia as you must make." In the Addison play, Juba is a soldier from the provinces, and Marcia is the Roman ruler's daughter. The devoted Juba never consummates his love for Marcia.

It is easy to imagine the secret pleasure George would have taken when Sally, dressed in silks and smelling of fine perfumes, would have said to him as he left for battle in accordance with her own given lines, "Go on and prosper in the paths of honor, / Thy virtue will excuse my passion for thee, / And make the gods propitious to our love." It was only a game, but in their literary references and gentle back-and-forth, George was no longer denied Sally's love. He could have embraced it as though it belonged to him, if only for a moment. This may well be a reference to at least one of the many "thousand tender passages" George shared with Sally.

The exchange of letters laced with innuendo came at a time when George—as Juba does in Cato—was going off to fight again and did not know if he would return. In the play, Juba hides his forbidden love, as George did. Toward the end, Marcia, not knowing if Juba has been killed, professes her love for him. The entire play is rife with a kind of delicate and clever word play that cultured young persons of this era engaged in. It displays a clever romantic nuance that is very much a lost art in our modern era of dating and texting.

Over the course of their lives, through refined thoughts and shared intimacies, Sally and George achieved a deeper understanding of their own sentiments and raised them to a higher plane. It is clear to me that their "romance" was a sophisticated courtship that managed to balance the passions of both partners. In large part thanks to Sally, and through all his edification at Belvoir, George acquired skills in the art of dancing, an abiding love for theater, and useful fine-tuning as a chivalric gentleman. Though these relations might be viewed as mere parlor play at first glance, Sally Fairfax undoubtedly was helping to coax a stronger character from George's solid virtue, polishing the social skills of a gentleman and Crown warrior.

When he met her as a teen, George, in awe of the svelte and alluring Sally, may have stumbled verbally, if not on the dance floor. But on other rare occasions, as the two danced together or alongside one another with different partners, George's immense physical presence would have been felt and admired, and he would have been in command of his surroundings as he directed his powerful sentiments into steps and gestures. With this ounce of speculation, it is easy to understand the thoughts of George after he had established himself as the father of a nation, when he would confess to Sally that the moments he had spent with her in his youth were "happy moments, the happiest in my life."

Thanks to the entire Fairfax clan, Sally included, the education of their young neighbor continued from the field to the manor house, and George gained insight into how all the world, from the battlefield to the manor house, was fast becoming his stage. With help from his patrons, he acquired a taste for elegant attire, dancing, riding to hounds, and the delicate arts of affection—all chivalric traits that would one day help him bask in the admiration of others.

George was no doubt spoiled, but in a rather good way, by the clan at Belvoir. In time, George became a romantic, probably to his dying day, as witnessed by a letter he wrote to Sally in 1798 when she was in Bath, England and alone. "When I cast my eyes towards [the ruins of] Belvoir, which often I do, to reflect the former inhabitants of it, with whom we lived in such harmony and friendship no longer reside there and that the ruins can only be viewed as the memento of former pleasures." His letter, though not poetic in a serious way, holds hints of Wordsworth's wistfulness, standing amid the ruins of Tintern Abbey. He also couldn't stop himself adding a woeful line about not understanding how Sally could "prefer spending the evening of your life . . . in a foreign Country."

George Washington would hang on to this past in his own waning years for good reasons. The Fairfax family helped him steer a course through his own unsteady emotions and better understand his own life within the context of hallowed and ancient traditions, a synthesis of Anglo-Saxon, Germanic, Greek, and Roman tradition that encouraged bravery, intense training, and unflinching service to a higher cause, including beauty—the very definition of a chevalier.

Of course, George's rather astounding character required more work and would not emerge in its full force or purpose until the Revolution. What strikes me from an examination of his softer side, however, is how much it echoes Western and ancient ideals of chivalry. It makes more sense to me in retrospect that some Americans prefer to gaze on the Houdon bust of Washington's head and think of him as a kind of epic hero. He was that and more, but solid clues of this emergent character came early in life.

11

Hog Wild in Winchester

IN WINCHESTER, VIRGINIA, where Lt. Col. George Washington set a series of frontier defenses just down the road from Greenway Court after his heroics at Monongahela, I checked in at the George Washington Hotel, whose major claim to fame is having guests Betty Crocker, Colonel Sanders, Lucille Ball, and Frank Sinatra as hosts of the Shenandoah Apple Blossom Parade.

Pat at the front desk was kind enough to give me a discounted rate for a well-appointed suite on the second floor with a view of the Christmas festivities below. At the hotel's bar, quaintly named George's Food and Spirits, a Saturday-night crowd had gathered to hear a local guitarist coo a tribute to Waylon Jennings.

"You know, George Washington went into politics here," Pat told me as I was signing my name to the register.

"I understand that he loved Winchester like a second home," I said, making light conversation.

"Yes, he did, and we are so proud of everything he accomplished here," Pat said. "You need to check out the new fiberglass pig statue near to his old surveying headquarters."

"Oh?" I made a mental note to do that.

I wasn't sure what she was talking about, but I promised to check it out after I put my suitcase aside. It was just down the road I'd driven in on, not far from the grave of Lord Thomas Fairfax. The dollar stores and Harley Davidson dealership on the edge of town had presented an odd juxtaposition of new and old for a town recently highlighted in an entertaining book titled *Deer Hunting with Jesus: Dispatches from America's Class War*.

Winchester, which changed hands during the Civil War literally dozens of times and represents the heart of America's first frontier,

Statue of George Washington, the surveyor, in Winchester, Virginia.
Phil Smucker

did not disappoint. A cordial mix of true-blooded Americans, it still balances a love of its native sons with its obsessions with guns, music, and biblical teaching.

In the historical district, I did not find bawdy women catering to lusty frontier soldiers, as George might have discovered on a night out. Instead, I strolled through a gentrified walking mall with family fun, rowdy pubs, and good eats. At my first stop, I had the roasted pork belly and a Miller Lite. I wanted to know if any of the taverns opened during the French and Indian War had survived fire, conflict, and development. I asked around, and the best answer I could get was that someone had a friend who owned "part of a log cabin that was one part of a tavern where George Washington once drank." It did not sound like a useful lead.

Fortunately, as I would discover, a handful of the town's buildings did escape the flames and cannon fire of the Civil War. I tipped the tavern's piano player, who was working on a jazzy version of "Rudolph the Red-Nosed Reindeer," before wandering back out on the street to sing Christmas carols. Between "Hark! The Herald Angels Sing" and "O Little Town of Bethlehem," I apologized for being out of tune and thanked a gentleman for handing me a songbook. His name, I soon learned, was Rev. Adam Sowder. I told him that I had recently learned about the unusual enthusiasm of eighteenth-century pastors for Virginia pastimes, including hunting, gambling, and, well, drinking. "Oh, yeah," he said. "That is fascinating, and, yes, true. I'm on my way to work on my doctorate in theology at Oxford. I'll be hitting the pubs when I'm there." I thought that idea would make Lord Fairfax quite happy, and when Adam offered to take me pheasant hunting, I jumped at the opportunity. We walked into a pub to warm up, and I struck up a conversation with an eighty-seven-year-old member of the University of West Virginia fencing team who was out for a drink with his daughter.

"Fencing?" I sounded him out. "I understand George Washington had fencing lessons in Winchester."

"He did?" he asked.

"No, really," I said. "He paid his instructor in August of 1756 a pound, a shilling, and six pence."

In the Winchester Book Gallery, three ladies on banjos and violins were playing Bob Dylan's "Blowin' in the Wind" against a backdrop of classics written by Harper Lee, J. D. Salinger, and Ralph Ellison. I wondered what George, who came to disdain the horrors of war in his old age, would have thought of the line "Yes, and how many times must the cannon balls fly / Before they're forever banned?"

My last stop before returning to the hotel room was to check out the fiberglass pig I had been referred to. As it turned out, one of George's important accomplishments as a legislator representing Frederick County, which includes Winchester, was to push for and pass a law banning pigs from running wild in the city streets. When Shenandoah University professor Sally Anderson dedicated the fiberglass pig, she helped her students put on a little skit titled *Hog Wild in Winchester*, about George Washington.

After Braddock's humiliating defeat, the French and Indian War evolved into a global conflict with major battles taking place in present-day New York, but it didn't look that way from Winchester. In the Shenandoah, the fight was an ambiguous war with an elusive foe, an indigenous population the English, Scottish, Irish, and German settlers in the Shenandoah and Ohio Valleys widely deemed to be what some Americans today mean by the word *terrorist*, or its equivalent. This attitude toward the Native American population, of course, didn't help George with his ongoing efforts to sway tribal chieftains to consider taking sides with the British. Native warriors, acting as French mercenaries and keen to plunder white settlements, roved the countryside in guerrilla bands, striking homes and farms in the dark and slipping away into the forests at will. George would eventually complain, "No troops in the universe can guard against the cunning and wiles of Indians," adding, "No one can tell where they will fall, till the mischief is done and 'tis in vein to pursue."

When Lt. Col. George Washington arrived to establish defenses, Winchester was little more than a collection of hovels, log cabins, and drinking holes. George had referred to the town on one occasion as a "vile hole," but he already knew his way around town. As soon as the word that the First Virginia Regiment was in the making, Winchester's economy, like small towns near military bases the world over, shifted its offerings as shop owners sought to reap profits by keeping soldiers liquored up and in hot pursuit of women. Hundreds of frontiersmen and ambitious second and third sons were on the prowl for booze, women, and glory.

As a surveyor in Winchester, George had first made his residence in stone-and-wood headquarters not far from the town's shoddy bars and restaurants. Outside his former redoubt today is a smaller-than-life-size statue of George the surveyor. His ambitions were soon too big for modest lodgings, and so he commandeered the immense stone home of one of the city's fathers. Here he began to plan, plot, and also entertain in style.

His new responsibilities were immense. They included control over some one thousand men and a mountainous three-hundred-mile-long swath of frontier. To his north, for a time, Lt. Col. Adam Stephen held down Fort Cumberland while George built up new fortifications, eventually named Fort Loudoun, in and around Winchester. This didn't stop marauding Indians in the pay of French officers from attacking nearby towns. As reports of new Native American strikes stacked up on his desk, George tried to assemble a strong team from an array of young aspirants, many of them from towns in Tidewater, Virginia, but from the start his officer corps began acting like a privileged class.

Tensions in Winchester rose quickly. Already wary of their new protectors, the local population complained. One civilian accused George's fellow officer, one Capt. Peter Hog, of taking his indentured servant as a lover. Though Lieutenant Colonel Washington frowned on the behavior, he did not abruptly end the affair either. Instead, he forced Hog to buy the price of his lady's servitude away from her master, in hopes of appeasing her former owner. George's broader priorities stood in the way of a better solution to the dilemma: Hog was an ally in the assemblage of new officers, and Washington wanted to keep him around to improve his force. Later, when Hog recruited black and mixed-race men into the Virginia force against existing British law, Washington gave him another pass because he needed all the soldiers he could get. The incident, and his decision to allow a handful of minorities to serve, foreshadowed similar recruiting decisions George would face as commander of the Continental Army.

Still just twenty-four years old, Colonel Washington was, in his own estimation, a stern disciplinarian and the embodiment of what his own corps should look up to. In some cases, he was stricter than his former mentor General Braddock. George announced, "Any soldier who is guilty of any breach of the articles of war, by swearing, getting drunk, or using an obscene language, shall be severely punished without the benefit of a court martial." He meant it at least some of the time. One soldier was harnessed to a pole and given six hundred lashes for so-called treasonable expressions. Such punishment was surely a deterrent if it did not also maim a man for life.

Shenandoah Valley residents, many of them Scotch-Irish and German, still unsure of the strapping young colonel who had been a mere surveyor sleeping in the wild a few years earlier, were not lining up in droves to join the new army. A local sheriff actually tried to stop Washington from taking more recruits but complained that he did not have sufficient force to arrest him. George would later joke to Dinwiddie that the local residents were threatening to "blow out my brains."

Saddled with local pleas and general disorder, George persisted but early on was forced to denounce the behavior of another of his recruiters, who had been accused of torturing and briefly imprisoning locals. Notably, there was no policy of forced conscription at the time, but dragoon squads could show up unanticipated at local taverns or homesteads. When the harsh recruiter escaped punishment, already poor relations with the local community slipped toward a precipice.

It may be considered a credit to Washington's emphasis on fair-mindedness—or good sportsmanship—that he suspended an ensign for cheating at cards, signing off on a court martial finding that he had "acted inconsistently with the character of a gentleman and scandalously for an officer." But this suggested disciplinary inconsistencies, and so there would have been some residents asking why cheating at cards, even in an age of accepted brutality, was a less egregious crime than torture.

Little Winchester in the 1750s was a dramatic, if also comic, front-lines town. After receiving a report on an "Indian raid," George galloped to the scene of the alleged attack only to discover three "drunken soldiers of the light-horse, carousing, firing pistols, and uttering the most unheard of imprecations." Such small teams of soldiers represented a new, albeit floundering, effort to cobble together a fast and mobile fighting force capable of dealing with swift enemy raids. The same initiative also sought to include, when possible, allied Native American fighters. The same light infantry forces had the added responsibility of standing guard while farmers, fearing for their lives, harvested their crops. It would have been hard not to sympathize with these farmers, who like the Native Americans were in a sense often little more than pawns in a great game of pawns and rooks played out between land barons and two royal courts, those of the French and the British.

Washington's earlier dealings with Half King had left him doubting the sincerity of all Native Americans. It was a distrust that had been maintained by four generations of Washingtons. Yet, while he warned against their "wolfish cunning," and called a group of them the "most insolent . . . wretches" he had ever met, he also surrendered to a cynical scheme to pay natives increasing amounts of hard cash for the scalps of French traders. In this way, Lieutenant Colonel

Washington's actions played a direct role in turning an international conflict—which began with the killing and scalping of Jumonville two years earlier—into a classic proxy war fought by indigenous Americans on both sides against enemies of the British or French Crown. It can be argued that Washington was just carrying imperial waters since Braddock had earlier practiced the payment schemes and Lieutenant Governor Dinwiddie approved. Still, he did not object and hastened the same efforts in some cases. The price of a scalp rose quickly when Virginia's House of Burgesses in Williamsburg upped the ante from one to ten pounds sterling for each scalp the natives delivered. Although he had not written the policy, it was an arguably cowardly approach to war, especially considering that neither the French nor the British recognized native land rights and would, by and large, discard them as erstwhile allies at war's end.

A few examples highlight George's intimate association with this pay-for-a-scalp program. His mate to the north at Fort Cumberland, Maj. Adam Stephen, who took the cliffs on George's flank during the Jumonville Glen attack, oversaw a raiding party of natives who scalped French ensign Dragreau Donville. Washington carefully packaged the scalp and sent it forward to Dinwiddie in order to gain a promised reward for the natives. Later in the war, George expressed great cheer upon learning that Gen. John Forbes was "so heartily disposed to please the Indians" with direct and timely payments for scalps, because he thought this might allow him to recruit more tribesmen to his side. When revenge was in order, George did not hesitate to dispatch mercenary natives to carry out the dirty work, remarking that "Indians are the only match for Indians." Though at least one prominent historian credits Washington for creating a "shared warrior culture [with the natives] as they fought together," it is a stretch to say that Native American and colonial warriors melded well; generations of distrust, cultural clashes, and imperial designs, including outright lies, stood in the way. Not only did George never fully trust his native allies, Native Americans sensed correctly that they were being used cynically for military ends.

The conflict ebbed and flowed, but in the Shenandoah Valley and farther north near Fort Cumberland, what had become Europe's Seven Years' War remained a low-burning, hit-and-run guerrilla conflict, not unlike modern conflicts characterized by night raids and heinous acts. Despite the best efforts that George put forth, the leading tribes in the region, including the Iroquois and Delaware, remained standoffish to his offers of cooperation. Even when he employed his old frontier colleague Christopher Gist to work with the natives, he came off sounding little different in his dealings than he had with Half King before the Jumonville Glen attack. "Gist should assure the sachems that they would receive provisions," he insisted. "And that we shall take every opportunity to testify the love we bear them."

From his petitions for more supplies, George feigned deep sympathy for both Native Americans and the white settlers they raided. But it was silly for him to think he could have it both ways. In one melodramatic plea on behalf of his fellow whites, he wrote that the tears of the women and cries for help of men "melt me into such a deadly sorrow that . . . I could offer myself as a willing sacrifice to the butchering enemy, provided that would contribute to the people's ease." George clearly wanted everyone around him to know that he was a leader with a sense of compassion. At the same time, it would never prove easy to hire on the same natives when you praised them as devoted allies in arms one day and disparaged them as butchers the next.

In his later years as the Revolution approached, Washington would mellow and acquire added humility, but in the first few years after Monongahela, his untamed ego was on full display. Officially he was already commander in chief of the First Virginia Regiment, having assumed the title from Dinwiddie, who bestowed it on him. He wrote that his own officers "should look to their colonel as an example to observe the strictest discipline through the whole of my economy and of my behavior." At the same time, Colonel Washington began to complain in 1756 to John Campbell, the Fourth Earl of Loudoun, that the lack of discipline in his own ranks was largely due to the lack of any uniform military code of conduct sent down to him from on high; he just needed better orders. "I can truly say and confidently assert that no soldiers were ever under better command," he gushed.

But George's task was great, and his attention to discipline had its natural limits. Adam Stephen looked up to his commander, and their correspondence suggests they shared social interests. Like Washington, with whom Stephen had barely escaped death in earlier engagements, he knew the joys of a good glass of wine, writing to his colleague that "after drinking the royal healths in a huff and a huzza at every health we passed an hour in singing and taking a cheerful glass. We then amused ourselves with acting part of a play and spending the night in mirth, jollity, and dancing." This unfolded at the military outpost, Fort Cumberland. By Stephen's own count, patriotism and sobriety could be measured by how many royals one toasted on any given evening. One wonders if that would have put him over George's proscribed limit, or if senior officers were given more leeway than lieutenants and commoners. But with such behavior from officers like Stephen, it is hardly surprising that his foot soldiers relished a chance to knock back a few at the local tippling houses of Winchester.

Commander Washington was more modest in his indulgences. He was a big man and could handle a few glasses of wine better than others. When he commandeered a large home in town, he began entertaining expansively, dressed in finery often purchased from London tailors. As a feather in his Virginia cavalier hat, he took up fencing lessons and often socialized with the "Good Lord" Thomas Fairfax and others at a safe distance from the main barracks, which housed his rowdy recruits.

George had assistants to help with some of the paperwork, and he made frequent jaunts on horseback to visit his own outposts, but he also begged Dinwiddie for extra time away to lobby for the martial cause and his own promotion through the ranks. The Scotsman, who considered Washington his man on the frontier, indulged him by approving a work-and-pleasure journey to Philadelphia, New York City, and Boston in the autumn of 1755. Though the locals hailed Washington for his deeds at the Monongahela, records show that he had some difficulty making appointments and spent much of his time being fitted for an elegant wardrobe, in addition to acquiring at least one new warhorse. In Philadelphia, George escorted a high-society heiress, Mary "Polly" Philipse, and her sister out on the town and then continued his journey to Boston by catching a boat in Newport, Rhode Island. Despite his aversion to cheaters, as a competitive Virginian, he relished the chance to gamble along the way, and his accounts suggest he was victorious at cards, at least until he arrived at the home of Massachusetts governor William Shirley. One ironic-sounding journalist for the *Boston Gazette* welcomed George to the city, calling "The Hon. Col. Washington, a gentleman of deservedly high reputation of military skill, integrity, and valor" and deadpanning that "success has not always attended his undertaking."

Regardless, in his first extended journey along the Eastern Seaboard, George won admirers and support for the struggle, further burnishing his image as a swashbuckling young officer. The accolades did not last long. After his return to the frontier, George's longtime mentor Col. William Fairfax warned him of what had seemed inevitable for some time. There was an ongoing investigation in Williamsburg into Dinwiddie's complaints about the "greater immoralities and drunkenness" of George's own officers' corps. These same officers were also being widely accused of wantonly "confining and torturing" new recruits. It was almost to be expected after the troubles George had dealt with, but the news deeply disturbed him and put him on edge, as witnessed by his return letters back to Colonel Fairfax. He viewed the criticisms as a direct attack on his own character.

At least some of the accusations were grounded in substance, as came to light a year later. For one, George had been required to confess to Lieutenant Governor Dinwiddie that his quartermaster had cut and run, adding that "Hamilton, the Quarter-master, hath misbehaved egregiously embezzling and disposing (in a clandestine manner) of some of the Regimental stores." A few days later, he wrote about other culprits. He suspected the credit that "tippling-house-keepers (with which Winchester abounds) gave to many of the Soldiers; we had reason strongly to suspect, that some there had received and concealed, some of the Stores, arms, and belonging to the regiment." He said he could give Dinwiddie more evidence of the "villainous Behavior of the Tippling-House-Keepers as would astonish any person."

Fortunately, George still had friends in high places as scandals in Winchester mounted. Members of the Fairfax family as well as his Potomac neighbor George Mason acted as Washington's eyes and ears in Williamsburg when he was away. From nearby Greenway Court, Lord Fairfax, who helped considerably with funds for the local militia, was always ready to fire off letters to powerful politicians in support of his protégé. Colonel Fairfax, in particular, knowing his young friend was feeling down on his luck, lauded George with praise, comparing him favorably to heroes in antiquity known to both of them through their readings. At one point, he wrote glowingly to encourage him:

> Your endeavors in the service and defence of your
> country must redound to your honor; therefore do not
> let any unavoidable interruptions sicken your mind in

the attempts you may pursue. . . . Your good health
and fortune is the toast of every table. Among the
Romans such a general acclamation and public regard
shown to any of their chieftains was always esteemed
a high honor.

The letter boldly demonstrates what lengths the Fairfax clan was
still going to in order to help boost the spirits of their friend—strok-
ing his ego and even comparing him to greatness personified. Fairfax
was telling George in so many words that his troubles went with the
territory. On trips to Williamsburg, George had been received as a
guest of distinction in leading homes, but Fairfax appears to have
been particularly aware that Washington had a prickly ego tied to his
well-formed personal views on honor. George bridled at the notion
that his own officers had "cast a slur" and "reflect[ed] dishonor"
on him. His anxiety grew more severe when the Williamsburg-based
Virginia Gazette wrote that his corps of officers were "rank novices,
rakes, spend thrifts, and bankrupts" who "browbeat and discouraged" the militia. If that wasn't scathing enough, the authors further
accused Washington's hand-selected lieutenants of "debauchery, vice,
and idleness." What could be worse? This was an infuriating attack
on George's honor. If it had not been for the constantly soothing
words of his Belvoir mentors, George might well have resigned his
commission or, worse, challenged someone to a lethal duel.

Instead, Colonel Fairfax was there to calm his nerves. He patted
the angry young man on the back, stating, "like Caesar," he should
expect to suffer "fatigues, murmuring, mutinies, and defections."
Even Dinwiddie, with whom Washington had been feuding off and
on, backed him before the *Gazette* accusations with calm and polite
assurances.

The correspondence between Washington and Dinwiddie is flush with
polite phrases, and the exchanges tell us a lot about how George
wanted to assert himself as a leader and also please his superior.
Deserters and traitors fighting under the British flag could safely pre-
dict that they might end up dead, but Colonel Washington wrote on
one occasion apologetically to Dinwiddie about his choice of execution styles. "Your honour will, I hope excuse my hanging, instead of

shooting them. . . . It conveyed much more terror to others; and it was for example sake, we did it."

While usually polite in his letters to Dinwiddie, George began to complain to friends, relatives, and associates about what he felt were the aging Scotsman's whimsical ways. He also expressed his direct ire, on occasion, to Dinwiddie. After asking for leave to visit Williamsburg and being politely refused, George sounded almost like a persnickety schoolboy whining to his teacher in his reply, remarking dejectedly, "It was not to enjoy a party of pleasure [that] I wanted leave of absence."

Dinwiddie, while handing down gruff demands on occasion, nevertheless had staunchly defended Washington after the calamities at Jumonville and Fort Necessity. By and large, their relationship benefited both sides. Since first authorizing him to tell the French to vacate the Ohio Valley, the governor had taken a steady liking to George. When Dinwiddie fell ill and contemplated his own retirement, however, he made clear that he was, himself, exasperated by George's newfound stridency and disrespect. He wrote, "My conduct to you from the beginning was always friendly . . . but you know I have great reason to suspect you of ingratitude." Without George's Fairfax benefactors or friends in the Mason and Lee families, Dinwiddie might well have ousted his former protégé outright. Unwittingly, George had come to embody the soldier's stage of life in Shakespeare's *As You Like It*, as one who is "Jealous in honour, sudden, and quick in quarrel, / Seeking the bubble 'reputation' / Even in the cannon's mouth."

His increasingly tempestuous relationship with Lieutenant Governor Dinwiddie can be interpreted on different levels. On a personal level, George looks like a typical commander in the field upset with the powers-that-be back in Williamsburg. As a former war correspondent, I heard from officers in the field the equivalent of the gripes and complaints Washington expressed throughout the French and Indian War. I heard the snipes and saw the head shaking of American colonels, majors, captains, and platoon leaders in places like Bosnia, Afghanistan, and Iraq. Soldiers, it must be said, rarely get all they want from civilian authorities. That is the way the system is set up, and it encourages a tradition of grumbling in the trenches at what military men see as unjust or inefficient.

On a more instructive level, though, George's relationship with the powerful Scotsman was a classic struggle between a young man and an older authority figure, a struggle that speaks to the revolutionary character Washington developed later in life. Of course, George had no father, or at least not one whom he could say he recalled well, so cautions, reprimands, and even encouragements from Dinwiddie were crucial to his development and emerging views of power. Blunt refusals appear to have impacted George's outlook as well. After the relative coddling he had from the Fairfax family, the stern back-and-forth with Dinwiddie became a special, however edifying, challenge for him. When George asked for more leave to settle some accounts, for instance, Dinwiddie snapped, "I think you are wrong to ask it."

Colonel Washington was not, of course, the first famous or father-less young man to spar with authority at his age, but his attitudes as they evolved toward British authority were central, in some ways, to his uniquely independent view of the world and how it worked to his advantage in the long run.

George was obsessed with doing the right thing in all circumstances, as is apparent in his letters to the Scotsman and other authority figures. Overall, this made him a good man to invest authority in, even though he did not always succeed. He was fully aware that his qualities were those of a soldier: smart, brave, and courageous like General Braddock, "even to a fault." But his inner ambitions would not allow him to accept everything he heard, not least of which was criticism of his own decision making or, God forbid, aspersions on his character like those cast by scribes at the *Virginia Gazette*. He sometimes bristled with an attitude that he was the best man for the job and that, despite his faults, others would be well advised to recognize this. His relationship with Dinwiddie grew to fit this pattern well. His frustrations, often expressed to others, including Colonel Fairfax and probably Lord Fairfax in private, tell the tale of a young, ambitious Virginian suffering unduly—as he believes—under the yoke of often demeaning and patronizing authority. Beneath his stridency, however, was a burning ambition to win out, even to defy authority.

Throughout the war, George's character traits bubbled to the surface. It isn't a stretch to look into the crystal ball of George's future and recognize that this penchant for rebelliousness was the forerunner of a vibrant spirit that would grow to maturity in his character over the next two decades. The young Virginian's stormy moods and ambitions were not necessarily what would eventually make him a great president, because that post required a more reserved and calm demeanor—that of a classic Virginia patrician. Yet, without this dogged desire to win a dispute with a superior, one wonders how

George could ever have become the leader of a revolution that dared to face down the world's most powerful empire. That war would require great management and arguably just as much audacity of spirit. For these reasons, he had his friend and sometimes nemesis Lieutenant Governor Dinwiddie to thank for more than he suspected in his midtwenties.

In Williamsburg he was taking a lot of grief, but in Winchester in the summer of 1757 George still had props. Within months, he would lead his First Virginia Regiment in a march to victory alongside General Forbes at Fort Duquesne. Before he set out with Forbes, George had written an old friend, Thomas Gage, to put in a good word for him with Forbes, who called Virginian officers "a bad collection of broken innkeepers, horse jockeys, and Indian traders." Washington joked that he wanted Gage to remind Forbes that he had been around from the start of the war, saying, "I understand there will be a motley herd of us." To George's dismay, the final battle of the war would prove humdrum for him by comparison to his other far bloodier and heroic engagements. In the end, what undermined the French presence in the Ohio Valley was as much a matter of population migration and sheer numbers of Anglo-German settlers and soldiers as it was military strategy or improved relations with Native American groups.

Before he set off with General Forbes, George wanted to make one final statement in the Shenandoah. As he contemplated settling down as a farmer at Mount Vernon, he now saw a chance to become a political player in his own right. If the notion that war is politics by other means was true, George had already been in the mix, and although he had run for office and lost three years earlier, this time he chose wisely to run as one of three candidates in a race alongside Thomas Bryan Martin, the nephew and right-hand man of Lord Fairfax. As sure as Lord Fairfax had lent him forty pounds sterling for new mounts during the war when he exhausted three horses in the field, the Fairfax family was now prepared to help him along with his political ambitions.

Both men trounced their sole opponent, garnering a vast majority of ballots cast. How county officials arrived at that final tally, however, is another story. In Frederick County, where two seats were on offer, the votes were cast in a process known as viva voce, in which each voter stood in a crowd and stated, sometimes yelled, the name of his preferred candidate. A sheriff duly recorded the individual votes, which were counted well after the polling parties had begun. To assure his victory, Washington paid for twenty-eight gallons of rum, fifty gallons of rum punch, thirty-four gallons of wine, forty-six gallons of beer, and two gallons of something called "cider royal." That totaled 160 gallons, and any way you mixed it for individual voters, it worked out to about a half gallon of alcoholic beverage per vote. Before he knew of his victory, Washington fretted that this wasn't quite enough to tip the viva voce balance in his favor, writing to his friend and organizer James Wood, "My only fear is that you spent with too sparing a hand." The victory resulted in the charming, less-than-democratic ring of bells in all the tippling houses of Winchester.

Washington's behavior during the French and Indian War is hard for some traditional historians to countenance against the man he would become. Many have frowned on his early military career for its many strategic blunders and for behavior that seems out of character, but there can be little doubt about the impact this war had on his outlook, particularly in the long run. One of my own favorite portraits of George Washington is a 1772 Charles Willson Peale, the first painting that George ever commissioned. It shows a rosy-cheeked, cheery, athletic-looking gent in full uniform, sword at his side, and Braddock's battle sash draped over his chest with his right hand tucked under his red shirt and placed over his heart. He looks dapper and ebullient. In the background are the rolling hills of his beloved Shenandoah.

The portrait suggests a dandified foxhunter turned warrior, albeit somehow removed from the rough frontier life and harsh realities of military command. In a sense, the portrait, painted over a dozen years after the close of the war, shows something that George still had not become during that war. In the picture, George is the essence of what we call now cool, calm, and collected. Though he had remained a work in progress during the war, the portrait tells a story of a statuesque and pleased leader of men who had, by his own admission, a deep love for his chosen profession.

In a real sense, the French and Indian War had a profound influence on the making of the leader we have come to know through myth and history. The war marked the birth of a compelling and amusing narrative of "George Washington" that would propel him to the heights of revolutionary leadership and would stick in the minds of his countrymen, including the scribes and poets who would tout him as a great man even before he assumed command of the Continental Army. George, in his own right, also had begun to shape and mold his own story as he struggled to live up to his own ideals. He embraced the key vignettes or moments of extreme courage, at least the ones he wanted to convey to a broader public, facing down critics and, in the process, strengthening our conception of him. Through word and deed, he helped write his own story, and he also portrayed the ideals he espoused, at least some of the time. Despite his well-documented flaws, George Washington had already become a great actor and director on the stage of American history.

The metamorphosis of a great Virginian had begun; George was becoming a master of the right action at the right time. Though some of his earliest childhood influences remain open to reinterpretation, often due to a lack of records and documentation, by the close of the French and Indian War, the lines of his character had come into public focus. He had developed a flexible mind and manner that allowed him to reach a broader audience from the halls of Williamsburg to the backwood haunts of the Ohio and Shenandoah Valleys. His friends and admirers were already on the edge of their seats, awaiting his next incarnation.

On July 20, 1776, as the turmoil of the Revolution was unfolding, George would write a nostalgic letter to his former colleague Major Stephen, who served by his side throughout the earlier war. He asked Stephen to please not "let the anniversary of the 3rd or 9th of this [month] pass off without a grateful remembrance of the escape we had at the Meadows and on the Banks of the Monongahela." Though Major Stephen had seized the left flank above the cliffs in the battle of Jumonville Glen, Washington makes no mention of that battle, one he also had attempted to gloss over in glowing terms at the time. Still, this note of recollection, coming as it did on the eve of another war, suggests that Washington still carried in his mind's eye a rarified sense of exceptionalism, the notion that he had been somehow saved for an even greater calling. This individual sense of being saved for a still-mysterious mission in life would evolve and contribute to a sometimes healthy and at other times dangerous national exceptionalism in the country he would one day help to found.

Even if Col. George Washington was at times standoffish, stubborn, and charged with a sprinkling of snobbishness, his character improved considerably after his first encounters in his first war. He also had some sage advice for his fellow officers in Winchester: "Remember that *it is action, and not the commission,* that make the officer—and that there is more expected from him than the title." One impressed fellow officer tipped his hat to George, writing, "Our colonel [Washington] is an example of fortitude in either danger or hardships and by his easy, polite behavior has gained not only the regard but the affection of both officers and soldiers."

III

Gentleman Sportsman

Washington and Friends After a Days Hunt in Virginia, lithograph by Charles P. Tholey, 1868. *Courtesy of Mount Vernon Ladies' Association*

12

En Garde!

IT ISN'T DIFFICULT TO UNDERSTAND George Washington's interest in becoming an expert fencer while stationed in Winchester, Virginia. It was not necessarily about improving his military skills, though that was certainly a part of the attraction. This was an ancient sport with obvious martial origins that British and European citizens cherished for several reasons. It allowed them to display their skill and prowess, and it also offered defense of a man's sacred honor. The sport fit George's vision of courage, bravery, and honor like a glove.

Since I inherited an unwieldy showpiece of a nineteenth-century cavalry sabre myself—one that hangs on a door as a means of last defense outside my bedroom—I decided that lessons at the Virginia Academy of Fencing in nearby Fairfax County might allow me to kill two birds with one weapon. I could bolster my home defenses and also gain some insight into the otherwise arcane—to me, at least—world of eighteenth-century fencing. The idea of taking up the sport of sword fighting also sounded like a lot of good fun.

The decor and general clientele at the academy reminded me vaguely of the archery range I frequented as a child. It had a slightly medieval air. The doors were guarded by a couple of dismounted Spanish explorers in tights with long spears. Inside, an armored knight, the kind usually reserved for German castles, guarded the entrance to the men's room. "Everything is for sale for the right price," said a gentleman at the front desk. That included a replica Roman legion helmet and a plethora of small and large fighting knights.

Across from the front desk, I noticed several intense fencing matches going on, all being scored by an electronic system that apparently rated a good stab to the face or torso much higher than a slash to the thigh. Dozens of enraptured family members sat on the edge of

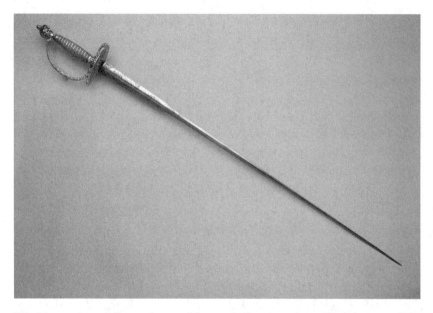

Washington's smallsword, possibly made by Appolone Rudkins, c. 1767 [W-84]. This sword appeared in the 1772 portrait of Washington by Charles Willson Peale. *Courtesy of Mount Vernon Ladies' Association*

their seats as if viewing a movie, facing the fencers, who included—to my surprise as a novice—several attractive and limber women in the requisite cage masks.

Though Washington was no historian, his early reading lists and subsequent book purchases suggest his keen interest in the classical eras of Greek and Roman civilization. Swordsmanship had been a cherished aspect of these ancient martial traditions, and one-on-one dueling often began or ended a battle between two armies. In the tradition of single combat, a great fighter would often be sent forth to take on a representative of an opposing army, with the expectation that the warriors would fight to the death. Homer's detailed clashes between Achilles, Ajax, and Hector are memorable for not only their drama but also the reverence they show toward the meaning of one-on-one combat. Romans also brought sword and spear fighting into the Colosseum and turned them into thrilling spectator sports, often with horrific finales. Though spears were often the weapon of choice for Roman soldiers, the soldiers also used swords and knives to help them conquer much of the known world.

During conquests of Europe, soldiers often clashed with horsemen, fights that required a longer sword. Men on horses carried long swords themselves, often fencing together in close combat. In a natural progression, medieval Europe saw the rise of one-on-one combat as both a regulated sport and a means of maintaining a man's honor. In England, knights fighting for the king were adept swordsmen, often with exceptional equestrian skills, and they were trained in other lethal sports also, including archery.

Like the Greeks and Romans, the Europeans also valued one-on-one combat. Swordplay became a means of venting anger and settling disputes. Eventually, dueling became accepted as a refined form of trial by combat to end a dispute, even when (counterintuitively) the innocent or wronged party might lose the fight. In other words, a fair duel between equals came to be accepted as the last word in a gentleman's disagreement.

In seventeenth- and eighteenth-century Virginia, a sword had come to be seen as a part of a gentleman's attire. Sword clashes during close combat and in naval battles were not uncommon, but by the middle of the eighteenth century the sword embodied a mostly symbolic function. Gentlemen did not often unsheathe their swords over a small dispute but rather kept them on hand as showpieces or for ready use in case of a great insult to their honor.

Antebellum society placed the highest premium on class and honor, and the classic duel was a way for gentlemen to prove both. Indeed, even in George's era, the legality of the duel held firm in many colonies and states. Proponents argued that keeping dueling legal worked toward the maintenance of public civility. The logic went like this: in order to avoid duels, proper gentlemen needed only comport themselves with honor and decency toward their fellow gentlemen. In other words, if everyone behaved decently—not hurling insults and slander around in wanton disregard of others, which was a tall order—there would be no need for a duel. Interestingly, dueling itself was an act of proper comportment, and elaborate rituals evolved around sword fighting, including saluting one's opponent, which included bowing gracefully. These actions and displays became an intimate part of a baroque protocol of civility, one with ancient origins. In the same way that the rituals surrounding foxhunting disguised the possible bloodletting in the field, swordplay also managed to cover the realities of a brutal duel with a charade of theatrics and ceremony. For Washington, who struggled to repress his anger and resentments, swordplay was just one more sporting outlet for his love of display and prowess. He traveled with fencing masters and took lessons early in his military career. Wielding a sword appears to have been something he was expected to learn at a young age, and his older half brother Lawrence may well have given him lessons, or at least a demonstration, prior to more formal, self-funded lessons.

George is not known to have sought justice through a duel. Despite numerous perceived slights and insults from gentlemen of his own class, he never provoked or accepted a duel. By all evidence, he was courageous in battle but did not seek to settle his disputes with physical brutality of any sort. He was known to wrestle on occasion with friends, and he sought to perfect his own martial skills, but when he finally became commander in chief, he worked during the Revolution to discourage dueling. This was a pragmatic call; there were so many rivalries and disputes among his fellow officers that accepting dueling as a means of settling differences held forth the likelihood of depleting his own staff.

His own rules against dueling did not diminish Washington's love of the sword, and he always carried one into battle. Later in life, he would become a collector of sorts, which was not uncommon for men of his stature. Archaeologists I met at his boyhood home in Fredericksburg had uncovered in the dirt the hand guard of an old sword, a telltale sign of George's family's veneration of swordsmanship. Lawrence, who served aboard a British ship, knew how to handle a sword in combat, as did many in his extended family. Lawrence, Austin, and their father, Gus, had attended the Appleby School in England, where understanding the use of a sword was considered essential.

I was excited to add swordplay to my repertoire, even after my agility was flagging somewhat. I was reading a book on modern swordsmanship in which author Nick Evangelista—an excellent name for a swordsman, to my mind—wrote, "The sword has been termed the 'Queen of Weapons,' and has been viewed as a symbol of justice, nobility, and male sexuality." The mix of gender metaphors threw me for a loop, but there were no women in my historical swordsmanship class, so I was eased off this potential quandary. A quick look around at my classmates, sixteen fellow fencers, suggested to me that wannabe knights, including me, would be more impressive when and if their beer bellies were fully disguised behind shining armor.

I whispered to a balding chap about my age, "We should have taken this up decades ago!" He nodded and smiled. Next to him were a few quaint father-and-son pairings, and finally at the end were several young men who appeared at first glance to have acquired an interest in fencing through computer gaming. Several of them were rather pale and scrawny. One in particular was tall and greasy, with long hair, and I immediately made a note to remember him as the Dungeons and Dragons guy. I had a vague feeling we would be stabbing one another at some point.

It was my good luck that I became a pupil of one of Virginia's most admired master swordsmen, Bill Grandy, who was coincidentally also writing a book—though his was about Renaissance-era swordsmanship. A tall, dark-eyed, and slender gentleman of some thirty-five years, Bill actually would look good with just a fork in his hand, and I soon came to know him, as my fellow classmates did, simply as Coach Grandy.

For our class in historical swordsmanship, we would be schooled in two main weapons, the German longsword and the Italian rapier. In the end, Coach Grandy assured us that we would also be able to wield daggers alongside our swords, a kind of crowning glory to our endeavors. The German longsword was a medieval instrument, the kind of weapon that King Arthur's knights would have wielded. I lifted a long sword up with two hands and discovered it to be extremely heavy, maybe more appropriate for Arnold Schwarzenegger or Russell Crowe.

Coach Grandy stressed that much of the success of a longswordsman was in footwork. You can't exactly hop around with a longsword, so stability is key and steps need to be deliberate and well timed. We learned the basic steps, including a passing step, which Grandy said could be modified to move to the side to help the longswordsman avoid being struck. I immediately assumed this would be a good defense short of running out the door. We weren't actually supposed to hit one another in the head with the sword, but I had a creeping feeling that Dungeons was already planning his next move and didn't play by the rules. (I wanted to try to think like my foe.)

With two hands on the sword, I tried out a few of the classic guards: the plow guard, good for farmers, I guessed; the roof guard, which involved raising the sword directly overhead and looked like what I had seen medieval executioners do; and the fool's guard, holding the sword pointed down in order to invite an attack. It was a kind of "Come and get me!" stance. Coach Grandy remarked, "This guard stance gives the appearance that you are open to an attack, hence it 'fools' your opponent into attacking you." There were two more key takeaways for me from the longsword instruction. First, a swordsman must never attack wildly and must always recover into a guarded position. There is, I was learning, very little room for error. Furthermore, a good cut comes from the body, not the arms or shoulders. As a former baseball player and a weekend golfer, I could relate to that, at least in theory.

I discovered through my research and from Coach Grandy that a sword was often the choice not only for barons but also for robbers. Some of the earliest fencing schools in England were considered little better than robbers' dens, so much so that an edict in 1286 outlawed such establishments, stating, "Whereas it is customary for profligates to learn the art of fencing, who are thereby emboldened to commit the most unheard of villainies, no school shall be kept in the city."

It was left to the Huns to come up with a more organized and systematic approach to lethal training. By the fourteenth century, a swordsman could earn a scholarly degree in swordsmanship in Germany. A general preference for longswords lasted through the Middle Ages, as they were needed to cut through thick armor, but by the end of the 1500s armor for personal defense was virtually abandoned. Not surprisingly, the use of guns in combat expedited the gradual demise of the knights in armor. It didn't much help to poke at someone with a sword if he was about to put a bit of lead through your heart. The art of killing, at this stage in history, became somewhat less dramatic and fun, I imagined.

Fighting with a sword hadn't lost its appeal entirely, however. It still served a purpose for individual showdowns and the settling of nasty spats. The Italian fencing master Achille Marozzo encouraged his students by insisting that there was nothing nobler than a swordsman. It took Camillo Agrippa, another great Italian, however, to better codify technique, stressing logic over silly romantic notions like slaying dragons and saving damsels in distress. A well-executed lunge came to take precedence over the slashing and hacking that sometimes occurred in a longsword fight.

By the fifth week in my historical fencing class, we moved on to a weapon that was efficient for killing, easier to handle, and served well, as one expert noted succinctly, for "cutting important parts off of one's opponent." Hmmm. As Evangelista writes in his tome on modern swordplay, "Suddenly, men were poking neat, lethal holes in one another." The stubborn Brits held out with their longswords for some time, as they considered men who played with the shorter and lighter rapier to be the equivalent of sissies. Nevertheless, by the seventeenth century, the rapier was all the rage, and between 1600 and 1780 nearly forty thousand noblemen were killed in sword fights, making the sword a rather useful tool for culling a nation's top one percent.

Coach Grandy explained that the choice of the right weapon could be the difference between victory or death. And it was important to be practiced in the art of everything from a rapier to an épée—a smaller, lighter, and slimmer sword—because when you were in a dispute, someone always got to choose the weapons, and it wasn't always you, he told us. "If you were not proficient at using a certain sword, and others knew this, your opponent could wisely choose that weapon for the duel." That could spell doom.

I learned that the classic rapier was longer than the shorter épée sword that Washington would have trained on in Winchester or when sparring with one of his older brothers in his teens. There is an entire and eloquent vocabulary of swordsmanship, but suffice it to say that the two main parts of the rapier worth remembering are the blade and the hilt. The hilt is comprised of the grip and the hand guard, and the blade is, well, the blade, much stronger and heavier at the base than it is at the tip. The footwork and thrusting motions for a rapier are very much the same for a sixteenth-century rapier as they are for an eighteenth-century épée. To take up one's guard, explained Coach Grandy, "the foot on the same side of the sword hand should be in front, pointed forward, and the other foot should be at a right angle, with the heel in a straight line as the front foot. About three-quarters of your weight should rest on the back leg, removing your torso from being easily struck."

Indeed, a lot, but not all, of swordplay is what you feel most comfortable with. The whole point of en garde posture, with knees bent slightly, is to allow you to advance forward and retreat back without bobbing up and down or moving wildly, which would be a recipe to get sliced open. I experimented a bit, trying to move up and down from this position in a quick but deliberate shuffle step, and I found it much easier than moving about with a burdensome longsword clasped in both hands like Attila the Hun. Keeping the rapier at the ready was also a key, as Grandy made clear, also pointing out that an actual lunge—an offensive move, which is also a good defense—begins with the extension of your arm. "Once your arm is extended, you can lift your front foot slightly off the ground and kick it forward into the air," he told us. "Touché!" I spat out, feeling a bit of the bloodlust of my ancestors rush to the fore.

On the last day of my historical swordsmanship class, we finally had a chance to compete directly with our classmates in a genuine, somewhat brutal, but bloodless duel. I ended up paired with Dungeons, not immediately recognizing him, as he had bundled his long, greasy locks under his mask. I didn't complain, however, as I relished a chance to test Coach Grandy's advice.

A delegated third and two assistants were set to keep score. It would be three points for a body blow or a good head strike and a single point for any of the limbs. We saluted each other by holding our hilts at belt level and the tips of our swords above our heads to our noses and then rolled away and assumed the ready position. Earlier we had been trained in how to use a small dagger to deflect an attack, and so I now held a dagger a bit awkwardly near to my cage mask in order to have an added defense. Though I had no acquired skill as a swordsman beyond the instruction Coach Grandy had provided me with over eight weeks, I felt at a slight advantage as I glanced over at my foe, a lefty whose sword hand was shaking severely. This bolstered my spirits some because I hadn't thought of myself as looking in any way intimidating.

We played with our swords for ten or fifteen seconds in rapid advances, pokes, and hasty retreats. I performed a feint or two, and then, as Coach Grandy had instructed, I provided an invitation for Dungeons to strike at me—if he dared. Such an invitation is considered a good way to win a sword fight, for when an opponent lunges at you, you can quickly turn his sword away with a twist of your wrist, usually inward, as you simultaneously slide forward onto the base of his sword and into his belly or face. Despite its lethal potential, it is a motion that carries with it a certain poetry of motion. As Coach Grandy described the move, the tip of your sword should be slightly raised in order to cross against the opponent's blade. Moving the forearm from the elbow only, you will "press the incoming blade out of the way by using the strong part of your sword against the weak part of theirs." That is when you, in theory, go for the jugular.

I did this twice, deflecting Dungeons's incoming blade and stretching my rapier as far as it would lunge. It worked much better than I had expected it would. Despite my opponent's unusually long arms, I managed twice—by thrusting forward as far as I could move—to slip the tip of my rapier forward into the front of his mask for two successive three-pointers. I drove the tip in for added emphasis. This felt overtly cruel, but it appeared to elicit some frustration in my opponent, and in short order I felt my moment of Zen arrive unexpectedly. We were only fighting to eleven points, and so the duel soon ended in my favor.

I enjoyed this little day in the sun immensely. I was almost sad that Virginia allowed concealed carry for guns but not open carry for swords in bars. After eight weeks of lessons, I felt about ten years younger, though no more popular with the ladies. At least I understood a little better the attraction that fencing would have held for George Washington.

The sword would remain for George an emblem of honor and service throughout his life. He acquired a large number of swords, not least of which was the sword that General Braddock bequeathed him when he was mortally wounded in July 1755. It is the one he wears in his first self-portrait. George seemed to have embraced a love of the symbolic value of swords. Accordingly, in his last will and testament, he carefully divided up his weapons to the sons of his brothers. He wrote:

> To each of my nephews, William Augustine Washington, George Lewis, George Steptoe Washington, Bushrod Washington and Samuel Washington, I give one of the swords or cutteaux of which I may die possessed; and they are to chose in the order they are named. These swords are accompanied with an injunction not to unsheathe them for the purpose of shedding blood, except it be for self defense, or in defense

of their Country and it's rights; and in the latter case, to keep them unsheathed, and prefer falling with them in their hands, to the relinquishment thereof.

This eloquent passage makes it clear that George's swords were not to be used to settle personal disputes, as was his preference across his storied lifetime. Ironically, one George Washington's favorite swords would end up at the center of an uprising against slavery led by John Brown at Harper's Ferry.

13

Minuets and Other Gentler Conflicts

THOUGH GEORGE'S LAST BATTLE of the French and Indian conflict did not win him any more fame than he had already garnered, he was still the toast of tiny Williamsburg. On horseback and in a carriage, he was a big fish in the small pond of only about two thousand inhabitants. When there was a ball at the Governor's Mansion, it was sometimes in honor of George, and if it was not, Colonel Washington almost always was asked to attend.

Invites for mere plebeians like me were harder to come by, but with some finagling at the Colonial Williamsburg ticket booth, I managed to secure an invitation to an exclusive ball held in honor of a pair of local lovelies.

I had been trying to connect with colonial etiquette expert and historian Cathy Hellier, and my path finally crossed hers on the candlelit dance floor beneath full-length portraits of King George III and his wife, Charlotte. Conveniently, Cathy, a soft-spoken young lady with blonde hair and a quick smile, was also a polished dance instructor, and I watched her demonstrate steps to a set of young ladies attired in frilly, hooped dresses.

Her instructions to all of us began with bows and curtsies for what was known as a square-formation dance. After my earlier lessons in Alexandria, I thought I might impress her with a step or two of my own, so I accepted her kind offer and took to the floor. I was soon eating humble pie. It was my lot in life. Cathy explained to me in the aftermath, as I mopped my forehead, some of what had gone wrong for me.

"You did fine," she said, attempting to soothe my trodden ego.

"You tell fibs, dear," I replied.

"The generally received wisdom was that a man could not appear outwardly genteel without the assistance of a dancing master," she said.

"But I've already had lessons," I exclaimed.

"If you didn't get the proper lessons early in life, one could still comport oneself well by judicious imitation."

"Aha," I said. There might still be hope—even if "judicious imitation" sounded complicated.

"But not likely a minuet," Cathy added.

The steps are complicated. There are degrees of grace, and there are a lot of variables on the dance floor; most minuets were spontaneously choreographed on the dance floor because in the eighteenth century people partnered with those with whom they had never danced before.

I was pretty convinced that I would never perform a spontaneous minuet, so I chose a chaise longue and decided to become an admirer instead. My place in the hierarchy as a bad dancer, I guessed, would be that of a candle lighter, but before it got better, the news got worse.

"These young gents were the future leaders of the colony," Cathy explained. "A young man who couldn't dance was also hampered when it came to courtship.

"Mastery of the minuet was important because this dance began every dance event. It was an exhibition dance, stepped one couple at a time, in order of social rank—that is, with the highest-ranking gentleman and lady dancing first and so on down the line. Everyone else watched and commented, often recording their impressions in their diaries. Whenever minuets are mentioned in letters, diaries, novels, etcetera, an evaluation of the dancers almost inevitably follows."

Cathy continued, "The eighteenth century was a pretty socially cruel age—if one 'exhibited himself' in the minuet, a dancer could expect to be critiqued by the others in attendance. It wasn't enough to slog through a minuet; a man had to look good doing it."

Virginians saw dance as both fun and an outright competition, particularly when "the company formed a circle, observing and informally adjudicating the performances in the center," wrote Rhys Isaac, who penned a Pulitzer Prize–winning book on culture in colonial Virginia. "A kind of challenge and response was rendered explicit in the cutting out ritual." This jovial custom, of course, continues to this day.

I was beginning to understand why George, up and through the French and Indian War, had been so obsessed with learning to dance. It was also a pastime that allowed him a light rapport with women. If George hadn't known how to dance, his detractors would have sharpened their knives and laughed heartily. He might have been known merely as an accomplished dodger of musket balls. Like everything, though, he took his performance on the dance floor deadly serious, once referring warmly to dance as "the gentler conflict."

When he was in Williamsburg in the company of fellow legislators, friends, and scholars, George Washington learned to distinguish himself less as gentleman-warrior than as gentleman-sportsman. As the legacy of the English Civil War faded and the age of knights and castles came to an abrupt close, a gentleman needed new ways of displaying his talents. A man's intonation, his steps, his carriage, and his facial expressions mattered more than ever. All of it, if performed in synchronicity, bespoke a portrait of a fine gentleman; the right stance and a stoic visage could win as much favor with royal authority as killing a foe of the Crown on the field of battle.

Colonel Washington's relentless determination to improve his actions and character had carried him through the war. He wanted to move on after achieving relative fame and good standing to become a master of his own estate. He also knew Sally would be nearby but forever unavailable.

In early spring, during an easing of the fighting on the western frontier, George had traveled to visit Williamsburg, where he learned through his ties to circles of elite Virginians that Martha Custis Dandridge, who lived nearby, was now a widow—and a wealthy one at that. On March 16, he paid a cordial visit to offer his condolences. Little is known of that visit except that he tipped her servants well, apparently as a down payment on his affections. Nine days later, he was back for another visit.

Despite earlier romantic failures, his diligence paid off with Martha. On January 6, 1759, still twenty-eight years old, George married Virginia's wealthiest widow. Apart from the fact that photography still had not been invented, it is odd that so little is known about the wedding day, which leading historians believe took place at Martha's White House plantation, not far from Williamsburg and close to present-day

Richmond—or, if not on the plantation, at a nearby Anglican chapel. Though George had a dapper blue velvet suit shipped earlier from England, it is not clear that he wore this to the wedding. Martha wore a stylish yellow dress draped in lace and a pair of purple silk pumps, which have been preserved.

Their marriage lifted George instantly from his earlier, often ham-handed existence into the upper echelons of Virginia society. Suddenly he was within reach, on the social scale, of the polished and polite Fairfax family he so admired. If he couldn't have his first love, he would certainly now be her equal in any social setting. George had eclipsed Old World expectations, even if some historians would be left with few lingering doubts about his true love. Why, after all, did he become obsessed with Martha? Research tells us little. A portrait of Martha close to her wedding date suggests she was by no means the prettiest lady in Virginia at the time. Her face was round with rosy cheeks and her brow had an appropriate widow's peak, but her nose was a bit hooked and her gaze in the picture has an avian quality, a bit quirky compared to the more dainty loveliness of Sally Fairfax's face as depicted in an earlier but equally bad portrait. Female historians at Mount Vernon have informed me that Martha was far more attractive than any portrait did her justice—indeed, the artist that depicted her in said portrait was particularly inept—and if this is true, I stand corrected. Beauty is, in any case, in the eye of the beholder, and George wasn't in the market for eye candy. In Martha, he found a soul mate that would last him a lifetime, supporting him tirelessly across war, hard times, and also through ill health. With her two charming young children, Jack and Patsy, she presented a delightful and inspiring prospect. She immediately gave over all of her fortune in land, slaves, and money to George's management. He also became the legal guardian to both children.

Martha was indisputably a good catch: she was devout, modest, well read, and a good letter writer. Her own White House estate was not far from Williamsburg, and she had long-standing ties to the town even before it was incorporated. Her great-grandfather Rowland Jones had been the first rector of Bruton Parish Church, one of the town's most important houses of worship, from 1674 until his death in 1688. She had married well on two occasions because she was polite, modest, and enjoyed the company of others. After the unexpected death of her first husband, her net worth was the equivalent of millions of dollars in today's money. Her inherited estate consisted of some three hundred slaves and 17,500 acres of land.

George brought to the marriage significant prestige as well as a polished and chivalric comportment and a lively but controlled passion for the opposite sex. After escaping with his life intact from a frontier war, he was now intent on providing for stepchildren and establishing a brood of his own. In his first formal purchase from London, George matter-of-factly put in for four ounces of the well-known aphrodisiac Spanish fly. This is an amusing anecdote when juxtaposed with the knowledge that he would eventually tell a friend who was marrying late in life to make sure his guns were maintained and his ammunition intact.

George wanted to be certain that his domestic life started out on the right foot. After passing through Williamsburg for a few days, he penned instructions ahead to the servants who worked for him at Mount Vernon, the large estate that he would soon own but still leased from his sister-in-law, Ann Fairfax Washington. He was adamant with what he wanted done: "You must have the house well cleaned. . . . You must get two of the best bedsteads put up, one in the hall room and the other in the little dining room that used to be and have beds made," adding, "You must also get out the chairs and tables and have them very well rubbed and cleaned. The staircase ought also to be polished in order to make it look well." Such attention to detail, often in the form of assigned labors for his servants, was to become a standard fixture of his domestic life.

Though George, as a colonist, could never become an aristocratic courtier, by all indications after his marriage to Martha he did his level best to imitate and maintain the lifestyle of a landed English baron. Any Virginian of his social standing aspired to a balance between hard work and social engagement, which furthered one's standing. George, who had fought for God and Crown for several years, returned to the plantation to work hard, but he would not exclude playing hard. This meant excursions with friends, socializing at homes, attending the theater, and playing cards. In short, he intended to see and be seen.

When George set up house with Martha, he began to spend on interior decorations, everything from mirrors to decanters to silverware. Improvements to lifestyle ran parallel or surpassed changes taking place in genteel society circles. In nearby York County between 1700 and 1709, only 3 to 8 percent of the population owned table forks. By 1768 to 1777, a quarter of the poor and half of the middle class used forks. Tea drinking, a British obsession since its discovery in the Far East, was now all the rage. Naturally, not all families could afford the lifestyle of the Washingtons, Masons, or Fairfaxes, but even a single silver spoon had become popular as a keepsake in many homes. Many colonists still ate with wooden spoons off of rough wooden tables while dressing in animal skins or linsey-woolsey. But that was also changing. In the decades to come, they would afford and acquire metal and silver forks, better education, and a love of new entertainments that had once been the exclusive domain of the wealthy. (Even before it became a nation, America had begun the competitive cycles of keeping up with the Joneses.)

Flush with money for a change, George's own life followed a pattern of increased refinement very much in line with Mary Ball Washington's wishes for her children when they lived with her at Ferry Farm. When he had first visited Belvoir Manor in the company of his now deceased brother Lawrence, George had packed nine white shirts and an equivalent number of stockings. As he grew older, his obsession with appearances evolved to include much finer threads. He wanted to be seen as a sharply dressed man, and Martha, no doubt, encouraged him. In 1762 he ordered "a superfine blue broadcloth coat with silver trimmings" and "a fine scarlet waistcoat" fully laced. George was, in more ways than one, resplendent. Such bright colors distinguished him as a fashionable man of wealth and pleasure, though in the halls of London he still might have looked out of place. George sometimes flirted with the garish, but his taste would one day evolve in charm and modesty, and, by the example of his prominence, set the tone for a new nation.

The evolution and democratization of good manners and refinement in America accompanied changes taking place on the political front, as well. Men whose writings inspired the American Revolution openly promoted the notion that power and moral authority fit hand in glove with good manners. John Locke, who inspired Thomas Paine's screeds on liberty, wrote, "Good qualities are the Substantial Riches of the Mind, but 'tis good Breeding sets them off: And he that will be acceptable, must give Beauty as well as Strength to his Actions . . . A Graceful Way and Fashion, in every thing, is that which gives the Ornament the Liking." Locke's strict conception of "Graceful Way and Fashion" was, in any case, not to be found in the backwoods of the Shenandoah nor with the riffraff hanging out in the bawdy taverns of Winchester. It could be earned in the right circles, though, through the practice of good manners and attention to detail. In this thinking, courtly manners were introduced broadly—and gradually accepted as useful to anyone and everyone. In a sense, there was a democratization of good manners in play, and every man had the right to look good and act well in public.

Regardless, there were conflicts and contradictions enough to confuse both the rich and the poor. The rising American colonist—man or woman—found his bearings around a well-appointed dinner table with friends, during walks through a trellised garden, or while riding in a new horse-drawn carriage with a spouse or friend. It wasn't so much what you did as much as where and how you did it. In this regard, Virginia's gentry had long since set double standards: the high gentry had passed laws against commoners drinking in public, but as Governor Spotswood's Knights of the Golden Horseshoe party had proved, drinking innumerable toasts in the woods with fellow gentry was not only acceptable but also won you a smile and a pat on the back. At the same time, while gambling was often discouraged at taverns, the elite, including George and his aristocratic pals, played cards for money on polished hardwood tables in the finest of parlors or private rooms. While it was illegal for a commoner to place a horse bet, a landowning "gentleman" could wager his home or the services of his servant on a single race, with few questions asked.

In the middle of the eighteenth century, some three hundred families made up the ruling classes in Virginia. They shared a cherished genteel life. For the sake of their children and for their own entertainment, a traveling dance master, who often doubled as a fencing instructor, made the rounds from one estate to the other, bringing students and family from nearby plantations for evenings of fun and excitement.

After the French and Indian War, George Washington exhibited the qualities of an extroverted gentleman about town. There is no indication that in the 1760s (or later) George went gallivanting about or philandering, but he was often out and about, bedding down in the home of an acquaintance, often after a friendly night out at a local tavern. Of course, he wasn't holding up the bar and bending elbows with just anyone. In many cases, he and his associates would settle into their own private club quarters at a local restaurant, often a large semiprivate room considered suitable for card playing and conversation.

In 1760, only a year into his marriage, George stumbled into a ball that wasn't quite up to the standards he had seen elsewhere. He recounted, "Went to a ball at Alexandria, where Musick and dancing was the chief Entertainment, however in a convenient room detached for the purpose abounded great plenty of bread and butter, some biscuits, with tea and coffee, which the drinkers of could not distinguish from hot water sweet'ned." George added that "pocket handkerchiefs servd the purposes of Table cloths & Napkins and that no apologies were made for either." He gladly dubbed the event the "the Bread & Butter Ball," assuring that it would be celebrated annually in Alexandria into perpetuity. The organizers of the dance event in my hometown certainly had not meant their event as a joke, and, to be clear, George meant no harm with his light asides. He sat on the board of trustees of the city for which he had helped his brother Lawrence draw up a street grid over a decade earlier. Yet his comments made him a social critic, so to speak, and no doubt amused his friends.

After his war in the woods, George, while suddenly wealthy, was not a spendthrift. Still, he knew how to mix pleasure and politics, and it was a secret to his still-growing acclaim. In order to remain an active member of the House of Burgesses, he switched from the Winchester area to Fairfax, remaining engaged in the same aggressive campaigning that had worked for him in the Shenandoah Valley. In two successive runs for the Virginia House, he spent lavishly again on drinks and balls, noting his expenses: "54 gallons of Strong Beer," "52 Do. of Ale," "£1.0.0. to Mr. John Muir for his fiddler," and "For cakes at the Election £7.11.1."

14

Augustan
Man of Manners

DURING THE LONG HIATUS BETWEEN THE TWO WARS that would continue to shape Washington's character, Williamsburg was at least as
dear to him as was Alexandria. He once remarked that Williamsburg
had the "manners and etiquette of a court in miniature," suggesting
he enjoyed playing the courtier there with the town's bigwigs. If he
wasn't in a fine carriage with Martha, he often rode two successive
fifty-mile sprints on horseback to get to Williamsburg, or to return
to Mount Vernon. He was addicted to speed and wasted no time
between engagements. It is worth contemplating such a distance,
which would give most men today saddle sores or a very bad back.
Twenty miles on a horse for many men, even in the eighteenth century, would be a brutal day out. Maintaining a social life could also
be taxing. George was lucky he could hold his drink well, though he
would later complain, with a hint of the occasional overindulgence,
that with the constant social rounds, "it was not possible for a man
to retire sober."

Not everyone would share George's love for the small town. When
prudish northerners arrived in Williamsburg, the royal capital of the
Commonwealth, they invariably remarked on aspects of Virginia life
that made them uneasy. Ebenezer Hazard, who would become the first
postmaster general of a new nation, said that "the poor are ignorant
& abject" and far worse off than the men and women he knew in
his native Connecticut. Rather, he stated, the Virginians were "much
addicted to Gambling, drinking, swearing, horse-racing, Cock-fighting,
and most Kinds of Dissipation." Hazard complained of the sweltering

weather in Virginia and that the only meal to be had in the summer months was a cheap slab of bacon.

What Hazard was missing, however, as he hurried through Virginia in the late eighteenth century was the slow and steady transformation of a colony that would give a new nation many of its boldest and brightest leaders. Virginians in the higher ranks were far more obsessed with manners than they were with morals. They gambled, they drank, they bet on horses, and, for better or worse, they did it with a certain panache not seen in the North.

There was already a growing divide between North and South, but there was more at play in Virginia in particular. Citizens accepted some of these vices with caveats: in the 1760s they may have already sensed that their golden age was approaching and that with the right risk taking, brain power, and persistence, they would be able to seize power in the New World. That was no reason, in their estimation, to curtail the good times through the kind of excessive moralizing that restricted pastimes and pleasures in northern colonies.

President Franklin D. Roosevelt, on visiting Williamsburg in 1934, called the old town's main thoroughfare, Duke of Gloucester Street, America's "most historic avenue." He certainly had a point. If you want to relive colonial history and converse with the living spirits of the founders, the majority of whom happened to be Virginians, there is, arguably, no better place than Williamsburg for this. From rolling horse pastures to the stately Georgian Governor's Mansion, across the bowling greens to the steps of the House of Burgesses, and to the infamous Raleigh Tavern, some of the greatest conspiracies and denunciations of tyranny in American history have unfolded here.

The restoration of the city and the re-creation of the eighteenth century is an intriguing story in itself. If it hadn't been for a speech given by a humble but determined Anglican minister at a Phi Beta Kappa celebration in New York City, none of us would have the pleasure of strolling the tree-lined streets of the old capital and reliving American history. By a stroke of luck, John D. Rockefeller Jr. was in attendance as Rev. William Goodwin preached the dire need to restore Williamsburg to its former glory. A few years later in 1926, Rockefeller took his own children on a visit. Shortly thereafter, and with some extended consideration of the potential uses of his philanthropic war chest, he reached deep into his pockets to begin restoring the town to its authentic eighteenth-century self.

My own excuse for spending several weeks on end in Williamsburg was to track the fingerprints and hoofprints of George Washington, the young politician and later Revolutionary War leader. I was rarely able to sleep where George slept. My budget pushed me out of town and into a wooded deer park surrounded by golf carts, Canadian geese, and screaming kids. But when I reached out to the Colonial Williamsburg Foundation, the Rockefeller family's brainchild of experts, historians, and "character interpreters," I was welcomed with huzzahs and open arms.

As one young historian, Brandon Bruce, told me, "You are writing about what we do all day!" Out of the blue, and to my surprise, Brandon soon suggested that I sit down and talk to George and Martha Washington, both of whom are played by brilliant character actors employed by the foundation.

"You really need to get their perspective if you are going to write about their lives, the sports they played, and how they looked at the world," Brandon insisted.

I agreed quickly, adding that I was a little nervous at the prospect.

"We'll set that up for you, but first you should take the tour with Thomas Jefferson," he said.

"Huh? Well, OK."

With that, I popped into a colonial shop to purchase a bar of eighteenth-century chocolate to tide me over until I met Mr. Jefferson. I looked forward to meeting the master of Monticello; I had wanted to study the character of the loquacious Jefferson in order to contrast him, in my own mind, with his slightly older contemporary George Washington. In many respects they were similar: both country squires, both punctilious gardeners, both lovers of the outdoors, including foxhunting, and both astute politicians with a style suited for greatness. Their known differences had also amused me. Jefferson was an intellectual, known more for his big ideas and grandiloquence than as a man of action or as a field commander. Mr. Jefferson also happened to have lived in Williamsburg in the 1760s and attended William and Mary under the tutelage of George Wythe.

Our walking tour began during a light drizzle on the well-manicured front lawn of the Governor's Palace amid a flurry of passing horse-drawn carriages. Accompanying a crowd of history buffs were a slobbering bulldog and several boys wielding fake wooden muskets. Jefferson first launched into an account of his own childhood:

"When my father shed his mortal coil at the age of forty-nine years, I was but fourteen, and he allowed moneys in his estate that I could continue my education. I had attended a Latin school that was conducted at Tuckahoe plantation. Lessons were conducted by the Rev. William Douglas, a Scot, and somewhat of a superficial Latinist. He had a great deep 'burrrr' in his accent, so I learned so I learned the Latin language to a great disadvantage of poor perrrrnunciation. I was able to continue my Latin education out on the frontier, . . . [which eventually] led me to attend the old Royal College of William and Mary during the winter of '59 and '60. I fell under the tutelage of one Dr. Small. I don't know if any of you have heard of Dr. Small. I hope history does not forget him. He had gentlemanly and correct manners. I have never ever forgotten the element of good manners as recognition of a civilized society."

At this point the bulldog in attendance growled and flashed his teeth at him. Jefferson ignored the beast. He comported himself with studied rectitude in a suit, scarf, and wide-brimmed straw hat. The drizzle increased, and we, his faithful followers, set off at a fast pace in the direction of the Governor's Palace. At last, the tour had begun.

"The roads in Williamsburg were not errant configuration of cow paths, nay indeed," Jefferson rambled on. "Williamsburg and a town in Maryland, Annapolis, were both purposefully designed by a royal governor in Virginia, Francis Nicholson. The ridge you see here continues to run down our peninsula. It commences at the falls of the James River at Richmond town and then runs all the way down to the Hampton Roads and ultimately to the Chesapeake Bay. It is what was originally an ancient Indian path."

As we rounded a corner, I put on my tricornered reporter's cap.

"So, I understand you admire George Washington's riding skills?" I said.

"Oh, yes. Mr. Washington is a fine—our finest—equestrian and a great foxhunter as well," he replied. "I do not as much fancy the foxhunt, but I also love to ride."

Since all this checked out well with my previous readings, I shot him another query: "And do you gamble—I mean like Mr. Washington does here in Williamsburg?"

"He loved to gamble, though not at high stakes. I don't gamble like he does—I'm not that kind of a risk taker, unless you consider that I've put some of my properties up for sale to the highest bidder."

The bulldog was getting anxious again, so I shut up.

Jefferson led us to a large oak tree, sat us down, and explained the trials and tribulations of the Jamestown Colony, extolling in four-syllable words how he was quite proud of his American "progenitors," including one Samuel Jefferson, who he said "stepped foot in James-town in sixteen and twelve" and invested heavily in flour, eventually taking up a seat on the original House of Burgesses in Jamestown in 1619.

As we approached the steps of the House of Burgesses, Jefferson perched himself on a bench overlooking the crowd. There were now nearly two hundred tourists hanging on his every word. Claiming he was strapped for income, he offered them all a chance to buy some of his properties. I made a note to investigate the deeper causes of his financial woes.

In the eighteenth century, Williamsburg, along with its role as the heart of the Old Dominion, became the venue for a new and unique American culture, one in which both Thomas Jefferson and George Washington would play a key role. George's own future as a leader of men remained to be decided. In the meantime, his own love of gentility and sport led him to seek amusement through dancing, hunt-ing, racing, politics, and also at the theater in the Virginia capital.

An ideal gentleman in this era maintained an elegant appearance, a noble disposition, but also eloquence and humor. At the same time, a gentleman had to avoid the perception of being undereducated or, heaven forbid, a boor in public. In the same way that one could learn to dance in step with the rest of the company, wit and wisdom also were acquired talents. Even stodgy Bostonians believed that a man should enliven his taste and build his character with attention to the arts and proper discourse. Their own Brahmins, however, did not share the same taste or love of drama that many Virginians held.

Arguably to the benefit of the minds of many of the Founding Fathers, in Williamsburg there was far less moral scrutiny of literature and drama than there was in colonial Boston or Philadelphia. Virgin-ians desperately longed to keep up with the times in Mother England.

Their fascination with the Augustan Age of literature guaranteed them a steady fare of comedies of manners, works that mocked conventional behavior. Leading characters in such dramas were marked by their acute character flaws, which—more often than not—made them misfits in society. Some stories delved into scandal. Laced with subtle and not-so-subtle morality lessons, actors used clever and cutting dialogue. Though William Shakespeare's plays, including *Much Ado About Nothing,* can be seen as the forerunners of the Augustan Age, it was Jonathan Swift who had earlier set the tone for the new dramatic genre. Though Swift mocked the upper classes and their obsession with manners, at the bottom of his biting satire was an urge to improve almost everyone's behavior. Swift is important to the era also because he was a political satirist. He, and other writers like him, helped set the stage for the revolutionary spirits that emerged in the colonies. By no coincidence, George Washington, already fixated on his own manners, would become bent on helping to improve the manners of an entire nation. Without the Augustan Age's drama and ideas of refined and instructive drama, it is hard to see how he would have become the same leader and trendsetter he eventually became.

In Williamsburg, the names of new British satirists and critics quickly gained currency. To quote a line or two did not always require cracking a book. The first purpose-built theater in the colonies opened in Williamsburg in 1716 and ran off and on for over two decades, finally closing in 1745. A few years later, though, in 1752, actors were again entertaining locals and Virginia legislators. Lewis Hallam was the company manager, and when he died, his wife remarried a man who would become the greatest innovator of stage productions in the New World, David Douglass. Douglass would build new stages in Williamsburg, Newport, Philadelphia, Annapolis, Williamsburg, Charleston, and Kingston, Jamaica.

The going was by no means easy for Douglass's thespians, but, along with playing the occasional key role in some plays, he became the chief advocate for the merits of good drama, turning on its head a standard criticism that drama instigated moral decay. He went so far as to claim that the stage provided "models of elocution for budding ministers and lawyers," which was hard to deny. Such arguments would be crucial in the years ahead as colonists were exposed further to the arts, satire, and political invective in the world beyond their plantations and small farmsteads. Douglass was also a marketing genius. He staged his performances in Williamsburg when locals and politicians streamed into the town for court days, horse races, and other seasonal festivities.

Though he sometimes did take Martha along—and later their two children—more often than not, George attended the theater alone, albeit often meeting up with friends and his fellow burgesses. Men who spent the day arguing politics often retreated to the theater to discuss ideas, smoke, drink, and watch others entertain them on a stage that in many ways mirrored life in London.

To get a better idea of what the whole theater scene looked like for George and his eventual good friend Thomas Jefferson, I ran down Williamsburg's chief architectural historian, Professor Carl Lounsbury, who had recently completed an investigation into the Williamsburg stage. I found Carl in an office cluttered with copies of eighteenth-century playbills. He had a good excuse for his obsession: as a young man growing up in Winston-Salem, North Carolina, he had fallen in love with the theater, later going to work at the Smithsonian Institute in Washington.

"We know from diary entries and such that when Williamsburg's legislators finished work at the House of Burgesses in the afternoon, they would go to see plays," he explained. "On one occasion, Jefferson attended the theater for eleven straight days, Washington for five straight." Financial records and other evidence suggests that in 1760, just after his marriage to Martha, George helped with several other investors to underwrite the construction of David Douglass's new theater in Williamsburg. "The appeal of this was that this was a very genteel thing to have in town: a polite entertainment with the latest fashions from London," Carl explained. "In effect, it was a kind of little London in a box where you could take in the latest jokes and catch up on the slang, latest songs, and even the new magical sleights of hand."

Leading politicians were soon addicted to the sparkle and glow of the candlelit theater. On numerous nights, a young Thomas Jefferson and war hero Washington headed to the theater at the same time, negotiating dusty streets on horseback and running "a gauntlet of hucksters selling a variety of foodstuffs," explained Carl. Starting in 1760, George probably sent a servant ahead to reserve his seat. A large wooden box that seated up to a dozen provided a comfort level not unlike a typical wooden church pew in the day. Pipe smoke and friendly banter filled the air, and in the colder months, a potbelly stove warmed the chill.

In 1728 John Gay's controversial *The Beggar's Opera* opened in London to rave reviews. Mixing in popular tunes, it was full of witticisms as well as political and cultural satire relevant to the scene in London. The play's success is often credited with unleashing a stream of new invective and satire onto the eighteenth-century stage, and a few decades later in Williamsburg, Douglass himself played Macheath, the curious womanizing rogue ensnared in a love triangle with Polly Peachum and Lucy Lockit. Viewed by many critics as a satirical attack on government corruption, the play also did exceedingly well in Virginia. Their mutual records show that both Jefferson and Washington attended the opening night of *The Beggar's Opera* in Williamsburg.

I was still having trouble imagining the atmosphere, and so Carl walked me over to a two-by-five-foot model of a similar theater. "Every time there was a new backdrop to be painted, stagehands, including the actors, would go to work," he explained. "The set was more complex than you might imagine. They brought in the latest light machines from London." For the sound of thunder, someone would simply roll a giant cannonball down a trough, making a loud rumble. "On at least one occasion, we know the cannonball dropped into the audience," he added.

"Ouch," I replied.

Young Thomas Jefferson preferred the riotous pit to the more luxurious box seats held by George, said Carl. From the sound of things, the evening could get rather wild. "There was a problem with the audience actually crawling onto the stage, and so they eventually put up a set of spikes in front of the stage." From the pit, where Jefferson liked to sit, young men, sometimes ensconced alongside ladies of dubious repute, hurled insults, apple cores, and orange peels at the actors when they didn't approve of an act. I told Carl that it sounded as fun as the rock concerts I attended as a youth.

An evening at the theater might last three or four hours. I wondered how anyone could possibly stay seated that long, but then I recalled that a lot of folks these days watch television for hours on end. In the eighteenth century a night out at the theater provided entertainment, socialization, and edification—a kind of package deal.

I became just too jealous of all the fun that our Founding Fathers had at the theater to pass it up, so I bought a ticket to the English playwright David Garrick's comical satire *Miss in Her Teens*. The title alone sounded a little naughty, and when I discovered that this play was not recommended for young children, I slouched up to the ticket booth with a feeling that I might end up in bad company. A smiling ticket master suggested that I stop off at the bar on my way to my seat to whet my whistle. My kind of theater, I thought.

Miss in Her Teens was typical of the age. It was a comedy of manners, a short afterpiece, actually, that made fun of the idea of false gallantry, a subject that George Washington, in his regular theatergoing, showed continued interest in. Such interludes were often performed between a major play—quite often a Shakespearean tragedy in Williamsburg.

In the eighteenth century the audience was encouraged to participate in the drama, I learned. Somehow the peanut gallery had ended up several rows just in front of me. They began guffawing and calling out insults as Biddy Bellair, the lead character, was romanced by several flawed characters as she swooned and plotted her catch. King George III and his family attended a similar performance in London, and I noted that a critic had panned it somewhat, noting that Garrick, in the role of one Mr. Fribble, was so "ridiculous" that he "mimics eleven men of fashion." I think the critic may have missed that this was often the point of a comedy of manners.

Along with the rest of the audience, I was taken by *Miss in Her Teens*. The Williamsburg actors were brilliant, and the dialogue did not disappoint. I was surprised to discover that it held forth as much sexual innuendo as any modern drama. It was clearly not made for a prim and proper audience, I decided. The twenty-first-century audience cheered, jeered, and called for repeated encores in the middle of an act, though no one crawled onto the stage. As Carl and Brandon had warned me, on-the-spot encores were standard practice in the era. In the end, one Captain Lovet, recently returned from some distant war, managed to win the hand of the lovely Miss Biddy Bellair, also acquiring her fortune in the process. All's well that end's well, I thought, watching the crowd stumble, half-drunk, for the nearest exits. It wasn't any kind of political satire, like *The Beggar's Opera*, but it was good, fun entertainment.

For insight into the Garrick performance I had seen, I arranged to again meet with historian and theater scholar Brandon Bruce, who sometimes worked as an eighteenth-century actor himself. In an office hung with fencing swords, Brandon described the changes that George would have witnessed as a regular attendee. "Shakespeare's day was darker, bloodier, and—in some ways—a more sexual age," he said. When the Puritans seized the reigns of authority in England during the interregnum, the stage went virtually silent. "Later, in the 1740s, David Garrick and a new crowd of dramatists and writers took things in a new direction," Brandon said. "Enter George Washington as an enthralled stagegoer."

Garrick revolutionized English theater, often reworking Shakespeare with a modern touch and obsessing over what Brandon called "emotion in the moment." The point was for an actor to actually, as he explained, "let the emotion take over so he or she could really start to emote. This came with a lot of gesture, usually bordering on the melodramatic."

I dug up an actors' manual of the day, titled *The Thespian Perceptor*, which made the idea of expressing wonder sound a little silly: "The eyes should be open, fixed upon the object of wonder, if visible, with the look of fear. If the hands hold anything, immediately allow it to drop. The whole body should be fixed in a stooping posture, with the mouth open and the open hands held up." Brandon insisted that this new world of expressing individual emotions—or emoting—was all a little revolutionary. He insisted that without the eighteenth-century stage revolution that George Washington and Thomas Jefferson enjoyed and that Garrick inspired, we wouldn't have gotten to Marlon Brando screaming "Stella, Stella!" in *A Streetcar Named Desire*.

"I think I prefer Lady Macbeth screaming at her dagger," I commented.

"Yes, me too!"

In tiny Williamsburg, the capital of Virginia, everyone had been starved for culture, and when they could get a taste, they indulged—George especially. "Washington went to the theater just about more than anyone we have recorded," Brandon said. "He loved comedy, he loved tragedy, and he loved it all!"

George's own character, held up to the mirror of eighteenth-century drama, also evolved. Williamsburg itself reflected a world whose concepts of conduct and freedom were churning and turning, approaching a breaking point. Friends said they never saw George Washington so lively and amused as when he attended a play. The drama—including the tragedy, comedy, and farce—he witnessed onstage had parallels with his personal experiences of love and conflict. If it wasn't cathartic, it was a constant exposure to ideas and behaviors that were fashionable and informative. It kept him on his toes and thinking about his own actions, and provided him a new prism through which to view his own idea of a gentleman with manners.

15

In the Garden with Martha Washington

IN MY QUEST TO UNDERSTAND George's pre-Revolutionary lifestyle and his relationship with Martha, I had secured an interview with Lee Ann Holfelder, the "character interpreter" charged with portraying Martha Washington at Williamsburg. I had caught her splendid act two years earlier and had spoken to her in some depth about the nuanced differences between her own Christian beliefs and those of George's more enigmatic devotions. There was no one who portrayed Martha, and had studied her character traits and cadence of speech, more than Lee Ann, and so I had been pleased to have her confirm our meeting near the center of town in an e-mail, which she signed "Your Humble Servant."

When we met, Martha apologized for not being dressed for a ball. She was wearing a long yellow dress covered with an apron, more appropriate for the smokehouse. We found a quiet garden off the main street and sat down for a chat. If there are two people I hope to meet first when I get to heaven, it would be George and Martha, so I considered this my first wish granted. I decided not to engage in an aggressive line of questioning but instead to allow Martha to reveal herself. I did make my interest known in advance and told her that I was quite keen to know more about George's physical prowess, equestrian skills, and romantic bent.

Martha obliged. She replied to my initial queries in a sweet southern drawl by way of explaining George's love of riding. "It takes a special kind of man to keep up with my husband on a horse," she said, flicking a bumblebee off her arm. "To give you an example, if my husband were to come to Williamsburg from Mount Vernon, where it would take five days in a carriage, he can ride alone and make it to Williamsburg in two days on fast horses, sometimes changing out his horse for a postman's horse to finish his travels."

I dared to ask Martha if her husband rode not only for pleasure but also to maintain his constitution and good physical health.

"Well, my husband is one who is not well confined behind a desk for long. He likes to take the air. Early in the morning, he will arise and ride his plantations before I am even up and have breakfast settled. I have to get up fairly early to give him a small breakfast but to sit down for breakfast for his whole cakes and time with his wife—this takes place after he has done a bit of riding—taking the air and getting that great glow upon his cheeks.

"I must say that for most of the Washington men, well, they died in their forties. My George, I dare say, will live a lot longer than that. And I believe, as much as I hate to say it, that part of it is the constitution of his mother, Mary. The other reason, though, is the way that he takes so vigorously to his outings on horseback. He will not sit and wait for the grave. He wants to be always doing things, doing what he loves. And that is riding his horse about his properties, looking over his land, and taking in the air."

Since I knew they often saw one another socially, I wanted to know how Martha viewed the influence of the Fairfax family on George's outlook.

"My husband is not a first son of his father's first wife, and his father, Augustine, paid his debt to nature early. For this reason, his mother could not send him for proper schooling in England. But Lord Fairfax saw in my husband what I see in him: a man of great integrity. And he took him under his wing and helped him in so many ways to finish his education as a fine gentleman. There was the horseback riding, the hunting, and that is probably why my husband loves it so. The Fairfax family gave him what he needed to be a man of society. All the Fairfaxes helped, and that was largely due to the fact that his half brother Lawrence, whom he loved so much, married into that fine family.

"Lord Fairfax and my husband have always maintained a great friendship, and that started with Lawrence, but it was first the horses and hunting that brought them together."

I knew I wouldn't be in heaven in all likelihood for several decades to come, so I decided to pry a little further into the unusual relationship that George had maintained with Sally Fairfax both before his betrothal to Martha and in the aftermath. I knew, by asking, that I was stepping into uncharted territory, and I prepared myself for the worst. What I heard from a jovial Martha, however, on this warm autumn day tracked closely with the observations of a lot of leading historians who also have delved into the quandary.

I tried to put it delicately: "So I understand that in his youth George had quite the eye for the ladies," I started. "And then there are the stories about Sally."

Martha did not hesitate, suggesting to me that she had already given the issue some serious thought.

"Every young man at a certain age, in flight of fancy, turns to the ladies. For my husband, he did not have much luck with it at first. It is not that he was not a fine figure of a man. But my husband is very—if I can take you into my confidences—he is very unsure of himself at times due to the lack of formal education that he was afforded early in life. It always made him think that people saw him as less than equal to themselves. So with the ladies sometimes he was a bit awkward.

"Sally Fairfax saw that. She wanted him to come out of that shell and be more accepted in society. It is a custom of intelligent ladies to want to show men that they are witty, to show that through a sensual banter with a gentleman. Not to play the coquette. That is something quite different. I believe Sally Fairfax was trying to help my husband, to learn the ways of man and romance. She took him upon a tour of it.

"My husband, though, thought that she meant that romantically or that she had a bit of an interest in him. But my husband would never step upon the line of having relations with a married lady, let alone one that is married with a man whose family has been his benefactors and so close to him, not to mention besmirching the name of his brother that he cared so much about. Still, he thought that perhaps Sally was not as interested in her husband as she might be and that perhaps they were estranged from one another, so there were letters that went betwixt them. Of course, the letters from her are quite gone. Perhaps he did not want me to see them. But I believe it was all a great misunderstanding of a man who did not understand the ways of a woman."

I was more certain, as she continued, that the concept of "complicated" relationships probably wasn't a twenty-first-century invention. I still wondered how Martha managed to curtail her jealousy.

"I have never found her to be want of my ire or anger. To tell you the truth, that when I came down with a great illness shortly after Mr. Washington and I married and there was some fear that I would not survive it, I asked Sally Fairfax to come to Mount Vernon to help nurse me. Would I do that if I thought perhaps there was a chance that there was anything going on betwixt her and the man I had just married?"

"No," I replied, a bit embarrassed at my own questioning. "I do not think so."

Given that Martha was off to a social engagement, I had only one or two questions remaining, so I decided to stick to sports—well, foxhunting. I wanted to know if Martha ever felt neglected by George's apparent obsession with foxhunting.

"Well, there is one area where my husband and I may have some vexations with one another, and that is when he brings the hounds in the time of their mating seasons within the household, which I do not quite approve of.

"The hunts always begin early with the howls. It will start very early in the morning, and I can hear the hounds going. Then it is to the horses that my husband goes next. He and my brother or a neighbor getting the horses all riled up. And, of course, in the winter air there is the smoke coming from all the mouths and noses of the horses. It is a sight to see with the foggy air, a bit of dew upon the ground, or some snow in the morning. Then you will hear the sound of the horn, and it is off to the hunt, waiting for the hounds to tell you that they are onto a scent. It is this moment of anticipation that I believe Mr. Washington lives for, perched upon his horse, waiting for that sound, and then he is off in a shot.

"I will try to have dinner on the table at half past the hour of three—for Mr. Washington does not care for dinner to be late, but sometimes he will make it barely in by the time dinner is placed upon the table.

"My husband takes as seriously everything in life. He lives by a code. It is something he has laid down for himself. That is what has made him a good sportsman as well as a gentleman: attending his animals, seeing to the overseers, seeing to his land, and riding his lands. He does not walk his land; he rides his land. It gives him great pleasure to be out in the air."

16

Good Masters
and Petty Tyrants

Past the shuffle of schoolchildren and whiff of fast food, I headed off on another long stroll through the grounds of Mount Vernon. At George's grave, two veterans and a young lady in a wheelchair volunteered to lay a wreath and say a prayer. It was a moment of solemnity as a light rain fell over the crowd. As I descended a hill and passed a newly dedicated memorial to George's slaves, I soon arrived at the riverfront, where a pair of young men dressed as eighteenth-century carpenters were constructing a small fishing boat. It was the kind that George's slaves used to pull in their nets and that the master of Mount Vernon also commandeered on occasion when he wanted to fish with friends. He fished purely for sport, sometimes with nets and other times with bait, including bloodworms.

"George Washington ran his fisheries as an industry on the side," said one of the two white carpenters, a tall gentleman in a floppy hat and sipping coffee from a tin cup. His more rotund colleague explained the boat-building process: "What we are doing here is bending the cypress boards to fit the length of the boat. Washington used small wooden boats like this one to help carry the nets out into the river. The nets were attached to the shoreline, and fish would swim as they raced up the river."

George wrote to a friend that his waters were "well supplied with various kinds of fish at all seasons of the year; and in the Spring with the greatest profusion of Shad, Herring, Bass, Carp, Perch, Sturgeon &ca." Eventually his extensive fishing would become an industry and a major source of his income. His catch would be salted and put in wooden barrels to be sold in nearby towns and in trade, sometimes to the West Indies in exchange for rum.

When he switched away from tobacco farming to wheat in the 1760s, Washington had been left with a surplus of slave labor, which he put to use building up his fishing industry. Modeling his new endeavor at least partly on that of his neighbor George Mason, he would bring his slaves together from their other assigned work on certain days, particularly when the fish were running. When the haul was particularly good, he might reward his servants with rum. From his diaries and tackle kits that Mount Vernon possesses, it is clear George enjoyed fishing and also encouraged at least two of his three younger brothers, Jack, Charles, and Samuel, to build up their own industrial fishing prospects. On September 3, 1770, for example, he remarked, "Want in the Evening a fishing with my Brothers Saml. And Charles," and five days later near Mount Vernon, he "went a fishing towards Sheridine Point. Dined upon the Point"—a known fishing landing. He sometimes stored fishing lines inside his canteens.

On any given day at Mount Vernon, George was up at the break of dawn and off on his horse to survey the work that needed to be done. Visitors reported that when an example was required, he would strip down to his shirtsleeves and work alongside his slaves. His passion for farming was almost as great as his love of hunting, and he often combined the two. Like Thomas Jefferson, he had a green thumb and took immense pleasure in discovering new varieties of plants, flowers, fruits, and vegetables. He marked his patches carefully and, like a scientist testing new theories, he took notes on what grew well and what did not.

I strolled through the upper gardens of Mount Vernon, where on one occasion George had forbidden slave children from playing their game of Prisoner's Base. Beside the garden, not far from George's eventual bowling green, stood an immense poplar tree dated to his years in residence. There were fresh specimens of decorative dogwood, redbud, and mountain laurel, which George loved for its pink flowers. His upper garden would evolve into a formal pleasure garden, a miniature of those kept by European royalty and the British governors in Williamsburg. Here he would also create a fruit-and-nut enclave, a kind of garden within a garden where guests could stroll and admire his lemon and orange trees. The plantation's lower gardens, which were apparently overseen by Martha, supplied vegetables like cabbage, cauliflower, broccoli, and lettuce.

When George first moved in with Martha, Mount Vernon, whose land had been in the family since its acquisition by John Washington, was little more than a glorified farmhouse, yet by the end of the 1760s it had the makings of a lovely manor house. From their back door, which opened onto the Potomac, Martha and George could see a great stretch of the slow-rolling river that runs between Maryland and Virginia into the Chesapeake Bay.

Since he had grown up in the shadow of Nomini and Stratford Halls in Westmoreland County, George knew what a well-appointed plantation manor looked like. Though his would become an architectural model for many Virginia homes in the future, it never would match the grandiosity of Nomini or Stratford, nor their more extensive gardens. Such grandeur required considerable money and manpower, and while he expanded his own home steadily over the next three decades, he also sought modesty and a sense of place, which are still apparent today in a walk through the interior or a stroll along the pebble paths he set forth. George's taste stands as an example of how Americans sought through innovation and labor to live as well as most of their European peers. The home he built—its majesty and simplicity—was and is symbolic of his core identity. Even its private spaces, including his isolated study, speak to his ideas about independence, privacy, and prosperity. Everything about the estate is in one way or another a reflection of Washington's own character.

For Virginia's wealthy planter class in the eighteenth century, the master of a big house was expected to want to beautify his environment through attention to the kind of minute detail that George loved in his own life. (If Sigmund Freud was right about childhood fixations, he might have enjoyed analyzing the master of Mount Vernon.) Indeed, George's peers, including Richard Henry Lee, George Mason, and Thomas Jefferson, were similarly engaged with external architecture, furniture design, and landscaping. George, obsessed with symmetry and his views from the house, would add wings and a classic back porch to his home, improving both the landscape and the interior design by making his estate flow seamlessly from one pleasant scene to the next. The estate became in many ways a monument to his virtue, common sense, and to the ideals of gentility his mother had instilled in him.

Yet, despite his obsessions with landscaping, farming, and interior design, George also had a certain pleasure principle. He frequently took time out to hunt and fish, even more than most of his neighbors. In the years following the French and Indian War, George fell in love with "the pursuit of happiness"—a phrase his neighbor and friend George Mason would one day coin in the Virginia Declaration of Rights, but that would end up more famously in the Declaration of Independence.

Maybe it was in part because he had never been to London that he sought out the latest English fashions, a habit he had acquired as a teen. Now, thanks to his good investments and Martha's wealth, he did not have to limit his taste as much as he had growing up in Fredericksburg or even serving as a surveyor for the Fairfax clan. Through his wife's purchasing agent, he placed orders for foreign and exclusive goods. In addition to clothes, these included jellies, sweetmeats, and new silverware with handles made of ivory.

George, as indicated by his diaries, couldn't resist an exciting horse race, a puppet show, or a carnival barker's display of a wild animal. He gave money on one occasion to a showman who walked an immense elk down his pebbled drive at Mount Vernon. His fun and games included boat races—with black oarsmen—on the Rappahannock and Potomac rivers, and at some point he invested in a bow and arrow for target practice.

His neighbors were his best friends, by all accounts in the 1760s. Apparently Martha did not object to spending long days and evenings with Sally Fairfax as well as George William Fairfax, who remained a close friend of both Washingtons. Martha surely had an inkling of George's past love interests, but she did not let on and by all accounts was happy to entertain her neighbors. The absence of jealousy went both ways.

When he so desired, the master of Mount Vernon could run off into the woods. According to recent archaeological research, the grounds of George Washington's five farms were probably once inhabited by Native American hunters, including the Dogue, for which one of the nearby creeks was named, the Patawomeck, and the Piscataway, among others. But by the mid-1700s, these tribes were long gone for the most part, pushed into the Shenandoah and beyond, and the woods were the domain of white hunters and black slaves, who sometimes helped procure wild game for the table. Washington called his cherished hunting grounds his "wilderness," and he would spend hours on end traipsing about the wilds, mostly on horseback but also on foot, with a fowling gun.

A glance through his diary entries in 1768 and 1769 alone suggests that in the run-up to the Revolution, George was a more avid hunter and fisher than he had ever been. On February 24, 1768, he wrote, "Went a ducking between breakfast and dinner and killed 2 Mallards and 5 bald faces." He had time on his hands to renew his friendship with Lord Fairfax, who often came out for the hunt in the company of his nephew and friend George William. On six occasions between November 15 and November 29, 1768, he hunted with the seventy-five-year-old Fairfax, whom he still referred to as "My Lord." On the fifteenth, he noted, "Went a Fox hunting in the Neck. Catch'd a bitch fox—after an hour and 40 min chase." Later in the month, George dined with Sally, her husband, and a guest visiting from England. Through his agent in London, he sent away for a new hunting horn in July 1769. He stipulated that the horn, which is now on display daily at Mount Vernon along with his riding crop and spurs, be "bound tight and round."

Too much attention to George Washington's diary entries might lead you to believe he was a dry character. On the surface, he sometimes seems overly obsessed with finances and how many ducks he shot or fish he caught earlier in the day. Actually, nothing could be further from the truth. His life as a country squire also provided the future president with added leisure to reflect and cultivate his ideas. While George did not, as Thomas Jefferson did, study Greek, Latin, French, or Hebrew with a mind to read great works in their original text, his letter writing before the Revolution reveals a man of growing culture and with an interest in liberal ideas, including a special concern for the role of women in society. Washington's excellent writing and penmanship—marked by near-perfect curls and slants—put him almost on an even footing with his better-educated peers. (He had his own writing paper drawn up with a watermark, including his family crest, a lonely leaf, which I have framed in my study in case I begin to suffer from a bad case of writer's block.) His associates and relatives, who still acted as sounding boards, allowed Washington to begin to reflect more widely on the world. Exceptional manners enabled him to win friends and influence others.

During his presidency, George Washington, burdened with civic duty even when he might have preferred to be chasing foxes, acquired a reputation as an icon of solid virtue. It was a polished reputation its bearer had well earned. But there was also a jovial side to George that sprang up in the company of friends and close acquaintances. For anyone who has trouble imagining the gentle jabbing he could give a friend, a light missive to his newly married friend, Burwell Bassett, is instructive. He wrote, "But harkee! I am told you have recently introduced into your family a certain production which you are lost in admiration of, and spend so much time in contemplating its just proportions of its parts, the ease and conveniences with which it abounds, that it is thought you will have little time to animadvert upon the prospects of your crops." The passage reveals some objectification of the opposite sex, standard for the day, but it also displays a playful charm that George often exhibited in person. At the same time, most of his letters are infused with an endearing quality, particularly in correspondence with family members, including distant relatives. They prove that he wanted to be liked by everyone he knew, and even by those he still did not know.

His business affairs were exacting and determined, but they also reveal a gentle nature. On the one hand, if he was somehow cheated in a deal, he might complain vociferously. On the other hand, he did not always seek recompense through legal means. For instance, in the case in which a young captain stole some of George's goods from a ship, George politely deferred pressing charges, writing, "It is not my wish to proceed to any harsh and rigorous measures by which a man just setting out in trade may be injured if there is any possibility of avoiding it." He understood that a man's honor stood in the balance and that his own forgiveness might sustain it. In this regard, he often gave men he dealt with, including those who worked for him, second chances to restore their merit.

George did not tolerate fools or drunkards well, but oddly he broke his own rules of civility when he kept regular company with Capt. Thomas Posey, a colleague from his French and Indian War days who was well known for his love of women and wine. Washington ended up loaning Posey over £1,000. Though Posey spent time in jail and was even caught trying to bilk money from him, George remained unusually loyal to his friend, sending his son to school and offering him a bed to sleep in and regular companionship on the foxhunting trail. Washington acknowledged that life dealt bad hands, and he remained tolerant of friends even when they exhibited bad judgment.

George's own financial management was stellar. He loved to play cards, but he knew it could become a vice, writing years later to his nephew Bushrod that gambling could result in the forfeiture of honor and was "the child of avarice, the brother of iniquity and the father of mischief," adding that "the successful gamester pushes his good fortune till it is overtaken by a reverse. The losing gamester, in hopes of retrieving past misfortunes, goes on from bad to worse."

Attending his own advice, Washington played cards for hours on end, but, based on his account books, clearly knew when to hold them and knew when to fold them. This behavior was in stark contrast to his wealthy contemporary William Byrd III, who gambled heavily in London as a student. Byrd reportedly lost £10,000 to the Duke of Cumberland in one sitting. In 1765 at Mrs. Vobe's Tavern in Williamsburg, Byrd, according to a colleague, was "never happy but when he has the box and Dices in hand." His associate continued by saying Byrd was a "gentleman of the greatest property of any in America [but] has reduced himself to that Degree by gameing that few or nobody will Credit him for Ever so mall a sum of money." Ironically, wealthy scions like Byrd were behind the antigaming laws that sought to forbid almost anyone except a gentleman from gambling. George's favorite card game, loo, a forerunner of poker, had a standard three-card limit with each player laying a stake in a pool before the deal. If a player did not win one of at least three hands, he was considered "looed." In this pastime, George appears to have treated gambling as a light social entertainment, in contrast to some of his more obsessed brethren. He likely enjoyed the company as much as the game.

As the crow flies today along the Potomac River, it is just about two and a half miles from Mount Vernon to Belvoir Manor, where Sally and George William lived, and two miles farther in the same direction to George Mason's Gunston Hall, a classic Georgian brick home with manicured gardens and a view of the Potomac. All three families shared an interest in hunting, which served as an excellent excuse to run horses through each other's plantations and then get together for drinks and a meal afterward. As was the case across rural Virginia at the time, guests would come and stay with the Washingtons and then take them along to balls and horse races farther afield. Distances were long and tedious, so guests often spent more than a night or two with their hosts.

Though the Masons, Washingtons, and Fairfaxes—arguably the wealthiest families in the Northern Neck—suffered from their share of common diseases, their lives were far removed from those of even the middle gentry into which George had been born. The Mason and the Fairfax family lifestyles, for instance, embodied some of the highest levels of gentility available to anyone living in the American colonies before 1760, and with his marriage to Martha, George had caught up and was riding right alongside his neighbors.

George's immense fortune gave him the luxury to contemplate his future and that of a nation-state, which still existed only in his mind's eye. Personally, I'm always amazed when I take time to think about the universal depth and value of the ideas that emerged from the minds and pens of America's Founding Fathers. It reminds me of the brilliance found in ancient civilizations—Egypt and Greece, for example—when the ruling classes had the luxury to consider and act on big ideas. Surely we were lucky that the American founders had time to amuse themselves and, more important, to read and engage as thinkers and creators.

Of course, there is another crucial parallel with antiquity that casts a shadow over many aspects of life in Virginia, and one that it would be foolish to ignore. It is also not possible, in my view, to discuss George's code of honor without addressing the issue of slavery and its impact on his time and lifestyle. After all, George Washington was born to be a slave master and would remain one for all of his life. He was part of a system that was intended to maximize production based on curtailing the rights of others, notably persons from different cultures and ethnicities.

The largest plantations in pre-Revolutionary Virginia produced a luxurious lifestyle and an outlook that influenced the American road to revolt. Friends and some historians I know see the American Revolution—at least until we established a Constitution—as a kind of baron's revolt that served the interests of the largest landholders and slave owners in the colonies. My views differ somewhat. Washington's financial standing and landowning ambitions fit well into this so-called baron's revolt argument, which contends that the War of Independence was a self-interested affair aimed at the enrichment of land barons and other well-off colonials who led the revolt. I can accept parts of this argument, but it falls apart when the Revolution first appears on the horizon. For despite Washington's solid business acumen, which makes him American to the core, he also exhibited a deep interest in the revolutionary ideas about liberty and fraternity that were already being articulated in Europe, namely in the writings of John Locke, Jean-Jacques Rousseau, and Charles-Louis Montesquieu. This, in my view, became the rub on his conscience when it came to considering his own slaveholdings. The bondage of his own servants, who aspired to freedom, undercut his own aspirations at all turns.

How George Washington dealt with slavery as an institution redounds to his own code of honor, to his ideas about fair play, and to our notions about his evenhandedness. Though the title of my book would not suggest an examination of George's relationship to the institution of slavery, I felt compelled to examine it. Slavery impacted his financial standing and shaped his character. It represents a troubled and often violent part of his life—one in which he could never live up to his own ideals, particularly as they developed in the lead-up to the Revolution and in its aftermath.

A look at the correspondence on the subject between George Washington and George Mason, his early confidant and close neighbor, reveals the tortured thinking of both men. Their hypocritical stances in regard to the institution of slavery are too striking to ignore, but looked at in tandem the views of both men shed light on the nature of slavery in Virginia both before and after the Revolution. Mason, a far more bookish plantation owner than Washington, often articulated his ideas about slavery more clearly than did his younger friend. In other respects, Mason's influence on Washington as a young plantation owner are well documented, and several leading historians credit Mason, who usually preferred to work behind the scenes rather than up front as a politician, with helping to "radicalize" his neighbor against the severe policies and encroaching power of Great Britain. In a sense, their demeanors and comportment were quite different, but the same albatross around their neck, slavery, defined them both.

In 1700 only 9 percent of Virginia's population was enslaved, but by the Revolution in 1775, that figure had risen to 40 percent and an estimated 186,000 slaves. As Joseph Ellis states in *Founding Brothers*, despite an internal debate about the value of slavery as an institution, most Virginians did almost nothing in their lifetimes to end the institution. Indeed, after the Revolution, Ellis says, Virginians were "overwhelmingly opposed to relinquishing one iota of control over their own slave population to any federal authority," adding that "[George] Mason's vehement opposition to the slave trade [not slavery] rested cheek to jowl with his demand for a constitutional guarantee to protect what he described as 'the property of that kind which we have already.'" Washington also went out of his way to protect the rights of his fellow slaveholders before and after the Revolution. Both Mason and Washington would eventually oppose the further importation of slaves to Virginia, but only Washington would eventually free his slaves upon his death.

When George married Martha, he had only twenty-two slaves of his own to work the vast five plantations he owned, including the 2,400 acres just at Mount Vernon. With their marriage, he gained the eventual services of some 250 more slaves. Soon he was on his way to cultivating 17,000 acres, but not without the help of enslaved labor, the value of which he measured well. Indeed, his diary entries pay close attention to the health of his slaves, particularly in 1760 when an outbreak of smallpox swept through his Mount Vernon slave quarters. There are hints of genuine sympathy, but the writings can also be interpreted as the thoughts of a cold administrator merely anxious to see that his slaves regain their good health so that they can get back to work and start making him money again. As an example, earlier in the same year, George had carefully calibrated the work output of four slave carpenters, recording and timing how fast they would turn raw wood into planks for use in everything from beams to boats. In his doing this, we witness a calculating taskmaster raising expectations and maintaining efficiency.

Slavery has never been an easy institution to uphold, and the examples of the challenges at Mount Vernon were many. On April 18, 1760, Davy, a trusted slave, returned one of George's runaway slaves, Boson, and was paid ten shillings for doing so. Over the course of George's life, dozens of slaves fled Mount Vernon, some of them escaping either to freedom in cities like Philadelphia or into the ranks of the British Army and farther afield. Washington acquired a man named Henry (also known as Harry Washington) in 1763, but Harry ran away from Mount Vernon before the Revolution and joined the

British Ethiopian Regiment of freed slaves fighting for the British side. After the war, Henry made it to Nova Scotia and eventually left for Sierra Leone, where—somewhat ironically but true to the form of his old master—he helped lead a failed uprising against British rule. Between 1760 and his death, at least forty-seven of the Washingtons' slaves, an estimated 7 percent of the slaves George owned and managed over his lifetime, became fugitives. Almost always, down to the last man and woman, Washington actively sought that his "property" should be returned to him in full form.

Washington maintained cordial relations with many of his slaves, particularly his personal servants, and he rewarded them for hard work, allowing them—at least on several documented occasions—to borrow his nets on their days off to fish on the Potomac River. In 1761, however, he bought a slave master's whip, one of many held for use and for warning on his plantations. "Overseers were not allowed to whip unless the case had been looked into and someone was definitely found guilty of a bad deed," said a historian employed today at Mount Vernon. "We know this stipulation was not always heeded, however."

Though later he would show a preference for black overseers, Washington constantly struggled with disgruntled slaves and he appears to have driven them as hard as he could without purposefully impinging on their health, the measure of an increasingly efficient slave manager. He informed his overseers that they should treat their charges with "humanity and tenderness when Sick" but at the same time should prevent the slaves "from running about and visiting without his consent; as also to forbid strange Negroes frequenting their Quarters without lawful excuses for so doing." In other words, he ran a tight ship, and while he might go hunting foxes or even fishing for days running, he did not tolerate excessive fun in the slave quarters. There is no evidence, despite extensive historical research, suggesting that Washington, like many other Virginia, southern, or Caribbean slave masters, took sexual liberties with his slaves.

To the credit of the Mount Vernon Estate, today they have made George's history of slavery a central focus for millions of annual visitors. A short distance from the carpenter's hut on the waterfront at Mount Vernon is a reproduction of a slave family's cabin, which stood on the grounds of the plantation at Washington's Dogue Run Farm. "The father, 'Slamin' Joe,' was a ditch digger who slept in the slave quarters near the Mansion, returning home for visits on Sundays," according to the estate's historians. They added that "his wife Priscilla (Silla), was a field hand." Slamin' Joe and his wife are believed to have had six children, not unusual for slaves in the era. All of them lived in the one-room cabin I visited, which had a large fireplace but a dirt floor and stiff beds that offered little in the way of shelter. Even with this rather sad and depressing display, however, the more violent aspects of slavery at Mount Vernon remain well hidden from the gaze and contemplation of most modern visitors.

In time, George would improve his efficiency as a slave master. In 1766 he began to lean more on black overseers, putting three of his five plantations in their hands. This suggests that he trusted some black men to serve him and control their brethren. He developed firm and friendly ties to his slaves, particularly to William Lee, his personal valet, whom he first acquired when Lee was a horse jockey and eighteen years old. Lee, who had the rare honor of being able to use a last name, became one of George's most trusted companions, particularly on lengthy foxhunts and in the heat of battle. Another slave, Davy, who had served him well by helping to return runaways, gained special praise for his steady and firm efforts that did not involve excessive shouting.

Unfortunately for George, passing along the burdens of slavery to black men did not end his ongoing problem with runaways. In my walks across the plantation, I noted that the carefully excavated graves of Mount Vernon's slaves faced toward Africa in a symbolic gesture of the slaves' desire in death to return home to their native lands—as Harry Washington had done. In 1766, after capturing a runaway named Tom, George decided it was in his interests to send Tom off to the island of Saint Christopher in the West Indies. Describing him as "exceeding healthy, strong, and good at the Hoe," Tom was, George wrote, a hopeless "Rogue & Runaway." In order to be certain that Tom did not cause trouble onboard or jump overboard, his master suggested to the captain of the ship that he should "keep him handcuffed till you get to sea." In 1771 he would take the same course of action to avert internal strife, sending another slave to Saint-Domingue.

Though he would state his opposition to breaking up slave families, in 1769 in Williamsburg, as one of seven managers of a lottery of fifty-five slaves, Washington bore witness to a major sale—one of several over his lifetime—that did divide slave families. Shortly thereafter, when a debtor owed him money, George urged him to sell his slaves to repay the money, writing that the market was at its best and that he should know that "his Negroes & stock never can be disposed of at a more favourable juncture than in the Fall . . . when they are fat and lusty and must soon fall of[f] unless well fed." He purchased more slaves for his own purposes in 1772, advising the purchaser that they should be "strait Limb'd, & in every respect strong & likely, with good Teeth & good Countenances."

The entire system was cruel beyond what most Americans today can imagine. Argument, even from my own relatives, that George Washington was a compassionate and "good master" ring hollow for me. Washington, to his credit, did not try to persuade anyone in public on such counterintuitive grounds, and on some occasions, he admitted in so many words—and mostly in private writings—that slavery was wrong.

In 1765 George Mason wrote to George Washington about how the institution of slavery was undermining the "morals and manners of our people." Mason said of slavery, "The primary Cause of the Destruction of the most flourishing Government that ever existed was the Introduction of great Numbers of Slaves—an Evil very pathetically described by the Roman Historians." In short, any society that enslaves others has doomed itself to long-term repercussions. Both Washington and Mason knew the evils of slavery, and both men wrestled with their better angels, but neither man relinquished his hold over the lives of others in his lifetime.

George Mason had to deal with a small slave uprising in 1767, two years after he wrote the aforementioned note to George Washington. In this case, some of Mason's slaves conspired to poison their overseers. They were not given a hearing that could be deemed fair in our own age, and for their alleged offenses, four "conspirators" were executed (and then four more subsequently), their heads chopped off and set atop the chimneys of the Fairfax County Court, according to the county's *Annual Register* of 1768. At the same time, Mason sought and received £350 in compensation from the government for his "loss of property."

Washington would have known what happened to Mason's alleged conspirators. "The government was making a statement," said Mount Vernon's Mary Thompson, who is completing an extensively researched book on Washington's slaves, titled *They Work Only from Sun to Sun*. "Other forms of resistance to masters were more common, but this did happen," Mary told me. "People feared uprisings, and this was a way to send a message."

Oddly, Washington may have listened more closely to Mason's advice than Mason did himself. Mason, one of Virginia's best minds of his generation, penned the 1776 Virginia Declaration of Rights, which served as a model for other state declarations as well the French Déclaration des Droits de l'Homme et du Citoyen (Declaration of the Rights of Man and of the Citizen), which was written with the help of the Marquis de Lafayette much later. Yet as early as 1773, Mason had called slavery the "slow Poison, which is daily contaminating the Minds & Morals of our People," adding that in Virginia "every Gentleman is born a petty Tyrant. Practiced in the Acts of Despotism and Cruelty, we become callous to the Dictates of Humanity, and all their finer feelings of the Soul. Taught to regard of our Species in the most abject & contemptible Degree below us, we lose that idea of the Dignity of Man, which the Hand of Nature had implanted in us, for great and useful purposes." The words are a scathing indictment of all slave owners, his neighbors and himself included.

Mason, a more devout Anglican than his younger neighbor George, also worried about the wrath of his own God and what the practice of slavery might bring down on future generations. He continued his 1773 diatribe, "The Laws of Impartial Providence may even by such Means as these, avenge upon our Posterity the Injury done a set of Wretches, whom our injustice hath debased almost to a Level with the Brute Creation." In other words, his message was a cold and cautionary one: the Lord would avenge the sins of the fathers over time.

Apparently aware of Mason's troubles with his slaves, Washington was not nearly as articulate about the moral decay inherent in slavery, but after the Revolution he would write about it as well. Washington and Mason had a falling out after Mason repeated many of the same harsh condemnations of slavery at the Constitutional Convention. Mason added his contention that slavery was bound to "bring the judgment of heaven on a Country," in keeping with an "inevitable chain of causes and effects." He contended that God "punishes national sins, by national calamities." Washington was looking for national consensus between a divided North and South. Yet Mason's insistence on the inevitable fall from grace that all slave owners would one day face was not the likely cause of a complete eventual collapse in their friendship.

George Washington's role as a gentleman, soldier, sportsman, and revolutionary overshadows his role as a slave master within the context of this book. But there are blunt and ugly facts in this personal tale that cannot and should not be ignored. Slavery and the violence it implies are a part of America's shared heritage, and slaves and their labor undeniably helped found the new republic in myriad ways. Without his slaves and the luxury of time they provided to think and act on his own, it is hard to see how George Washington would have become the leader of all men that he became in the Revolution.

I have asked myself, with slavery in mind, whether it is fair to consider George Washington a magnanimous gentleman of impeccable manners. I have settled in my mind that we must all decide this question on our own and leave the contradictions and ambiguity for others to weigh as well. I have no doubt that Washington's role as a slaveholder left his character flawed and scarred in life and even upon his death. The institution of slavery, which he played an instrumental role throughout his life, remained a heavy weight to bear—as we will see—and it dragged him down like a ball and chain in his later years. Indeed, America's greatest president—and I believe that is the correct description until another arises to take his place—was never able to release himself from the mental shackles that slavery held him in.

17

Gentleman Rebel

WHEN I FINALLY RAN into George Washington at the end of Duke of Gloucester Street—better known by Williamsburg's locals as DOG Street—I was pleasantly surprised, though I probably shouldn't have been. My long-awaited formal meeting with George, his handlers promised me, was still a few days off. But I still managed a good taste of his wisdom as he urged his fellow colonists (tourists) to engage in a voluntary boycott of British goods. The episode, as all reimagined historical moments at Williamsburg, had a very specific—and realistic—date in history. George was talking just after the Boston Tea Party, an event he still disapproved of, and the questions he fielded were straightforward enough.

"What are we supposed to drink other than tea?" asked a tourist, whose floppy blue hat was falling over her eyes.

"Tea is a luxury, ma'am!" George replied. "We have been drinking it for only about the last one hundred years. Let me assure you, if I can do without my Madeira, you can do without your tea."

I was reminded that George had once encouraged the Marquis de Chastellux to scare off "la grippe," or influenza, with a proper dose of red wine. The marquis had written, "The General observing it, told me he was sure I had not met with a good glass of wine for some time, an article then very rare, but that my disorder must be frightened away; he made me drink three or four of his silver cups of excellent madeira at noon, and recommended to me that I take a generous glass of claret after dinner, a prescription by no means repugnant to my feelings."

The gentleman performing the role of George Washington rousing the masses to action was no slouch. Ron Carnegie, a professional actor from California, had studied George's character and pastimes

219

not for a few weeks but for two years before assuming his role as the Colonial Williamsburg Foundation's one and only George Washington. He was schooled by one of the greatest ethnohistorians of Virginia history, Rhys Isaac, a beloved foreign scholar who had moved on to the library in the sky only recently. Carnegie knew from his own research of George that his character could be reserved and taciturn but otherwise cordial, cheery, and blessed with that certain gentility of character that I had learned about and enjoyed in all my own research. Ron's attention to detail in everything he said was always on the mark, albeit often with an extra dose of George's famous dry humor to further entertain a twenty-first-century crowd.

Advising his fellow colonists to curtail their tastes for luxuries, George was, on this occasion, rather serious in his tone. It surprised a few in the audience that a Virginia gentleman who had grown up as a law-abiding subject of the Crown had actually disapproved of the Boston Tea Party. He explained his view of that action but quickly condemned the British government's reaction.

"And yet regardless of the crimes that were committed in Boston last September," he contended, gesticulating mildly, "they have replaced a civilian governor. And they have suspended habeas corpus. They will stop at nothing less than the complete destruction of our abilities to maintain those rights and liberties, which we gained through the labors of our forebears."

Alas, another man was worried that purchasing British goods might be akin to treason, to which George replied with a stinging Socratic interjection: "What have I asked you to do, dear sir? Not buy anything! That is not treason, sir. You have the right to determine if you are going to buy things or not—nobody can force you against your will. And I can promise you that the merchants won't send you these goods if you don't buy them." The crowd unleashed a collective guffaw.

George's new incarnation as a revolutionary leader evolved rapidly in the late 1760s and early 1770s. He was ripe for radicalization. After all, his burning ambitions had been stymied on numerous occasions by British authority, both as a military officer and as a land prospector. His immense personal wealth, largely a product of his marriage and sound investments, rendered him self-sufficient, and his self-education made him very much a man of his own free will. His views had emerged in a milieu of new thinking about rights of individual men and the inherent liberties with which their creator had endowed them. Poets and journalists out to take down kings and dictators sharpened their daggers before his eyes, everywhere from the teahouse to the theater. In his late thirties at the time, George was the right man in the right place to seize the historical moment, which he did not without thoughts about the consequences.

Apart from his land acquisition interests, he still had other concerns, including his crops, their value, and the deteriorating health of Patsy, his epileptic stepdaughter, who was experiencing increasingly severe seizures. In his role as a Fairfax representative to the House of Burgesses, George had often deferred to men like Patrick Henry and sometimes George Mason, who spoke with great eloquence. That hadn't prevented him from taking a keen interest in taxation issues, and his close correspondence and friendship with George Mason appears to have set his mind on the road to revolution as early as 1769. In April he wrote to Mason in a cutting tone:

> At a time, when our lordly masters in Great Britain
> will be satisfied with nothing less than the deprivation
> of American freedom, it seems highly necessary that
> something should be done to avert the stroke, and
> maintain the liberty, which we have derived from our
> ancestors. But the manner of doing it, to answer the
> purpose effectually, is the point in question. That no
> man should scruple, or hesitate a moment, to use arms
> in defence of so valuable a blessing, on which all the
> good and evil of life depends, is clearly my opinion.
> Yet arms, I would beg leave to add, should be the last
> resource, the dernier [last] resort.

The letter is a sign that George's patience is running thin and a hint that he is about to unsheathe his sword in the name of honor. It carries an unusual sense of his own thinking—a kind of soliloquy over the question of whether to fight or not to fight. That he sent it to Mason is yet another sure sign of their close confidences. Then on May 18 Washington did something uncharacteristic: he took a proposal, drafted by Mason, to the House of Burgesses and introduced it himself. It called on all Virginians to boycott English-manufactured goods—an immense undertaking in itself that would also include an end to the brutal trade in slaves from Africa and beyond.

Though he began to follow his own prescriptions by making sure his slaves and other workers produced almost everything his family required to live up to his boycott, George's vibrant social life did not reflect any special austerity. Instead, he continued to pursue his love of socializing, foxhunting, and hobnobbing with old-school aristocrats.

When the governor of Virginia, Lord Botetourt, inaugurated a session of the House of Burgesses, His Lordship blazed through Williamsburg in a carriage drawn by cream-white horses. Instead of thumbing his nose at the British peer, George decided to purchase the splendid horses for his own stables. It was proof both of his acquisitive nature and his taste for luxury. It was also apparent that George still favored his special friendships with titled aristocrats sent to oversee Virginia real estate or run the ship of state. In 1771 John Murray, the Fourth Earl of Dunmore, took up the governorship of Virginia, having moved down from New York, where he had held the same post. George became fast friends with the man, a fiery-eyed, redheaded Scotsman, like Dinwiddie. In 1773 George persuaded Dunmore to grant him additional land for his fellow French and Indian War vets on the western frontier, and the two began to hunt together in and around Williamsburg.

In 1774 Dunmore's wife, Charlotte, and six children would sail from Scotland to join him. They settled into a plantation home of their own, Porto Bello, which rested just outside Williamsburg. Upon Charlotte's arrival, George graciously offered up his carriages in case Lady Dunmore desired to use them.

During my stay in Williamsburg, I had heard high praise for the "lovely" Lady Dunmore from several colonial-era impersonators, who informed me about George and Martha's curious friendship with the Scottish couple, whom they were near to in age. "She is one of the most gracious ladies you'll ever meet, and she has a way about her!" a gentleman in a tricornered hat and breeches said of the governor's lady. "When they were at home in London, it was not unusual for the lord and lady to have breakfast with His Majesty," he added. "That is the sort of company they keep—well, along with George and Martha."

George's personal dilemma of whether or not to be a revolutionary is further highlighted in a 1773 trip he took to New York City to enroll his unruly stepson, Jack Custis, in Columbia College. On April 27 he attended an "Entertainment" given by the citizens of the city to honor his old French and Indian War colleague Gen. Thomas Gage, who for much of the last decade had been the senior commander of British forces in North America. Of course, Gage would soon return and become Washington's rival in arms on the front lines, but not just yet. The next day, George joined James De Lancey, the son of the governor of New York, and attended—as did Gage—a showing of *Hamlet* and a new farce called *Cross Purposes* at David Douglass's John Street Theatre in New York.

Through all his engagements, George had managed to transform his thinking. By the autumn, George was fairly committed to an idea of greater independence, bouncing his ideas off George William Fairfax, who had heard the war drums beat often and hard and had already left for Mother England with Sally. In one letter, George worries that hell is about to break loose, but uses an unusual analogy:

> God only knows what is to become of us, threatened as we are with so many hovering evils as hang over us at present, the Indians, between whom and our frontier inhabitants many skirmishes have happened, and with whom a general war is inevitable, while those from whom we have a right to seek protection are endeavoring by every piece of art and despotism to fix the shackles of slavery upon us.

George was all set to free himself from his lord and master, a crime that would be punishable by death on his own plantation. Yet, apart from gambling for higher stakes than usual, little in his robust schedule was altered by the storm clouds overhead. On May 26, 1774, just days after news arrived from Boston that the British would close the harbor until reparations were paid, his diary notes that he rode out to Lord Dunmore's "farm," likely Porto Bello, and "breakfasted with him there." Washington and Dunmore returned to Williamsburg together. Dunmore, facing a political insurgency led by Thomas Jefferson and Richard Henry Lee, and with Patrick Henry calling for a day of "fasting, prayer, and humiliation," angrily dissolved Virginia's House of Burgesses.

George met with the conspirators in the hallowed Apollo Room at Williamsburg's Raleigh Tavern and resolved with them to support the constitutional "liberties of America" against the "oppressive" British Parliament. Still not deterred from his social rounds, he attended a ball given by the House of Burgesses to honor none other than Lady Dunmore, his hunting partner's wife. The colonies were collapsing from Boston to Williamsburg, but the dancing and drinking continued in earnest. Some still saw the coming storm as a difference of opinion among friends, but subtle changes were in play. By June 14 George was throwing an election ball and party with a "Hogshead of Toddy" in Alexandria. The merrymakers, including George, made a point of drinking coffee and hot chocolate, but, of course, no tea, in respect for the Boston Tea Party, which George had condemned for its rash tactics earlier.

Anyone familiar with the British colonial mind-set or even with the island's reaction to the imminent invasion of Germany during World War II will recognize the odd spirit of good sportsmanship that consumed the American colonies on both sides of the debate in the days leading up to war. Manners, a stiff upper lip, and a stiff drink when necessary were part of the general facade of pretended normality. It was important to keep up appearances, smile, and entertain the idea that the world wasn't crumbling around you. George still was part of that world, and he acted the part down to his last hunt breakfast before the war.

On the way to the First Continental Congress in September of the same year, Patrick Henry stopped in to see his friend George Washington at Mount Vernon on August 30. George Mason joined the party the night of its departure for Philadelphia. The following year, 1775, after blood had been shed at the battles of Lexington and Concord, George packed up the French and Indian War uniform Charles Willson Peale had painted him wearing two years earlier. George Washington then mounted a buffed coach with Richard Henry Lee of Stratford Hall. He could not have chosen a more august orator and travel companion. In due time, the tall, erudite Lee would put forth the motion in Philadelphia "that these United Colonies are, and of right ought to be, free and independent States, that they are absolved from all allegiance to the British Crown, and that all political connection between them and the State of Great Britain is, and ought to be, totally dissolved."

Washington and Lee prepared for a hero's welcome. Near Philadelphia, farmers, merchants, and townspeople emerged from their homes to pay their respects to the two men in an English-made carriage, which had recently been repaneled in American wood. Six miles outside the town, five hundred horsemen and scattered fife-and-drum crews and foot soldiers joined their procession as it entered the city. It would be weeks before Washington would actually be all but forced to accept the role of commander in chief, and until that time he attended session in full military uniform, the only delegate who chose to do so—a clear indication of his intentions, if not his ambitions. At night George dined with important figures from across the colonies and often ended his night out with a few drinks and a game of cards at one or another of Philadelphia's many bustling taverns.

He said almost nothing of political note in public. Men who admired his style and grace kept making up very nice things about George Washington. Witness the wildly fabricated praise in John Adams's own diary, which read, "Col. Washington made the most eloquent speech at the Virginia Convention that was ever made. Adams insisted erroneously that George had said, 'I will raise 1,000 Men, Subsist them at My expense, and march myself at their head for the Relief of Boston.'" Adams would add to a friend that Washington was "leaving his delicious retirement, his family and friends, sacrificing his ease, and hazarding all in the cause of his country!" The second point was true, but the first was a bald-faced exaggeration. Adams and others needed a brave and perfect saint, and their imaginations already were fast at work conceiving one. All George had to contribute to keep the rumor mill churning was his mere presence in a uniform.

Later in the year, even before a Virginia regiment fired a shot in anger, George's fellow Americans would start naming their offspring George Washington, applying both his names to their newborns. Like other Americans dreaming of independence, Dr. Solomon Drowne of Rhode Island imagined openly that a great showdown between the colonies and Britain could be won in a single mano a mano duel between none other than George III and George Washington. It was a notion—far-fetched though it was—that would have saved everyone a lot of blood and treasure. It would also have put to good use George's Winchester fencing lessons. Meanwhile, journalist and writer Philip Freneau, who would become a nemesis later in life, wrote George Washington an ode of affection, suggesting that George was soon to be America's knight in shining armor:

> No fop in arms, no feather on his head,
> No glittering toys the manly warrior had,
> His auburne face the least empoly'd his care,
> He left it to the females to be fair.

George had become, almost overnight, a walking, talking, physical specimen of what it meant to be handsome, selfless, and courageous in the new age of revolution. Freneau was also trying to make it clear that Washington was no namby-pamby aristocrat.

Such adulation, of course, had everything to do with the old-school image of a soldier and sportsman that Washington had cultivated so carefully through his teens, twenties, and thirties. If an eighteenth-century portrait painter had sought a model with the right look, and one painted with ease to impress people, he or she would have been hard-pressed to find a better model than George on the cusp of the Revolution. He knew this, of course, which was precisely why he had sported his uniform. Even the light pockmarks on his face from his bout of smallpox in Barbados helped him fit the mold of a rough and rugged American hero. George's future sculptor William Rush would gush of his stature and carriage: "I have viewed him walking, standing, sitting, and have seen him in a game of ball for several hours, [and he possesses] the most manly and graceful attitudes I ever saw."

All that said, George hadn't lost his good humor, even after the death of his dear stepdaughter Patsy a year earlier. When his friend Joseph Reed sent a rather bad portrait of George from an anonymous English printmaker who signed his name as "Alexander Campbell," George was more than amused. The rudimentary portrait had him perched on a horse rearing up on its hind legs. But there was something acutely wrong with the picture, to his mind. Washington, though fully in charge of his steed, looked scornful, not his usual cool and reserved self in the least. Even Martha took notice. George wrote back to Joseph, "Mrs. Washington desires I will thank you for the Picture sent her. Mr. Campbell whom I never saw (to my knowledge) has made a very formidable figure of the Commander in Chief giving him a sufficient portion of Terror in his Countenance." The new American hero could not be seen looking mean, yet George did have something brutal on his mind late in 1775. He was ready to kill his old foxhunting friend Lord Dunmore. He would write to Richard Henry Lee in December that taking Lord Dunmore prisoner wasn't enough:

> Lord *Dunmore's* letters to General *Howe*, which very fortunately fell into my hands, and were enclosed by me to Congress, will let you pretty fully into his diabolical schemes. If, my dear sir, that man is not crushed before Spring, he will become the most formidable

enemy *America* has. His strength will increase as a snow-ball, by rolling, and faster, if some expedient cannot be hit upon to convince the slaves and servants of the impotency of his designs. . . . I do not think that forcing his Lordship on ship-board is sufficient. Nothing less than depriving him of life or liberty will secure peace to *Virginia*, as motives of resentment actuate his conduct to a degree equal to the total destruction of the Colony.

Even as the future general appeared on the surface to be as calm as the eye of a storm, deep down George was fully prepared to kill the governor to achieve his revolutionary designs.

18

Bowling with George

AFTER SPENDING A FEW WEEKS in Williamsburg researching George's hoofprints and carriage tracks, I was still hanging out in the Virginia lowlands, waiting for a formal interview with the future first president in the form of his character-interpreter, Ron Carnegie. Though I'd listened to him rally the citizens to boycott British goods, I wasn't at all sure if he would be able to fit me into his busy schedule. After all, he had to mount a horse almost every day and review the troops, in addition to kissing small babies, petting dogs, and rallying support to oppose British tyranny. That was a lot of work for any historical figure.

It wasn't until I heard from Martha that George was an avid lawn bowler that I came up with a reasonable plan of attack. I wasn't going to trouble George to lend me a steed in order that I might ride alongside him. But if he didn't mind, I wrote, did he think he might be able to make an appointment for lawn bowling? Martha informed me kindly, with an instant message, that I was to meet her husband in the flesh on Duke of Gloucester (DOG) Street at precisely 3:30 PM on a Wednesday. I arrived at the appointed time, still believing my chances of meeting the great man were slim.

Then from behind a tree, striding toward me on foot, George Washington emerged in his patriotic splendor. He wore a neatly tailored blue uniform and knee-length breeches with gold lapels and epaulets. His hair was tied back in a bow, and he smiled, but only lightly, possibly to disguise his bad teeth. He appeared in a fine spirit.

It wasn't my first big interview, but I did have a few butterflies. I once interviewed the Dalai Lama in a very small town in Russia, and he had put me at ease almost immediately by hailing me from about a hundred feet away after stepping out of a black limousine. This meeting was quite different, and though I had prepared my questions in advance without showing them to Washington, there was an added anticipation on my part since I'd researched my book for nearly five years and still had several key questions about moments in George's life that *only he*—a scholarly impersonator—could shed light on.

"If you don't mind, Mr. Washington, we can make our way down DOG Street to the Williamsburg Inn and the bowling green around back," I suggested. "I thought we might take a cup of tea first and chat."

"Not at all, good sir."

Though I was almost certain George would refuse to answer a few controversial questions, I was determined to press him on several points. I knew that actor Ron Carnegie had studied George's life, played his part for over a decade, and acquired his manners and habits of speaking. As we crossed DOG Street toward the inn, a young lady curtsied. George politely doffed his hat and bid her a pleasant day. I felt awkward shadowing the man I was writing a book about; the waves and handshakes all made me feel, soon enough, like just another of his many admirers.

It was a lovely day to hit the bowling green, and in the distance we spotted several older couples enjoying a lively bowl. We arranged to play following our tea. What I would hear over the next two hours would enthrall me and in some cases surprise me. What didn't shock me, however, was that George was a consummate gentleman throughout, with impeccable manners. And while sometimes reluctant to discuss personal matters, he opened up to me and revealed his personality, which of course helped me to further understand the genuine eighteenth-century George.

Our table was wrought iron on a red brick patio that faced the green in the distance. Carefully, I attached a microphone to George's lapel. I did not want to misquote him. I cleared my throat and began with a few queries about his youth, his education, and his under-reported teen years when he was still in the sway of his mother, his brother Lawrence, and the entire Fairfax clan.

"Can you tell me a bit about how the Fairfax family helped to make you the man you are today?"

"Well, it is worth a mention, sir, that I have suffered a deficiency of education from my early years. It had been my father's hope that like my elder brothers, and like himself, that I would be educated at the Appleby School, but my father passed when I was eleven and those opportunities were denied me. I owe a great deal to my relations with the Fairfaxes, with George William, the colonel, and Lord Fairfax. They were my patrons in my youth—when I was in need of patrons. They provided me a start in life, some education, particularly a social education. They also opened important doors for various connections that were necessary later in my life."

"I believe they may also have encouraged you in the reading of the classics—Alexander the Great, and Caesar's campaigns?"

"Yes, and Tacitus [the Roman senator and historian] and others. I've always endeavored to guide myself by the principles put forth by Seneca—a philosopher, not a soldier—and also the author of our faith."

I thought of George's conception of Providence but worried about going too far with any probes into his faith, which I knew he cherished as a private matter. I thought to stick to more pragmatic issues and I wasn't disappointed by a lack of interest: "What was it about your surveying career that prepared you for soldiering?"

"The main advantages of being a surveyor did not apply directly to my military service, though some of the skills I acquired certainly did. Surveying gave me some familiarity with distance, for example. One gets a good eye for the land. But the real advantage that I gained through surveying is that I gained land. I have come to think of land as the only true form of wealth."

I also had a few lingering questions about the French and Indian War, questions that even the most accomplished historians in America often had failed to shed much light on.

"During your return journey from Fort Le Boeuf, an altercation took place with your native guild—can you explain your version of the incident?"

"Yes. It was an attempt to assassinate me."

At that moment, our waiter, dressed in a tie and jacket, arrived and we both ordered. I offered George a glass of wine, thinking it might loosen his tongue, but he politely refused.

"And what of the untimely death of the Frenchman de Jumonville in your first battle?"

"I was overly suspicious of the French party because they were skulking in the woods, sir. They were clearly endeavoring some attack upon us, so we turned the tables on them. We took the advantage of surprise away from them and attacked them before they could begin such a thing. A soldier never forgets any encounter he is engaged in, sir. No, Jumonville fell in combat, sir. Naturally, there was some difficulty in controlling the Indians. But I will remind you that—perhaps not what you have heard or read, sir—over half of the men that we were engaged with at Jumonville were made prisoners. They were brought here to Williamsburg and held in the jail here. They were not all slaughtered. There was some claim made by France and by Jumonville's brother later that they were engaged in a diplomatic mission, which is pure chicanery."

I nodded and thanked him for clarifying.

"To what, Colonel Washington, do you ascribe your ability to dodge bullets successfully, particularly at Braddock's awful defeat along the Monongahela?"

"Certainly it was Providence, sir. I wouldn't be here if it were not for the generous interposition of Providence. At that battle, as I recall, two horses were shot out from under me, sir, so there was something more than luck involved."

I wanted to know more about how Colonel Washington had managed to control his horses in the same battle. "Can a good horse be controlled under intense fire?"

"It depends entirely on the horse. A proper horse is trained for warfare. At that time, I didn't have any choice in the matter you are speaking of. I was making use of any horse I could find. I wasn't in the line of command, sir, at Monongahela. But I was there when Braddock fell—I was there when he died."

"Have you had any regrets about that war?"

"Nobody prays as much for peace as those of us who have seen war, sir. Of course, looking back, I had no idea what direction my life would take. In my youth, like many men, I had hoped that I would do so in combat and in glory—in fact, originally as a sailor—as I wanted to join the Royal Navy. My experiences in that late war led me to believe that, if I had a future at all, it was not under arms. So shortly following the war, I looked to other matters and I engaged myself more deeply in the governing of Virginia and I gave more consideration to what a man should be."

I noticed that up to this point in history, which was the late 1760s, still well in advance of the Revolution, George did not let on that he was concerned about any future conflicts. Earlier I'd noticed some wrestling and cudgeling in the streets of Williamsburg, but there had been no sign of an imminent revolution. It probably wasn't worth asking him to look into his crystal ball and prognosticate. I did, however, have some questions regarding his code for living—his "code of honor," so to speak.

"By what advice do you guide your good behavior, sir?" I asked.

"I gained from Seneca and the author of our faith some ideas about how a man should respond in public life, and I have endeavored ever since—to the best of my ability to meet that—to curb my irregular passions and desires and to guide myself instead by reason and conscience. I am still, like all of us, you included, a mortal, and there are occasions when my natural weakness prevails and I lose the reigns of my behavior, but I have to keep it curbed, and so I try."

Since George had begun to relax, sitting back in his chair as the sun slipped back over the pine and oak trees, I ventured a couple of rather sensitive questions that I knew he might well balk at.

"Dear sir, it is said that you have a certain way with the ladies. Would you say that is correct? And would you mind, for the sake of history, expounding a bit on what Sally Fairfax really meant to you?"

I noticed, even as I spoke, that the question wasn't going over well, and, frankly, I wasn't surprised when George parried my question abruptly.

"Sally was the wife of a dear friend, sir."

With that, George gave me a stare that nearly sent me ducking beneath the wrought iron for cover. He grit his teeth, or what was left of them, and looked at me like I was a rotting log.

"But she had a role, in her own way, of teaching you etiquette and some dance steps, no?"

"In fact, I learned to dance while I was still in Fredericksburg, sir, well before I was living at Mount Vernon. Dancing is a love of all Virginians, and if they are of true blood, they will dance or die. But it is more than just that. Dancing shows a man's education, his breeding. It shows he is a gentleman, and of course it helps when one is courting. It didn't help me as much as I would have preferred. In your question you suggested that I might have some great ability with women. I certainly do not, sir. In my youth I had very little success in that, but in the end I did with my dear wife, Martha."

"And what of your love of the hunt—foxhunting in particular?"

"The point of hunting the fox isn't so much to get the fox; it is the riding. The fox determines the route the horsemen will take.

And of course the best riders are the ones who can keep up with the hounds and are there when the mask is taken. I don't usually tend to my fields without the attendance of my foxhounds. And if a fox should foolishly make itself known, well, I'm engaged in this ride on this property for work, but if a fox makes itself known, we will chase that fox."

"Sounds a bit dangerous."

This comment elicited a chuckle from George.

"Even if you are good, it can be dangerous, sir. Good horsemen do die."

Next, without my prompting, George cut to the chase, so to speak, and began to reminisce about his rides to and from Williamsburg. "When I used to come here in the halcyon days of old, I would ride here to Williamsburg in two days' time," he said, sitting forward. "It is 150 miles as the crow flies from Mount Vernon. My wife certainly wouldn't ride the distance, and even if she did, it would not be in two days' time. I enjoy riding, and I enjoy riding quickly, sir. I always have. Perhaps that is a vice, sir, and perhaps that is one that should be curbed."

As I had suspected, George was something of a speed freak. I wanted to offer him a ride in my sports car but worried he might object on the grounds that it was an import. Next, I listed the sports I thought George had engaged in and enjoyed as a young man. I left a couple out, as he pointed out.

"Don't forget that one of my greatest enjoyments in my youth was throwing weights for distance, sir."

"You mean like the old Scottish Highlands sport?"

"I would argue it was a Greek sport long before it made its way to Scotland."

The sun was dipping behind my shoulder, and we still had an appointment on the bowling green. I confessed to George that I'd only played the equivalent French sport, which was a little embarrassing to admit. I recalled, however, that it was at nearby Jamestown, where the British governor tried rather unsuccessfully to ban lawn bowling in the 1600s. George then recounted the tale of Sir Francis Drake staving off his lieutenants to finish an exciting round of bowling even as the Spanish Armada appeared on the horizon. I felt lucky to learn from my sources at Mount Vernon that a final inventory of George's estate upon his death had revealed a pair of wooden bowling balls stashed away in a storehouse. Clearly the general or his guests had used them on the bowling green he had set up on his manicured lawn in 1785.

George was a long-standing member of the Williamsburg Lawn Bowling Club. He was something of an expert, familiar with other versions of the game, such as the French and the Spanish varieties, and he insisted on showing me the difference. He walked over to an amused set of British bowlers, and I asked them if they wouldn't mind letting him show me the bowling ball.

"Can I hold one?" He turned to me, holding out the lopsided painted ball. "One of the things that is different about the English game than most of the others is that the ball is not a sphere, you see. I don't know if you can see that. See how it is flatter on this side? And because of that, it doesn't roll straight; it must be curved in for a good score."

"Can you roll one? Do you mind?"

"The question would be if *they* mind, because it is not my bowling match and I'm not wearing the right shoes."

As I expected, George was being excessively polite—even humble—in public. In the process, he was managing to amuse all of us. "Do you see that little ball at the end?"

"Yes."

He rolled and placed the "jack," as he referred to it, just next to the smaller target ball.

"See how it curved in? The grass has a grain to it. The speed will change with the moisture and the temperature, which is hard to believe until you see it happen."

We were getting down to some real minutiae, I noticed. He apologized again to the other players for interrupting their game, so I explained that I was bothering them on their green because I was writing a book about George the sportsman.

George rolled again.

"That's a little too narrow and not fast enough," he said, narrowing his gaze. "See, now I have to get around the other one. Still a little wide. You were asking about the goal. It works kind of like horseshoes. The goal is to be closest to the jack."

"I remember when I was in France—they played a similar game on the dirt," I said.

"Did they roll or did they throw?"

"Tossed it."

"Yes. That is what they do. They toss it—and it is on dirt. Now you see, she has points"—he gestured toward the kind lady, who had managed a very good roll. "What they want to do is either come in closer, or they could knock the jack out and knock it closer to the other. So there are different tactics involved."

I noticed George was being treated like an honored guest, and he couldn't stop explaining tactics to me. I suddenly wished I had been with him on a battlefield.

"Either way," he added, providing me a play-by-play, "he at least took a point away from her because you get a point for every ball you have closer to the jack. So, you see, she had two!"

We bid our adieus and headed back against the sunset toward our original table. I was feeling wistful about our imminent departure and I asked if someday we might go fishing together. He said it would be his great pleasure and explained how he had tried, to little avail, to get Alexander Hamilton and Thomas Jefferson to stop feuding by taking them on a fishing trip.

"The fish weren't biting, and they wouldn't take my bait," said George.

"At least you gave it a try," I said.

When we finally parted ways back near DOG Street, I was left with a very fine impression of George. He was, as the poet and biographer David Humphreys once remarked, a serious and kind man who "perfectly relishes a pleasant story."

I asked for his phone number, but he appeared not to understand my question.

IV

Clever Like a Fox

Washington at the Battle of Princeton, after Chappel, published by Johnson, Fry & Co., 1857. *Courtesy of Mount Vernon Ladies' Association*

19

The World Is His Stage

FROM THE RED BRICK WHARF at Cobble Hill on most afternoons, the whitecaps churn up and around the green hues of the Statue of Liberty, and the sun dips in the west without a hint that Brooklyn, New York, was the scene of slaughter and flight at Gen. George Washington's first major battle of the Revolution.

Backed with man-of-war gunships from of the world's most powerful navy, British forces had landed on Long Island weeks earlier before cornering and nearly annihilating a contingent of Marylanders under Washington's control at Cobble Hill. Farther north, some ten thousand redcoats slipped through the loosely defended Jamaica Pass and tightened the noose around tens of thousands of Continental Army fighters. Then something strange and unpredicted happened. It wouldn't be the first or the last time in the Revolution that the stars and the weather aligned: on August 30 and 31 heavy rains let up, generating an intense fog that enveloped most of Brooklyn and Manhattan, including the positions of the Continental Army.

With the British Army digging trenches and preparing to take the main body of his fledgling army, General Washington ordered troops to light campfires that evening to confuse British commanders into thinking they intended to stay and fight. Meanwhile, hundreds of seasoned cod fishermen in knit voyager caps from the Boston area commandeered every available flatboat, fishing vessel, and rowboat to begin evacuating nine thousand Continental soldiers along with all their guns. The evacuation took place near to the watermarks of today's Brooklyn Bridge. Pacing up and down the shoreline, George anticipated an attack. None came; his campfire ruse had worked. In the dead of night, he dismounted and stepped onto the last boat headed over to Manhattan Island.

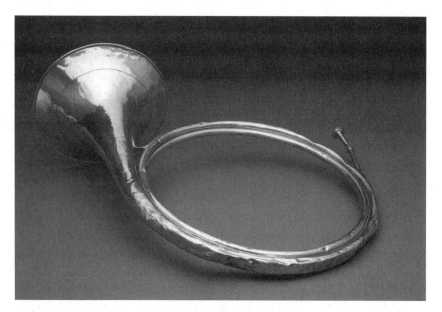

George Washington's hunting horn, George Henry Rodenbostel, c. 1764–1789 [W-81]. *Courtesy of Mount Vernon Ladies' Association*

What looked on the surface like a defeat in Brooklyn was the first of several clever maneuvers that would preserve the Continental Army to fight another day over the course of the next two years. Over and over again, Washington would manage to hold his army together when military experts and even his own soldiers believed it was collapsing. He made his name as field commander and escape artist.

As General Washington struggled to build his character in the French and Indian War, his new revolutionary task would be to cobble together the character of an entire army, one that could stand toe to toe with the British in its last and decisive battle. Throughout the new war, George's confidence in his own army would waver, often sending him reeling into depression. He still could not fathom the idea of defeat, since in his mind, the Continental Army became an extension of his own character, and when it failed, he felt that he had somehow failed as well.

In the summer of 1775 General Washington mounted his horse near Boston and conducted the first military review of his new army.

What he saw was strikingly familiar in appearance, albeit on a much larger scale, to the fighting forces he had assembled years earlier from indentured servants and ex-prisoners in Alexandria and Winchester. Soldiers carried arms of varied function and performance, everything from fowling guns to pistols. Some men were shoeless or nearly naked, but these men had a cause and a will to fight that surpassed anything he had ever known or seen in that earlier war. At the Battle of Bunker Hill in June 1775, just before Washington's arrival, the colonial militia inflicted two times the casualties, a total of 226, than they suffered in return as the British charged up the hill at them. Though the colonials would retreat, in many cases literally losing their shoes, they had proven their mettle, and that was something George now could hang his hat on.

As he took charge, however, he was not overly encouraged. He remarked of his own officers' corps that they weren't "worth the bread they eat." Yet he also understood that he had the core of a great army in the making. He described the ragtag force of some 14,500 men as "able bodied, active, zealous in the cause and of unquestionable courage." Almost immediately, he projected onto this force, which had already proven itself at Lexington and Concord before his arrival, the same qualities he had admired in the brave Virginians who had fought alongside the British and perished at his side when Crown warriors had run for cover at Monongahela. Many of George's colonials were also expert marksmen, often better than their foes.

Washington's longtime friend Richard Henry Lee from Westmoreland County described the Continentals as frontiersmen and hunters, men with "amazing hardihood" grounded in "their method of living so long in the woods without carrying provisions with them, the exceeding quickness with which they can march to distant parts and above all, the dexterity to which they have arrived in the use of the rifle gun. There is not one of these men who wish a distance less than 200 yards or a larger object than an orange—Every shot is fatal." They were, indeed, highly skilled woodsmen and sportsmen, if also sometimes suffering from severe character flaws. Their fortitude from exertion was beyond reproach, thus giving the entire force several traits shared by their new leader.

Washington set himself up in relative style in July in Cambridge, Massachusetts, at a home recently abandoned by departed Loyalist John Vassall. The general carried with him several leading members of his Mount Vernon staff, including a clothes tailor, Giles Alexander, and his ever-loyal foxhunting companion and personal valet, William Lee. On December 11 Martha arrived with her adolescent son, Jack, and the wife of Gen. Horatio Gates. Frequent visitors to the Vassall house would include George's admirer John Adams, his young wife, Abigail, and the ornery Gen. Benedict Arnold. The new leadership did not suffer from bad rations; records show that guests helped the Washingtons consume large quantities of beef, lamb, wild fowl, barrels of cider, rum, and 217 bottles of Madeira wine.

As he glanced out his window onto the Charles River and rode out to observe British forces in control of Boston, George reminded himself that it was his duty to stand as a symbol of calm resolution amid the wildfires of revolt. He even wished away his own fiery disposition, writing, "My temper leads me to peace and harmony with all Men; and it is peculiarly my wish, to avoid any personal feuds with those, who are embarked in the same great National interest with myself." He knew he would need all his patience to survive the war.

Throughout the Revolution, Washington exhibited manners and behavior that endeared him to his fellow officers, and also to women, who in the eighteenth century were the true arbiters of good etiquette. Mercy Otis Warren, a prominent author and social critic, astutely contrasted George with one of his early competitors for the position of commander in chief, British-born Charles Lee. Her observations are especially instructive. Lee was a mercurial commander who had served with Washington in the French and Indian War and eventually married the daughter of a Mohawk Indian chief. He was proficient in Latin, Greek, and French, but despite his extensive education, he was often rude to those around him. Upon meeting both Washington and Lee near Cambridge, Warren wrote, "The first of these [George] I think one of the most amiable and accomplished gentlemen, both in person, mind and manners that I have ever met with. The second, whom I never saw before, I think plain in his person to a degree of ugliness, careless even to unpoliteness—his garb ordinary, his voice rough, his manners rather morose; yet sensible, learned, judicious, and penetrating." In other words, Lee might have been held in greater esteem had he only maintained a more pleasant set of manners. For George, good etiquette was a given.

When he assumed his new incarnation, General Washington's habits and lifestyle as a wealthy planter and sportsman were fast turned upside down. Just as he would have to give up or curtail his favorite pastimes, the rest of the nation braced itself for a similarly broad regimen of austerity. Delegates at the Continental Congress vowed to "discourage every species of extravagance and dissipation, especially all horse-racing, and all kinds of gaming, cock-fighting, exhibitions of shows, plays, and other expensive diversions and entertainments." In short, war meant that testy Mayflower Puritans, who had never vanished from the scene, could weigh in again on America's emerging moral texture. However, their influence would never entirely damp down the rowdy and lusty behavior of the Continental Army, which was at least now governed by a firm hand.

Though he would allow ball playing and encourage his fellow officers to enjoy the occasional theater performance during the long war ahead, George was for the most part on board with the restraints on recreation. He asked his officers' corps to "be strict in your discipline" and to "discourage vice in every shape, and impress upon the mind of every man, from the first to the lowest, the importance of the cause, and what they are contending for."

The new commander in chief sought to build a new corps of officers, drawing to his side eccentric individuals accomplished outside the martial realm. Senior military appointments were at the discretion of the Continental Congress, but Washington was given leeway to assemble a team of brilliant and savvy counselors at his side. The choices of Henry Knox, Joseph Reed, and Nathanael Greene stand out.

Knox, the three-hundred-pound artillery commander whose father died when he was twelve, had owned and operated a bookstore in Boston before the war and had taught himself military strategy by reading in his spare time. Washington was doing the same throughout the struggle. At the same time, Knox was no bookish character: he had scrapped in fisticuffs with rivals as a member of a Boston street gang.

Nathanael Greene, born into an austere Quaker family, served in the Rhode Island General Assembly. Unable to march with his men due to a bad leg, he also immersed himself from a young age in military tactics, and would become one of George's closest friends and best generals.

Washington also convinced Joseph Reed, a lawyer and delegate to the Continental Congress, to join him as close aide. By 1763 Reed had studied law for two years in London and married the British daughter of the most senior official in Massachusetts Bay. He would be one of the first to notice that Benedict Arnold, as an assigned commander in Philadelphia, was corrupt to the bone. It did not matter to George that Reed knew very little about soldiering; he valued Reed mostly for his political savvy and social skills.

General Washington and his officers' corps recognized early on that winning wasn't all about shots fired, dead redcoats, and the number of prisoners taken. On October 26, 1775, a recently emancipated black poet, Phillis Wheatley, who had been adopted by a white family and sent to England to show off her writing talents, wrote to George with a poem praising his virtues and martial talents. She was an accomplished author, and George would have ignored her at his own peril. His former foxhunting associate John Murray, Fourth Earl of Dunmore and Britain's acting governor in Virginia, already had offered in writing emancipation for Virginia's African slaves who would be willing to side with the British as the Revolution took hold. Washington forwarded the poem to Joseph Reed in Philadelphia along with a suggestion that it was simply too flattering for him to deal with, indicating that he was leaving the poem in Reed's hands to dispose of. Reed forwarded the poem to the *Virginia Gazette*, which published the poem praising Washington in the following fashion:

> Proceed, great chief, with virtue on thy side,
> Thy ev'ry action let the goddess guide.
> A crown, a mansion, and a throne that shine,
> With gold unfading, WASHINGTON! Be thine.

In her optimism, Wheatley, who had developed friendships with Native American Christian leaders in her youth, also praised the new nation in the making as "The Land of freedom's heaven-defended race!" In addition to the Virginia paper, her poem also soon appeared in the *Pennsylvania Magazine*. Like other minorities, Wheatley had hopes of a broader freedom for her kin, which she hoped could be delivered through revolution. But the poem, once published, became a publicity coup for wealthy white slave owners in Virginia, who worried intensely about their slaves running off to fight with the British if a full-blown war broke out. Publishing the poem in the *Virginia Gazette* helped in part to keep the lower castes, both blacks and whites, in their place and also to rally them to the patriotic cause. At the same time, it partially undercut Lord Dunmore's promises to liberate blacks, who fought with the British, since it suggested that at least some blacks did not support the Loyalist cause. Washington, ever the eloquent correspondent, wrote to Wheatley and offered her a meeting: "If you should ever come to Cambridge, I shall be happy to see a person so favored by the muses." Historians believe they met, though the content of their discussion, possibly laced with controversy either on the surface or beneath, was either not recorded or the account was lost to posterity.

From Cambridge, Washington intensified the Siege of Boston, his first significant move in a martial chess game that for the Continental Army rewarded patience and punished haste. His first face-off—thanks to Knox's engineering feat of successfully hauling heavy guns over the mountains from Fort Ticonderoga—would prove to be an exceptionally bloodless engagement considering the scale of forces in play. In early March, the Continental Army fortified Dorchester Heights above the Boston Harbor, creating an indefensible fait accompli. Faced with a barrage of cannonballs raining down on his entrenched positions, Gen. William Howe accepted Washington's offer to evacuate over one thousand troops from Boston on the condition that British forces did not set fire to the city.

Victory assured in Boston, George turned yet again to his younger brother Jack in order to express his satisfaction at what it meant to his stature in the eyes of his fellow countrymen:

> I believe I may with great truth affirm that no man perhaps since the first institution of armies ever commanded one under more difficult circumstances, than I have done. To enumerate the particulars would fill a volume. . . . I am happy, however, to find and to hear from different quarters that my reputation stands fair, that my conduct hitherto has given universal satisfaction. The addresses which I have received, and which I suppose will be published, from the General Court of the Colony—the same as our General Assembly—and from the selectmen of Boston upon the evacuation of the town and my approaching departure from the Colony, exhibits a pleasing testimony of their approbation of my conduct and of their personal regard, which I have found in various other instances, and which, in retirement, will afford many comfortable reflections.

These words display the hyperbolic outlines of George's earlier boasts to Jack during the French and Indian War, but are slightly tempered by age and reason. There is some modesty, but the letter is laced also with a vanity that is easy to miss if you just buy entirely into the myth of General Washington's selfless leadership. Most of what Washington did in this era, as during his earlier war, was aimed at winning "universal satisfaction" and "approbation." This letter to Jack is telling, and it also marks a mountaintop that George would tumble from in the months ahead. It was written at a heady moment in the Revolution. Without fighting a pitched battle, George had already emerged as the shining star of the coming struggle for a still-to-be-declared independence. Jack, as he had done during the earlier war, remained a sounding board for his older brother's love of honor and duty. Events had changed the dynamic somewhat, and this time George was fighting for new ideals different from those that had fueled his ambitions in the French and Indian conflict.

Asked to send along congressional thanks to his troops, George wrote to Philadelphia that he was fighting to selflessly win his "American brethren a restitution of their just rights and privileges," adding with a note of ancient chivalry, "I shall constantly bear in mind that, as the sword was the last resort for the preservation of our liberties, so it ought to be the first to be laid aside when those liberties are firmly established."

General Washington took his role as an evenhanded peacemaker seriously. Clenching his teeth in public and attempting to maintain an outer cool, George, now in his midforties, inserted himself into fights between his own troops when he thought it would help calm the fray. In one instance, the infighting began when members of an unruly southern rifle regiment had squared off with New Englanders. Reportedly, northerners were taunting the southerners for being slave owners. In a brawl that spread through the ranks like a wildfire, scores of Continental soldiers punched one another and shouted obscenities.

A Massachusetts soldier, Israel Trask, recorded Washington's quick reaction. In his eyewitness account, Washington appeared alongside his turbaned servant, William Lee, before charging into the fray on horseback. In a rare look at George's physical strength, Trask wrote that the general, "with the spring of a deer . . . leaped from his saddle, threw the reins of his bridle into the hands of his servant, and rushed into the thickest of the melees, with an iron grip seized two tall, brawny, athletic, savage-looking riflemen by the throat, keeping them at arm's length, alternately shaking and talking to them." The commander in chief's manhandling of the two soldiers stopped the brawl as others dropped their own scuffling to gawk at Washington's feat. Trask concluded that through this one act, the "hostile feelings between two of the best regiments" were "extinguished by one man." George had always been quick to avoid fights, but he wasn't deterred from exhibiting his strength in a show of force, which also enhanced his role as a peacemaker. Though his intervention involved some violence, it also set a pacifying example for his men to live by.

The uncertainty of trying to keep his men in line, fight a war on several fronts, including in Canada, and deal with his own fear of failure still elicited private moans. As he prepared to defend New York with a Continental Army that was undermanned, undisciplined, and threatening to disband, he wrote again to Jack: "I am wearied almost to death with the retrograde motions of things, and I solemnly protest that a pecuniary record of [£]20,000 a year would not induce me to undergo what I do; and, after all, perhaps, to lose my character." Again, we hear echoes of an earlier war, but these words were private ramblings only.

Tougher days lay ahead. Thomas Paine would write that Washington's true character emerged in "difficulties and in action." Disappointed with losses in Boston, the British tried to double down with the might of their army and navy. This time, to seize New York, King George dispatched both viscount Adm. Richard Howe and his brother Gen. William Howe to launch what would be the largest British seaborne assault until the twentieth century. Nearly thirty thousand fighting men were destined for New York, arriving just in time to learn of news that the Declaration of Independence had been signed in July in Philadelphia.

George had parted with Martha and arrived in New York amid fresh reports of behavior that was fast pushing civilians into the Loyalist ranks. On Manhattan, soldiers were drinking heavily and frequenting whorehouses, giving rise to court cases involving public drunkenness. Though Washington knew his forces were still not prepared to defend New York, he agreed that, for the sake of the struggle and as a matter of honor, the Continentals needed to make a stand and act with courage in the face of the predicted British onslaught.

On July 12 two British ships sailed up the Hudson, firing their cannons in a classic show of force. George, who bore witness, described the moment in this way: "When the Men of War passed up the River the Shrieks & Cries of these poor creatures running every way with their Children was truly distressing." The Howe brothers hoped their power play would force Washington to rethink the idea of American independence. Out of earshot, Admiral Howe referred to George and his forces as "rascally banditti." When an envoy requesting negotiations arrived in a small boat with a letter addressed to "George Washington, Esqr. New York," Joseph Reed turned him back briskly, remarking, "We have no person in our army with that address."

After repeated rebuffs, Howe's secretary, Ambrose Serle, remarked in his journal on the "vanity and insolence" of George and the Continentals. After more ham-handed British diplomacy, Washington agreed to meet British colonel James Patterson for a brief parley. When Patterson placed before him a tweaked letter addressed this time to "George Washington, Esq., etc., etc." Washington asked what precisely that meant, and Patterson replied, according to Henry Knox, that the etceteras meant, well, "everything."

Visibly irate, George shot back, "It does so—and anything?" He added that while he understood Howe had come with powers to pardon, the admiral had come to the wrong place, because Americans needed no pardoning.

Finally, Colonel Patterson asked, "Has your Excellency no particular commands with which you would please to honor me to Lord [Admiral] Howe and General Howe?"

"Nothing, sir, but my particular compliments to both," replied General Washington with his classic—this time ironic—politesse.

The encounter is archetypal George Washington in several ways. In the French and Indian War, when he was upset with Lieutenant Governor Dinwiddie, he would write long-winded replies to his British superior, declaring how offended he was. The more mature Washington, however, was a man of sparing words, solid protocol, and gentlemanly conduct. Henry Knox wrote to his wife that at this meeting, General Washington had looked particularly dapper, saying he was "very handsomely dressed and made the most elegant appearance," adding that Colonel Patterson looked shocked, as though before "something supernatural." Appearances mattered as much as or more than words, as George had learned long before the Revolution.

Gen. George Washington was finally standing up to the rulers who had denied him a commission in the British military. In the years since, he had become their nemesis as well as their peer in the field, and he took time to relish it—at least for a minute or two. Just as he would when he would send General Howe's lost dog back across the front lines, George was striking at his foe with his special savoir faire and a gesture of defiance to inspire his men. In one stroke, he had turned the British petition for surrender into a show of esprit de corps that would add a fresh layer of gloss to his personal legend.

When General Washington and almost his entire army slipped away at Brooklyn Heights and traveled by boat into Manhattan, the Howe brothers were kicking themselves for waiting him out despite their numerical advantage of nearly two to one.

George's subsequent retreat through Manhattan was ugly but did not allow the British to corner his forces as they had in Brooklyn. Knowing he would not be able to defend himself for long from a force with superior naval power, he urged his men, most of whom were on foot, to head north through what is today Central Park. It was a rocky terrain camouflaged in green trees as far as the eye could see. When British forces landed to the northeast at Kip's Bay, General Washington rode forward to hold the line. When his forces broke and ran, he was left astride his horse, looking dumbfounded. He turned and followed in another moment of disgrace, but not in total defeat.

All was not lost. Joseph Reed appeared to inform General Washington that the Continentals had made a brave stand at Harlem Heights but were now considering retreat. Could he send reinforcements? Even as Washington considered his next move, British forces appeared, a bugle blasting. They played a foxhunting call known as "Gone Away," normally invoked when a fox has been killed or gone to ground. It is meant to call hounds and foxhunters off the hunt. In this case, it was meant to taunt the embattled Continentals. One young American officer stated that he had "never felt such a sensation before, it seem'd to crown our Disgrace."

Bridling at the ridicule, Washington ordered parts of two remaining Maryland regiments into the fight alongside the Fourteenth Continental Marblehead Regiment columns. They soon defeated the advance British forces—those who had dared to mock the Continentals. Though he was anxious to pursue the fleeing British, Washington called off his forces to regroup and then to flee across the Hudson River into New Jersey (near the current Fort Lee) for a full-on retreat moving south. Always the competitor, George would write to Congress that, despite a string of defeats, the stand at Harlem Heights had "greatly inspired the whole of our troops."

20

Victory or Death

FOR THE REENACTMENTS OF WASHINGTON crossing the Delaware and the Battle of Trenton, I showed up dressed in the same Virginia regiment uniform I'd worn to the French and Indian War. The Virginia regiment that I was hoping to follow through the battle was a complete no-show. They had either missed the train or purposefully skipped the Christmas Day event on the Delaware. I immediately met up with a German American reenactor, Georg Schaeffer, dressed, he insisted, "as a spy," in a tricornered hat, wire-rim specs, a light flannel jacket, and breeches. He looked a bit like a young John Lennon on the *Sgt. Pepper's* album.

"I'm working the woods on this one," Georg told me. "There is a rumor that the British have sent spies around back to track General Washington's movements."

"I can believe the limeys might do that," I said.

It was a little embarrassing to have to admit to Georg that my fellow Virginians couldn't make it out of bed on Christmas Day, but at least I had already connected with George Washington, in this case a Pennsylvania police chief, John Godzieba, who had just the right height and stature to play George, as long as you overlooked his Philly accent.

We spoke right before he powdered his face.

"I've been doing this twenty-three years," he told me. "I auditioned for the part of the general two times and finally landed it seven years ago. This will be my seventh year playing George." John had owned his own horse and dabbled a bit in foxhunting. "I think that's really a part of who he was. I really only hunted as a means to an end, to better understand his character and his passions."

"And did it help?" I asked.

"Absolutely. I don't think you can be George and not go foxhunting."

John's theory was that George, at least as a young man, aspired to be a Virginia nobleman. "If he could not be nobility, he wanted to act like it," he insisted. "This included everything he did. How he rode and how he dressed had everything to do with upholding a certain status. He wanted to be a true gentleman at all times. As a military tactician, his main goal was to keep the army together and maintain the morale of the troops. He managed that in spades."

The Howe brothers had maintained, while chasing Washington up into, through, and out of Manhattan, that they would eventually link up with victorious British forces fighting alongside Native American allies in Canada in order to deliver a knockout blow to the Continentals. That strategy did not pan out. With their chief foe now on the run with his fellow "rascally banditti," the British command sent Gen. Charles Cornwallis in hot pursuit. When he was a youth at the elite Eton boys' school, Lord Cornwallis's face had been slightly disfigured in a field hockey match, which gave him a scar-faced look that didn't quite suit his compassionate personality. He would eventually regret his hunt for George Washington. As he moved south chasing George, Continentals and their supporters interrupted the British aristocrat by blowing up bridges and felling trees in his path. Satisfied that they were in control of events, a confident but frustrated general British command called Cornwallis back to winter quarters for a rest. At the same time, they dispatched German Hessian divisions to hold down central Jersey across the Delaware from General Washington's bedraggled army.

With 40 percent of his army's enlistments due to expire on December 1, Washington faced tense morale issues, writing, "[If] every nerve is not strained to recruit the New Army with all possible expedition, I think the game is pretty near up." Since Manhattan, George's troubles had only deepened. His top commander, the British-born and trained Charles Lee, was acting outlandishly as usual, refusing to answer General Washington's petitions to combine their forces. George wrote again to Jack, calling the eccentric Lee—who was of no relation to the prominent Lees of Virginia—"rather fickle & violent I fear in temper." He was being kind. Lee was dragging his feet, and with some four to five thousand soldiers under his command. His presence, in any case, would not bear on the coming winter campaign. Stealing away one morning from the main body of his own forces, and casually breakfasting in a nearby farmhouse, Lee was surrounded by a British patrol and seized without a fight. The arrest, fortunate in many respects, would keep Lee's bizarre mannerisms off the battlefield for months to come.

By early December, Washington massed his forces on the southern side of the Delaware River. To the northwest in Trenton, some fifteen hundred elite Hessian troops made their own winter camp. George was itching for a fight, and he had a corps of inspired supporters, including the forty-year-old radicalized pamphleteer Thomas Paine, who on December 19 would publish the now famous entreaty to all true patriots, remarking, "The summer soldier and the sunshine patriot will, in this crisis shrink from the service." Paine was one of several key figures on the campaign, but Washington also had young fighters from his own home county of Westmoreland County by his side, including the future president James Monroe and a cousin, William Washington, related to him through the Chotank, Virginia, clan of Washingtons with whom he spent time as a youth.

George was embattled, but he wasn't on his last leg as some historians have contended. He had lost thousands in Manhattan and Brooklyn, but as he had descended south from New York, his forces had increased, not decreased, in size and strength. The cause itself was still popular, despite its early failures. Apart from a successful fight and retreat at Harlem Heights, Washington still had no solid battlefield victories to boast about. His trusted aide Joseph Reed now urged that "something must be attempted to revive our expiring Cred—give our Cause some Degree of Reputation."

Though the tide in the war would ebb and flow in the next five years and finish with a fortuitous stroke of genius and luck, the ten days at the end of 1776 and start of 1777 are celebrated today—correctly, in my view—as the most glorious days of the long American Revolution. Washington's reputation has always fared better in the eyes of historians than it has in the view of military strategists, but almost no one questions the brilliance and stealth of George's decision making at the battles of Trenton and Princeton. The tactics and planning he invoked at those battles are still used at military academies around the world as examples of how to surprise and confound an enemy. It remains an example of modern guerrilla warfare at its best and most daring. Both battles also stand as examples of how George's courage and penchant for risk taking, innate qualities he cultivated early in life, paid incredible dividends when the chips were down.

Before his famous crossing of the Delaware, the weather again turned weird on George Washington and his assembled forces. In the days and hours before the crossing, temperatures rose rapidly, giving way to heavy rains and hail, then, with temperatures plummeting, it began to snow. Massive slabs of ice swept down the Delaware, threatening to scuttle the crossing. Washington hoped to ferry his men across the river on Christmas night and arrive the next morning at dawn to surprise the Hessians.

The weather did not cooperate for my own crossing, in the sense that everyone present was trying to relive a similar day in history. It was a lovely day, unseasonably balmy and sixty-five degrees Fahrenheit as John Godzieba and hundreds of his loyal followers lined up to cross the river. The hot dog stands and beer vendors were doing a brisk business as Col. John Glover's Marblehead Regiment, the same guys who made the earlier escape from Brooklyn Heights possible, paced the riverbank in their signature pantaloons and red stocking caps, lugging giant oars on their shoulders. True to the day, some of the fife-and-drum bands were now armed with rifles.

John Godzieba had just finished a local radio interview, so I knew I had one last chance to query George Washington as he prepared for his daring crossing. I started with an obvious question: "I understand you are planning to surprise the Hessians?"

After clearing his throat, George spoke: "Well, yes. Today, it is victory or death." It came out sounding a little lackluster, but since I knew that was the secret password for the mission, I kept pestering.

"So, any good reasons to cross the Delaware on Christmas Day?"

"Well the weather isn't on our side, that's for sure," he said, looking skyward. Except today it was so warm that he could probably have asked his entire force to swim across the river in briefs with their packs held overhead.

"The hand of Providence is sure to guide us directly to the Hessian rum supplies," George added.

"That sounds like motivation enough to take on this unseasonal weather," I said.

For the actual crossing, I situated myself on the riverbank with a bird's-eye view of the action. Christmas Day tourists grabbed me and pulled me in for family photos, forcing me to smile and drink with them. I latched onto Paul Donahue, an aging member of the Pennsylvania riflemen corps. In a farmer's broad-brimmed hat stuck with a large turkey feather and green flannel uniform, he looked the part.

"I started coming here as a Boy Scout when I was just thirteen years old," he told me.

In fact, many of the soldiers who crossed the Delaware in 1776 were under the enlistment age of sixteen, but the average age of the Americans who crossed in the ice that day was forty-four, rather astounding given that this was close to the life expectancy at that time.

"If we hadn't won the battle of Trenton in 1776, though, I can tell you I would have been right back on the farm minding my animals," Paul told me.

With little warning, General Washington popped up ahead of us, live on a speaker system and in a chat with his artillery commander, Henry Knox, waddling along to keep his bulk moving apace.

"Henry," said George, needling him. "You are falling behind. I want you to make sure you sit in the middle so you don't swamp my boat." Not everyone was lucky enough to have the carriage of General Washington, I thought.

How we remember the actual crossing is part of a legend that sprang from truth and tall tales. A brilliant depiction by Emanuel Leutze makes the three-hundred-yard crossing look more like the Bering Strait. But elements of the painting are close to what the scene looked like, particularly the black oarsman at General Washington's knee. For many of the black reenactors of the Revolution—and I met many on the day of the crossing—the sole oarsman is a symbol of the contribution African Americans made to the victory at Trenton. On the actual day of the crossing, General Washington's forces were clothed in extra rags to ward off the cold, and the snow they walked over was marked by blood from their feet. The men boarded the giant flat-bottom Durham boats usually used to transport products like pig iron to Philadelphia. And when they embarked, a few men fell overboard, including one Col. John Haslet, who was soon hauled back on the boat, flustered but alive.

I watched the first several crafts cross and then volunteered myself as a lifeguard in case anyone fell in. Perhaps as a tip of the hat to my enthusiasm, I was asked by one of George's lieutenants, who could find no space on his boat for me, "Swim if you can!"

The real George Washington crossed the river early to oversee the operation but landed at 3 AM, a full three hours after his own midnight target time. Each boat had six oarsmen and a captain, usually a cod fisherman. There were steady delays amid the ice floes, and the element of surprise was slipping away. Maybe worse, Col. John Cadwalader's Philadelphia Associators, units of craftsmen and farmers attempting to cross the same river directly opposite Trenton, failed due to thickening ice slabs. Earlier General Washington had written to him, "If you can do nothing real at least create as great a diversion as possible," but even that was impossible due to the weather. Colonel Cadwalader had actually tried to make the other side, but he turned back when the ice at the edge of the Jersey shore prevented him from landing two cannons.

Finally in New Jersey with some 2,400 men, George split his forces into two columns, with Gen. John Sullivan taking the route closest to the river and Washington marching his own soldiers on a slightly more inland route. He and his commanders leaned forward into what had become churning northeastern blizzard. It made the march more of a challenge but at the same time camouflaged the massive troop movements. Mysterious Providence had again entered the fray.

I managed to slip into Trenton ahead of George and his men thanks to my use of twenty-first-century horsepower. The first thing I noticed was that Trenton had changed a bit since the eighteenth century. It had become a crime-ridden midsized city now famous for its indicted mayors and its blighted decay. It reminded me of Washington, DC, in the 1980s, at the height of the crack epidemic. Adjusting for population, Trenton's annual homicide rate per hundred thousand people stood at twenty-two, surpassing Newark's rate of fifteen, Detroit's seventeen, and more than doubling nearby Philadelphia's eight.

There were a few nice corners, but many homes were boarded with BEWARE OF DOG signs, and the liquor stores had bars on the windows.

When I dropped into one to ask where the reenactment crowd was hanging out, a kind cashier told me, "Sorry, I'm not from around here."

When at last I reached my destination, I found myself surrounded by dozens of armed men. I had landed in Trenton with the Von Prueschenk Feldjager Corps, whose ornately clad Hessian fighters were just about to get some shut-eye over at Trenton's Old Barracks, where some of their forces had actually lodged the night before the big battle in the eighteenth century. The Old Barracks have been turned into a museum and refurbished to their original look, including bunks and an apothecary with leech-bleeding facilities.

Molly, a former Fulbright scholar who had studied the early life of Mahatma Gandhi abroad, was cutting cheesecake and sausage, offering the Hessians rum shots as she worked.

"I do this every year," she told me.

I was frankly a little surprised to find a camp follower who was also a follower of Gandhi, but it just went to show how Revolutionary War reenactors buck the trends.

"Since my days abroad, I've become a labor organizer," said Molly. "If I'm not reenacting, you can usually find me walking the picket lines."

Molly's friend Jere Bethune was also a character actor. She was wearing a gray silk dress she had made herself. A ballet dancer and fencer, she had me beat across the board on the colonial sports front.

"I also foxhunt," she said. "But in New Jersey, it is all in good fun and no one is really trying to kill a fox. If the fox does get killed up here in Jersey, there are lots of people who get upset."

In the real Battle of Trenton, George had done his best to keep female camp followers to their assigned duties. He had a few cautionary tales from the French and Indian War to remind himself that they should stick to assigned battle chores, including swabbing down the cannons and carrying water to parched mouths during heated engagements. He had issued repeated orders for women to stay off the moving wagons, where flirting and liaisons often began. The British and the Germans, however, hired women in some cases specifically to "service" the troops, most of whom were far from loved ones. Unlike the camp followers I met, many of these colonial women were destitute and willing to do just about anything to support their families.

At the Old Barracks, there were no reenactors better dressed than the leading Hessians. Their cone-shaped gold hats and curlicue mustaches made them look like gentrified Coneheads. The guys I spoke to were surprisingly obsessed with German history, and although they were indeed American reenactors, several of them had developed a peculiar disdain for George Washington through the years.

"Not my favorite Rev. War commander," one of them told me. He provided no reason, and I was reluctant to probe further out of fear of being accused of spying in advance of the battle.

The real Hessian commander, just before his clash with the Continentals, reportedly said, "*Scheisse* [excrement] on them!" adding, "Let them come. We will simply fall on them and rout them." Indeed, Johann Gottlieb Rall, six years older than General Washington, had been sometimes referred to as the "child soldier" since he is believed to have commanded his first regiment as the age of fourteen. He had a much better military résumé than his rival. He had served in Scotland during the Jacobite rebellion and fought with success for Catherine the Great under her lover Count Grigory Orlov in the Fourth Russo-Turkish War.

"But Rall and his men were mercenaries, as I understand," I said in an effort to egg on several of the Hessians, who were eating cheesecake with a schnapps-induced passion.

"That's not really true," said Mark Worthington, whose name did not sound quite German enough.

"We weren't mercenaries," he said. "Remember, George III was of German stock, and he basically hired us through the House of Hanover, so we were under a contract with Frederick II. He paid all the Germans who came to fight." Mark was more affable than most of the Hessians I met. In fact, he was right. The Hessians were only one of six princedoms that fed the imperial fighting interests.

As Washington's fourteen hundred soldiers approached Trenton, they stepped up the pace, moving their horses and strikers into a long trot. George rode up and down the lines, encouraging his men to go faster. When a courier from General Sullivan arrived to say that his men's gunpowder was soaked, Washington replied, "Tell General Sullivan to use the bayonet. I am resolved to take Trenton."

To everyone's surprise, as the columns moved forward, trusted Brig. Gen. Adam Stephen and dozens of his men emerged from the forest. Stephen, who struggled with drinking issues after Jumonville and Necessity, could not explain how he had launched an advance patrol into New Jersey that George knew nothing about. George snapped at his old friend, charging that Stephen had helped to destroy the secrecy of the assault. But George was wrong this time, for although Hessians had skirmished with Stephen's patrols, Rall had already called off his regular dawn patrols due to inclement weather. By eight in the morning on the day after Christmas, Washington and Sullivan had joined forces and were only a half mile out of Trenton. A young Alexander Hamilton moved to take down a Hessian picket on the outskirts of town, and General Washington's column moved to strike.

❧ **21** ❧

A Fine Fox Chase

By the time I caught back up to the Continental Army on the outskirts of Trenton, the city's new mayor was inspecting the troops. A few minutes earlier, an organizer asked the assembled fighters to please give the mayor their utmost respect.

"He isn't the indicted one!" insisted Richard Patterson, words that prompted a few awkward chuckles. The new mayor arrived, he walked down the line, and, not missing a beat, Continentals began to march toward their Hessian foe through the streets of Trenton. It was Sunday morning. Thousands of residents emerged from their homes and from historic churches along the route. With or without the Lord's blessing, blood was about to flow.

Several Vietnam veterans exited the doors of Trenton's VFW office and began urging the Continentals forward. I jumped in line with the cod fishermen of the Marblehead Regiment, prepared to duck incoming fire, but found myself suddenly marching alongside the Vietnam vets.

"Yeah, man! People gotta know!" hollered a black vet, who told me his name was Alfonso McCray. "It all started here in Trenton. We helped free America! It all started here!"

Alfonso was clearly elated, so I asked him just what he thought about the "freedom" everyone had been fighting for back in the day. We walked along and then stopped near a line of American line riflemen who were about to unload on the Hessians.

"Washington was, after all, a rather prominent slave owner," I added as emphasis to my query.

"There are times when I find myself debating this with myself," said Alfonso, a hefty and muscular man who had lived through several wars and the civil rights movement. "Well, I've spoken to the

George Washington's silver spurs, c. 1775 [W-1912/A-B]. *Courtesy of Mount Vernon Ladies' Association*

VFW about this. I think you have to put yourself in the shoes of George Washington. It was in that era of slavery, and everyone was involved, including Thomas Jefferson and Benjamin Franklin. Few wealthy white men could say they didn't have a hand in it. As Jefferson once said, maintaining slavery was like trying to hold a 'wolf by the ears.'"

I did not interrupt, because Alfonso had clearly thought about my question long before I asked it. He continued, "George Washington was from the South, an agricultural area, and he didn't want the blacks to fight at first, but by the end of the Revolution, he had to concede that they did fight, fought well, and that they wanted their freedom. It meant everything to them, and I think he saw that. George Washington's idea, at least by the time he died, was that slavery would wither on the vine. Of course it did not, and it took another war to resolve that great controversy."

I wanted to talk more with Alfonso, but black-powder shots were erupting all around us as he spoke. There were booms and crashes, and then Alfonso grabbed me and pushed me to safety on the sidewalk as a stampede of soldiers trampled past.

The first Continentals to plunge into the real Battle of Trenton and surprise their German foe were the Virginians fighting under Capt. William Washington and Lt. James Monroe. The Hessians had been caught with their guard down—and in some cases pants off—and many of their big guns were seized immediately. Rall, the former child commander, was still in bed when the Americans rolled into town. His brigade adjutant had to wake him up to tell him that his horse was being saddled. The Hessians, who had slept off Christmas at the Old Barracks, were far luckier. Many of them ran with a group of British dragoons toward Assunpink Creek, where they crossed a bridge or flung themselves into the water, heading north toward Princeton. They ran while firing only a few shots. Naturally, in the aftermath, I had to ask their spokesman about the apparent cowardice.

"So, you guys just hightailed it out of town?"

"Well, the problem was that we were disorganized," he said. "We were quartered according to our companies but not our platoons, so we weren't able to get into action."

"But you did manage to run pretty fast," I said, trying not to chuckle.

"Well, yes, we weren't able to get our cannons into action, but Henry Knox had the Continental guns in location and firing. He could sweep most of the town with the Continental Army's guns."

It was, in this case, all true.

"This was typical of European-style warfare," he added. "If you can put an enemy in an untenable position, you win."

"You mean like checkmate?"

"Yes. You just die or surrender."

"Or run," I added, reminded that George's motto and password for this particular battle was a fair bit tougher to live up to.

I looked down the street. The Hessians were in full flight. One German manning a camera keeled over, his head hanging over the wheels. He looked up and someone mockingly hit him with the butt of a gun. It must have hurt, because he let out a squeal.

In the real Battle of Trenton, George was able to close the door on further retreat once his men had seized the northern exit route at the Assunpink bridge. Still on horseback, George took the high ground, watching his soldiers struggle with the Hessians for control of large guns. When Rall's formations dissolved, he led his forces down into the center of town, shouting these words: "March on, my brave fellows, after me!" It was a moment to savor—a sense that a day of total victory was in hand.

Rall finally made it onto his horse but soon enough was shot through and through by a musket ball and died. The remainder of his forces were surrounded and taken in an orchard with their backs against the creek. The Continentals seized nearly nine hundred German prisoners; some twenty-five to thirty Germans had died in combat. It had been an utter capitulation. Not one American had been killed in the lightning strike, though two reportedly froze to death in the blizzard after they crossed the Delaware. James Monroe was wounded in the shoulder, but a savvy field surgeon saved his life by clamping shut a severed artery. A Hessian army captain described the defeat as follows: "Since we had thus far underestimated our enemy, from this unhappy day onward we saw everything through the magnifying glass."

As the Hessians surrendered, the American commander remarked to a young officer that it was a "glorious day." To form, George's overjoyed foot soldiers, weary but elated, soon discovered the Hessian rum supplies and were toasting one another. In contrast to his defeat at Fort Necessity when his soldiers started drinking to ease the pain of an ongoing defeat, this celebration was well deserved. Hours later, George's tipsy fighters boarded boats to return across the icy Delaware into Pennsylvania.

Trenton had been more than a game changer for the course of the war. It also helped alleviate long-standing fears among colonials and their commanders that they were incapable of fighting head-to-head with elite European forces. The nature of the victory, something of a small miracle considering that there had been no Continental losses amid a raging battle, inspired everyone, including George Washington. The gargantuan gamble had paid off. If the Hessians had been on alert, the fight would have been far bloodier and may well have ended in an icy stalemate, with American forces stranded in New Jersey.

General Washington wasn't about to let the moment go to waste. Back in Pennsylvania, on the opposite shore, he called a new council of war to plan yet another assault into New Jersey. But before his men boarded the same river craft that transported them to victory at Trenton, he offered a deal he hoped they would not refuse. He lined up his forces on the banks of the Delaware and offered a ten-dollar bonus to any soldier who would agree to stay in the army for another six weeks after the expiration of their due date, December 31. Pacing up and down the lines, he entreated them, "My brave fellows, you have done all I asked you to do, and more than could be reasonably expected; but your country is at stake, your wives, your houses, and all that you hold dear. You have worn yourselves out with fatigues and hardships, but we know not how to spare you." Implied in his words was that each man's honor was as important to him as his own was to him. It was a dramatic plea to the men's consciences. One man stepped forward and looked around. Another stepped up, and the line began to thicken.

By the time Washington had decided to cross the Delaware River yet again, British forces, embittered by the defeat of the Hessian stronghold at Trenton, had deployed south from Princeton, again under the command of General Cornwallis. Earlier the British left fourteen hundred men back in Princeton in the charge of the eclectic Charles Mawhood and planned to call them south if and when they were needed. Continental sharpshooters held up the main force of the British Army as it moved south, giving time for Washington to dig in south of the Assunpink Creek for another confrontation. As the British approached, Americans unleashed a withering fire on their foe from their side of the creek. Unable to ford the waters above the bridge, the British massed to try to cross the bridge at Assunpink in columns set to proceed in waves. As they charged, though, General Knox's big guns and Continental snipers cut them off at the knees, piling attacker one atop the other, and repulsing the British onslaught.

That night Cornwallis, catching up to Washington at last, arrived to survey the bloody scene. He still had George where he wanted him. Aides urged him to attack at once. He is reported to have replied in British hunting lingo that he had the "old fox"; Washington had finally been cornered. Like the Howe brothers in late August 1776 at Brooklyn Heights, Cornwallis unwisely decided that he would wait and order a massive attack in the morning.

It was another British blunder for the ages. Rather than risk a perilous escape back into Pennsylvania, Washington, thinking like a clever prey, chose a far riskier route: the less traveled road that flanked the British on his left as he moved through the night toward Princeton. Again, George kept a rearguard with campfires burning, and his men covered their transport wagon wheels in rags to silence them on the road. His men slogged north. Quaker Road, as it was called, led toward a less protected corner of Princeton. Colonel and doctor Hugh Mercer, George's longtime friend, was sent to the front of the Continental columns.

Even as the Continental Army descended on the college town, British colonel Mawhood, who had two barking spaniels at the hooves of his horse, had already been called to move south to link up with Cornwallis. Washington's movements on Quaker Road had, until he spotted Mercer's forces, gone virtually unnoticed.

British forces, making haste to get to Trenton, spotted the oncoming Continentals. They faced down Mercer on an ice-encrusted orchard. In the field, the two sides squared off for a classic eighteenth-century musket battle, lining up in neat rows like pawns on a chessboard, exchanging timed volleys as men began to drop into the ice and snow. Within minutes, as Washington was still approaching the confrontation, Colonel Mercer fell, his horse shot out from him as he shouted for his forces to fall back. British soldiers, their bayonets drawn, swarmed in over the elegant and well-dressed American commander, who some of them initially mistook to be the American commander in chief.

"Call for Quarters, you damned rebel!" they reportedly shouted as Mercer defied them, denying that he was a rebel at all. In keeping with other cruelties that were fast turning American popular opinion against the Crown, the British forces stabbed Mercer to death as he lay injured on the ground. For George, it was a devastating blow. Dr. Mercer had served at his side during the French and Indian War and more recently cared for his ailing mother. (Indeed, he still owned the main apothecary in George's hometown of Fredericksburg.)

As Mercer's life expired on the icy field, Col. John Cadwalader's Philadelphia Associators—soldiers with mostly artisan backgrounds—did not flinch. Poorly clothed, many with rags bound around their feet from the night's march, the Associators made a stand but eventually also began to back away from the torrential British fire. The snowy field was now thick with corpses from both sides. Pools of blood congealed on the ice, according to eyewitnesses.

Arriving as heavy fighting was under way, George, his battle-hardened Virginia riflemen at his side, swept in front of the embattled Continental forces, urging them on. He rode, literally prancing on horseback, before the Pennsylvanians. With added drama, he waved his tricornered hat and reportedly shouted, "Parade with me my brave fellows! There is but a handful of the enemy, and we will have them directly." British guns fired. Bullets whizzed through the lines. Turning back several fleeing soldiers, Washington led the way, charging up the hill, stopping only when the American column was within a hundred feet of the British guns. Face-to-face with his foe, he shouted for the troops to halt, step up to the line, and then to fire!

The general's aide-de-camp, John Fitzgerald, later told Washington's grandson that, fearing to witness his general shot dead, he "drew his hat over his face" before removing it moments later to see Washington wreathed in smoke but unscathed and still in full command. Colonel Mawhood, his terrified spaniels at heel, turned to defend the town of Princeton. It proved too late for a defense of the college town, and he abandoned this idea and fled in a gallop.

The sight of their commander in chief in full stride was all the Continentals needed to muster their own courage. They turned toward the fleeing British, and, their general in the lead, joined the pursuit. "It is a fine fox chase, my boys!" shouted George, racing down a gully in the direction of the fleeing redcoats, only to be called off the trail by his own men. The poetic justice in the mockery directed at what was still considered to be the world's greatest army was not lost on anyone. Three months earlier, British officers had ordered a bugler to blow a special foxhunting call known as "Gone Away!" which signaled that Washington had fled Harlem Heights with his troops and was beating a craven retreat. The idea that George also carried foxhunting notions into military battle wasn't so surprising, but his lively spirit in the face of horror and gore was, well, astounding.

Even more than at Trenton, George's demeanor and actions at Princeton, when he was forty-four years old and in the prime of his life, had everything to do with the athleticism, sportsmanship, and prowess that he had cultivated over four decades. He was a specimen to behold as he dashed forward amid the incoming fire, barking orders before pivoting on his horse and charging up the hill. When he shouted and clenched his jaw, the well-defined bones of his weather-beaten face jutted out beneath a wide brow and striking Roman nose. British musket balls and cannon shots missed their mark yet again. It was déjà vu for anyone who knew George's history and was watching.

Observing the general race off after the British, only to be restrained by his own men, was more striking, however, for reasons beyond heroic appearances on that day in January 1777. Like Trenton, Princeton put Washington's sporting and competitive spirit on full display. Daring his foe to make him a martyr set him apart as a leader. At Trenton, at Assunpink Creek, and again at Princeton, George had asked his troops for nothing more and nothing less than what he demanded of himself as their leader—qualities that included courage, daring, speed, stamina, stealth, strength, selflessness, and fair play. In his moment at Princeton, the general leading his army became indistinguishable from the army itself. Poetically speaking, the dancer had become the dance.

Military maneuvers at Trenton and Assunpink Creek set the stage for a resounding victory at Princeton. They had the mark of genius as well as determination. General Howe, quartered in Manhattan for the winter with a romantic interest, was forced to admit, "The Enemy moves with so much more celerity than we possibly can with our foreign troops who are too much attached to their baggage." In the case of the march to Princeton, the Continental Army had moved at an amazing wintertime pace: nearly two miles an hour, even as his men left behind blood in the snow.

Since the start of the Revolutionary War, the Continental Army had employed unconventional fighting tactics—in many cases hit-and-run or stalking skills, which mimicked those American Indians used against British forces in earlier conflicts. In an approach that Sun Tzu would certainly have approved, Washington stubbornly and repeatedly refused to allow the larger and better equipped British forces to attack him in any one battle with the brunt of their full force. Throughout the New Jersey campaign, Continental irregulars shadowed British forces and sniped at redcoats from behind trees, sometimes setting up ambushes in camouflaged terrain that resembled bear- and deer-hunting blinds. In advance of his attack on Princeton, Washington ordered his troops to harass British regulars marching toward him at Trenton and to beat a fighting retreat when they arrived. These tactics delayed a full-blown British assault on Assunpink Creek and permitted the Continentals to issue a crushing blow at Princeton.

In order to direct traffic and secure the crossing in advance of the Trenton attack, George had departed on one of the first boats to cross the Delaware, showing that he preferred to lead from the front, not from the rear as many of his polished British foes, including Cornwallis and the Howe brothers, did. At Princeton, Washington chose to dash into the heart of the battle rather than remain in the back with a view overlooking the fray. This urge to inspire his soldiers was nothing new for Washington, who relished danger even when on a foxhunt in the Shenandoah Valley, where he had learned about courage and equestrian skill. That was the way he rolled as a young man, and this did not change with maturity.

But there is another, often ignored aspect of George's essential sportsmanship on display during the early years of the war, one that won him popular support among both civilians and his own men. In keeping with the code of honor and fair play that he lived by, he insisted on proper rules of war, almost always more humane than those of his British foe. His officers' corps insisted that "quarter," or mercy, be extended to the enemy, particularly captives. In contrast, European forces, including the British and Hessians, believed quarter was only a privilege that victors should bestow on a defeated and contrite foe. After Trenton, Washington ordered that the Hessian captives be treated with the same human rights for which the Continental Army had vowed to fight. When Philadelphians called for the heads of the Hessians, many of whom had earlier executed Americans in and around New York, Washington made a point of publicly stating that the German mercenaries were "innocent people in this war," insisting they be treated as friends rather than as enemies. (Given George's generosity toward prisoners, it becomes clear why so many Hessians ended up voting with their feet and settling families in the new nation.) Despite the redcoats' bayoneting his friend Dr. Mercer on the cold earth, Washington insisted on decent treatment for all prisoners after the Battle of Princeton, arguing that they should "have no reason to complain of our copying the brutal example of the British Army in their treatment of our unfortunate brethren." Ever the sporting foe, he even made a point of politely commending the "gallantry" of Colonel Mawhood and his two spaniels. Such sporting and chivalric virtues were at his core.

22

Drama in the Valley of Death

ON MY WAY TO THE BATTLE OF WHITE MARSH, I dropped in to sample the fare at the Valley Forge Casino and take the pulse of America's twenty-first-century pursuit of happiness. Frankly, it felt awkward to observe promotions for bikini-clad bachelorette parties and all-night gaming at the scene of the Revolution's most pressing hour, but I'm not sure George's fairly libertarian spirit would have really objected that much. From my vantage point inside the casino beneath a sign for Samuel Adams Boston Lager and an American flag flying over a Krispy Kreme donut shop, I looked out over a vast sea of slot machines with spinning rows of lemons and apples, manned by aging, desperate, hobbled, diabetic, overweight, chain-smoking types.

In any case, I suspected George would have shunned such kitsch for a comfortable back room with his fellow revolutionaries. A common punter, I stood in line to buy thirty dollars of credit on the blackjack table.

"I watch my pockets here every time I come here," said an old guy in a baseball cap, pulling his wallet out of his back pocket and transferring it to his front. "There are people just floating around here looking to make a hit."

"Oh!" I said, not knowing what else to say.

Chits in hand, I still wasn't sure I could go through with it.

"Please stand back from the rail, sir!" A very large guard ushered me past a "Wheel of Fortune" toward a bar surrounded by roulette tables and dozens of TV screens, on which NFL gladiators prepared to smash one another into the artificial turf.

My luck ran low fast enough. I lost all my credits in an hour, and since it was too early for a drink, I made a beeline for the door. A tout stood over a table lined with presidential faces, George's head in the middle.

"Was George a big gambler?" I asked in passing.

"Of course he was—he was the biggest gambler of them all!"

At Valley Forge, Thomas Paine's writings set the tone for the commitment through the harshest of seasons in a horrid place that defined American resolve and stamina better than any one pitched battle. As much as Valley Forge represents a transformation of a military into a professional fighting force, it also gives us an inkling of what a new multiethnic patchwork nation, in its varied stripes and colors, would look like after the Revolution.

As General Washington's forces swept toward Valley Forge in late 1777, they were still reeling from the loss of Philadelphia and a defeat at Germantown in early October. George had conceded the capital of the new nation, Philadelphia, to the marauding British regulars and their cheery officers. A string of losses and continuing recruitment issues due to expiring enlistments dogged him as he tried to settle his forces in for the winter. Nearby towns weren't crying out to house the ailing Continental Army, so the general and his lieutenants chose the desolate wooded hills and high ground twenty miles from Philadelphia as their winter encampment. Soldiers were required to build their own shelters, mostly small log cabins carved out of foraged wood. Ravines and trenches caked in snow and mud provided a fatal cocktail of disease, often the dreaded yellow fever. Meanwhile, men with bare feet set about making their own shoes and repairing their gear. It would be months before everyone had sleeping quarters, and there was little straw to go on the frozen ground to keep the biting cold out at night. By comparison, what a visitor sees today is sanitized, a bland National Park Service presentation of the past. The scene carries little of the wretched air and disgruntled cries that marked Valley Forge when the Continentals arrived.

When General Washington rode through the encampments, he heard chants of "No pay, no clothes, no provisions, no rum." These were the cries of men who had, despite the spread of disease, the urgings of their families, and wavering faith, decided to remain with their commander in chief. They came not only from North America but also from Europe because they believed in what the Revolution had come to embody. Valley Forge, in addition to being a cesspool of disease, was a melting pot of races and aspirations. There were runaway indentured servants, idealistic young men seeking a future in the New World, and an odd panoply of professional soldiers from abroad who weren't sure what to make of it all—including what to think of the American commander. Though dearly loved by his men, to many observers Washington began to appear aloof and preoccupied.

After a number of Revolutionary War reenactments, I had become more comfortable with eighteenth-century idealism than I was with twenty-first-century materialism. Apart from rampant disease and bad medicine, which did not apply to reenactments, I decided I had surely been born in the wrong century. Besides, fake wars were a bit easier on my nerves than the real ones.

At the entrance to the Battle of White Marsh, on the outskirts of Valley Forge, a woman with rosy cheeks and wearing a hoopskirt and puffy white bonnet greeted me.

"Are you with the reenactors?" she asked.

"Well, not exactly, but I'm writing a book about George Washington," I replied.

"Oh, then you'll want to get with George Washington," she said.

"Naturally," I agreed.

As a reporter I was always trained not to take freebies, so I paid her the small entrance fee as a contribution to the fun.

Moments later, I was surprised to find a dapper old chap actually named George Washington, dressed in epaulets and a tricornered hat and serving in the Pennsylvania command. I had a hard time finding him because I assumed foolishly at the outset that he was a black man. I was dead wrong. He was lily white, about eighty years old, and dressed to a T like the real George. He explained to me that he was playing a senior officer under, well, General Washington's command.

"Maybe you are a very distant cousin of mine," I suggested by way of introduction. Wrong again.

"My family came over as Irish immigrants."

I was stumped, because I thought that Washington was a very English name. He explained further.

"You see, we faced immense discrimination from the Protestants in Pennsylvania," he said. I guessed he was talking about the Anglican relatives on my mother's side, who regularly sang mean little ditties about the Pope. (My ninety-two-year-old mother still remembered these after a glass or two of sherry.)

"I'm sorry to hear that. I know they can be mean-spirited sometimes," I replied.

"Well, my grandfather got around that by changing his name to George Washington, and the rest was history." He smiled, then checked his powder magazine and headed over to a mock execution.

As he spoke, a matronly woman struck up a tune on a dulcimer and an impeccably dressed preacher stopped by to sing in tune. I watched a group of riflemen lining up to shoot a Continental Army deserter. A few muscle-bound enforcers blindfolded him and spun him around to disorient him. Muskets were lowered, and last words were offered.

"I was only going to see my girl for three days!" he hollered. The executioners squinted and took aim.

At the last minute someone came running with an official order from General Washington calling off the execution.

At Valley Forge in 1778, slovenly Continental Army soldiers were about to get a special dose of discipline in the form of an out-of-work, gay, German-speaking baron. Benjamin Franklin, who was running the American cause in France with his usual panache and humor, had already heard about the flamboyant and heavyset Prussian, Friedrich Wilhelm von Steuben, and he took an interest. For his part, Washington had grown tired of the myriad foreign officers who wanted to be paid well to help the American cause, so Franklin had been unable to promise the baron any special rank or pay. Discouraged, the baron returned to Prussia to learn he was facing allegations that he had engaged in homosexual relations with fellow soldiers while in the service of Prince Josef Friedrich Wilhelm. Under threat of prosecution, he asked again for a way over to America. Determined to preserve his honor and long-standing military career, von Steuben applied for and this time obtained, with Franklin's help, a special congressional stipend to train and fight with the Americans. He was given travel money and set out from Marseilles in September 1777 to meet General Washington.

In his letters, von Steuben's young French aide, Pierre-Étienne Du Ponceau, described meeting General Washington on February 23, 1778: "I cannot describe the impression that the first sight of the great man [Washington] made upon me. I could not keep my eyes from that imposing countenance; grave, yet not severe; affable, without familiarity. Its predominant expression was calm dignity." Turning to the strange but collegial conditions at Valley Forge, Du Ponceau also spoke of a dinner that von Steuben threw for the ragged Americans: "Once with the Baron's permission, his aids invited a number of young officers to dine at our quarters; on condition that none should be admitted, that had on a whole pair of breeches. This was, of course, understood as pars pro toto; but torn clothes were an indispensable requisite for admission; and in this, the guests were very sure not to fail. The dinner took place; the guests clubbed their rations, and we feasted sumptuously on tough beef-steaks, and potatoes, and hickory nuts for our dessert. In lieu of wine, we had some kind of spirits, with which we made Salamanders; that is to say; after filling our glasses, we set the liquor on fire, and drank it up, flame and all." He added, "The Baron loved to speak of that dinner, and the Sans-Culottes, as he called us," a moniker that "honored the followers of Washington."

"Sans-Culottes" were nonaristocratic citizens of the French Revolution who could not afford the fashionable silk knee breeches popular with the upper classes. They came to represent the noble ideals of social equality and democratic rule that soon would sweep monarchs from power in Europe and open the floodgates to popular rule around the world. (Eventually, they also helped oversee the guillotines, but that is another story.) By all accounts, the baron, like George, was as comfortable in such a ribald martial setting as he was in the parlors of Europe.

At Valley Forge, Washington and von Steuben both did their best to keep spirits up. Washington hadn't lost his biting sense of humor either, as Du Ponceau would explain, providing a rare insight into how Washington playfully needled his own men. When Benjamin Walker, a young officer also attached to the baron, approached Washington for leave to visit his Quaker belle, he begged to go, insisting, "She will die."

"Oh, no!" said George, according to Du Ponceau's account. "Women do not die for such trifles."

"But general, what shall I do?" inquired the distraught young man.

"Why, write her to add another leaf to her book of sufferings" was George's reply. He was referring to what American Quakers documented in their *Great Book of Sufferings*, which was filled with woeful tribulations of, among other things, the whippings and other punishments patriots and enlisted soldiers often meted out for the standard Quaker refusal to serve the cause. It was an excellent play on words.

George sought in other ways to uphold the sagging esprit de corps. He made a concerted effort to support the arts, particularly drama, insisting on its value, despite the reservations of more puritanical-minded members of Congress. Though patriots like Samuel Adams condemned theatrical performances, saying they led to "Vice Idleness Dissipation and General Depravity of Principles and Manners," Washington, long a lover of both the fun and moralizing impact of good theater, thought and acted to the contrary.

From his first Barbados adventure, General Washington had not forgotten the work of playwright George Lillo, whose dramatic dialogues contained famous phrases like "inalienable rights" and "sons of liberty," which American patriots would later employ.

The lead production at Valley Forge in 1778, however, was another play, Addison's *Cato*, equally loved by George from his early days at Belvoir. As George matured, its lines resonated more and more with him, reflecting the kind of moral leader he wanted to be remembered as. In it, Cato himself says, "What pity is it that we can die but once to serve our country?"

The staging of *Cato* at Valley Forge represented a symbolic moment in Washington's spiritual life as well. In his fight for independence, he had found a moral, political, and social cause worth dying for. Though he was still riding through a hail of bullets, he wasn't doing it in the name of a crown anymore.

George's inherent faith in independence and his ideas of freedom from tyrannical rule buoyed his belief that a battle of ideas was worth engaging in. The arts provided a means for him and his fellow Americans to envision their own ideals—to put meat on the bone, so to speak. It was this faith in his own ideals that guided his evolution as one of America's earliest and most influential patrons of the arts. This evolving role was never a given, considering that George had no formal education, yet in Williamsburg he had already become an American of the Augustan Age. From his desk at Valley Forge, he wrote to the young poet Timothy Dwight to encourage him, stating that nothing would please him more "than to patronize the essays of Genius and a laudable cultivation of the Arts & Sciences, which had begun to flourish in so eminent a degree, before the hand of oppression was stretched over our devoted Country." In the wake of the Revolution, his adamant belief in the new nation's need for literature, drama, and art would remain with him. He would remark that "every effort in genius, and all attempts toward improving useful knowledge ought to meet with encouragement in this country." Patronizing the arts, particularly drama, was not universally approved of, particularly in the former northern colonies. But George understood its critical value to the Revolution.

As admirable and eloquent as his love of the arts sounds today, it was also part and parcel of a radical new era. Throughout modern history, rebel leaders have promoted freedom for "the muses," often burnishing their own heroic images onto the world. With many revolutionaries, however, a respect for the independence of art and literature dwindles once they have achieved their ends. Not so with George Washington, who would to his dying day be pleased to see artists, poets, and even critics unfettered by moral and legal restrictions.

Scholars, soldiers, and poets regularly dedicated their works to George as both a revolutionary hero and later as a patron of the arts. An artist's hand could as easily wash his own, as he could theirs. He grasped the import of this symbiotic relationship, writing in later years to the Marquis de Lafayette, "Men of real talents in Arms have commonly approved themselves patrons of the liberal arts and friends to poets, of their own as well as former times," adding that, "In some instances by acting reciprocally, heroes have made poets, and poets heroes." He was of course a great actor, but he knew that no great actor could survive without a proper playwright or two—the taste of whose fruits he had already begun to savor.

In comparison with today's spectrum of journalists, in eighteenth-century Europe and America, a far greater proportion of them also doubled as poets. Washington knew well that these men held the key to breaking down the old symbols of power and building up the new ones. He would write to Irish journalist and poet Mathew Carey after the war that his publication was "more happily calculated than any other, to preserve liberty, stimulate industry and meliorate morals of the enlightened and free People." At the time of the Revolution, however, he could not have known how or why some of the most polished scribes in America would eventually turn on him and write scathing indictments of his government's alleged corruption and his own "royal aspirations."

Artistic expression as it developed out of the Revolution helped the new nation establish a truly American identity infused with the ideals of the Revolution and unique to the New World. Some of George's dogged openness to artistic freedom is likely also attributable to his old friend George Mason, who in 1776 had written in the Virginia Declaration of Rights "that the freedom of the press [and speech] is one of the great bulwarks of liberty, and can never be restrained but by despotick governments." This idea of preserving a free press was growing in currency even in Europe. The last thing George Washington ever wanted to be accused of was setting up a new form of despotism. Beyond that, however, there was ample evidence, particularly from Williamsburg, that he actually loved the arts.

For these reasons beyond his prowess in the field, the identity of the Revolution and the new nation became closely identified with George Washington. He was the most dramatic actor on the stage of the American Revolution, particularly during the war years. Unlike many other revolutionaries in his day he recognized the value of art in his own life and in the life of the new nation. Unfortunately, his support for lofty ideas and ideals did not always translate into liberating actions on the ground.

A visitor to Valley Forge in the spring of 1778 might have been amused to see the diversity of all the young soldiers, including the teenage farm boys, who had signed on to serve in the Continental Army. Some had been indentured servants; others were fighting with a guarantee that they would be free from their masters.

Camped out on the lawn in front of me was Deonte Hannah, a young reenactor from New Jersey who was a member of the First Rhode Island Regiment, a mostly all-black unit of the Revolution. He was dressed in full uniform and was warming his hands beside a small fire. He could have been one of George's adolescent recruits—also known today as child soldiers.

Deonte explained to me that a kind, older lady had purchased his uniform for him because she thought it would be good for him to learn about the role of African Americans in the Revolution.

"Where is your home?" I asked.

"Oh, the Jersey Shore."

"Nice. So what do you think about our first great war?" I asked.

"It was about revolution," Deonte told me. "People did this for others—to help the cause of freedom."

We didn't get very far discussing the Revolution before Joe Becton, a former Valley Forge park ranger, and Noah Lewis, a fellow reenactor, overheard us talking and came over to warm their hands on Deonte's campfire.

Noah was playing the persona of Ned Hector, a black hero from the war who had served courageously at the Battle of Brandywine on September 11, 1777, only a few months before retreating to Valley Forge. At that battle, Ned Hector had shouted at the Brits as he rallied his cavalry horses, "You can kill me, but you'll never get my horses!" For his service, and after his years of pleas as an upstanding citizen in the new United States, the government granted Ned Hector a one-time forty-dollar gratuity the year before he died of old age.

"That's not much," I said. "How did you find out about Ned?"

"In the public library," said Noah. "I found him on the mustard rolls from 1777. He was born in 1743 and died in 1834."

Noah wanted to know about his own family roots, which, like those of many black Americans, are not easy to uncover, often because slaveholders kept poor records and usually provided only one legal name for their slaves. That's precisely why Noah started digging into the American Revolution. What he discovered shocked him: African Americans fought in almost every major battle of the Revolution, including the siege of Yorktown, where their seizure of British pickets proved crucial. Within a few years, Noah's obsession to know more became a profession, and he was visiting schools up and down the East Coast, speaking out for Ned Hector and other black veterans of the Revolution.

"I wanted to tell modern Americans all about it," he told me.

From his arrival in New England to take charge of a new army in 1775, George Washington struggled morally and logistically with what was already taking place in the ranks of the new army. His first reaction when northern advisers suggested he enlist blacks was that enlistments and reenlistments would disturb recruitment drives in southern colonies. That didn't sound right to northerners who had already fought alongside blacks. They argued that the free blacks would be "very much dissatisfied at being discarded." Black soldiers would jump ship and fight with the British if General Washington didn't step up and allow blacks who fought at Lexington and Concord to reenlist, his close advisers warned. So, open to the views of others, the general relented and allowed reenlistments. Then at Valley Forge in the winter of 1778, after fighting for nearly two years and listening weekly to his officers' corps tell him about feats of black heroism, Washington had a more significant change of heart toward black soldiers. The pendulum swung toward full rank and pay for all blacks as equals, as Joe explained. "For Washington, this was a war for independence, not necessarily for freedom," he told me. "There was an irony. For a lot of blacks who served, the sentiment was, 'If we serve, we'll be freed.'"

Noah agreed, "By 'a citizen,' Washington first meant landowning whites. But that changed when he started listening to people around him, including Alexander Hamilton, John Laurens, a fellow southerner, and the Marquis de Lafayette. His conscience really started to bother him. I think he was also influenced by his meetings with free blacks, including a brilliant black poet, Phillis Wheatley." (I remembered Wheatley, of course, from her visit with General Washington at his Boston headquarters.)

There had been a lot going on: from Cambridge to Valley Forge in 1778, the Continental Army's position changed from exclusion of blacks to new experiments with active recruitment of men both free and enslaved. Much of Washington's own thinking was calculated on British offers—successful in some regions—of freedom for service. Still, it was a hard row to hoe. Over the course of the war, British forces would recruit nearly double the number of blacks into their own ranks than did the Continentals. In the end, British promises of freedom often paid out less often than those the Continental Army made.

Valley Forge was a desperate time that required desperate measures. Major cities, including Philadelphia and New York, had fallen, and overall morale was sagging to new lows. That winter Washington urged the Continental Congress to enroll free blacks under new quotas set for states. The commander in chief wrote to Rhode Island governor Nicholas Cooke, who oversaw a state legislature stacked with well-heeled slave traders now down on their luck due to British blockades. On February 23 Rhode Island approved a plan allowing individual slaves to enroll and offering freedom once they passed muster. The legislature also allowed for a $400 compensatory fee for slaveholders whose "property" chose to serve. Though the same legislators would attempt to terminate the agreement, the floodgates were opened, and enlistments rolled in even as local white men tried to discourage it. In Rhode Island, some 250 black men signed up to fight in the newly formed First Rhode Island Regiment, whose records would show an extremely low rate of absence from post as well a limited number of desertions.

Integrating black soldiers was more than a little awkward for a Virginia planter whose moral quandary over slavery would deepen over the 1780s and well into the 1790s. George's personal valet, William Lee, rode next to him in most battles. This meant that when he was reviewing troops whose freedom he had guaranteed, these same troops were observing him in the company of his personal slave.

I asked Joe and Noah why they thought William Lee remained loyal.

"I think it had a lot to do with the way Washington treated most people," said Joe. "He [William] was loyal until the very end, never said a bad word about George Washington. But I do admire George for this. I researched his relationship to his slaves and the decision-making process that led to the final decision to free his slaves upon his death."

"Maybe they could see that Washington was grappling with the issue," I offered.

Noah nodded. "You don't get the kind of respect he garnered by pulling the wool over people's eyes."

The expediency of needing more soldiers, of course, did not resolve Washington's quandaries. When the new Rhode Island line had been trained and reorganized, George ordered that the troops not be segregated. He wanted them assigned in such a way "as to abolish the name and appearance of a black corps." Though George had come around reluctantly, his policies would set an early precedent for integration within the US military, yet one that would prove extremely hard to uphold.

23

Two Old-School Chevaliers

WHEN THE ELEVEN THOUSAND SOLDIERS of the Continental Army marched into Valley Forge in December, nearly a third did not have shoes on their feet. Many of them were dying or suffering from disease. By the spring, the brutal winter was winding down and, thanks to the efforts of Baron von Steuben, professionalism and general discipline had improved. More than training, however, a new alliance with France was about to turn the tables and make the Continental Army a more aggressive force, not an amalgam of flighty souls who often retreated at the first sign of defeat. On May 5, 1778, General Washington issued a decree for his forces to toast and celebrate the alliance, which he ascribed to both the intense diplomacy of Benjamin Franklin and the "Almighty Ruler of the Universe," whom he said favored America's pursuit of "liberty and independence."

Months before the celebration of the official alliance, Washington had met the nineteen-year-old Marquis de Lafayette, an idealistic young military officer who hailed from one of the wealthiest families in France. Lafayette was born in a decaying manor house far from Paris. His father died at the Battle of Minden in 1759. In 1770 his mother and grandmother died in the same week, leaving the young aristocrat orphaned but extremely wealthy. The next year, just into his teens, he joined the British Army as a lieutenant in a contingent known as the Kimip (Black) Musketeers. Though he was little more than a mannequin soldier, he already was on a fast track to becoming a noble warrior. Socially speaking, it was expected that the Marquis's courtly manners and agile comportment would one day make him useful to the royal family in the battlefield. But Paris was a playground, and Lafayette went out carousing with some of the city's finest young men and women. In 1768, after he entered the famed Collège du Plessis, he described his own nights out with "children sporting épées" and wearing "embroidered suits, their bourses, and their curls garnished with powder and pomade." His social set included the famous Marie Antoinette, but he was not all suave and debonair; he is alleged to have accidentally stepped on at least one young lady's toes while dancing.

The marquis still managed to marry well, and one of his high-flying Noailles relatives was known in the Versailles court as none other than Madame L'Étiquette for her insistence on good manners. The formality of Versailles was also influenced by Charles Rollin's treatise on education in 1726, which insisted noble boys would be better to "emulate the selfless actions of ancient heroes rather than the fanciful tales passed down through family lore." It was a notion that young George would have readily accepted, I expect.

Before embarking for America to fight for George Washington, who was at the time the enemy of France's worst enemy, Lafayette fell in with the grand masters of Freemasonry, the secretive society that George had already joined as a young colonist. In France, Freemasonry, despite the standard suspicions about its mystical cliquishness, was already advancing progressive political views, including constitutional monarchy and a society built more on merit than on birthright. For Lafayette's early designs, however, money meant as much as merit. After he determined that he wanted to fight in the American War, a wildly popular cause, he handily bought his own ship, *La Victoire,* and set sail for American shores with colleagues in tow.

There was nothing like fighting in another nation's revolution when your own kingdom was rotting from within, and Lafayette, who had not made an adequate commission in the British Army, saw his future—at least at the outset—as a rebel allied with America. In the summer of 1777 he first came upon General Washington, reportedly in Philadelphia's City Tavern, remarking, "The majesty of his figure and his size made it impossible to mistake his identity." Impressed with his zeal, George immediately invited the young marquis to join him the following day on an inspection of his Delaware River forts.

As George had done in the French and Indian War, the marquis was ready to brave enemy fire to prove his honor and courage, which he soon did at the Battle of Brandywine, fighting the battle with a wounded leg and earning the rank of lieutenant general, which George

Washington bestowed upon him. In only months, Lafayette, who peers had been seen as a somewhat awkward courtier in Versailles, had become the same kind of gallant, young hero that George had fancied himself to be over two decades earlier in the Shenandoah Valley. The marquis had also trained for this role as George had, albeit mostly in the Shenandoah. A mature George likely saw in the marquis his own early aspirations for fame and gallantry. This was a fairly solid foundation for, as they say in the twenty-first century, a serious bromance.

On the surface, the two men looked to be worlds apart when they first met. Lafayette had studied literature and chivalric comportment in Versailles with three future kings. He was born into an actual manor house and, unlike George, traced his recent lineage to a string of renowned warriors. By comparison, Washington had needed to study courtly behavior in books before finally meeting palpable models in the Fairfax family. His half brother Lawrence had served as the only recent military hero in his British American family. While George developed into a fine dancer and equestrian, he was never entirely comfortable in high society.

But the marquis shared some of George's earlier challenges. He, too, had lost his father as a boy. And he struggled to overcome his size and awkwardness but soon became a sinewy extrovert, and—by field accounts—an accomplished equestrian and swordsman. He greeted almost everyone with his unique aplomb, which included hugs and abundant kisses on the cheek. He was exquisite and polite, a courtier in the old sense of the word.

This peculiar friendship between fellow chevaliers probably flourished for other reasons as well. Lafayette's public buoyancy was an excellent foil to Washington's born pessimism, which often exhibited itself in his brooding private correspondence. As George wrote freely to his younger brother Jack, he also wrote with pluck and unusual trust to his new French friend. It was almost as though George felt more comfortable confiding in a stranger than he did in some of his contemporaries. (At least with the young and foreign Lafayette, he could safely expect he was somewhat safer from being double-crossed.) With his forces already ensconced at Valley Forge, George wrote to the marquis, "I have no doubt everything happens for the best, that we shall triumph over all our misfortunes, and, in the end, be happy; when, my dear marquis, if you will give me your company in Virginia, we will laugh at our past difficulties and the folly of others." Lafayette wrote to a friend a few days later that Washington confided in him and liked him because he was direct, contending, "[I] tell him the truth." Though he sounded sometimes like an overzealous sociopath, he easily endeared himself to George, a notoriously hard man to get to know. George would entrust Lafayette, still only nineteen when he was commissioned as a general, with the survival of a large division within the Continental Army. It was yet another a huge gamble, but another one that paid off. In a sense, General Washington was playing a kinder, gentler Lieutenant Governor Dinwiddie to the marquis's George Washington. In doing so, he gave Lafayette the military authority that the British Empire had stubbornly refused to bestow upon him in that earlier war. It must have secretly pleased Washington to know he was throwing up a French teenager as a leading general for the Continental Army against his polished set of British rivals.

After Brandywine, General Washington assigned Lafayette to secure Canada, but Lafayette quickly became bogged down with a lack of material and recruits. The marquis's complaint sounded like that of a troubled son to a father, as he wrote, "Why am I so far from you, and what business had the board of war to hurry me through the ice and snow without knowing what I should do." Such complaints from the hinterlands may well have reminded George of his own far-flung troubles in the French and Indian War. Playing the mentor, he quickly wrote to reassure his young friend, suggesting he rein in his ambitions. "However sensibly your ardour for Glory may make you feel this disappointment," he wrote, sounding strikingly like Colonel Fairfax, who had buoyed him in a similar circumstance, "you may be assured that your Character stands as fair as it ever did, and that no new Enterprise is necessary to wipe off this imaginary stain."

Despite differences in upbringing, the ambitions of these two men, one from the New World and one from the Old World, were quite similar. George's own early exploits had led others to banter about the parlors of England and Europe in both rude jest and high acclaim. Before he married the wealthiest widow in Virginia, George had, like the young marquis, remained laser focused on glory and fame, on admiration from fellow aristocrats and Virginia cavaliers, men who habitually watched out for one another and regularly honored each other with accolades.

This odd couple of the Revolution would correspond and chat across the course of the rest of the war, sometimes on a daily basis. Though a generation apart, both men had emerged at a young age onto an Old World stage of classical taste and desires. They both had sought and were seeking affirmation by asserting themselves through displays of prowess, as well as within their exclusive social circles. Lafayette recovered from his first failed invasion of northern British redoubts and soon retreated to France to drum up more support for General Washington and his cause. He casually offered to murder a senior British diplomat in a duel that was never accepted. He wrote, "I have nothing very interesting to do here, and even while killing Lord Carlisle, I can make some more important arrangements at White Plains." He claimed that Lord Carlisle had impugned the honor of all of France by insisting France was only interested in the American colonies as an "instrument of their ambition." Honor for this young knight—as it had for George at a young age—meant everything.

Yet time for these two old-school warriors had not stood still. When the two men became acquainted, their worlds were spinning with new ideas. George Mason's Virginia Declaration of Rights, penned in 1776, would become a seminal influence on a French document that Lafayette soon would help to articulate, the Déclaration des Droits de l'Homme et du Citoyen, or Declaration of the Rights of Man and of the Citizen. In a matter of years, classic courtiers, who wanted to garner favor with persons born to power, were fast becoming obsolete. The new international demand was not for classic courtiers but for dedicated patriots and egalitarian-minded leaders. For both Washington and Lafayette, this impact would be felt in their lives and across the spectrum of their public engagement. Though they were in similar respects born of a much older world, Lafayette and Washington both understood the implications; they would have to roll with the changes or surrender their bigger, grandiose personal goals.

New notions of liberty, equality, and freedom were now up for discussion in parlors and back alleys, on the tips of tongues of foot soldiers and generals. I thought back to what Joe Becton had said about Washington, that he was "for independence, not necessarily for freedom." He had a good point, at least when you considered Washington's early years as commander of the Continental Army. In some respects, he did not have freedom to gain, only to lose. He was fighting to maintain it—fighting, that is, to live in the genteel manner and comfort of the Washingtons, Masons, and Fairfaxes that he had become so accustomed to. George's model of independence had been that of the Virginia gentleman whose property and wealth liberated him from dependence on anyone, including authoritarian rulers at home and abroad. In his character, as well, Washington was fiercely self-governing and self-made, preferring to remain aloof and at a distance from others. The day he had quit fighting for the Crown at the end of the French and Indian War, George had taken up a happy life as a country squire, one in which he had become truly independent in his own mind, despite being dependent on slave labor for his growing wealth. In letters to his friends and relatives, he pined to get back to that life, which the same new and broad interpretations of freedom he was allegedly fighting for had suddenly called into question.

Yet over the course of his life, George Washington remained open to change. He liked to weigh alternative points of view, and, particularly when planning, he reserved his own opinion until an abundance of facts and ideas were made available. His ideas of independence and the inherent rights of his own soldiers were changing in the process. These ideas were au courant and familiar even to British lords and masters. They sprang from Locke's writings, flowered through Thomas Paine's poetry, and were the very substance of Jean-Jacques Rousseau's *The Social Contract*, which argued that all law should be an expression of the "general will" intended to promote equality and liberty.

The American Revolution, made possible through the blood and sweat of the common soldier opposed to authoritarian rule became, in essence, a new battleground of ideas. Lafayette and Washington, who would look at one another as genteel fellow courtiers, were now required to not only speak about but also actively promote equal rights and freedoms for all men, regardless of origin. That was the challenge, but their collective past, chiseled from marble in an age of imperial rule and chivalric deeds done to honor monarchs, was still a hindrance. If they held on to their pasts, they risked becoming subjects of ridicule, pilloried by the public and in the press as aristocratic dinosaurs of the Old Regime.

The first major test of George's new army after Valley Forge arrived as his forces set off from Valley Forge and the British, for strategic reasons, ended their occupation of Philadelphia. The battle did not unfold as planned. The mercurial Gen. Charles Lee, recently liberated in a prisoner exchange, petitioned for a chance to command on the front lines at the Battle of Monmouth Courthouse on June 28, 1778, just as a suffocating heat wave swept the East Coast. Though he had preferred to put Lafayette in charge and almost did, George, after deliberations, agreed reluctantly to put Lee in charge and staked out an overview position on the field for himself. Anxious about the imminent clash of thousands of Continentals against elite British forces, Washington rode closer to the front and met with an awful surprise. He was quickly surrounded by fleeing American forces, who explained that General Lee had ordered their retreat.

When General Lee approached on horseback, George exploded with vitriol, accusing Lee, in essence, of cowardice. He flew into a rage that lives now in infamy but was cut short by the necessity to save the day. General Washington was forced to implement an alternate strategy, so he looked around the hill where he had halted with his forces and discovered that to the east was a viable hedgerow fronted by a swamp, which could provide position and cover. Here he would make a stand with reinforcements and fleeing troops, which he quickly turned around. Continentals, again inspired by George's presence among them, rapidly fell in line behind the hedges and prepared to fight. George's young aide-de-camp, Alexander Hamilton, would remark that the commander in chief took charge with "coolness and firmness," blocking the British advance and allowing the full thrust of the Continental Army to move forward into the fray. As it turned out, it was a belated but well-set trap; the British cavalry charged forward into a withering Continental fire that came at them from three sides. With the help of his top commanders, including Lafayette, Washington drove the British back through the swamp as von Steuben's men stepped forward into the heat of the battle.

The Continental Army prevailed at Monmouth Courthouse, if only after looking squarely into the jaws of humiliating defeat yet again. The British left some 220 badly wounded or dead soldiers behind on the field as fighting ended. The enemy's forces had been cut down by nearly twelve hundred men, losses that were estimated at five times those suffered by the Continental Army. Though thousands of British and Hessian troops had escaped to fight another day, the battle, in the end, was a victory for George—though still one of few to date. Until Yorktown, the Continental Army would not line up again to face the British in such a consequential clash. In the aftermath, Gen. Charles Lee, accused of a "shameful retreat," would be forced to step down, guilty of breaching Washington's direct orders to stand and attack at the outset of the battle. He soon retired to a life as a gentleman farmer in Virginia. Though the tempestuous relationship of Lee, the British immigrant, and Washington, the fourth-generation American, would come down to a nasty court-martial case, what most divided the two senior Virginia commanders in the field was George's caution-to-the-wind courage, his superior public manners, and Lee's spinelessness.

Victory at Monmouth did not put an end to criticism of Washington's strategic decision making. In fairness, however, once he had the French on his side, his strategy to fight a relatively cautious war of attrition—trying not to pit thousands of Continentals against their British foe all at once—soon became a viable approach to winning. Critics of George's conventional tactics often ignore a basic tenet of rebellion: rebels don't have to win most battles; they merely need to keep fighting on indefinitely. (Most imperial powers don't lose wars in the battlefield; they lose them when they go home.) Maintaining a viable force in the field was always George's greatest strategic success. He now put off any plans to march major contingents north to take on the British in Canada. French admiral Charles-Hector d'Estaing wrote reassuringly that he had orders from Paris to second all of Washington's commands. But dissuaded in 1781 from using the full thrust of combined French and American forces to retake New York, Washington agreed—begrudgingly at first—to march with Gen. Jean-Baptiste-Donatien de Vimeur, better known as the Count de Rochambeau, south to meet up with General Lafayette, who was conducting lightning strikes on British forces near Charlottesville, Virginia. General Cornwallis's embattled and increasingly diseased army had dogged the marquis's forces through Virginia up the James River Valley toward Charlottesville. As they traveled through the South, British forces, still flush with means to pay, collected hundreds of runaway slaves for their cause. The former slaves, who came for the pay and dubious promises of freedom, worked mostly as bearers and cooks and also readily seized horses from farms along the way.

On his journey through Virginia, Washington persuaded General Rochambeau to rest with him briefly at his beloved Mount Vernon. In the company of scores of his servants, George feted his guests in classic Virginia style. Only months earlier, his chief overseer and distant cousin, Lund Washington, had personally boarded a British frigate in an effort to dissuade the king's forces from burning the estate. He handed over rations to the enemy as a means to save the plantation. Learning of what his trusted relative had done to save Mount Vernon, George was outraged that any attempt had been made to placate the British. He would have preferred to see his beloved home burn to the ground, he insisted. It was, of course, a matter of personal honor to not ask for special favors from the foe.

On the route south with Rochambeau, George learned that Cornwallis had moved north and out to the port of Yorktown, where the British general had begun to petition—in a desperate tone—for naval power. Along with him had come hundreds of black workers, many of them ill with smallpox but irreplaceable for the building of fortifications. Cornwallis's aide, Charles O'Hara, openly worried that disease, famine, and their enraged masters would soon kill off hired black hands if the workers were cut loose for lack of food and their own sickliness per his general's orders.

If the British military hadn't grown tired, and arguably lazy, the war might well have run on much longer. Victory, never assured, suddenly appeared like the sun cutting through a thunderstorm in Tidewater, Virginia. The combined French and American forces stopped in Williamsburg, where on any given weekend you can witness reenactments of George's review of his troops as they head off for a victory at Yorktown. I arrived back in Williamsburg just in time to see the marquis prance forth in all his regalia on a large white steed to announce to the masses, "Your day of glory has arrived! General George Washington has just given the order that a grand army of twenty-one thousand French and American soldiers shall begin their march upon the town of York and there shall besiege our enemy Lord Cornwallis, and, by the grace of God above, we shall have the greatest victory in this war to date!"

As Lafayette cried forth at the top of his lungs in a rather good French accent, the assembled crowd raised a cheer for him and a general hiss of disdain at the passing mention of the traitor Benedict Arnold, who was still lurking nearby. The marquis's gestures were grandiose and his praise of General Washington excessively effusive, but he was a crowd-pleaser. It reminded me of how the marquis had actually injected a bit of royal zest into the long and bloody Revolution. What I didn't see that day was the well-documented moment when George Washington and the marquis reunited after not seeing one another for nearly a year. An observer remarked that General Lafayette "embraced him [Washington] with an ardor not easily described," adding that he "absolutely kissed him from ear to ear."

Arriving in Yorktown just a few hours later, I looked around for a horse to ride. Nothing. My closest option would be to borrow one in Williamsburg and ride the ten miles by highway back to Yorktown. I settled on a modern, clean-energy option: a Segway. Had that mode of transportation been available in his time, I imagined that George would have enjoyed it as a quick and efficient means of reviewing his troops.

Yorktown is marked by an out-of-place-looking windmill, a replica from colonial days, and like Williamsburg, the city looks very much as it appeared in 1781. Several homes and stores from the era still stand on sparsely populated street corners. On the heights above the town, you can watch video reenactments of the surrender and talk with a colonial-era doctor about how the Continental Army tried to treat the rampant camp fever that swept through their ranks. The first cure was from a potion made of South American tree bark, and then, of course, if the shivering did not subside, the leeches were brought out of the medicine jar. Looking out over the port from the heights, General Washington would have seen thousands of British troops swarming below but blocked at the mouth of the James River by a bullying French fleet.

With a tour group of chummy Ohioans, I gazed out across what would have been the British defenses, imagining the final days that spelled the end to British domination in the colonies. I sensed, if only for an instant, the imminent victory with a sharp hint of revenge. George faced off yet again with the hapless General Cornwallis, whom he had outfoxed at the second battle of Trenton and then again at Princeton. Due to his emphasis on appearances and self-control, George looked as dapper, stern, and polished as Cornwallis in the field, yet he was still a novice in classical military training compared to his British peer. None of that mattered now. After years of grinding conflict, Washington was the better commander, a product of his many experiences, including his failures. Before leaving New York, he wisely employed elements of the spy craft that had served him throughout the struggle, making sure that British forces intercepted enough of his false orders to become confused about where he was headed next. It had been doubly humiliating for Cornwallis to realize he was trapped with even his maritime escape route across to Gloucester shut down, by elite French naval forces. The redcoats were at long last, like so many red foxes gone to ground, surrounded by hounds, hunters, and twenty-five-pounder cannons. George hastened to his end game.

To get a better look at the battlefield, I rode down from the heights above town near to the British embattlements below. Replicas of huge iron stakes shot out of the immense circular gun positions. They had been put in place to withstand a full-on assault from American forces, and General Washington knew his men would have to breach and seize them in order to intensify the bombardment of British positions on the water's edge.

The Marquis de Lafayette ordered Alexander Hamilton to charge one of the last outposts with bayonets, because bullets would have ended in far too many friendly-fire incidents. Nearly a quarter of the attack force was lost in the assault. Likewise, the First Rhode Island Regiment, replete with black Americans, took another picket in hand-to-hand combat. Their horrific work was over in about ten minutes. One French officer was genuinely impressed with the esprit de corps left in the ranks of the bedraggled Continental Army, commenting that, though many of those he viewed were barefoot, underage, or just too old to still be fighting, "a quarter of them were negroes, merry, confident, and sturdy."

In initiating the siege at Yorktown, George Washington swung a pickax to break the first ground. Camping on the outskirts of town with his men, he slept out under the stars on some nights with Martha's last son, Jackie Custis, who would not survive the campaign—yet another victim of camp fever. (No record of their last words to one another survives.)

With each successful frontline assault, Continental forces dug new trenches in order to tighten the siege. Still, on the cusp of victory, the final days of Yorktown were a bittersweet reminder of the horrors of war for everyone. As cannonballs rained down on Cornwallis's forces, he expelled scores of maimed and diseased blacks into no-man's-land, betraying their newly professed loyalty to the Crown. Amid intensified shelling, a courageous British drummer boy emerged onto a hillock to gain the attention of the American side. Moments later, an officer appeared amid the smoke and thunder, waving a flag of surrender.

In the end, some eight thousand British prisoners were taken. American casualties, mostly from the direct final assaults, totaled only about three hundred. When a humiliated Cornwallis failed to show up for a formal surrender, General Washington, on horseback, snubbed the British colonel sent in his place and forced him down the line to surrender to his junior. Military protocol, which the British had schooled George in, was observed to the last detail. General Washington wrote the terms of surrender, but he was not able to dictate terms to Virginia's runaway slaves, who hobbled into the forest and, in some cases, stowed themselves away on the HMS *Bonetta*, General Cornwallis's return vessel bound for New York.

Independence and freedom had come at a high price, but Washington's French allies stood in awe of the American accomplishment. After withstanding so many defeats and gaining only a handful of victories in the field, George Washington stood tall on his saddle, a symbol of a selfless citizen-patriot, a representative of a new revolutionary spirit, which was on the verge of sweeping much of Europe.

The Revolution secured George's place in history far beyond his military and political leadership. Yet his unique ascent to the pinnacle of fame in the Western world presented a stark dichotomy of sorts: even before the war, he had begun to embody the ideal of a citizen-patriot, but his rise to fame as the third son of his father was still a romantic tale of patrician connections, courageous feats, and a lifestyle that was, in many respects, Old World and elitist.

Regardless, and somewhat counterintuitively, America's old-school chevalier would become the de facto model of good behavior and manners in this New World order. In the eyes of his peers, the American public, and admirers around the world, George Washington was the "New American Man," a fungible idea that after the war remained open to change and interpretation. Even George felt compelled to find out more about what was commonly acceptable behavior for modern men of refinement. To this end, as the Revolutionary War was winding down and he was encamped with fellow officers in Newburgh, New York, he wrote to a close aide, requesting the purchase of a two-volume set titled *A View of Society and Manners in France, Switzerland, and Germany: With Anecdotes Relating to Some Eminent Characters.*

The book, which I viewed in the form of George's own copy at the George Washington Library at Mount Vernon, is both entertaining and instructive. For instance, the author, John Moore, comments on the French nation's love of manners, pointing out that "politeness and good manners, indeed, may be traced, though in different proportions, through every rank, from the greatest of the nobility to the lowest mechanic." He then adds, "This forms a more remarkable and distinguishing feature in the French national character." Embracing such information as empowering in the wake of the Revolution, Washington would seek a universal and parallel acceptance of good manners in America. These writings were also about how European leaders can and should behave in public. They deal with emerging issues of liberty and freedom, including with the case of a German leader supporting free expression in the face of tyranny. From Mannheim, the German statesman observes, "Many windows were broken, and the chariots of a few members of parliament were bespattered with dirt by the mob—what are the frivolous disorders when compared to the gloomy regularity produced by despotism; in which . . . men are afraid to speak their sentiments." As surely as he had studied military strategy before the war, through his readings, George was preparing himself for the new battle for hearts, minds, and manners that lay ahead.

It is fair to say, however, that after his rise to glory, which was well earned in the eyes of his compatriots—as well as in his own mind—George still was not ready to apologize for his aristocratic tastes, which had not changed much. These would include, in the years to come, more of the fine dining, foxhunting, and ballroom dancing he loved so much. Such pursuits would remain a part of his character, but they would also come under increasing attack as the arcane habits of an obsolete aristocracy.

❧ V ❧

Master of Manners

George Washington actor Dean and guest Barbara at the Gadsby's Tavern Birthright Ball, Alexandria, Virginia, 2014. *Phil Smucker*

24

Leading the Revolution in Style

IF GEORGE WASHINGTON PREFERRED REPUBLICAN virtue and simple modesty, it was not terribly apparent in April 1789 as he trotted on horseback through the cheering throngs that awaited him on the outskirts of Philadelphia as he made his way to New York. George dismounted and crossed the Schuylkill River in a glorious scene that, as one newspaperman remarked, "even the pencil of Raphael could not delineate." A twenty-five-foot liberty pole bore a banner reading DON'T TREAD ON ME! and BEHOLD THE RISING EMPIRE. The scene, which would never be equaled, held trappings closer to those of a coronation of an ancient king or emperor than it did to the birth of a new republic. One young lady worked a contraption aimed at lowering a crown of laurel onto George's head. That night, Philadelphia's City Tavern hosted a dinner for the president-to-be, described by the Pennsylvania Packet as "an elegant entertainment" for over 250 guests, with an orchestra inside and fireworks later blasting through the streets and over the harbor.

Back on his steed the next day, George was greeted by church bells ringing upon his arrival in each town along the way to New York. George rode through a chorus of young girls in Trenton dressed in white and decked in wreaths as they pulled flowers from straw baskets and tossed them at the new chief. They sang, "Virgins fair, and Matrons grave, / These the conquered arms did save." If there was any doubt as to the zealous veneration for the new president as America's father, another banner crowed THE DEFENDER OF THE MOTHERS WILL BE THE PROTECTOR OF THE DAUGHTERS. The great patriarch was a

friend and defender to all. From Elizabethtown, New Jersey, George
and his entourage caught a barge described as "festooned with red
curtains, manned by New York harbor pilots and thirteen oarsmen
in white smocks." The barge measured some fifty feet in length, the
centerpiece of an entire flotilla, which converged on what is now the
financial district of New York City. In another sign that encouraged
the royal rumors, a string of porpoises, dipping and leaping into the
air, played in the vessel's wakes. Despite the pomp of the procession, the new American leader did appear to dress down for the final
swearing in. He sported a red overcoat, a dark brown suit made in
America, white stockings, and shoes adorned with silver buckles. Lest
anyone think he really intended to become a monarch, George had
come to state otherwise: he raised his right hand above his sheathed
sword and took a solemn oath to serve his country as its first president, whose duties were in line with the Constitution he had already
carefully checked off along the margins of his own personal copy.

In a sense, though he sought to encourage the concept, George
Washington never quite became the New American Man. In many
respects, he was too much of the past, a lost age of chivalry when
charging knights on royal steeds rode to glory and won the fair-
est damsels as a reward for their service. That's how a lot of men
and women—particularly those who did not grasp the complexity of
his character—would always see him, no matter what he did to try
to dissuade them. He was America's knight on a white horse, but
by the time he took office, George's armor had lost some—but by
no means all—of its glint. His fair damsel, Martha, was soon to be
known as the nation's most consummate and polite hostess. Abigail
Adams adored the first couple though often became jealous of what
the Washingtons represented to the new nation. In the same way that
John F. and Jackie Kennedy would come to represent some bygone
ideal—an age of Camelot—George and Martha projected a legacy of
manners and old-fashioned decency that would resonate across two
terms and well into the future.

Though General Washington could look the part of the new
American leader, he could hardly project, on his own, a revolutionary aura of, for instance, a Simón Bolívar. In its immediate aftermath,
his revolution did not so much liberate the oppressed masses as it

did restore the rights of certain men, particularly those already with substantial means. And even though the new nation had written its ideals into the Constitution by 1787, George Washington was still very much a part of the old establishment.

As America's new patriarchal leader, George became and remains our most chivalric president and, unless we switch back to horses for transportation, probably always will be. What other American president—not to ignore second-tier competitors like the hard-charging Old Hickory Andrew Jackson or the rough-riding, half-crazy Teddy Roosevelt—led the charge, rode through flying ordnance, and wooed the ladies—well, at least, later in life—with such pluck and aplomb? As it was on the day of his inauguration, it remains so today: there is George Washington, and then there are all the rest.

As a gentleman and a sportsman who eschewed scholarly discussions when he left his secluded study, George soon became a transformative character in American history. He bridged the past with the present. In 1855 former news reporter Rufus Griswold wrote a book aptly named *The Republican Court: Or, American Society in the Days of Washington*, which shifts the focus on Washington from his political and military exploits to the civility and gentility that surrounded his reign as president. Griswold was one of the first modern writers to recognize that Washington's extraordinary social skills, which included a determination to include educated women in the shaping of a new nation, established a uniquely American gentility in the expanding theater of the nation's early public life.

George sought to hold on to and also to display his manners and what were essentially aristocratic habits in order to help fashion the nation. He was unapologetic, and for good reason: as an adolescent and as a soldier, he had utilized his studied gentility as an advantage, and that would not change through his two terms as president. He sought to balance his love of manners and sportsmanship with his newfound love for liberty and equality, so he usually tempered his style in such a way as to avoid ostentation, but lest anyone forget who he was, he remained proud of his full-feathered presentation. He knew, in short, that he was as much a symbol of a new nation as he was a mere mortal with personal flaws, which he disguised efficiently. Elegant, reserved, and virtuous, he rode into his new political role, gliding past the flying daggers of his detractors as he moved through the throngs.

The idea of the New American Man was in a sense schizophrenic from the start. Even at the inauguration, it wasn't clear what the American Revolution would mean for Europe and the world. To some it still looked more like a baron's revolt led by wealthy men who were protecting assets. To blacks, indentured servants, other minorities, and anyone who didn't own land and would not be enfranchised in the new system, including women, it still wasn't clear what real ideals the Revolution stood for or, for that matter, for whom it had been fought.

A raging internal American debate as to what "revolution" really meant and how it defined the New American citizen would spark tensions across the colonies in the aftermath of the war, through George's two terms in office, during his retirement, and after his death. Even today, of course, Americans are still hammering away at their own ideals and trying to come to terms with who they are and what kind of nation they want. In truth, the process that leads the nation to question the progress of its revolution is precisely what many of the founders, including Washington, looked forward to and encouraged. In the eighteenth century, however, there could be no doubt that the authors of great documents like the Declaration of Independence and the Virginia Declaration of Rights had been inspired by the ideas of Rousseau and Locke. Just what they had wrought or intended in terms of fair play, the pursuit of happiness, and equality for all still required defining through action.

George's unique ascent to the presidency offered him a chance to adhere to his own independent and personal tastes. Preserving them was made easier by the changes in American society writ large. Pastimes once considered the domain of the wealthy in the 1750s and 1760s were now, with the exception of foxhunting, spreading in interest to other groups, including a growing middle class. The process was slow and sometimes hard to detect, but it was also inexorable and evolving over time. As sure as the next century would bring an expansion of manners, it would also bring about a democratization of sports. In other words, the attributes of a sportsman could and would one day be recognizable on new and different levels, particularly in the company of an active middle class. This meant, in practice, more local fairs, balls, and other events for men and women to exhibit their social and physical skills, as well as a more competitive and polite society across the board.

There was a catch, however. For many, including those myriad Americans still very much in possession of the puritanical and socially conservative values of their forefathers, the preference after the Revolution was not for elegance in the least but rather for republican simplicity. The courtly life was anathema to their thinking, including to the stated goals of the Revolution. Ironically, even some true American aristocrats with vast slave holdings, like Thomas Jefferson, championed varied versions of this allegedly humble and modest character—in Jefferson's case that of the independent, no-nonsense, and self-sufficient farmer. The idea would prove to have great populist appeal, particularly in the small farming communities scattered across the new nation. A stripped-down, back-to-the-land, anti-elitist life remains an American ideal in some quarters even today.

At the time, this new concept of republican virtue meant different things to different people, but overly formal behavior was seen, by and large, as buying into the old monarchical authoritarianism that the Continental Army had fought to eradicate. Washington's own lifestyle, naturally, fell under the microscope of often well-meaning scrutinizers intent on keeping American ideals free of infection from what were seen as the evils of luxurious living. These ills, as it turned out, were associated in the minds of critics with pompous behavior in public, theatrical fun, and extravagant parties.

One particular case relates to how Thomas Jefferson expressed disdain for the regal behavior of his old friend George at a ball in Philadelphia. Some background on Jefferson's critique is essential because it relates to courtly behavior going back centuries, one based on a strict monarchical hierarchy. In England in the seventeenth century and even before that, a king (or prince in smaller regions) and his spouse would preside at formal occasions—particularly at balls. The organizers of the American ball in question set themselves up to look silly in Jefferson's eyes from the start. They raised a couch several steps for George and Martha to sit on. Worse, dancers were informed of a protocol that required them to approach George and Martha before every dance. This they did, adding a bow at the feet of the president and his wife, which provided the appearance of a kowtow to their overbearing power, as far as Jefferson saw it. In his view, it wasn't the image that a leader attempting to embody the "will of the people" should project.

It didn't help that George spent much of his leisure time with a set of friends who were also some of the richest men and women in Philadelphia and New York, as well as in the entire nation. This raised eyebrows among some newly minted American republicans, particularly when George and his associates were pursuing leisure often deemed to be excessive "high living."

For Washington, some such behavior came naturally. His debonair displays of grace and power were in keeping with the role of a refined Virginia gentleman within a society that remained highly stratified after the Revolution. Also, despite Jefferson's somewhat conspiratorial view that the new nation might soon slip into authoritarian rule, for many common citizens, especially for most southerners, George's manners and virtues were something to hail and admire, not to abhor. For them, the hero of the Revolution was largely beyond reproach. He had already made his sacrifices and paid his dues at that altar of liberty. So, whereas some men might have been skewered and pilloried more severely by their public, this crowd gave him the benefit of the doubt. Some northerners were also unfailing admirers of George's charm. Abigail Adams, for instance, the loquacious wife of the future second president, early on would describe the new president as moving among the masses "with a grace, dignity, and ease that leaves Royal George (of England) far behind him." Many Americans didn't want their president to be a king, of course; they wanted him to be a great man, like a king, but yet greater than any European monarch.

Such admiration had begun even before the war, with the image of George, sword in hand, dueling with a monarch, and so it was linked in the public psyche to older Jungian concepts like that of a knight slaying a tyrant or a dragon. In essence, the adulation for George's style and demeanor harked back again in many ways to the age of King Arthur. Abigail's husband, John, though somewhat puritanical in other respects, admired George for his ability to stride effortlessly into a room, pay his courtesies, and stand as an icon of style. (Adams first cited these skills at a Continental Congress meeting before the Revolution.) In a sense, it served the new nation to have an iconic figure like Washington, grandfatherly in later days, presiding over both festivities and matters of state. In any case, the new state wasn't about to become a dictatorship, nor wither away into an egalitarian commune, for that matter. Few in the new nation expected a bricklayer or carpenter to stand for the highest ideals yet envisioned by man.

John Adams, who had first met George Washington in Philadelphia during the Continental Congress, once said of the man he liked to think of as largely his own creation, "He was the best actor of the presidency we have ever had." Washington tried hard to mold his actions to fit his new title. His actions displayed an acute awareness of the public wanting to adore him, often combined with his own disdain for too much glitz and glamour. He could not and would not consider turning his victory over the greatest European army of the day into the makings of a monarchy in America. Despite his efforts, monarchical conspiracy theories swirled and were given undue and, in retrospect, puerile credence by men as great as Thomas Jefferson through both of Washington's presidential terms in office.

Even if there were those who would install a King George I on American shores, their hopes were futile from the outset. That he was simply not interested did not mean he could not have become something close to a king if he genuinely had wanted to. It would have taken some astute use of his powers and politesse, but it is a safe bet—though still debated by historians—that Washington soon could have become something close to an American Napoleon. The notion that he had the power to make it happen also served as a lightning rod to provoke further criticism. But it was all for naught. He never wanted that final crowning glory—and for a sound reason of course: it was everything he had fought against during the war.

As sure as he tested his own powers and checked them when necessary, others struggled to help the new American leader better define his role. An example of this is seen in deliberations over a title for the head of the new American government. Some of the illustrious choices under consideration were His Highness the President of the United States and His Serene Highness. In the end, of course, these were put aside for President of the United States.

25

Southern Persuasions

IN THE FIRST HALF OF HIS FIRST TERM as the first president, despite his complaints that he wanted little to do with public service, it was still nice to be George Washington, basking in the glory of a new republic. But there were added responsibilities, and George saw one as putting his authority on public display while taking the pulse of the new nation. If there was one way to make his points in life, George knew it meant going on the road and engaging with the broader public. His own writings while in office suggest that he was anxious to escape the confines of an office, and after short trips to several northern states, he began to plan for a grand tour of the South to begin in the spring of 1791.

It would be one of the most entertaining presidential tours in history. In essence, it would be about manners, propriety, and a leader's intimacy with his constituency, including his ability to gauge regional happiness and local grievances. It lasted three months and covered some eighteen hundred miles, and the old wayfarer planned it himself as though he was arranging one of his original mule trains for mission in the wilderness. As few presidents would be in the future, he was in control and hands-on throughout, so much so that he would, on his own volition, ask that his own overtaxed horses be replaced to keep up with the pace of the tour.

In anticipation of some of the criticism that would follow, including an attack from Benjamin Franklin Bache (a grandson of Benjamin Franklin) lambasting George's "stately journeying through the American continent in search of personal incense," George vowed from the start to avoid appearances of favoritism by lodging in public houses along the way. When he failed his own stipulations, it was only by error or to stay with his distant relative Col. William Washington, who had served with him in the Revolution.

Though the southern trip would put on display the South's near deification of their war hero, it also brought out Washington's best leadership qualities, including his ability to embrace his new calling and inspire respect for the new nation and its groundbreaking Constitution. Though he sought to accomplish only a few crucial matters of state while on the road, he behaved not like a jovial, fun-loving Virginia cavalier but rather more as a standard-bearer and friend of the public. That was not to say that the joys of travel, fine dining, and cordial interaction were not on his mind as he embarked on the well-planned excursion. Not surprisingly, Martha, who probably foresaw some of the hardships, including a shortage of powder rooms, would not be along for this great adventure.

The president announced to his cabinet that he would proceed on the low road along the Atlantic, and return on the high road in the foothills of the eastern mountain ranges. In his own words, "My equipage and attendance consisted of a Chariot [with his family coat of arms] & 4 horses drove in hand—a light baggage wagon & two horses—for Saddle horses besides a le[a]d one for myself—& five Servants including to wit my Valet de Chambre [William Lee], two footmen, Coachman & Postillion." It was, in its design and trimmings, a sharp-looking presidential cavalcade with a dedicated staff.

That he fully intended to take some pleasure and enjoy the healthy air on the journey can be assumed from a letter he wrote stipulating that he wanted to be out of the southern states by end of May, when it often gets brutally hot, and that the entire trip should "be made slow and easy."

Over the course of ten days, as I followed the president's course by boat, horse-drawn carriage, and car at an unduly furious pace—which landed me a speeding ticket—I gained an immense respect for George's own initiative, often wondering how his good health stood up amid the rattling of his aging bones over poorly kept southern roads.

My own trip began in Annapolis, Maryland, where General Washington had earlier resigned his commission. I took a jog around the perimeter of the US Naval Academy in order to pinpoint the landmass on which George's entire party ran aground in foul weather. The sail into Annapolis hadn't been smooth in the least. As the president wrote, reminding me vaguely of his other wartime crossings, "Unluckily, embarking on board of a borrowed Boat because she was the largest,

I was in imminent danger, from the unskillfulness of the hands, and the dullness of her sailing, added to the darkness and storminess of the night."

A near-fatal mishap amid "constant lightning and tremendous thunder" took place, in George's words, due to the "ignorance of the People onboard," which was probably much nicer than the language he mumbled to his aides after "having lain all night in my Great Coat and Boots, in a berth not long enough for me by the head, & much cramped." His barge became stuck on a shoal for a night, and George's coachman, attempting to switch boats midstream, narrowly escaped drowning. Days later near Colchester, Virginia, after another familiar ferry crossing, a horse leapt overboard and three others, spooked by the commotion, followed it into the water, splashing around for dear life. For a man who grew up at a river crossing and was trying to project the authority and good sense of his new office, the events must have been mortifying. "Slow and easy" just wasn't on the horizon, at least until he arrived in Charleston and Savannah.

After a stopover on March 28, 1791, that he had made to meet with, among others, Pierre Charles L'Enfant to confirm plans for the new national capital—the future Washington, DC—he made a trip home and then dropped in on his sister, Betty, and his infirm mother, Mary, in Fredericksburg for a short visit. Before entering Wilmington, the president, ever mindful of perceptions, stepped out of his chariot and rode into town on his own horse, likely the white steed named Prescott. Four dragoons rode in front with a royal-sounding trumpeter. It wasn't the first time he had jettisoned a carriage ride for a true equestrian's mount. It was a crowd-pleaser, and he knew it. While he was honored and admired in the northern states, he was a virtual deity in the South, and, though he stuck to military-like protocol and repetitive but polite speeches, he seems to have soaked up positive sentiments at every turn. A fifteen-gun salute greeted him as he entered the city. One newspaper described Washington's entry with a wink to his standard hauteur: "Through an astonishing concourse of people of the town and country, where, as well as the ladies that filled the windows and balconies of the houses, he saluted with his usual affability and condescension." In the harbor, impressive even today for its festive spirit, festooned ships nodded in the tide as gun salutes resounded.

On the sandy strand that was once called Long Bay but is now rife with the beach bum kitsch of Myrtle Beach, I discovered no obvious signs of George Washington's earlier passage. I had my first speeding ticket, and to cool off I dropped into the Hard Rock Café, where I was met by Elvis Presley's silk, sequined cape and Johnny Cash's lace-up black boots on display in glass cases. Though his legacy competes heavily with such modern commercialism as well as Civil War paraphernalia and nostalgia today, the president's only journey through the entire South (as it existed in his day) is still fondly remembered farther south, as I soon discovered.

In nearby Georgetown, where he arrived by ship, the gift shop was sold out of George Washington bobbleheads. "We just can't seem to get rid of the Abe Lincolns," the shop owner told me. A stone's throw away, I signed on with docent Douglas Schmersal for a tour of the sprawling manor where some fifty ladies, by George's own count, showed up for an impromptu tea with him.

Douglas explained that day's events as a yellow shrimp boat bobbed in the alluvial waters out back. "This would have been about where he stood to greet the ladies," he said, striking a pose at the foot of the fireplace of what was once the home of Daniel Tucker, a prominent merchant. The house was intact, including its original pine floors, but it was missing its original furnishings. "If you stand where I am for a moment, I think you'll be able to sense the great man's presence still."

"I think you have his pose down well," I remarked.

I drove down the road to the Hampton Plantation, all hung with spooky Spanish moss, where George's entourage had been a couple of hours late for breakfast the next morning. Breakfast soon turned into lunch. Legend has it that one of his hostesses, Mrs. Horry, confided in the general that she wanted to cut down an oak tree, which still spreads across the entire front yard of the big house. George is said to have advised her, "Let it stay. It can do no harm where it is and I would not think of cutting it down," since it takes generations to grow a great tree. (The story sounded to me to be a little too antithetical to the cherry tree tale to be correct.)

As George headed into Charleston, twelve ship captains dressed alike rowed him in a barge as a chorus clad in white sang, "The hero comes, / Sound your Trumpets, / Beat your Drums!" George was pleased, recounting that "there were a great number of other boats with Gentlemen and Ladies in them; & two Boats with Music."

I happened to arrive in Charleston in the same month (May) that the presidential party entered in 1791. His weeklong visit to the city, in and around which major Revolutionary War battles had earlier raged, was the centerpiece of his trip, and his hosts provided well for his arrival in accommodations he paid for through his office. Emma Biggs, my guide to the Heyward-Washington House, as it is now known, opened the doors onto the lavish possessions of the wealthy Heyward family, whose scion Daniel Heyward owned a rice plantation farther south in Beaufort and commanded some one thousand slaves. "Here is the bedroom—though not the bed—that George slept in," she offered, ushering us into the hallowed chamber. Our tour went around back to the stables and the servants' quarters, which housed up to seventeen slaves in close proximity.

Almost everywhere I traveled, retracing George's southern trip, the legacy of slavery resonated, sometimes in awkward ways. Fortunately, I had an old friend—a South Carolinian reporter I'd shared time with in West Africa—to guide me through some of the nuances. "When George Washington visited in the eighteenth century, Charleston was very much still an African city in many ways, with 50 percent of the population enslaved," said Herb Frazier, an erstwhile reporter at Charleston's *Post and Courier* newspaper who also has written a history of local black communities in South Carolina.

We strolled the waterfront and took the time to eat shrimp po'boys before retiring to Herb's favorite cigar shop for a long smoke. "Black men and women worked here on the docks, loading indigo, rice, and then cotton," he told me. "Some of them even won their freedom through hard labor." An elaborate and unique system of badging slaves with copper plates marked a servant's status. "Africanisms vibrated through the city and across into the remote sea islands, which were isolated and worked by slaves. Within this crucible grew the Gullah culture." This was a unique Creole culture that melded West African traditions with southern plantation life. In many ways, Herb pointed out, the Charleston and Savannah region's African American communities occupied a universe parallel to the lavish world of their masters.

Herb traced his own roots to West Africa, where I had first met him working to improve journalistic practices there in the modern era. He was also a member of the African Methodist Episcopal congregation, which was attacked by a racist white man in 2015. "The church's founder, Richard Allen, who opened the first AME church, in Philadelphia, in 1794, genuinely aspired to help form a nation in which all men are created equal," Herb explained. Out of immense respect and because both Herb and I had enjoyed the company of Allen's direct relative of the same name, who had taught us journalism at the University of Michigan, I visited the AME church in Charleston, which sits at the heart of the old slave labor port district.

"We said, 'We forgive you,' which makes some of the whites in this city feel comfortable and less threatened," said Herb, who has cowritten a new book about the killings, *We Are Charleston*, with South Carolina's white poet laureate. "Some of them thought we blacks would actually burn the city down," chuckled Herb. About that time, a car full of rowdy white teens with beer cans passed by sneering and shouting.

George would have heard a lot from local plantation owners on his trip. He decided to send a presidential dispatch to the Spanish governor of East Florida to help stop the flight of black slaves into Spanish territories, which had been taken back from the British in 1783. "Back then it was a lot easier to run south than it was to try to make your way north," Herb had told me. On the advice of Thomas Jefferson, George wrote that he hoped to make "arrangements for the prevention of these evils and, if possible, for the restoration of the property—especially those slaves." The diary note displays Washington's continued vacillation over the issue and also makes clear that on this occasion he stood in solidarity with southern plantation owners, despite the petitions to the contrary by friends like Col. John Laurens, his former aide-de-camp during the Revolution and also a previous resident of Charleston who before his untimely death had devised a plan to recruit blacks into the Continental Army.

Though George's southern trip was arguably overly "perfumed with the incense of addresses," it was also peppered with near-constant adoration, the variety that gave his critics hesitation and stoked their worries of an impending American monarchy. These were, of course, not his own concerns; the new commander in chief again paid particularly close attention to the women of Charleston in his own diary of the journey, writing that he, "was visited about 2 O'clock by a great number of the most respectable ladies of Charleston—the first honor of the kind I had ever experienced and it was flattering as it was singular." The next day, with Martha patiently awaiting her husband's return like an American Penelope, George had a chance to meet (and dance) with 256 elegantly dressed southern belles, whom he described as "handsome ladies." That night, the president dined under a canopy set up along the riverbank, where he witnessed, in his words, "a tolerable good display of fireworks."

In lovely Savannah, Georgia, the fanfare was just as wild, arguably because, like Charleston, the city had suffered the brunt of the urban slaughter during the Revolution and residents had still never met General Washington in the flesh. I managed a boat into port to get an idea of how it might have felt for the president riding into what is even today one of America's loveliest small cities. Just as I was about to give up on the notion of living vicariously through the first president, a fully grown bald eagle swept down from above and snatched a large fish from the Savannah River, wafting gracefully to a perch on the opposite shore. Surely this was a sign from Providence, I mused.

The presidential party had arrived by the same route in the early evening. Onshore, one alderman's front yard was festooned with lights in a giant *W*, and fathers and mothers with babies lined up to welcome the president. In a sampling of the hero worship at play in 1791, city fathers read out a statement that sounded, at least today, like a religious invocation:

> We make it a prayer to the Almighty God that you may be long continued in your country her Ornament & Father, and that it may be more & more exemplified in you, Sir, that to know how to conquer & to improve the advantages of conquest into blessings to a community, are faculties sometimes bestowed on the same mortal.

I took a carriage ride through town with a lively narrator whose voice reminded me distinctly of a female Forrest Gump, which seemed appropriate since the bus bench where the movie begins is set in Savannah. "George Washington danced with about two hundred southern belles, and no one bothered to tell Martha," joked Tammy. "Well, if you asked me, thaaat is a weee bit muuuch!" We passed a sign for a drag show put on by Lady Chablis, famous for her role in the book and movie *Midnight in the Garden of Good and Evil*. "I recommend it for aaall y'all," Tammy sang out.

George makes the pleasure he took in more conventional festivities crystal clear in his diary. On his second night in town he met with a "dancing Assembly at which there were about 100 well-dressed handsome ladies." A night later, a local scribe noted that, "after a few minuets were moved, and one country dance led down, the President & his Suit retired about 1 o'clock, [AM]" adding that, "dances continued to 3 o'clock [AM]." Such were the late southern nights out typical of the era.

A Washington family member would describe a similar dance scene several years earlier, remarking that the "minuet was much in vogue at that period, and was peculiarly calculated for the display of the splendid figure of the chief, and his natural grace and elegance of air and manners. . . . As the evening advanced, the commander-in-chief yielding to the general gayety of the scene, went down some dozen couple in the contre [country] dance with great spirit and satisfaction." By accounts, George was still doing minuets into his fifties. The president, who sometimes stood stiff in crowds and found it hard to smile through his now entirely false teeth, was at ease on a dance floor in any town he entered. If there was any doubt that George, in addition to also being a politician, was also a ladies' man, the southern tour confirmed this beyond a shadow of a doubt.

During his trip, George paid close attention to the lay of the land and the mood of the population. He was not always impressed with what he saw, but he concluded that southerners had "abundant means to live well the grounds where they are settled yielding grain in abundance and the natural herbage a multitude of meat with little or no labr. to provide food for the support of their Stock—especially in Georgia where it is said the Cattle live through the winter without any support from the owner of them."

Along the way, George had done his best to show people that their leader was civil, polite, and concerned with their lives. He further observed, "The manners of the people, are far as my observations, and means of information extended, were orderly and Civil. And they appeared to be happy contented and satisfied with the government under which they are placed," adding, "Where the case was otherwise, it was not difficult to trace the cause to some demagogue, or speculating character."

These southern injustices, though overlooked for the enslaved, did not go entirely unnoticed. Though George received word that Georgians and South Carolinians had "buried the hatchet" with their Native American brethren, he worried that land speculators, disavowing principles of "justice to the Indians & policy to their Country would, for their own immediate emolument, strip the Indns of all their territory if they could obtain the least countenance to the measure."

With his ear to the ground amid all the pomp and protocol, the president accomplished what he had set out to on his tour. His very presence on the southern stage—apart from the ferry accidents—emanated power and certainty of purpose. Maybe his most lasting legacy is the example he set of style, grace, and decent behavior in public. Despite city fathers' throwing splendiferous balls, rollicking fireworks displays, lively processions, and fancy dinners—none of which he could have easily turned down—he had stuck to his original plan to avoid signs of outright favoritism, with the possible exception of his effusive speeches to the Freemasons on a few stops.

America's changing world of manners was as much in the eye of the beholder as in George's actual behavior or demeanor. Though he had learned much about patriotism and even new ideals, George, in truth, didn't act so differently in the decade after the Revolution as he had acted in the decade before the Revolution. He did not have to reenter a school of manners; he was already a polished emeritus. The social patterns in his life, as reflected in his diary, show that his tastes and interests were steady. He loved to ride his horse and attend dinner parties, and he enjoyed the company of beautiful women on whom he looked admiringly but did not touch romantically. In his southern tour and throughout his presidency, he honored his wife and remained cordial, if not warm, with almost everyone he met. However, as he would find out over two terms, the president's actions and demeanor were not nearly enough to please all of the people all of the time.

26

Fear and Glory
at the Races

WHEN I ARRIVED IN CHARLES TOWN, West Virginia, my idea of a great day at the Thoroughbred races was some Tinsel Town fantasy of Grace Kelly in a big hat and pearl necklace, cheering at the top of her lungs as the horse I bet big on thundered down the stretch on the outside and won by a nose. Men in hats and ladies in bigger hats, cigars, everyone's hearts thumping. You get the idea.

I had come back to West Virginia's eastern panhandle, just a ninety-minute ride from Alexandria, with a touch of nostalgia for my childhood spent playing on the lawn of a gingerbread mansion and rummaging through the attic in search of secrets. I recalled gawking at the grounds where hundreds of US soldiers guarded the hanging of the would-be emancipator John Brown. Before Robert E. Lee and his forces seized Brown in a fight at Harpers Ferry, Brown had swept down on the plantation of Col. Lewis Washington, taken him hostage, and, for its talismanic value, stolen an heirloom sword that George Washington wore in the Revolution. Brown reportedly cradled George's sword at his side as the men who brought him to "justice" slashed him nearly to death.

There are probably more Washingtons, including the last Washington heir to Mount Vernon, buried in the Zion Episcopal Church graveyard than anywhere in America, almost all of them relatives of George's three younger brothers, Jack, Samuel, and Charles, the last after whom the town was named. The brothers, setting themselves up on Shenandoah lands first surveyed by their famous full brother, erected sprawling plantation homes, some nearly as spectacular as Mount Vernon.

Built on a hilly and fertile crescent five miles south of Harpers Ferry at the confluence of the Potomac and the Shenandoah, Charles Town still should be a quaint small town. Instead it survives on tenterhooks in the shadow of gambling kingpins who reap immense profits from weekend gamers but give little back to the local community. Main thoroughfares are lined with homeless persons and pawnshops that do a brisk business with old-timers selling their life's possessions to get back to the casino for one more hand of blackjack. With some trepidation, I approached my grandmother's now dilapidated Victorian-era home to discover that the former grass tennis courts in the front had become a parking lot. The horse pasture out back had been sold off for low-income housing units.

But I wasn't in town to take toll of the demise of small-town America. I was in Charles Town after a hiatus of several decades to taste what was left of the horse racing, which began here in the eighteenth century and sustained the economy long before a casino opened. I wanted a taste of the winner's circle and to enjoy the thrill that George Washington had experienced betting on similar-style Thoroughbred races, sometimes with his own horse, at the races in Alexandria, Fredericksburg, and Annapolis. From his diary entries, it is apparent George was an avid horse breeder and an even more passionate racing fan. His affection no doubt stemmed from a childhood in which race days were a veritable carnival of delight in Fredericksburg.

During the Revolution, George, spotting a group of Connecticut cavalry officers on fine gray horses, sent a Captain Lindsey to inquire about a strain of Arabian horses sired by a stud named Ranger. As it turned out, the sultan of Morocco had gifted Ranger to a British captain who had left the horse on American soil as a breeder. Washington bought the horse, which crossed with another famous Arabian offspring, the mare Othello, and sired one of George's favorite racing horses, Magnolia, or "Magnolio" as George wrote. On one recorded occasion, Magnolio, a chestnut stallion, raced and lost at the Alexandria track against a horse belonging to George's friend and sometimes rival Thomas Jefferson. Apparently Magnolio wasn't a keeper, and George sold him in 1788 to Henry "Light Horse Harry" Lee for several thousand acres of land in Kentucky.

In his later years, George held posts and was master of ceremonies on occasion at the Fredericksburg and Alexandria jockey clubs. From his account books, I had learned that George generally bet small amounts on horses. This gave me some confidence that, as a novice,

I could afford the thrills of betting without going entirely broke. Who knew? Maybe I would get lucky and make some money. It was John Steinbeck who said, "The profession of book writing makes horse racing seem like a solid, stable business."

On my way to the paddock on a warm Saturday afternoon in February, I did spot Grace Kelly. She stared wistfully down from a gigantic photograph above the head of a hulk of a man with a head of unruly gray hair, not unlike that of Albert Einstein. He was busy, like thousands of others, pulling on the slots inside Charles Town Races' sprawling 250-yard-long Hollywood Casino. Out along the rail, the manicured green turf I recalled from a childhood visit was mostly dirt and cracked concrete. There weren't any belles in bonnets, nor did I spot any gentlemen in blazers smoking cigars. In the track's covered stands, I saw a few hacks scribbling away on their race cards, assessing the night's odds based on victories, jockeys, and such.

It was still early. Most of the bettors were inside gorging on the buffet behind plate glass overlooking the track. My immediate thought was that the gene pool in West Virginia had taken yet another nosedive. As far as I could see, some of the horses had been better bred but were not better fed than some of the race fans at the track. Hostesses had reserved the first floor for roly-poly families that were gorging themselves on the all-you-can-eat buffet. The cheesecake, chocolate tarts, apple pie, and ice cream were all slipping off the counter at lightning speed.

I made a beeline for the bar. I wasn't hopeful, but I wanted to try to catch up with a few serious horse gamblers. I needed advice, so I glanced around for someone pacing himself or herself on beer, not whiskey. Perched on a stool monitoring ten television screens with races from across America, I spotted someone who looked relaxed and alone. The bar in front of him was littered with dozens of losing tickets, probably not a good sign.

"Hi. It's my first time. Can you give me any tips?" I asked, sitting down next to him and introducing myself. "I'd like to understand how to win, or at least not lose too much."

"Not really. I just play the numbers," said Mike, offering to buy me a beer.

"What's 'the numbers'?" I asked.

"Well, I was born in the year 1958, so I play variations on that number most of the time. For example, I will bet on the five and the eight horse or on eight-to-five odds. What's your birthday?"

"1961."

"OK. I'll go bet on that," he said. He ambled off to an electronic betting machine and bet my birthday on a race about to start in California. He returned with a sparkle in his eye.

"That doesn't sound like a winning formula," I said. "How can you win doing that?"

"I don't bet much," he said, and laughed. He wasn't concerned. His girlfriend, Chrissy, was on the way, and when she arrived they both settled on stools beside me. We had a nice chat about George Washington and low-income housing. On the video screens overhead, Mike's bets produced no wins. There wasn't much excitement either until a jockey got squeezed off his mount on the screen above us and went bounding in a fetal position down the track like a misfired cue ball. A horse on his immediate right trampled him, and a great howl went up in the bar. Blood sport, I thought. I'd seen a replay of a race a few years back at Charles Town in which one horse tumbled and five more came crashing down behind him like dominoes, leaving only one horse and one jockey to finish the race.

I was sandwiched between Mike and one of his good friends, a guy named Dantel. I was hoping Dantel had a better formula for winning than Mike had.

"I study the books closely," he told me. "A lot of it has to do with jockeys and trainers. I know most of them."

"Oh," I said. "So you win more than you lose?"

"Not really," he said. "A lot of it is dumb luck. Mike"—he gestured past me—"was there one night when a lady walked in on her anniversary and told her husband to bet the anniversary date for a trifecta." A trifecta, I knew, was picking the one, two, and three placements in the correct order.

"She ran the house for $48,000 all on one bet," Dantel said.

"Yep," added Mike.

With that advice in hand, I made my way past the mussels in wine sauce and bleeding roast beef, outside, and back down to the rail. Still short of any logical system, I decided to just bet the race favorites to win or place.

I lost the first two races, and with my patience running dry, I decided to bet on cute names. So I bet on Ello Govna in the third race.

I once had an editor in London who answered the phone, regardless of who was on the line, with those two words. It was a good hunch, and he beat out a horse named Retirement Plan for my first win.

Whether you are standing and cheering wildly or—as George Washington probably did—watching the race with aloof resolve, horse races give you a healthy adrenaline rush. It all comes down to a great finish line when your horse or horses, still in contention, barrel down the backstretch to victory or defeat. It was a lot more fun, I thought, than sitting in a dark casino, pulling on a cigarette, and waiting for three rows of cherries to pop up. Racing is usually outdoors in the open air, and it has the sense of a splendid spectator sport. If you love horses as much as you love your pets, as I do, there is also the added thrill of watching a lovely animal sprinting all out at speeds often between thirty and forty miles an hour. When you win, usually folks—if they aren't too busy sulking over their own losses—turn to you and actually smile.

Horse races pack a punch of Americana as well. The track at Charles Town is shorter than several larger, more famous Thoroughbred tracks. In this regard, it is more like the eighteenth-century Thoroughbred races that usually pitted about a half dozen horses against one another on an oval track, usually grass or turf, not the soft dirt that is preferred now.

The big races these days are outside the area, but Virginia, of which West Virginia was a part until 1863, is where it all started. Racing arrived in Virginia in the 1600s and flourished early, mostly with quarter-horse runs. New York's British governor Richard Nicholls, who had been groom to the bedchamber of King Charles II's younger brother James, built an actual track on Long Island in 1665. Tracks followed in Virginia, several of them between the Potomac and Rappahannock, George's home turf.

At its outset, horse racing was mostly the domain of the upper classes, at least when it came to wagering. In York County, for instance, a tailor tried to bet £2,000 of tobacco and a cask in a race against a wealthy neighbor, Matthew Slader. Because the tailor was not a member of the gentry, he was fined £100, with the judge declaring it "contrary to the Law for a Labourer to make a race being a Sport only for a Gentleman." Everything from the dress to the language of betting spoke of a class system. Not so anymore.

In many ways, gambling on horses in the eighteenth and even nineteenth century was easier than it is today. Gentlemen who bet on horses knew each other; they knew their horses, including the bloodlines of the opposing horses. The riders were often servants or slaves, and after the middle of the eighteenth century, riders were often black and small in stature. George Washington's valet and companion during the Revolution, William Lee, who was of a similar race and build, began his life as a horse jockey.

An eighteenth-century racing venue provided more than amusement. While the races were an often brutal sport for the riders, for the gentry, they allowed for stylish displays, including exhibitions by ladies sporting new dresses and parasols. Men and women often arrived at the races in carriages and remained seated while individual male riders, often just spectators themselves, pranced and preened about the infield on steeds to impress the ladies. In this way, horse racing always maintained a romantic air. Race days, which often coincided with court days, legitimized aristocratic values, including wealth, competition, and independence. The scene also allowed men to let off steam and to settle financial scores in a peaceful, even genteel manner. But if an eighteenth-century race was a good place to see and be seen, it was also a place to witness who held the reins of power and control.

To that end, the race day was well regulated with stipulations for good and decent behavior. Early in the eighteenth century, an announcement advised that "All Persons resorting there are desir'd to behave themselves with Decency and Sobriety," the sponsors being "resolv'd to discountenance all Immorality with the utmost Rigour." The general public could almost always attend, if not always bet, and the same announcement suggested a good reason: for "cultivating friendship."

I vowed, after my first win, to make more friends myself. I sat down next to Guillermo, who had long, stringy hair and appeared to be wavering somewhat on his bar stool.

"First time at the Charles Town races?" I asked.

"Yes," he replied. "My first, but I know a horse."

"You know a horse?" I repeated.

I pegged Guillermo for a slightly inebriated South American horse trainer. There were many in the Shenandoah area. He wasn't very coherent, though, so I could not be sure.

"You can call me Villiam."

"OK, Villiam," I said. Guillermo then tried through a series of incomprehensive vowel sounds to buy us both a round of shots, but Brittany, our young waitress, cut him off abruptly.

"You are going to have to pay your tab now," she said, flashing him what I took to be a scowl.

Moments later, two dour men in black suits arrived and ushered my new friend out of the casino. So much for cultivating friendship at the races, I thought. Certainly it must have been easier for George.

At that point, however, an older, gray-haired gentleman, very Anglo-Saxon looking, arrived at my side and ordered four bottles of dark beer. It turned out that Larry Angus—"like the cows"—had been a joint owner of the Charles Town Race Track in the 1990s and had sold his stake to the current casino consortium.

"Historically speaking, horse races have meant everything to folks around here," he began. "Even before this track came up in the 1930s, horse racing was big in Charles Town. Everyone was in on it, and everyone wanted to make money from it." During the Great Depression, bootlegging and horse racing in West Virginia went together hand in glove. They were a formula for survival. Both often involved some avoidance of the law.

"Things have changed a lot since the heyday," Larry continued. "It is not clear that horse racing will even survive. Kids these days want instant gratification, you know. They can't be bothered to study the daily listings. They just want to push a button and 'bingo'—they win something."

"That's a casino in a nutshell," I said, looking out at a sea of money-crazed locals spending hand over fist as bells and whistles sounded near and far.

"And then you have the drugs," said Larry.

"You are talking about the horses or the people?" I asked. I had read an earlier report that in a two-week time span, one county emergency dispatcher fielded twenty-six heroin overdose calls. Across the entire state of West Virginia, the number of people dying from heroin overdoses had tripled in the last five years.

"No, I mean the horses," said Larry. "They were drugged constantly, and some of it was legal because the horses suffer, like humans, from allergies."

"Oh, you mean like the doping of athletes?" I asked. "Major League Baseball a decade ago?"

"Yeah," Larry said. "There is testing, but you can't get it all. It is widespread."

Less betting and renewed fears over doping scandals now threatened to take a toll in Charles Town's Jefferson County, said Larry. A lot was at stake: racing still employs 14 percent of the county's workforce, according to the local news reports. Across the board, in a state whose citizens struggle to make ends meet, Thoroughbred racing produces 3,844 direct jobs and $40.5 million in pay for employees.

Several leading watchdog groups have cited the Charles Town race track—a kind of minor league for bigger tracks in Maryland, Kentucky, and New York—as having a doping problem. Breeders, owners, and racing executives concerned about the impact of rumors have agreed that better federal regulation is now essential. Even my trusty foxhunting friend Col. Dennis Foster weighed in on the side of regulation. "There is no question that racing needs medical regulation reforms, including standardized laboratory testing," he told me.

Top Thoroughbreds are often selected for having speedy, champagne-glass legs, which experts say can break down when pushed too far and too hard with drugs. The physical stress from drugs can lead to falls and dead horses or, worse, mauled jockeys. Naturally, doping horses wreaks havoc on anyone's effort to understand and play the odds, since a drugged horse on any given day can beat a horse fed on oats and hay.

It's a sad state of affairs that needs correcting, particularly with more and more average punters believing the fix is in on horse races.

Larry, who had a lovely lady to attend to, had some betting advice for me despite my fears of never understanding the odds. He pointed up to a television screen showing the horses moving about the track before the next race.

"Watch that horse's gate closely," he told me. "You see it is favoring its back right leg?"

"Yeah," I said.

"Watch for that when you are betting," he said. "He won't show, and he can't win tonight. Another thing I can suggest: don't bet on the favorites. If they don't win, which they often don't, you just go broke. I like a horse with a shot, decent odds to win but still not a sure thing."

That made sense. I started to look out for limps and drugged animals, including humans. Frankly, they all looked drugged after what I had learned, but I settled on a couple of bets in the last two races based on two long shots that weren't too long. I made my way to the betting machine and laid down thirty-dollar bets on two horses, Thunder Lord and Wild Ham. They were both about seven-to-two odds, and their numbers in the books, recent finishes, and jockeys looked respectable.

Before the races, I went back inside to have a gander at all the sad casino clients stuck with losing hands. It was still early, but more drunks were being shown the door. I was pretty sure Uncle George would have been appalled by all the sordid behavior in his former backwoods. The dance crowd had arrived, and a middle-aged rocker at the far end of the casino belted out the lyrics of "Brick House" as I ran back up the ramp and down a flight of stairs to the rail.

Moments later, Thunder Lord was powering down the stretch, his jockey holding on tight and slapping his hindquarters. The race caller caught a wind: "And it's Thunder Lord taking the rail." The horse clinched it at the finish.

I had only one race left, but if I won it, my total earnings would pay for my weekend at the races. I'd stuck with the same formula, but when the race got under way, my pick, Wild Ham, was nowhere to be seen near the front. He hadn't shown at the halfway point either, and I resigned myself to a final loss and further research. Then, from out of nowhere, Wild Ham appeared on the rail, legs pounding the dirt with fury. Panicked jockeys in front started flailing their steeds. The home stretch arrived. Momentarily, I lost it, cheered madly, and waved my program in the air. I looked to my side, and I knew my luck would not last indefinitely. I saw two officials in black ogling me as though I were behaving as poorly as Guillermo. I was fine with that, considering the circumstances. I cashed in my two winning tickets, straightened my gait, and headed back to the Turf Motel for a relaxing beer in a quaint little pub appropriately named Turf's Winners Circle Lounge.

27

L'Aristocrate Meets la Guillotine

I ARRIVED IN PHILADELPHIA in the heart of winter and settled down for a history lesson at the downtown City Tavern, which, according to the colonial-era *Pennsylvania Packet*, in 1774 was "erected at great expense by a volunteer subscription of the principal gentlemen of the city for the convenience of the public, and is much the largest and most elegant house occupied in that way in America." The tavern served for George Washington and his many friends as a warm retreat from the rigors of both the Continental Congress and the Constitutional Convention. John Adams would call it the finest tavern in America, and the modern American historian David McCullough would tout the tavern—rebuilt in the 1970s to the precise architectural specifications derived from original insurance records after a nineteenth-century fire—as a place where "we can come to know them [the Founders] through . . . their music, their architecture, the ways they worshipped, and yes, God be praised by the food they ate."

I looked over at the tall, burly bartender clad in eighteenth-century garb and added to myself, And by the spirits they imbibed. After seating myself at a wooden bench beside the bar, I was presented with a stark, dumbfounding choice between Alexander Hamilton's Pale Ale ("citrusy and smooth") and George Washington's Dark Porter ("rich, hoppy, and smooth"). I chose what I believed might be George's favorite, his namesake, also ordering the most inexpensive menu staple, a German sausage.

Several guests soon plopped down beside me.

"What brings you here?" I asked, by way of making conversation.

"We are on our way to a stage play, but we thought we would drop in for a bite first," said David, who was out for the evening with his best friend. A Philly-area traffic engineer, David was also a supercharged history buff. He was currently reading a book about the spy craft of the Revolution, and he confessed to me that he enjoyed "living in the eighteenth century."

"I grew up taking field trips to Independence Hall and Ben Franklin's old haunts in Philadelphia. Now I take my son. We just visited Fort Ticonderoga and Colonial Williamsburg, my favorite."

David had his own theory as to Washington's ascent: "He had pretty serious issues with the British as far back as the French and Indian War, so it doesn't surprise me that he became a revolutionary," he said. "But George really moved up in life—into the upper echelons of society, I mean—by taking a fine wife, who was quite wealthy."

"Never a bad idea," I agreed.

We both were well into our first beers when we looked up to see a gentleman sporting a tailored brown jacket with gold lace and white knickers with buttons running along the seams. Bearded and erudite looking, he bore himself with a friendly modesty. He was, as it turned out, the City Tavern's own harpsichordist.

"We're in one of George's favorite haunts," said the harpsichordist, whose name was Mark Carroll. The City Tavern was the place gentlemen met after hours and a place dances took place and political deals were made, he added. "George first met John Adams at the Tavern and probably, as far as we can tell, also the Marquis de Lafayette."

Mark suggested I hurry down my beer and join him over at his colonial-era replica harp. David bid me adieu and left for his performance, and I sat down beside Mark as he started strumming several bars of Handel. The eighteenth-century model harp was Mark's own creation, hand-carved down to the twelve bridges and swirling baroque inlay.

"George Washington's men captured several talented Hessian musicians at the Battle of Trenton and allowed them to settle in as artists in Philadelphia in exchange for giving up the struggle to kill Americans," he said. It sounded to me like a straightforward and fair exchange.

"George was quite friendly with musicians," Mark added. "He wasn't all business, you know."

Other musicians flocked to Philadelphia's music scene after the Revolution. These included John Proctor, who had been George's Revolutionary War artillerist and band director. Washington had earlier used Proctor's services "mostly to blow things up, like houses," said Mark.

"Oh?" I said.

"Another local musician who often entertained dignitaries in Philadelphia was Francis Hopkinson," said Mark. "He was a playwright, a poet, and a lawyer but also the organist at Christ Church." Hopkinson's poem, "The Battle of the Kegs," is a satirical indictment of British admiral Richard Howe's befuddlement when faced with colonial kegs of dynamite floating toward him in the nearby Delaware River.

As it turned out, in addition to being a historian, Mark was a part of the legacy of colonial-era music in Philadelphia. A former navy cook, he traveled the world and spent a lot of time in Spain before returning to his hometown to raise a family. He didn't have a formal education, but he played the violin, the flute, and the fife, as well as the harp.

"My dad was a pianist, and my Revolutionary War relative was Salisbury Carroll, the pianist," Mark said. "We still have his piano." Mark's two children, now grown, paid their respects to us as they left the tavern on the way to a nearby musical gig.

As the complex business of the Constitutional Convention got under way in 1787, George filled his diary with new entries about his visits to the tavern, where delegates hammered out much of the after-hours business of creating a nation. Ale, wine, and other sundry spirits greased the wheels of the political process and guaranteed a less-than-perfect union of states. On May 29, 1787, George—who habitually drank two or three glasses of wine in a sitting but never drank to excess—entered into his diary that he "dined with a club at the City Tavern and spent the evening at my quarters writing letters." On June 12 George "dined and drank tea at Mr. Morris's" and "went afterwards to a concert at the City Tavern." Then on June 18, in what was a raucous salute, the former commander in chief appeared as the guest of honor at a "meeting of the Sons of St. Patrick, held at the City Tavern." Not all get-togethers were at taverns, and the same month, he "dined with Mr. John Penn [of the Quaker founding family], and spent the evening at a superb entertainment at Bush-hill given by Mr. Hamilton—at which were more than an hundred guests." On September 14 of the same year, he dined again at the tavern "at an entertainment given on my account." The delegates were in a celebratory mood, and on the day, September 17, their new document was signed off on but still not formally ratified, they all, according to George, "adjourned to the City Tavern."

Mark ushered me upstairs to the grand ballroom, which was one of the largest ballrooms in Philadelphia during the Convention. It was magnificent and sprawling for the day, with showy fireplaces on either end, ornate wooden mirrors on the walls, and an elaborate chandelier overhead.

"Just imagine the events that went on here," said Mark. "Many of the balls here were held in honor of George and Martha, and the dancing often went on into the wee hours of the morning." I pictured the guests lined up to pay their respects to George and Martha and Thomas Jefferson looking on with his usual suspicions.

Philadelphia, which would become the seat of the presidency for the lion's share of George's two presidential terms, did not have a reputation as the best place in the new nation to party—even after the Constitution was signed. It was flush with persons we might call social conservatives today. These were the same folks who had tried for years to ban theater performances anywhere north of Baltimore. But Philadelphia was also a city of contrasts and contradictions, the largest metropolis in America in the colonial era, with a reputation for religious tolerance and a population of close to forty thousand. It had a circus, a good line of taverns with acceptable menus, and an art museum. At the same time, it remained under the moral sway of its first European inhabitants, men and women who set the wheels in motion in 1682, the Quakers. Tolerant of others because of their own history of persecution and the value that they placed on education, the Quakers created a city open to all races and religions. They made known their strong views opposing slavery, a divisive issue that would provide added momentum for the eventual shift of the nation's capital to lands that abutted George's native Virginia.

Washington admired the Quakers deeply, but it is apparent from his diary entries that both George and Martha preferred to spend most of their leisure time with another set. As George wrote tellingly, Philadelphia "possessed a very gay fashionable circle, despite the large Quaker element in its population."

George and Martha, by the logs of their social visits, preferred fashionable and lighthearted to austere and moralizing. Their elite social circle included Philadelphia's rich and powerful, led by Robert Morris, who at the time of the Constitutional Convention was deemed the "richest man in America." He had helped finance the Revolution. George would stay with Morris when in town and eventually would lease a two-story home from him when the capital moved from New York to Philadelphia in 1790. I visited the walls of this former presidential dwelling, excavated and reconstructed today. They stand only about a hundred yards from the city's glass-encased Liberty Bell. Much of the writing on historical markers inside the walls attests to the difficult lives of the servants who worked within.

Both Washingtons were also close to Samuel Powel, the former mayor and eventual owner of the City Tavern, and to his erudite wife, Eliza Willing Powel, who would correspond in writing with George frequently. The couples had lived side by side during the Revolution in 1781 and 1782. Even before assuming the presidency, George and Martha had been frequent guests of Annis Boudinot Stockton at her estate, Morven, not far from Philadelphia in New Jersey. Her parlor served as a venue for discussions of everything from the novel idea of promoting women's education in the new nation to dark political intrigue to the latest literature from London.

Martha was herself a trendsetter. She began George's first presidential term by hosting small public receptions in New York City that encouraged good manners and decency while discouraging ruffians and rapscallions. A visitor to one of Martha's early assemblies said it represented "all that was fashionable, elegant, and refined in society," adding, "but there were no place for the intrusion of the rabble in crowds, or for the mere coarse and boisterous partisan." Abigail Adams described Martha as "unassuming, dignified and feminine," without even a "tincture of hauteur about her."

George was not the same and often struck an awkward nervousness into his visitors. When his friend Gouverneur Morris (his actual name, not his title) wagered Alexander Hamilton that Hamilton could not get the president to just act like one of the guys, Hamilton took the bet and approached George in a chummy manner, put his arm on his shoulder, and remarked, "My dear General, how happy I am to see you so well!" Washington took a step back and froze the younger man out with a frown, which spoke volumes about his demanding sense of protocol.

For her part, Martha did her best at her semipublic gatherings to set the mood of the new nation, but her events didn't always come off as planned. The ubiquitous step-grandson George Washington Parke Custis, about nine at the time, later would describe women sporting ostrich plumes at one such meeting, including one "Miss McEvers," who had "plumes unusually high to the ceiling of the drawing room." He added that Miss McEvers's feathers "were ignited by the flames of the chandelier," and George's right-hand man had to "spring to the rescue."

Thomas Jefferson, who relentlessly championed ideals of a rustic, rural life, frowned on such salon gatherings and railed against the influences of big-city vices, while Hamilton and his "Hamiltonians" championed the allure of parlor life and what one historian, referring to women's styles, joked was the "fashionable nakedness of their women." Though he remained above the fray most of the time, George began to suffer guilt by association with the Hamiltonians in the eyes of many quick-witted pundits who bought into protocols of republican virtue.

After the ratification of the Constitution on December 7, 1787, George was all too aware of what he would need to do to help the new nation live up to its ideals and to set a new fashion for independence. If he was going to help in any way to craft a New American Man and Woman, he knew he needed help of his own. In 1788 he wrote to Annis Boudinot Stockton, whose poetry and social influence were then flourishing, stating, "And now I am speaking of your Sex, I will ask whether they are not capable of doing something towards introducing federal fashion and national manners?" It were an extraordinary moment for an individual who as a youth read advice from the pens of European clerics intended for courtiers in order to polish chivalrous manners. Yet there is also ample evidence from his early years that Mary Ball Washington is to thank for George's trust that women should be the purveyors of good manners not only in the house but also across society as a whole. Two wars and several decades later, it made sense that he was reaching out to a woman to help him set the style and fashion for a new nation.

He wanted American style to be designed and made in America, warning against the dangers inherent in "purchasing foreign superfluities and adopting fantastic fashions, which are, at best, ill-suited to our stage of Society." This was one of several signs after the Revolution that Washington was keen to assume a central role, with the help of friends, as a leader in the realm of behavior and fashion. He also wanted women to play a greater role in the public space, and he encouraged help from Martha, who would prove talented at organizing ladies and getting their input.

Despite a hankering for more indigenous fashions and manners, George and Martha were sometimes too consumed by politics to notice all the changes that were about to explode in Europe and stretch across the Atlantic in waves and ripples. Though George had never been far from the spinning gyre, the changes brewing in Paris were profound. The French Revolution, which ripped through the courts and salons of Paris in 1789, spoke to a longed-for equality and liberty valued by the masses, which included intellectuals, artisans, day laborers, indentured servants, slaves, and farmers. Initially, before mass bloodshed descended on France, shared ideas of liberty and equality remained all the rage in allied America. As bloodshed rose, though, the tide would turn. The French Revolution, at its core, posed a danger to the privileged political classes everywhere and aristocrats of all stripes, including the American patriarchs who signed the Constitution.

As the Revolution took hold, old-school aristocrats attempted to change course and join the mass revolt. Many were sincere in their undertakings. George's aristocratic protégé the Marquis de Lafayette led the charge to break open the Bastille, and he came away with at least one key, which he gifted to his friend and mentor "Mon Général" Washington. Lafayette's mind burned with idealistic fire, and he helped write the first draft of the French Declaration of Rights of Man and of the Citizen. It stated unequivocally, "Men are born and remain free and equal in rights. Social distinctions can be founded only on the common utility."

French men and women took the meaning of such ideas literally. They began to express new egalitarian aspirations openly and in the public arena. This did not pose great obstacles at the start of the French Revolution as for centuries France had been a nation of elaborate manners and fashion. Indeed, European chivalry was born there, despite what the British might contend. Its citizens based much of their social interaction on polite habits, which were handed down to the British royal courts after the Norman Conquest. For these reasons, the French did not initially suffer intense dissonance at the thought of combining aristocratic and republican virtues. Many of the Frenchmen who had fought alongside Washington in the American Revolution saw him as a kind of selfless citizen-patriot, the variety of man they hoped would inspire and lead their own country. It was true that Washington stood as a kind of model, even outside America, for the selfless patriot bent on freeing the masses from the grip of tyranny, but, of course, the truth was more complicated, particularly within the borders of the new nation.

In America, George Washington still represented different ideas to varied groups. His own life provided a metaphor for a clash between perceived republican values and a preference for aristocratic taste. In a sense, this showdown between who America was and who we would become had been brewing since its founding. America had imported its blue bloods—most from Mother England, Scotland, and Wales, though others from mainland Europe—and bred many more of its own. Of course, George wasn't really from an imported blue blood family, and he was not even much interested in his distant relations in England. As a child, he had grown up as a neighbor to the Lees and Carters, but it had taken him most of his adult life to acquire their wealth and power. Through dedication, hard work, and displays of courage in the field, he had risen to the level of these great Virginia dynasties. The Fairfax family's examples of manners and taste had stuck with him through the decades. In any case, he had earned (and not been gifted) his fancy stripes. In his youth he may have been a dandy who enjoyed parlor life at Belvoir, but his character had been shaped on the anvil of the frontier life, including through camping, hunting, and riding rough in the wilderness with strange men and their stranger ways. For George, nobility was not a birthright; he defined it through his actions.

The impact of the French Revolution was felt early and often in the streets of Philadelphia, both in the fashionable and poor districts of the city. Along with thousands of refugees who streamed into the city, major parades took place supporting the Revolution. Women wore handmade "liberty caps and French cockades." Both American men and women sang "La Marseillaise" and imbibed liberally to much discussed but poorly defined freedoms. In contrast, a local magazine argued that a locally designed "Federalist Bonnet" would be more appropriate than the flashy French fashions, which also included turbans for women.

Revolution caught fire in the streets as pure entertainment. A pair of life-size automatons that could be wound up to perform in public appeared a few blocks from the City Tavern. Citizen Sans Culotte and the opposing Mr. L'Aristocrate represented the two feuding sides of the French Revolution. Records show that Martha and her granddaughter attended a show and returned with George in tow. The robotic opponents saluted the audience and competed against one another for their attention. To the delight of all the spectators—probably the president included—they also danced, although Mr. L'Aristocrate reportedly refused to dance to any songs of the French Revolution.

A songbook available in Philadelphia bookstores made available the tunes and lyrics of a pro-French song, "God Save the Rights of Man," and another lengthy title, "Patriotic Stanzas on the Anniversary of the Storming of the Bastille." Street hawkers, exhibiting an entrepreneurial spirit in 1794, also charged for demonstrations of a guillotine, often twenty or twenty-five times a day. A dummy's head was severed from its body and dropped into a basket as gawkers stood on. The contraption was invented by Joseph-Ignace Guillotin, a Frenchman who had for years opposed the death penalty but settled for a faster means to kill people. (Guillotin himself once boasted to a public audience, "Now with my machine I take off your head in a twinkling of an eye, and you never feel it!")

Because it was charged with new ideas, The French Revolution helped Americans think and debate their own freedoms. Women, in particular, became conversant in politics. This didn't mean they were all wild-eyed revolutionaries, however. In truth, many of them—even aristocrats—had already played a role sustaining the American Revolution. Eliza Powel threw some of the best soirees in Philadelphia and she wasn't afraid to express her opinions in public. A French visitor to her home, George's friend the Marquis de Chastellux, praised her as "well read and intelligent," adding, "but what distinguished her most is her taste for conversation." Along with her niece Anne Willing Bingham, who was critiqued locally for wearing dresses made by Marie Antoinette's designer, she managed to keep women's issues at the front of polite conversation. In one exchange, Thomas Jefferson railed against the political activities of French women, describing them as "Amazona" in contrast to his preference for American "Angels," who he said were intelligent enough to know that politics was not their domain. Such quips by men were typical of the age. Bingham, who had studied in Paris a few years earlier, defended American women, shooting back that they had "obtained that rank in society, which the sex are entitled to, and which they in vain contended for in other countries."

Other leading male figures in Philadelphia adamantly opposed Francophilia and, in particular, the new French fashions and mind-sets that were creeping into American life. Periodical editor and pundit William Cobbett put his misogyny on display in the process, arguing that many women in Philadelphia had become "daredevil, turban-headed females," the kind he loathed. He said that he would as soon have a "host of infernals" in his house than a gathering of "Frenchified dames." He added that "of all the monsters in the human shape, a bully in petticoats is most completely odious and detestable."

George was in the middle of this controversy, but due both to his aloofness and closeness to opinionated female friends, he usually let others do the talking in public. And though he made an effort to look disinterested, evidence suggests that he never really was. It might be argued that since he was frequently out and about the town, attending the theater and engaging in regular conversation with educated women, he actively encouraged openness, inclusion, and new roles for women in the new nation. In his other role as patron of the arts, President Washington was "an unpaid performer, ably filing his role as leader to an often-admiring crowd."

George in his iconic way remained at the center of Philadelphia society, and at the theater he enjoyed the ongoing social debates that were played out through varied stage performances. He was also, as a product of the vibrant Augustan Age, entirely capable of laughing at his own class. This goes a way toward explaining why his name pops up on the dedication pages of a young American playwright, Royall Tyler, the author of a play titled *The Contrast*, which foreshadowed the imminent and bloody clash of aristocratic tastes with republican virtue. The play, which opened at the John Street Theatre on April 16, 1787, was another comedy of manners but somewhat more sophisticated in subject matter than the play I attended in Williamsburg, *Miss in Her Teens*. *The Contrast* is a rich satire that takes apart the character of one Billy Dimple, the epitome of foppish, Frenchified aristocracy. Dimple's actions are set against a classic backdrop of republican virtue, including that of the character Manly, who contends, "I have humbly imitated our illustrious Washington, in having exposed my health and life in the service of my country, without reaping any other reward than the glory of conquering in so arduous a contest." Manly stands up to Dimple, an eighteenth-century version of Eurotrash who comes off as a hypocritical rake, the very embodiment of what can go wrong when a man's taste is subsumed by luxury, drinking, and dueling. In short, Dimple is gentility run amok, and there was more here than met the eye, particularly since Royall Tyler, the playwright, was a bit of a fop himself and had, in his early years, sought and failed to date John Adams's daughter. It was the new kind of homegrown American drama that pleased George and not only exposed societal tensions but also provided a young nation with needed perspective. President Washington led a list of subscribers to the printed edition of the play in 1790, and he no doubt saw the nuance and humor in the story. (In Mount Vernon's 1799 inventory of possessions, I discovered a copy of *The Contrast*, suggesting George's extended appreciation.) The real lesson was that an obsession with fashion and manners could become a threat to republican virtue. It was all a delicate balance worth considering and exceptionally relevant to salon discussions. After all, George had spent much of his life trying to look good and charm his friends, but not look like a fop.

A performance that one day might begin with "La Marseillaise" and the next a tribute to America's great commander in arms represented a battle of ideas that further defined the values and ideals of the New American Man and Woman. Just to survive the critiques from the more puritanical-minded old Philadelphia establishment, one theater was renamed the "Opera House" in order to stave off the vice squads. Dramatists fought back against attempted theater bans, one writing satirically about concerns that theaters would be shuttered:

> No more they'll excite the lewd leer of the pit,
> Or set the whole house agrin
> The harlots, alas! Now their stations quit,
> Nor patches nor breasts need expose.

In practice, and in his heart, George continued to show his love for drama and theatrics for their edifying and moral value throughout the 1780s and 1790s. By his mere presence and attention to the exciting theater scene, he made it clear that he thought Americans were entirely capable of reconciling good virtue with sophisticated taste, including the occasional off-color joke.

On January 21, 1793, no one's favorite monarch, Louis XVI, found guilty of high treason, was placed beneath the guillotine. Along with the beheading of Marie Antoinette three months earlier, the ongoing slaughter of French aristocrats began to repulse many Americans. The defamation of the blue bloods finally had come to a horrific end. The satirical, usually underground press in France, including cartoonists, had played the key role in ridiculing aristocrats and vilifying monarchs for their manners and also for their sexual peccadilloes. The two well-publicized beheadings sent shock waves through the courts of Europe and indirectly impacted the behavior of American politicians, including Washington. As an ancillary result, pomp and circumstance, wildly popular through much of George's first term, were fully downplayed at the second inauguration. George had been reluctant to accept a second term, and his inaugural address suggested as much. It was over in just four sentences.

George's second round in office would bring infighting and accusations. Once the embodiment of all goodness and devotion born in America, George fell under further suspicion from America's biting press, which he had allowed to flourish without censorship. His unjust reward was that he was now accused openly of coveting a crown. There was still nothing to the rumor, but Jefferson, who once famously said he would rather have a free press than a government, was busy fanning the flames. The death of the French monarch brought to America's shores one "Citizen" Edmond-Charles Genêt. He was France's envoy to America, and as renewed conflict broke out between Britain and France, Genêt agitated to end Washington's national policy of neutrality toward French and British infighting. He wanted George to break his reticence and come down on the side of the increasingly bloody French Revolution, and through a shocking narrative, which he promoted in the streets from Charleston to Philadelphia, Genêt pegged George as a friend of that odious "counter-revolutionary Lafayette." (To his credit, Lafayette had been instrumental in helping the Revolution take off, particularly in moving ideals forward, but had later fallen out of favor. His aristocratic roots did not help him win friends in the broader masses either.) Washington could be accused of being an American baron and slave owner, but the charge that he treated the entire American people as "serfs," as Genêt insisted, was outlandish and did not sit well with most of Washington's broad constituency. Despite the false charges, Washington, chastened by a life as a soldier, continued to use his well-learned politesse to steer clear of a growing conflict between France and Great Britain.

Convinced of America's sound republican virtues, the commander in chief looked fairly unflappable. Well, almost. At a cabinet meeting, Gen. Henry Knox, who served as secretary of war, seized upon a newly published satire in the press titled *The Funeral Dirge of George Washington and James Wilson, King and Judge*, a playful drama in which Washington was dragged before the guillotine for alleged "aristocratic crimes." It was playful satire, but it went too far this time. George's temper, which he struggled to control all his life, blew another fuse, and Thomas Jefferson described the rage of the president in these words: Washington went into a tirade, and shouted that he would "rather be on his farm than be made emperor of the world, and yet that they were charging him with wanting to be king." It wasn't the first time he had been ridiculed, and it would not be the last, but even magnanimous George had his limits.

The attacks on his character continued, but the president resisted the temptation to crack down on the free press. When Jefferson, whom Washington admired despite his relentless political gamesmanship, decided to quit, George took it upon himself to saddle up his horse and go to him directly to dissuade him from leaving. In this, he succeeded in delaying Jefferson's departure. At their meeting, however, the lord and master of Monticello insisted without solid evidence that there were persons in the shadows conniving to put George on a throne. Considering this a silly suggestion, President Washington snapped back that such allegations were merely "proof of their insanity." Yet deep down, all the false insinuations still hurt.

George was at the end of his rope (and almost his presidency), and he wrote to a refined female friend—as he often did when he was down on his luck—that he certainly had no "ardent desire to be the butt of party malevolence," adding, "Having tasted that cup I found it bitter nauseous and unwholesome." George had done his best to set an example of good manners and an even temper for the nation, but now it was time to make a tactical retreat with his weary Martha to the relative calm and civility of Mount Vernon.

⊰ 28 ⊱

A Sportsman for All Seasons

LOOKING UPSTREAM FROM THE MUDDY brown heart of the Kanawha River, the banks are lush with pines, oaks, and tall grass. I tested my paddle against the relentless springtime rainwaters that flow north from the high, ravaged peaks of West Virginia coal country. Along the quiet shoreline where George made his way deeper into the American heartland, the waters were easier to traverse. I crossed over to get a better feel for the springtime currents. On the far bank, a great blue heron glided in the shadows near a Canadian goose gently urging her fluffy yellow offspring along with her beak. In the swift waters beneath me there were bluegill, catfish, and muskies in a river that, with the help of a coal mining community, has come back to life in recent years.

"He camped under that rock face up there above the train station," said Rush Finley, seventy-six, pointing to the Point Pleasant station. "The railway company knocked off the rock face when they built the train station, but folks still refer to it as Washington Springs. Daniel Boone is pretty big here, but George made his mark as well." Rush, who ran the desk at the historic Lowe Hotel at Point Pleasant, an hour north of Charleston, West Virginia, told me that his forefathers had fought begrudgingly for Virginia's Lord Dunmore in the Indian war he started just before the Revolution broke out. "That Brit started the war, as far as we know, just to get us all killed," he explained.

The Kanawha River still provides clues as to where George hunted and slept. Roads are named after the herds of buffalo he saw roaming wild in the valley, which runs south from the Ohio River.

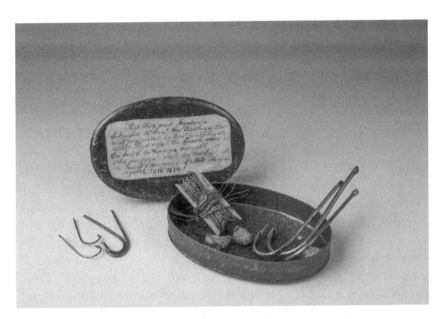

George Washington's tackle box, 1760–1800 [W-2201]. *Courtesy of Mount Vernon Ladies' Association*

Around World War I, a wealthy farmer built a rather precise replica of George's Mount Vernon estate along the riverbank not far from where I entered the river. But nearby, a historical marker makes it clear how George's first efforts to settle the land did not end well. An informative sign titled "Lost Colony" remarks on how Washington's attempts to send slaves and recent immigrants to farm the land failed. It reads, "Land was cleared, orchards planted, houses built, but when the war ended, the colony was gone." Another marker dolefully notes, "Here are graves of 'Mad Anne' Bailey, border scout, and Cornstalk, Shawnee chief, held hostage and killed here in 1777."

It said a lot about George Washington the woodsman and adventurer that after more than a decade as an established planter on the banks of the Potomac, he returned again to his great love, the vast American wilderness, in 1770. In his late thirties, with the drums of the impending Revolution thumping louder after the Boston Massacre, he still could not help indulging his passion for raw nature. It was an unquenchable desire, one that had driven him even in his teens.

The splendid descriptions that he wrote of his journey on horseback and then by canoe into the remote Kanawha River valley make clear his intense wanderlust for the great outdoors. In some moments, he played the role of a sharp-eyed surveyor, "gliding gently along," as he said, adding that the water "bottoms seemed to be getting a little longer and wider, as the bends of the river grew larger." At other moments, George was more of a rapturous explorer, remarking that "after a little distance from the river, we came (without any rising) to a pretty lively kind of land grown up with hickory and oaks of different kinds, intermixed with walnut, etc., here and there." He added, "We also found many shallow ponds, the sides of which, abounding in grass, invited innumerable quantities of wild fowl among which I saw a couple of birds in size between a swan and a goose, and in color somewhat between the two. . . . The cry of these was as unusual as the bird itself, as I never heard any noise resembling it before." Then, at turns, he reprised his old role as a hunter, writing, "Went a hunting; killed 5 buffaloes . . . and three deer." He sounded surprised to have found a land where the buffalo roamed in such large numbers.

In 1770 the acquisition of western lands appealed to George's gambling instincts and his dedication to his fellow officers, and so after years of delays, he sought to make good on Lieutenant Governor Dinwiddie's promise of some two hundred thousand acres for Virginia officers who had served loyally in the French and Indian War. Property speculation, which soon consumed George once again, was a game he knew how to play and one that his talents were already honed for.

Earlier, in 1763, George had written of his desire to "explore uninhabited wilds," despite prohibitions, adding to his own surveyor, William Crawford, a kind of speculator's creed that any person "who neglects the present opportunity of hunting out good lands and in some measure making and distinguishing them for their own will never regain it." At the same time, he shrewdly advised Crawford that surveys at that time should be disguised from what they really were "under the pretence of hunting other game." It was of course a white lie, but who would doubt a man's good word when he was out in the woods with a gun? (Actually, Native Americans could, and in 1782, while traveling nearby, Colonel Crawford was captured and sadly burned alive at the stake.)

Having Crawford on the prowl for him was not enough, in any case. In the early winter of 1770 George set out on horseback with a small survey party, which included his close friend Dr. James Craik.

It would not be George's last adventure into unknown mountains, but this particular six-week journey into the wilderness, one of so many, was extraordinary for other reasons. As one of Virginia's wealthiest men, George Washington had absolutely no sufficient reason to be wandering mostly on his own in the distant forests of Virginia and Pennsylvania in search of new farmlands, even if most of them were for his fellow French and Indian War veterans. He did possess several parallel ideas about expanding frontiers with connecting waterways, but none of them had yet gained serious financial backing in 1770. The western lands he was after were distant and still considered too dangerous to settle and cultivate. Nevertheless, throwing caution to the wind as he often would in the heat of battle, George, who still had no children of his own, decided to risk it.

In the lush valley of the Kanawha, sided mostly with jagged mountains on one side and flat, rich farmlands on the other, it is easy to see why our preeminent Founding Father headed out for another camping trip. Indeed, finally after decades of neglect, an environmental coalition, the Coal River Group, is helping to restore the natural beauty to the river region. The coalition organizes local families and resources to help clean out old tires and toxins, making the river water potable and navigable once more. The Coal River Group's chief, Bill Currey, though he was still closed for the long West Virginia winter, happily lent me one of his river crafts for my own journey from Point Pleasant to Leon, where George finally turned around and headed home to Martha after some extraordinary hunting and surveying.

George was always ready to gamble on the next tract of American wilderness. As a habit, he kept most of his long-term investments in land, not in gold or banknotes. He was, in the classic sense, always land rich and money poor, but he liked it that way. When he traveled after the French and Indian War, sleeping here and there in taverns or with friends, the conversation often turned to farming and the quality or value of the land. He was always curious about what grew where and how. Later, as president on his southern tour, enthralled with southern belles and rolling along past waving citizens, he couldn't help but stop and chat with fellow farmers about the lay of the American land, its trails and waterways. (In addition to being a good gambler, I suspect George would likely have been quite hard to beat at Monopoly had that game been invented. Not surprisingly, he would die one of the wealthiest men in the new nation.)

George had set off in October 1770 to stake his claims on the Kanawha River, and an old friend, Col. George Croghan, set him up with provisions and Indian guides, including one named the Pheasant. George wrote in his diary that he "received a Speech with a String of wampum from the White Mingo" and, referring to his first adventure with Christopher Gist, he added, "I was a Person who some of them remember to have seen when I was sent on an Embassy to the French, and most of them had heard of; they were come to bid me welcome to the Country, and to desire that the People of Virginia would consider them as friends & Brothers linked together in one chain." It was "their wish," he said, "to live in peace and harmy, with the white People, & that tho their had some unhappy differences between them and the People upon our Frontiers, it was all made up, and they hopd forgotten." With a hope and a prayer for burying the hatchet, George surely thought wistfully, if only for a moment, about his failed efforts to win Native Americans over to his cause in the early years of the French and Indian War.

Days later Washington and his fellow explorers, paddling against the currents, reached "Mingo Town," which contained some sixty native families. He noted, "Upon our arrival at the Mingo Town we received the disagreeable News of two Traders being killd at a Town calld the Grape Vine Town, 38 miles below this, which caused us to hesitate whether we should proceed or not, & wait for further Intelligence." The insecurities delayed but did not deter the party. The next day George wrote that the Indians said whatever happened had not been "done by their people." As it turned out, their word could be trusted. A single fur trader had drowned of his own volition.

On my own brief Kanawha trip, I discovered few traces of Native American life, but I did wind up for a time in a semipermanent trailer park full of unemployed but cordial coal miners. I spoke with a group of young men fishing on a Sunday. I learned they supported their coal mining union's efforts to uphold a sixty-dollar-an-hour mining income for jobs that were vanishing faster than the Indians ever had. They hadn't caught many fish, but they weren't giving up either. There was also plenty of venison left in the forest "when the fish are not biting," I was told.

As much as any American who came after him, George Washington bought into the myth of western freedom and limitless national
expansion. He had always believed in his own destiny as tied to rivers,
mountains, valleys, and wildlife. It was about who he was and what
we would became as a nation. He was an outdoorsman, a hunter, an
explorer, and a lover, but also a classic romantic enthralled with the
vastness of America. Though he wasn't an eloquent writer, George
Washington still contributed in his own way to the myth of the great
frontier. He spoke openly about his love of the land and how much
he cherished the steep, rugged trails and each new encounter. He was
as comfortable napping under a large boulder at the confluence of
two rivers as he was sleeping in an immense bedroom on a southern
plantation.

George never figured out what to do with his lands in the Kanawha
Valley. Though he talked about settling them, even breeding and raising tame buffalo on a ranch, his Kanawha tracts remained mostly out
of reach for him. Yet his western lands always held a special place in
his thoughts. During the Revolution, with victory against the British
unsure and his own demons of depression taunting him, he spoke
of a secret dream he harbored. If he did not defeat the world's most
powerful army in the East, he would retreat to fight with a loyal
band of guerrillas past civilized society to the ends of the known
New World, the Kanawha Valley. He would fight in the trees, over
streams, night and day to maintain his independence and his honor.
Clad in buckskins and moccasins and flush with black powder, he
would continue the struggle against tyranny—a veritable Robin Hood
fighting on against the odds.

As a youth, George loved the idea of legends, and that may be
the best explanation of how he became one. Like a character out of
an early Hemingway story, he tested his exceptional physical skills
in the backwoods, taking off in the early winter of 1753 to struggle
through the mountains on horseback and on foot, parleying with the
American Indians and ducking an assassin's fire. He always measured
his courage and his will against the cruelties of nature. The wilderness
alone gave him the affirmation he needed to survive and fight another
day. That's the way he cut his own path, and that's how the world
first took notice of him. Even when his romantic passions dragged
him to the precipice of the abyss in a forbidden love affair, he went
west to fight and dodge more bullets. Later, eschewing the comforts
of towns he might have holed up in for the winter, he dragged his

Continental Army into the frozen hills at Valley Forge and watched them fight for their own lives against snow and starvation. In the end, his army emerged from its test, as he had as a young soldier, stronger and more capable than before.

As president, George never managed to hang up his spurs. He still rode to get away from it all, to exercise, to survey, to farm, to put down the Whiskey Rebellion, and to fend off potential new foes. Few eighteenth-century artists depict George without a horse at least at his side. It would be like leaving out his legs. There was often a wilderness backdrop as well, for he was first a frontiersman and sportsman, who spoke to others through his gesture and stature more than through words.

The specter of death often appeared to George on the horizon, possibly because he was from a short-lived family, but it did not strike a lasting fear into his heart. In his seventh decade, it only increased his haste to complete his colossal tasks. The world was still his stage, and he wrote to his step-grandson, "As the curtain of my political life is about to drop, I am, as you may suppose, a great deal hurried in the closing scenes." His great and final goal would be to help mold well-mannered men and women to the land he loved. He knew this work would remain for others to complete, but from his observations, it is easy to see that he was satisfied with his work in progress. America was in the process of becoming what its citizens hoped it would be. He remarked at one point on a tour of northern states that he was "persuaded that the ill-boding politicians who prognosticated that America would never enjoy the fruits from her independence" were flat-out "mistaken." For George, proving his critics wrong had always been inspiration to keep going.

He suffered from occasional bouts of gloom, but deep down he remained optimistic. He believed as much as any founder in the great experiment that was the United States, and he wrote to the poet David Humphreys that if Americans were only "permitted to improve without interruption, the great advantages which nature and circumstances" had placed before them, they would surely be ranked "not only among the most respectable, but among the happiest people on the globe." He also wanted the new nation, with its vast expanses and its growing love of liberty, to be an eternal refuge, stating his hope that America would be "not only the asylum of the oppressed of every nation, but a desirable residence of the virtuous and industrious of every country." A man's honor and hard work, not his religious persuasion, would and should be his ticket in the New World, and despite his shortcomings on racial issues, George Washington articulated that as well as any president who would follow.

Ironically, the burdens of his presidency and his troubled conscience hindered George's own pursuit of happiness in his late years. George's word had always been his honor. In 1786 he said, "In the course of my life I never forfeited my word, or broke a promise made to anyone." Few Americans doubted him on that, but his code of honor, which affirmed his self-worth as a southern gentleman, was now butting up against his conscience. It is clear that he felt these pangs both on a personal level, as a planter, and on a national level, as a founder.

As president, Washington would become unpopular with groups of America's western settlers whom he angrily accused of trying, without paying the natives, to "strip the Indians of all their territory if they could obtain it" for free. Despite generations of distrust between his own family and Native Americans, he came to see people he sometimes referred to as "savages" as men with rights, however poorly defined. In an account from Philadelphia by John Adams, George smoked an unusually large peace pipe with a visiting contingent of Chickasaw Indians in his own home. He felt deep down that they deserved peace and happiness like everyone else. Yet, like the black slaves in Virginia and elsewhere, the natives would not—in his lifetime at least—receive this from the white man. (Indeed, their fate would be arguably worse than that of the slaves and former slaves.)

George Washington also knew that American Indians and black Americans understood liberty and freedom in different ways than did European settlers—and because of their own experiences at the beck, call, and subjugation of others. And so it was that the inherited institution of slavery returned to haunt him in his final years. When he had taken over Mount Vernon at the age of twenty-two, he had assumed control of just eighteen resident slaves, yet after two wars and two presidential terms, the figure would stand in 1793 at over three hundred humans in bondage, many of whom belonged to his wife. Though he tried not to treat them poorly, dozens of these men and women attempted to escape from servitude. There could be, as his friend and neighbor George Mason had stressed, no good slave owners.

In the Revolution, General Washington had myriad direct dealings with black men willing to die for freedom. Though he wrote little about how this impacted him, records prove beyond a doubt that he suffered growing dissonance in his own mind toward his slaveholdings. Pressures for him to lead on the issue were constant—and from all sides. Emancipationists approached him in Virginia and Philadelphia. In 1790, upon becoming our first president, he openly entertained Warner Mifflin, a Quaker gentleman who sought the gradual emancipation of all slaves. In his diary he wrote objectively that Mifflin had "used Arguments to shew the immorality, injustice and impolicy of keeping these people in a state of Slavery," adding that he listened attentively but "was not inclined to express my sentiments on the merits of the question" before the issue passed to his desk for a decision.

It wasn't the first time he listened to ideas about liberating black men. At the end of the Revolution, the Marquis de Lafayette had written to George with a plan that he advised could serve to help all enslaved men. A wildly idealistic Lafayette, still only twenty-five years old at the time, suggested George unite with him "in purchasing a small estate, where we may try the experiment to free the Negroes, and use them as tenants," or farmers. Such a project would become a model for the liberation of slaves, the marquis insisted. Washington referred to the idea as "laudable work," thanking his friend profusely for the idea and calling it "striking evidence of the benevolence of your heart." A few years later, Lafayette reminded Washington of the idea a second time. That same year, 1786, George wrote, "I can only say that no man living wishes more sincerely than I do to see the abolition of it [slavery]." Of course, this would have taken far more than the stroke of a pen when he became president.

He now began to trouble himself to think of ways to help blacks and unburden his own conscience—asking his overseer at one point the prices he might get for selling all his slaves and, short of that, then telling his associate and would-be biographer Humphreys that he was ready, in his lifetime, to help lay a foundation for the freedom of his slaves. This involved a plan he described in 1793 to liquidate his properties, keep his main house, and have slaves on his other plantation hired out as common laborers by the purchasers. They would, in essence, be free wage earners, he explained. The idea for gradual liberation bore a resemblance to Lafayette's original idea. George's slaveholdings were, he wrote to David Humphreys, his "only unavoidable subject of regret." The idea to begin to free his slaves would not, he hoped, "be displeasing to the justice of the Creator." Despite his tortuous thinking about ways to free his slaves in his lifetime, the elaborate plan remained a secret and was never carried forward.

Washington's thinking remained tied in knots. No one person was forcing him to reconsider his views about human servitude, but from Quakers to Frenchmen and several fellow aristocrats he had been urged to do so and to set an example for the new nation. Those who petitioned him to change knew that George's own decisions and model would make a world of difference. He hesitated at the river's edge and gave it more thought.

It would have been feasible, however impractical, according to Mount Vernon's Mary Thompson. "I've calculated that only 8.33 percent of his wealth was in slaves," she told me in her office stacked with essential books on slavery. "More common was having 33 to 75 percent of your estate tied up in slaveholdings, so he could have done it. But he thinks that a graduated approach is better, as it was being done in New York and New Jersey. They would be freed, and they would be prepared for it."

George knew that simply selling his slaves to another man would not solve the issue. In the end, he came up with a far from satisfactory moral compromise, which was to liberate his slaves upon his own death through his will. The will was detailed and specific: George also wanted his freed young slaves to have a chance to work as apprentices until the age of twenty-five so that they could find "some useful occupation." Though this was an incomplete resolution for George's own daunting dilemma, the final plan was far more than most of his fellow Virginia plantation owners would manage. By comparison, twenty years after George's death, Thomas Jefferson was still telling his overseer that making more enslaved children outweighed the money he could earn from a potential mother's slave labor in the field. It was a particularly unsettling stance juxtaposed with his long-standing affair with Sally Hemings, whom he had taken to Paris during his tenure there and with whom he had fathered several children.

Washington's old neighbor George Mason had been a soothsayer. No worse war has riven our shores than the Civil War, which was, despite some ongoing denials, very much about the unfinished business of the American Revolution and the promises it made to all men.

George Washington's relatives would have hell to pay for not forsaking the institution of slavery. Mason's premonitions that Providence would "avenge upon our Posterity" raised their ugly head for most of George's close southern relatives. Though my great-great-grandfather John Augustine Washington sold Mount Vernon in 1858, he moved many of his slaves with him to another plantation near The Plains, Virginia. Other Washingtons in Virginia and West Virginia also held on to their slaves. This happened despite George's admirable and reasoned intentions, which he clearly articulated in his last will and testament, of freeing all the slaves owned at Mount Vernon. When the Civil War broke out in 1862, John Augustine Washington, who had been educated at the University of Virginia and enjoyed many of the sporting pursuits of his forefathers, agreed to fight alongside Robert E. Lee. He was cut down by enemy fire in Lee's first battle, leaving nine orphans to be raised by relatives. Other Washingtons suffered similar but less dramatic falls.

George's final days are remarkable for what they confirm about his character and sense of self, including his extraordinary courage and his kindhearted and cordial nature. He would, as usual, rise early and ride out to survey his plantation. In the summer, when the morning sun crossed his lightly wrinkled visage, he covered his head with a broad-brimmed straw hat. To his saddle he sometimes attached a large parasol, which one visitor described swaying back and forth over his still-solid frame.

In his element at Mount Vernon, the gentleman farmer now indulged his love of animal breeding. After the Revolution, the king of Spain had gifted him a splendid jackass, which he immediately set out to pasture with his mares in order to produce what would become an American "super mule." He was so proud of his work that he set a team of four of these mules before his own carriage. For his hunting hobbies, the Marquis de Lafayette had sent him a pack of French hounds, which were nearly lost in transit on the New York docks. When they finally arrived, George set to crossbreeding them with local canines in an effort to produce a superior hunting hound. He also continued to hunt foxes into the mid-1780s until the pressures of politics left him with far less time on his hands.

About the same time, he decided that he wanted to bring more wild creatures to Mount Vernon, so he imported exotic European deer, which he vowed to defend with his life from poachers. Martha, who had issues with hounds running amok in her home, showed a preference for deer over foxhunts, and she embroidered the likeness of a deer to hang on the wall.

When he arrived home from his plantation inspections, William Lee, George's former personal valet, battle companion, and foxhunting friend—now a free man—sometimes greeted him after a few of his regular, well-deserved drinks. As it always had been, Washington's Mount Vernon remained open and accessible to visitors. When he would sit down in the afternoon for the main meal of the day, prepared under Martha's adoring supervision, he would, he confessed, invariably see strangers who had come to see him, they said, out of "respect."

"Pray, would not the word 'curiosity' answer as well," he joked to a friend. No matter the guest, whether known or unknown, the old soldier did his best to lead a round of toasts, singling out each individual and then raising a final drink "to all our friends." Even in his old age, George kept up appearances. Dapper, charming, and an exceedingly good sport well into his final days, he could rest assured that no one who knew him and what he had been through would foolishly venture to call him a dandy. When France threatened to interfere with American neutrality, the old general obeyed the trumpet call to arms and readied his sterling silver spurs. He sent in an order for a blue coat with yellow buttons and gold epaulets. He asked for no lapels but rather for an outer garment fully embroidered on the cape, cuffs, and pockets. To top it all off, he asked for a white plume, which would likely have been an ostrich feather had it arrived before he died.

Out of habit or maybe from a sense that one day the world would pay close attention to the precise details of his life, he kept up his diary until the end, marking before his last ride, "Morning snow and about three inches deep. Wind at northeast and mercury at 30. Continued snowing till one o'clock, and about four it became perfectly clear." Returning to Martha, he sat down for his midday meal with a few snowflakes still lightly encrusting his gray hair. When his personal secretary asked him to take something for a cold he appeared to be developing, George shrugged it off like we all have at least once. "You know I never take anything for a cold," he said. "Let it go as it came."

The next day, what had looked like a chill grew worse, and soon enough a slew of doctors gathered round his bedside, sitting near to him, with Martha and a servant, Christopher, in attendance. Medical advice being what it was in the eighteenth century, the agreed-upon remedy was to bleed George as long and as hard as his frail body would permit. Martha actually had to plead to put an end to the bleeding. George's close friend Dr. James Craik sought the opinion of Dr. Elisha Dick, who suggested an invasive surgery that was virtually untried to date. Though Craik worried that a tracheotomy might not work, Dick said he would bear the responsibility if it failed. In the end, doctors decided the operation, which held forth only a slim chance of success in that late hour, should not be attempted.

George let everyone know he was ready. He wanted to settle his books. Was there anything he had left out, he asked his personal secretary. Tobias Lear would recount, "I told him, that I could recollect nothing, but that I hoped he was not near his end. He observed, smiling, that he certainly was, and that, it was the debt which we must all pay." He later murmured softly to Craik these words: "I die hard, but I am not afraid to go," adding, "my breath cannot last long."

George Washington, though he believed in powers greater than himself, had not asked for a priest to sit with him or to forgive him his sins in his final hour. His very last words were "Tis Well." George had finally proven to all that he was a mere mortal after all. Poetic justice had been done.

ACKNOWLEDGMENTS

RIDING WITH GEORGE IS A living history flush with reenactors, historians, hunters, park officials, and trail guides, all of whom have contributed immensely to the story. They have put flesh on the bone of the scholarly texts that have guided my thinking on George Washington, the wars he fought in, and the history of sportsmanship as well as early American drama, politesse, and leadership.

For my first lessons in foxhunting, I'm indebted to Col. Dennis Foster, executive secretary of the Masters of the Foxhounds Association of America. Dennis's keen insights show up throughout the book, but he gets even more kudos for finagling rides on several magnificent hunting horses for me and for introducing an unkempt war correspondent to the well-healed fellowship of the Blue Ridge Hunt, among others. Mrs. Sam Snapp with the Wagon Wheel Ranch, also in the Shenandoah, took me riding on the back trails that George once trod, and provided insights into the still-vibrant equestrian and hunting life of the valley's longtime residents.

When in Middleburg hanging out with the "hunt crowd," I often stayed as a guest with my trusted ex-schoolmate Lizzie Mandros or at the nearby Welbourne Estate, still owned by the same Irish clan that lived there when General Washington rode through to round up war recruits. For further insights on the history of hunting, Col. Bob Ferrer of the Orange County Hunt was helpful with stories, texts, and facts down on his own farm.

For my days at George Washington's birthplace in Westmoreland County, Virginia, local historian and reenactor Dal Mallory played the consummate part of both friend and guide. He is an unforgettable gentleman with a deep love for George and the red clay of Virginia. At nearby Ferry Farm, archaeologists David Muraca and Laura Galke helped me touch and feel a much mythologized childhood. Across the river, Jo Atkins guided me through the cockfights and card games of Fredericksburg's roiling tavern life.

In my hometown of Alexandria, I tripped over my shoelaces with the help of colonial dance instructor Corky Palmer at Gadsby's Tavern, where George's elegant dance steps once turned heads. On the night of the great Birthright Ball, Dean Malissa, Mount Vernon's very own George Washington, provided insights, advice, and a dance photo with my date, Barbara, who also helped advise me on eighteenth-century wardrobe.

For George's first venture into the wilds to deliver his ultimatum to the French commander, Dr. Carl Robertson entertained me in his colonial home and then took me to venues where George defied death as a young envoy for the British Empire. I imbibed comradery (and great Caribbean rum) while hanging out with both French and Indian War and Revolutionary War reenactors from Virginia to Pennsylvania, and crossing the Delaware into Trenton and Princeton, New Jersey. They know who they are, but just to name a few, Bob Tohey, Native American actors Tom Hinkelman and Mike Shafer, and Jeffrey Graham (a.k.a. General Braddock), I thank you.

My insights into George's early romantic aspirations began with an essay I read by George Mason University's emeritus professor Peter Henriques, and he subsequently offered me chats, encouragement, and edits. Farther north in the hallowed halls of West Point, I befriended Adrienne Harrison, a young US army officer and an academic star, who was in the process of carving out young George's reading lists.

In the course of working on this book, I learned to foxhunt, I tried to dance, and I acquired some skills wielding a foil and épée. For the latter, I owe thanks to fencing coach Bill Grandy of the Virginia Fencing Academy, a master swordsman and author who provided unusual insight into both the obsession with fencing and the history of the sport, which George practiced as a colonel in Winchester.

The Colonial Williamsburg Foundation opened its doors and expertise to me in the weeks I spent there with Dr. Carl Lounsbury, Brandon Bruce, Cathy Hellier, Lee Ann Holfelder, and the impeccably dressed and erudite Ron Carnegie, who portrays the soft nuances of George's character as none other. One of the great thrills of my research was my chance to go lawn bowling on a perfect autumn afternoon with Ron in character as Colonel Washington. It gave me a genuine sense of how much his fellow Virginians really admired the master of Mount Vernon.

On the Revolutionary War reenactment trail, I'm indebted to another Washington reenactor, foxhunter and former police chief John Godzieba, as well as the loyal members of the Prucschenk Feldjager Corps. At the Battle of White Marsh, I finally met up with a real George Washington, who turned out to be Irish, and Noah Lewis, who played—and offered understanding of—the black Revolutionary War hero Ned Hector. (Until one finally meets such men dedicated to the memory of past wars, it is hard to understand the living and breathing patriotism that they embody.)

On my whirlwind southern tour, it was my old fourth estate pal Herb Frazier who offered an understanding of contemporary subcultures and the history of enslaved Africans. Without his insights, the journey to retrace George's one and only venture into the deep South would not have had nearly the same meaning.

Back in the Shenandoah at the horse races, I relied on Larry Angus, the former owner of the Charles Town track, as well as my cousin Warner Washington, who along with stories of George's brothers connected me further to local experts and my own family history. Warner, a soft-spoken elderly bachelor, lives surrounded by portraits of all my ancestors and a marble hearth sent to the Samuel Washington estate of Harewood by General Lafayette himself. (Warner descends directly not from one but from two of George's brothers, and it is worth listening to the story of how that came about!)

In Philly, harpsichordist Mark Carroll offered music and insight into the City Tavern's role in the Revolution as well as the Quaker city's central role in our national character. Finally, on the last leg of my journey, as I ventured up the Kanawha River in West Virginia, it was Coal River Group's Bill Currey, who provided the paddle, craft, and encouragement for my journey through George's cherished western landholdings.

I also want to especially acknowledge and praise the splendid and erudite staff at the Mount Vernon Ladies' Association, the Mount Vernon Estate and Gardens, and the National Library for the Study of George Washington. In particular, the library's founding director, Douglas Bradburn, and his director of programs, Stephen McLeod, welcomed me with a fellowship (and beers) to the tavern and library at Mount Vernon. Prior to that, I was offered constant and kind assistance from my dear friend Mary Thompson, Mount Vernon's longest-serving and most astute historian. Mary is truly an expert in everything from George's religious devotion to the moral conundrums he suffered as a master of slaves. In addition, Mount Vernon's incredible curators led by Susan Schoelwer and Amanda Isaac along with photographic archivist Dawn Bonner helped me immensely with illustrations, access, advice, and insight, as did Matt Briney in new media.

I would like to mention the hard work of Jessica Papin at the esteemed Dystel, Goderich & Bourret literary agency, who helped me transform a ragged first draft into what I hope has turned into a new and enjoyable take on the past. Likewise, the excellent editors at Chicago Review Press Jerome Pohlen and Lindsey Schauer lent me help at every twist and turn on the long and winding road to publication. When I went a little gonzo, they reined me in.

Surely there are others I've left out and whom I'll thank when I see them, but in particular, since I'm often away from Alexandria—though my heart still lies there—I offer a special and deeply loving thanks to my dear mother, Louisa Fontaine Washington Dawson Smucker, who, when I began my project, was still editing my grammar and pointing out what I might slightly reword. I dare say that I acquired a deep love of literature steeped in the modern classics from my dear mom, who also taught me all of the little modesty I manage to display in public.

In summary, people—including guides, sages, actors, and writers—are the parts that make up the whole of this text, and *Riding with George* is truly a book that belongs as much to those who lent a helping hand and advice along the way as it does to the author. Once again, thank you kindly, and if I can't return the debt I owe you here on earth, you can expect that I'll try to buy you your favorite poison if we meet again in the afterlife!

INDEX

Familial parenthetical qualifiers indicate family relationship to George Washington.